ROADSIDE HISTORY OF

ARIZONA

Second Edition

MARSHALL TRIMBLE

Mountain Press Publishing Company
Missoula, Montana
2004

Fifth Printing, January 2012

Maps © William L. Nelson

COVER IMAGE: "In the Bullpen" *by Elbridge Ayer Burbank. Courtesy of National Park Service, Hubbell Trading Post, NHS, HUTR-3457*

Library of Congress Cataloging-in-Publication Data

Trimble, Marshall.
  Roadside history of Arizona / Marshall Trimble.—Sec. ed.
    p.   cm.
Includes bibliographical references (p.   ) and index.
  ISBN 0-87842-471-7 (pbk.   :   alk. paper)
  1. Arizona—History, Local. 2. Historic sites—Arizona—
Guidebooks. 3. Arizona—Guidebooks. 4. Automobile travel–
Arizona—Guidebooks. I. Title.
  F811.T77 2004
  979.1'02—dc22

                                                    2003023021

PRINTED IN CANADA

MP Mountain Press
PUBLISHING COMPANY
P.O. Box 2399 · Missoula, MT 59806 · 406-728-1900
800-234-5308 · info@mtnpress.com
www.mountain-press.com

To my beloved son,
First Lieutenant Roger Trimble,
Fourteenth Armored Cavalry
United States Military Academy, Class of 2001

CONTENTS

CHRONOLOGY OF ARIZONA HISTORY

10,000 B.C	Paleo-Indians (big-game hunters) inhabit Arizona
2000 B.C.	Cochise Man begins farming primitive corn
300 B.C.	Hohokam Culture rises
A.D. 100	Ancestral Pueblo (Anasazi) Culture rises in Four Corners area
A.D. 500	Sinagua Culture rises
1064	Sunset Crater erupts
1276–99	Longest of many droughts in Arizona
1300	Casa Grande built in southern Arizona
1528–36	Eight-year odyssey of Cabeza de Vaca, Esteban, and others stirs Spanish interest in the Southwest
1539	Fray Marcos de Niza and Esteban search for golden cities
1540–42	Francisco Vasquez de Coronado claims a vast area of the Southwest for Spain
1582–83	The first prospector in Arizona, Antonio de Espejo, looks for minerals in the region
1598–1607	Juan de Oñate begins colonizing New Mexico and exploring Arizona
1629	Franciscans establish Arizona's first mission in Hopiland, in northern Arizona
1680	Pueblo Indians drive Franciscans and Spanish soldiers out of northern Arizona and New Mexico for twelve years
1687–1711	Jesuit father Eusebio Kino founds missions in southern Arizona
1736	Silver discovered at Ali-Shonak, just south of today's Arizona border

1751	Pima Indians revolt against Spanish
1752	First Spanish presidio (fort) in Arizona built at Tubac
1767	King Carlos III of Spain expels the Jesuits from Pimeria Alta
1768	Franciscans arrive in Pimeria Alta; Father Garcés explores the area
1772	The Royal Regulations of 1772 reorganize the Spanish presidio system
1774	From Tubac, Father Garcés and Juan Bautista de Anza explore overland route to California
1775	Tucson becomes a Spanish presidio
1775–76	Anza leads first colonists from Tubac to San Francisco
	Father Garcés explores the Colorado River, visits Hopiland
1781	Yuma Indians revolt against Spanish; Father Garcés is killed
1785–1810	Mining, ranching, and missions prosper
1786	The Gálvez Plan ("Establishments for Peace") goes into effect; Apaches sign treaties, beginning an era of peace in southern Arizona
1810–21	Mexican Revolution
1821	Mexican Republic is born; rule of Arizona passes from Spain to Mexico
1822	Santa Fe Trail opens
1824	American mountain men enter Arizona
1846–48	Mexican-American War
1848	Treaty of Guadalupe Hidalgo ends the war; vast Mexican territory ceded to United States
	Gold discovered in California; thousands of emigrants cross Arizona on the Gila Trail to the goldfields
1849	Fort Yuma constructed at Yuma Crossing
1850	New Mexico Territory (including Arizona) created in Compromise of 1850

1851	Fort Defiance, first U.S. military post in Arizona, established
1852	Steamboats begin plying the Colorado River
	U.S. government surveys of Arizona begin
1854	Gadsden Treaty ratified by Congress
	First American commercial mining ventures in Arizona
1856	Last Mexican troops, there to protect settlers from Apaches, march out of Arizona; Americans march in
	Arizonans begin petitioning to separate from New Mexico
	Fort Buchanan established on Sonoita Creek
1857	San Antonio and San Diego stagecoach line (aka "the Jackass Mail") begins operations in Arizona
	Camels used in expedition along 35th parallel
1858	Butterfield Overland stagecoaches traverse Arizona, offering the first reliable transcontinental transportation
1861	Bascom Affair sparks twenty-five-year war with Chiricahua Apache
	Civil War begins; troops pulled from Arizona posts for duty in the East
1862	Arizona briefly becomes a Confederate Territory
	Westernmost battle of the Civil War occurs at Picacho Peak
1863	Arizona becomes a territory
	Walker Party discovers gold at Prescott
	Rich Hill gold strike
1864	Territorial capital established at Prescott
	Navajos make the "Long Walk" to reservation at Bosque Redondo, New Mexico
1867	Territorial capital moved to Tucson
	Jack Swilling leads a party from Wickenburg to settle on site of present-day Phoenix

1868	Thomas Hunter brings the first cattle to the Salt River Valley
	Navajos return from Bosque Redondo, settle in Four Corners area
1869	John Wesley Powell explores the Grand Canyon
1871	Massacre of Apaches at Camp Grant outrages Easterners; a peace policy attempted
1872	Cochise accepts peace terms, ending ten-year war
	Gen. George Crook takes command of army troops in Arizona; goes on winter offensive against Tonto Apache and Yavapai
1873	Tonto Apache and Yavapai surrender and are moved to reservations
1877	Territorial capital moved back to Prescott
	Southern Pacific Railroad, building east along the 32nd parallel, reaches Yuma
	Ed Schieffelin discovers silver; Tombstone is born
1881	Southern Pacific Railroad completes route across Arizona
	Gunfight at OK Corral
1883	Santa Fe Railroad crosses northern Arizona along the 35th parallel
1886	Geronimo surrenders, ending Apache Wars
	Tempe Normal School (today's Arizona State University) opens with thirty-three students
1888	Copper surpasses gold and silver in economic importance in Arizona
1889	Territorial capital moved to Phoenix
1891	University of Arizona opens
1895	Santa Fe Railroad reaches Phoenix from Ash Fork, closing the frontier period in Arizona history
1898	Arizona Rough Riders win fame and glory at San Juan Hill in Cuba
1899	Northern Arizona State Teachers College (today's Northern Arizona University) founded

1901	New territorial capitol building finished and dedicated in Phoenix
1902	National Reclamation (Newlands) Act passed
1903	Salt River Water Users Association (Salt River Project), first of its kind in the nation, is created
1910	Arizona holds a constitutional convention in Phoenix to prepare its application for statehood
1911	Theodore Roosevelt Dam completed
1912	On February 14, Arizona enters union as 48th state
	Carl Hayden Tempe elected to Congress, to serve until 1969, serving more years in Congress than anyone else in history
1914	Women win the right to vote in Arizona
1917	World War I creates an economic boom in Arizona
	Striking mine workers and unionists deported from Bisbee
1919	Grand Canyon becomes a national park
1929	Sky Harbor International Airport dedicated in Phoenix
1936	Hoover (Boulder) Dam completed on the Colorado River
1941–45	Economic boom from World War II; cotton, copper, cattle, farming, and industry flourish
1949	Construction of a Motorola plant in Phoenix heralds new statewide era of high technology and manufacturing
1952	Barry Goldwater of Phoenix elected to U.S. Senate
1960	Arizona population exceeds 1 million
1961	Stewart Udall becomes first Arizonan to serve in a president's cabinet (as Secretary of the Interior)
1963	Arizona wins court decision against California over allotment of Colorado River water
1964	Barry Goldwater is the Republican candidate for president
1968	Central Arizona Project construction authorized

1978	Gary Tison Gang escapes prison and terrorizes Arizona
1981	Sandra Day O'Connor, from a ranch near Duncan, appointed to U.S. Supreme Court
	State Lottery begins
1984	Arizona population exceeds 3 million
1985	Central Arizona Project water reaches Phoenix
1986	William Rehnquist of Phoenix appointed chief justice, U.S. Supreme Court
1987	Arizona State University football team wins Rose Bowl
1988	In the National Football League, Phoenix adopts the Cardinals, formerly of St. Louis
	Governor Evan Mecham impeached and removed from office; replaced by Rose Mofford, Arizona's first woman governor
1990	The Dude Fire near Payson kills six firefighters and destroys the historic Zane Grey Cabin
1992	Former Arizona governor Bruce Babbitt appointed Secretary of the Interior
	Arizona voters approve a Martin Luther King Jr. holiday
1993	First Indian gaming contracts signed in Arizona
1995	Arizona population reaches 4 million
1996	Arizona hosts Super Bowl XXX
1997	University of Arizona basketball team wins the NCAA championship for the first time
1998	Inaugural season of Major League baseball's Arizona Diamondbacks
	For the first time in Arizona or any other state, women hold the top five elected offices: Governor Jane Dee Hull; Secretary of State Betsey Bayless; Attorney General Janet Napolitano; Treasurer Carol Springer; and Superintendent of Public Instruction Lisa Graham Keegan

2000	Population of Arizona exceeds 5 million
	Arizona voters are the first in the nation to vote online in a presidential primary
2001	The Arizona Diamondbacks beat the New York Yankees to win the World Series
2002	University of Arizona basketball coach Lute Olson inducted into the National Basketball Hall of Fame
	Rodeo-Chedeski Fire on Mogollon Rim burns 500,000 acres in the state's worst forest fire

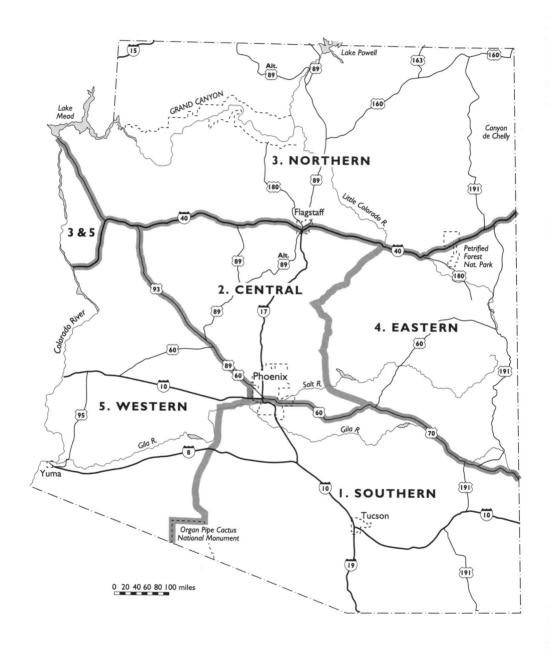

15

Alt.
89

Lake Powell

163

160

Lake
Mead

GRAND CANYON

160

Canyon
de Chelly

3. NORTHERN

89

180

191

Flagstaff

Little Colorado R.

40

40

3 & 5

89

Alt.
89

Petrified
Forest
Nat. Park

93

180

2. CENTRAL

89

17

4. EASTERN

60

60

89

60

60

191

10

Phoenix

Salt R.

5. WESTERN

95

60

Gila R.

70

Gila R.

8

10

I. SOUTHERN

Colorado River

Yuma

Organ Pipe Cactus
National Monument

Tucson

10

191

19

191

0 20 40 60 80 100 miles

The Land and Its People

There's nothing ordinary about Arizona. It's a state that combines the romance of the Old West with the challenges of space-age technology, where outdoor enthusiasts can ski the slopes of the San Francisco peaks in the morning and spend the afternoon water-skiing on the lakes near Phoenix.

Someone who's never been to Arizona is likely to associate it with the Grand Canyon, desolate deserts, or Wyatt Earp, while those who enjoy the sunbelt lifestyle might think of their own clean, modern metropolis with sprawling golf courses, man-made lakes, and high-tech industry. Old-timers reflect nostalgically on the changes that have taken place in recent decades—many lamenting their failure to invest their entire savings in real estate—while newcomers from all over the country and the world add cosmopolitan flavors to their adopted desert home. Occasional bumper stickers proudly proclaim the driver to be "Almost a Native."

Geographically, several large systems that characterize the American Southwest and northern Mexico converge inside Arizona. Many a traveler has noted wryly, "If you don't like the country you're looking at, just keep going a few miles farther and it'll be something completely different."

The state can be split into three zones, starting in the south: basin and range, mountain, and plateau. In the southwestern and south-central parts of the state where the basin and range system predominates, flat desert alternates with mountain ranges lushly timbered at the top with ponderosa pine. Most of these ranges run north-south, and in general they get progressively lower in elevation as they progress southwest. Phoenix and Tucson are in this part of the state, both in arid desert basins.

1

Ecologically, most of the southern half of Arizona east to the New Mexico line belongs to the Sonoran Desert, which continues west into California and south into Mexico.

Near Yuma, in the extreme southwestern corner of the state, the elevation is less than 100 feet above sea level. Some 300 miles north is the highest point in the state, the top of Mount Humphreys in the San Francisco Mountains, at 12,633 feet. Mount Humphreys lies in the next major geographical zone in the state: the narrow belt of high mountains that separates southern and northern Arizona. Cutting diagonally across the state from the southeast to the northwest, this belt includes the magnificent Mogollon Rim, a cliff as high as 2,000 feet in some places, which stretches roughly a third of the way across the state and forms a divide for rivers flowing north or south. In summer it is cooler and greener in this zone, which includes meadows and deep forests. The towns of Flagstaff and Prescott lie within this area, as do Jerome, Sedona, Oak Creek and Walnut Canyons, and Meteor Crater.

The great Mogollon Rim signals a significant step up into the third zone, the high country of the Colorado Plateau, which makes up most of the northern section of the state. The vast plateau reaches into southwestern Colorado, northwestern New Mexico, and southeastern Utah as well. The Colorado Plateau is actually a collection of smaller plateaus separated by deep canyons—the Grand Canyon being the largest and most famous. Elevations on the plateau range from 5,000 to 8,000 feet above sea level. Far from flat on top, the plateau features distinctive topographical features—mesas, eroded rock towers, arches, and bridges—celebrated in a plethora of parks and monuments. In the middle of the plateau is the Four Corners area—the only place in the United States where four states meet. In this country lie the Navajo and Hopi reservations, as well as majestic Monument Valley, the Grand Canyon, and Hoover and Glen Canyon Dams.

Only 18 percent of Arizona's land is privately owned; the other 82 percent is state, federal, and tribal. Annual rainfall varies from three inches or less in the deserts to more than thirty inches in the mountains of eastern Arizona. It is not unusual for the nation's highest and lowest daily temperatures to occur within Arizona's boundaries. All climatic life zones, from dry tropical to arctic-alpine, are found within its borders. A twenty-minute drive up the Mount Lemmon highway from Tucson passes from Sonoran Desert to alpine forests.

Yet, in this land of great contrasts, the most intriguing ones may be among its people. As a pluralistic society, Arizonans have been described as a mulligan stew rather than a melting pot. The state has been and continues to be home to people with roots from around the globe, from Arabs who came with Ned Beale's Camel Corps, to Japanese farmers before World War II, to the multicultural student bodies of today's universities. Arizona's diverse populations contribute wholeheartedly to the commonweal while maintaining pride in their heritage and a commitment to keeping it alive.

The state's Hispanic people, with their rich and varied cultures, are a foundational part of Arizona's past and present, as they are throughout the Southwest. Although some Mexican Americans

Lee Tan Grocery, Tucson (no date) —Arizona Historical Society/Tucson

in Arizona trace their ancestry back to the 1850s, most arrived during the twentieth century. Many were from mining communities in Mexico and brought their knowledge to Arizona during the copper boom of World War I. Even more have come recently seeking jobs, and they retain close cultural ties with Mexico. Hispanics are the fastest-growing minority in the state. The 1920 census showed only 2,323 Hispanic citizens in the state. Today Hispanics make up about 25 percent of the population.

Northern Europeans have also immigrated in waves. Some came to the state directly from their home countries; others came from the East, where their families had been for generations. They came to farm, ranch, mine, teach, pick crops, do business, fight for the military, and later, to establish or work in high-tech companies. Some, like the Mormons and the Russian Molokans, came seeking religious freedom.

The African American community in Arizona is small (an estimated 3.1 percent of the population, or about 160,000 people) but long-standing. Blacks have participated in nearly every aspect of the state's history since the earliest Spanish explorations.

Arizona's native tribes, in language, livelihood, physical appearance, religion, culture, and lifestyle, differ nearly as much from one another as they do from other peoples in the state. Near the Mexican border, the durable Tohono O'Odham continue to flourish in a land of little rainfall. In the lofty White Mountains, the once nomadic, warlike Apache operate a ski lodge, run Hereford cattle on high mountain meadows, and operate a lumber business.

In the Four Corners area, the Navajo, occupants of that high desert plain for hundreds of years, have found wealth in mining royalties. Atop the barren mesas overlooking the Painted Desert live the very traditional Hopi, or "peaceful people." Like their ancestors, these indomitable people dry-farm at the base of their mountain citadels. Farther west, in a steep-sided canyon of the Grand Canyon, live the Havasupai, the only native residents in that great abyss. The only way in to their remote village is by foot, horseback, or helicopter. Today the state's nineteen federally recognized native tribes occupy nearly 27 percent—20 million acres—of Arizona's 114,000 square miles. There are twenty-three reservations.

Arizona state seal

After Arizona was admitted to the union in 1912, the citizens chose *Ditat Deus* ("God Enriches") as their motto, the saguaro blossom as state flower, the paloverde as state tree, and the cactus wren as state bird. As for the state humans, habitation in such a challenging, inhospitable place seems to have bred a state character of self-reliance and independence. As the people continue to shape life and culture in Arizona, Arizona will continue to shape the people—air-conditioning or not—whatever their background.

This book is not just a history of place; more importantly, it is a tribute to the men and women who have made Arizona what it is today. They have passed down a legacy of toughness, perseverance, humor, and stories. Perhaps this book can help keep their spirit alive.

Note to the Reader: Some of the features described in this book are on private land. If you want to see them, be sure to obtain the owners' permission. Also, while this book provides some directions to sites, it is best to check locally about directions and road conditions.

A Historical Overview

From the earliest journeys of sixteenth-century Spanish *conquistadores* into the early 1900s, Arizona was seen as a desolate and forbidding place. It was one of the last areas in the continental United States to be "civilized." The hot, dry climate, rough terrain, lack of transportation, Apache resistance, and frontier lawlessness all discouraged settlement.

Negative first impressions expressed by visiting dignitaries added to Arizona's notorious image. When Gen. William Tecumseh Sherman paid a summertime visit in 1880, one of Phoenix's early-day promoters made the mistake of asking the straight-talking general what he thought of the place.

"Too damn hot and dry," Sherman declared.

"All she needs," the promoter said soothingly, "is less heat, more water, and a few good citizens."

"Huh," Sherman replied gruffly. "That's all hell needs."

Kit Carson, the legendary mountain man, once testified before Congress that parts of Arizona were so poor a wolf would starve to death there. Few people had reason to doubt Mark Twain when he said of the state, "The temperature remains at a constant 120 degrees in the shade, except when it varies and goes higher."

Among those who did settle in Arizona was an immoral majority of unchurched, unmarried, and unwashed citizens. Wild and woolly Arizona tales were fodder for Eastern journalists and writers of pulp westerns, who contributed to the territory's reputation as the devil's playground.

But several historical events led, over time, to a new, more favorable image for Arizona. After the great economic boost of mining, which began in the 1850s, the railroads arrived in the 1880s, opening up the heart of Arizona for commerce and settlement. By 1895 every major community of the time was linked by rail. When Roosevelt Dam was completed in 1911, the guarantee of water from the 13,000-square-mile watershed above the Salt River Valley ensured the future growth and prosperity of the area. The twentieth century brought new technology, such as the evaporative cooler, followed a few years later by air conditioning, which made the desert a habitable and even desirable place to live year-round.

Throughout its history, Arizona's growth has been cyclical. Teeming boomtowns evaporated into ghost towns and sometimes came back again. Others left no trace of their once thriving communities except for some weathered boards, melted mounds of adobe, or rusted machinery. In still other places, throughout Arizona, the past and the present exist side by side in apparent harmony. In the foothills just outside modern metropolises of concrete, glass, and steel, hard-riding ranch hands rope and brand cattle just like their great-grandfathers and great-grandmothers did. Near Flagstaff, scientists at Lowell Observatory examine the stars, while a few miles north on the windswept Hopi mesa, descendants of an ancient people gaze at the same stars with different interpretations. South of Tucson, retirement communities stand beside the ruins of an old presidio. Ancient Hohokam canals inspired the irrigation projects still used in the Salt River Valley today, and the capital city of Arizona is built on the ruins of several prehistoric Indian villages.

First Arizonans

Migrant big-game hunters called Paleo-Indians were the earliest inhabitants of Arizona. It is thought they came from the north, having crossed the Bering Strait from Asia in pursuit of prey, and arrived in Arizona at least 15,000 years ago. At that time, the state was much cooler and wetter than it is today, and it supported a variety of large animals of interest to the hunters, such as mastodons and mammoths. Paleo-Indians hunted together as a group, setting up kills near water holes. Living before the advent of bows and arrows, these hunters used spears, with launchers called *atlatls* to give added force.

About 6,000 years ago, great change began taking place in Arizona. The land was slowly becoming the desert we know today. The large animals disappeared. They may have become extinct due to the climate change or to hunting, or they may have migrated farther east. The Paleo-Indians adjusted to the new climate, becoming more sedentary. They hunted smaller game, gathered fruits and roots, and evolved into what is known as the Desert (Archaic) Culture, which lasted until about 100 B.C. With the exception of the Apache and the Navajo, who arrived in the area after A.D. 1300, most of today's Arizona tribes are believed to have descended from the Paleo-Indians.

Archaeological evidence found along creek banks in Cochise County sheds light on another prehistoric group, the Cochise Culture. About 4,000 years ago, the Cochise people became Arizona's first farmers when they learned from inhabitants of Mexico how to cultivate corn. Researchers don't know whether the Cochise people moved away or stayed and evolved into other tribes. Other prehistoric peoples may have wandered through or settled briefly in Arizona, but few artifacts survive from this far back and our knowledge is limited.

Hohokam, Mogollon, and Ancestral Pueblo Cultures

By A.D. 100, three dominant cultures had emerged in prehistoric Arizona: the Hohokam, Mogollon, and Ancestral Pueblo (Anasazi) Cultures. The Hohokam Culture spread along the river valleys of southern Arizona, including the valleys of the Gila and Santa Cruz Rivers. By A.D. 700 the Hohokam had reached the Salt River Valley.

The Hohokam Culture was rich and highly developed. By A.D. 1100 the Hohokam had created a network of cities and satellite communities with as many as 100,000 people. The name *Hohokam*, a Pima (Akimel O'Odham) word for "all used up" or "vanished ones," was coined by archaeologists. Scientists used to think the Hohokam came to Arizona from Mexico, but now it is believed that they evolved from earlier desert cultures.

Masters of creative arts, the Hohokam were using the lost wax process to make jewelry hundreds of years before the Europeans. With acidic cactus juice, they created elaborate etchings on seashells. They also introduced a game using a rubber ball that was knocked through a hoop; played in sunken, open-air stadiums, it may have been Arizona's first spectator sport. In addition, the Hohokam masterminded an advanced system of irrigation, including many miles of canals—some of them formed the basis for modern irrigation systems in Arizona.

Hohokam Culture reached its zenith around A.D. 1200. About 1250 the Hohokam people began to leave southern Arizona, and by 1400 they appear to have vanished completely. But some believe that their descendants are the Pima (Akimel O'Odham) and Papago (Tohono O'Odham) of today.

In the high plateau country of northern Arizona, the Ancestral Pueblo people, formerly called the Anasazi, lived. The earliest Ancestral Puebloans lived in this area from about A.D. 100 to 700. Referred to as the Basketmakers, they crafted wonderful baskets from yucca fiber.

The first Ancestral Puebloans lived in caves. We know from physical remains that they were slender and short with long, narrow faces. They used their hair to make ropes—mainly women's hair, but the men also plucked out most of theirs, leaving enough for a long braid down the back.

About A.D. 700, the Ancestral Pueblo settled in the arid high northern plateau. They abandoned their caves for pit houses and

Betatakin, Navajo National Monument
—Southwest Studies, Scottsdale Community College

learned to cultivate corn, beans, and squash. They traded in their baskets—more suited for nomadic life—and began creating durable pottery for household and ceremonial use. They also began using the bow and arrow.

Around 1250 the Ancestral Pueblo moved into dwellings in cliffs, probably for protection from nomadic tribes. Betatakin and Keet Seel at Navajo National Monument are the best examples of such cliff dwellings. The Puebloans also built small diversion dams, and agriculture flourished. Kokopelli, the hump-backed flute player from mythology, and kachinas both date back to this time and to Pueblo people.

Around 1400, the Ancestral Pueblo people began to abandon their settlements, and by the time the Spanish arrived in the sixteenth century, the Puebloans had vanished. Archaeologists generally agree that the Puebloans moved south and became the Hopi of today.

The Mogollon people ranged the central mountains and valleys of the state. By A.D. 200 they were farming, and by 1000 they had moved from pit houses into masonry pueblos. Casa Malpais, near Springerville, is a Mogollon ruin. Mogollon Culture flourished until 1150, then quickly withered. Their lasting influence was minimal, except that they were the first of the early cultures to cultivate a good variety of corn. The northern Mogollon people may have assimilated into the Ancestral Pueblo Culture, while the southern Mogollon migrated into northern Mexico. It is believed that no modern Indian tribe in Arizona is descended directly from the Mogollon.

Other Prehistoric Cultures

Several smaller prehistoric cultures lived in central and western Arizona, coexisting with the three dominant ones. The Sinagua people lived in an area from present-day Flagstaff down to the Verde River valley from about A.D. 500 to 1450. *Sinagua* means "without water" in Spanish. Dry-land farmers, the Sinagua relied on rainfall for irrigation and lived communally in pueblos. Ruins left from their settlements include Montezuma Castle, Walnut Canyon, and Wupatki.

In 1064 the volcano now known as Sunset Crater erupted, sending streams of lava over an area of 800 square miles (geologic evidence of the eruption is still visible from the air). The Sinagua fled their homes during the eruption, but returned later to find the soil much enriched by ash. Word got out and people from as far away as the Salt River Valley flocked there, introducing new customs and skills. Wupatki, a Sinagua ruin, has a Hohokam-style ball court and an open-air amphitheater similar to a Mogollon or Ancestral Pueblo kiva.

The Salado Culture settled in central Arizona. Tonto National Monument in Tonto National Park is a Salado site. The Salado are best remembered for their beautiful polychromatic pottery. The Salado mixed and married with both the Mogollon and Hohokam peoples, exchanging skills and culture.

The Patayan people lived along the Colorado River in northwestern Arizona. Another name for them was Hakataya, a Quechan name for the Colorado. The Patayan farmed the riverbanks; when the river flooded, they moved inland to hunt and gather in the high desert. The river washed away most evidence of Patayan Culture. Patayan subgroups included the Cerbat and Cohonina Cultures—people who lived west of Flagstaff and south of the Grand Canyon—and others. By the time the Spanish arrived in Arizona in the 1500s, the Patayan had evolved into the Quechan, Cocopah, Maricopa, Mojave, Yavapai, Hualapai, and Havasupai.

Late Arrivals: Shoshoneans and Athabascans

Nomadic peoples from two language groups migrated into Arizona long after the prehistoric peoples. These were Shoshonean and Athabascan speakers. Both groups came from the north between A.D. 1300 and 1600. The small number of Ute Indian people in Arizona are descendants of the first group. Both Navajo and some Apache tribes are descended from the Athabascans. Neither group tried to conquer the established peoples; rather, mainly, they coexisted, sharing skills and knowledge in a challenging land.

Three Centuries of Spanish Influence

Into this land of indigenous peoples came, in the sixteenth century, Spanish explorers. Rumors of fabulous cities of gold inspired the earliest European exploration of this land, which the Spanish called "the Northern Mystery." From present-day

Mexico, Francisco Vasquez de Coronado led the first great expedition in 1540. For two years Coronado searched Arizona and other parts of the Southwest for the mythical cities of gold as well as a water passage through North America, but he ended up returning to Mexico City a failure. His expedition did, however, give Spain claim to the vast regions of today's American Southwest. A few subsequent Spanish expeditions found mineral wealth in present-day Arizona, but they did not exploit it, in part because the rough and remote terrain made mining and transporting minerals too difficult.

Statue of Father Eusebio Kino —Arizona Historial Society

Some Spaniards came to stay, not to explore, and they had a more lasting impact on the place. These were Franciscans and Jesuits wanting to "harvest" native souls for the Catholic Church. Franciscans established the first missions in Arizona, among the Hopi in 1629. But the Hopi resisted the outsiders and finally drove them away in the Great Pueblo Revolt of 1680.

Among the Pima and the Tohono O'Odham (Papago), the Jesuits, who arrived in 1691 from Mexico, fared better. Foremost among them was Father Francisco Eusebio Kino, who worked tirelessly among the Indians for nearly a quarter of a century. This remarkable priest introduced cattle raising, agriculture, Catholicism, and Spanish culture to thousands of natives of the *Pimeria Alta,* Spanish for "Upper Land of the Pima."

The Spanish religious organized places and native people in several ways. A mission was a full-blown combination of church, village, and ranch. Many people lived, worked, and worshipped there. A *cabecera*—from the Spanish word *cabeza,* or "head"— was a head mission—the priest's home base from which he traveled to smaller missions and *visitas.* Visitas were villages too small for missions, but important enough to receive regular visits from priests. *Rancherias* were areas of fixed agricultural settlement, though their native inhabitants came and went according to the season and what needed to be done there or elsewhere.

In the late 1700s in the Pimeria Alta, mines were opened and mission life flourished. The Spanish government gave away large tracts of land, usually along rivers or creeks, to favored subjects. Settlers could also purchase land grants. These peaceful times were the result of new Spanish policies toward the Apache, whose resistance had severely hampered settlement. The Spanish fought back with aggressive officers and hard-riding troops while, at the same time, giving out rations of food, liquor, and inferior weaponry to pacify the Indians. This thirty-year time of peace made it obvious that in southern Arizona, Europeans' ability to thrive was dependent upon their success in dealing with the Apache.

Despite the years of peace, tension between Spaniards and Indians remained. In 1751 the Pima rose up against the Spanish, which led to the establishment at Tubac of the first of several presidios, or forts, that would arc from San Diego, California, to

San Antonio, Texas. In Arizona, the building of the presidios marks the true beginning of the Spanish colonial period.

In 1767 King Carlos III of Spain expelled the Jesuits from the Pimeria Alta, and Franciscans moved in. The best-remembered of these is Father Francisco Tomás Garcés. Like Kino, Garcés was an unflagging worker and had much success among the natives. In 1775 the Spanish moved the presidio from Tubac to Tucson, founding this historic city. During this time, Garcés opened missions among the Quechan at Yuma. In 1781, however,

Garcés monument, Yuma —Arizona Historical Society Library/Tucson

cruel treatment of the natives by Spanish soldiers led to a Quechan revolt in which Garcés was killed.

The Republic of Mexico came into being in the early 1820s, ending the golden era of peace with the Apache. The new government discontinued the policy of providing the Apache with food and amenities, and by the 1830s the Apache had returned to their traditional raiding. Soon, missions, ranches, and mines were abandoned, and most of southern Arizona passed back into Apache control for the next thirty years.

Much has been said, good and bad, about the Spanish impact on native Arizonans. The missionaries introduced new crops, animal husbandry, and adobe construction. In return they expected the natives to forsake time-honored customs and religion. There was some compromise, but sometimes tolerance reached the breaking point. Nevertheless, the Spanish priests and native farmers found they needed each other for protection against warring Apache bands, especially since military support for the settlements, missions, and rancherias was sporadic. Perhaps if Spanish explorers had found the vast mineral wealth they so desperately sought in the 1500s, or had discovered a river of the magnitude of the Rio Grande, the Spanish presence would have been more dominant. But neither thing happened. As it was, native cultures north of the Gila River remained intact because the fierce, nomadic Apache and Yavapai succeeded in keeping Spanish settlers out. And native cultures south of the Gila held tenaciously to traditional ways.

Anglo Americans Come to Arizona

The first Anglo Americans came to Arizona in 1824 from New Mexico. Parties of mountain men operating out of Santa Fe and Taos came to trap beaver along the Gila River and its tributaries. One of these, a young adventurer named James Ohio Pattie, recounted his adventures a few years later, providing the first written account of untamed Arizona for folks in "the States." During the next several years, other well-known trappers such as Bill Williams, Ewing Young, Kit Carson, Antoine Leroux, Michel Robidoux, Pauline Weaver, and Joe Walker ventured into Arizona's unexplored valleys and mountains.

In 1846, the United States government, interested in westward expansion, declared war on Mexico, primarily to acquire California. Col. Stephen Watts Kearny was appointed head of the Army of the West and ordered to take New Mexico and proceed to California. Kearny and 100 mounted soldiers, or dragoons, traveled through Arizona along the Gila River to Yuma Crossing in late 1846.

Arizonans still remember and celebrate several American exploits of this war. One is the achievements of the Mormon Battalion. During the war, a noncombatant battalion of Mormon volunteers was assigned to build a road for the Army of the West. The arrangement benefited both sides. The army needed a wagon road from New Mexico to the California coast. The Mormons wanted to show their patriotism, earn money for their church, and receive government-paid transportation to California, where they hoped to establish new colonies. Thus in 1847 a group of about 500 Mormon men, women, and children journeyed on foot from Iowa to Santa Fe, and approximately 400 of them went on to scout, mark, and prepare the road.

Commanded by Capt. Philip St. George Cooke and guided by Antoine Leroux, Pauline Weaver, and Jean Baptiste Charbonneau, the Mormons made history with their perseverance and conscientiousness on the 102-day, 1,000-mile expedition from Santa Fe to San Diego. Those who completed the entire journey— over 2,000 miles from Iowa to San Diego—earned the distinction of making the longest infantry march in American history.

The war with Mexico ended in 1848 with the signing of the Treaty of Guadalupe Hildalgo. The Mexican Republic ceded nearly half its territory to the United States, including California, Arizona, New Mexico, Nevada, Utah, and Colorado. The two parties agreed on a southern boundary in Arizona at the Gila River, north of where it is today. In addition to land, the United States acquired responsibility for the approximately 120,000 native people who lived on that land, some of whom were nomadic and did not recognize the boundary lines set by the newcomers. From then on, when Apache war parties raided south of the border, the Mexicans would insist that the *norteamericanos* control them.

Surveying the New American Territory

In the 1850s, the Army Corps of Topographical Engineers began conducting numerous surveys through Arizona along the thirty-second and thirty-fifth parallels for the construction of transcontinental railroad lines. One of these surveys also incorporated an experiment in transportation: the use of camels as pack animals in the desert landscape. As things turned out, actual construction of the railroads was a few decades off.

The surveys revealed that the terrain north of the Gila River was so rugged, construction of a wagon road or rail line to the Pacific in U.S. territory would be impossible. So in 1853, the government sent James Gadsden to Mexico City to negotiate the purchase of more land. The Gadsden Purchase established the present-day southern boundary of Arizona, increasing the state's size by 29,670 square miles.

For about three more years, until March 1856, Mexican troops continued to provide protection for settlers. Finally, the following November, the First U.S. Dragoons arrived in Tucson and assumed responsibility.

Wars Slow Progress

Beginning in the 1850s, stagecoach lines and steamboats on the Colorado River connected Arizona with the rest of the country. Not long after these lines of transportation were established, however, they were disrupted by war within Arizona and within the country. In 1861 the Bascom Affair—a tragic misunderstanding between the army and Chiricahua Apache leader Cochise—inflamed already poor relations between Anglos and the Apache. For several reasons—including the toughness and wiliness of the Apache and the conflict's setting in their home terrain—the Apache Wars would stretch on for decades.

In the East, the American Civil War raged. While only a few confrontations connected to that war actually took place on Arizona soil, the war's greatest impact on the state was the withdrawal of federal troops from its forts for fighting in the East. With troops gone, settlers and miners in southern Arizona felt the full force of the Apache's wrath. During the next few years, whites in Tucson lived, for all intents and purposes, under siege. Only the bravest dared to travel through Apacheria.

Arizona Becomes a Territory

During the Civil War and the overlapping Apache Wars, discoveries of rich, easily recoverable gold deposits in the Bradshaw Mountains in 1863 brought settlers to the land north of the Gila River. These and other mineral discoveries gave Congress the impetus to create the Territory of Arizona from the western half of New Mexico that same year.

Names legislators proposed for the new territory included Montezuma, Pimeria, and Gadsonia, as well as variations on what would be the final choice, such as Arizuma and Arizonia. At least two theories exist about the origins of the name Arizona. The most widely accepted suggests that it came from the name of a place about twenty-five miles southwest of Nogales, in present-day Mexico. In 1736, a Yaqui Indian miner struck a rich silver lode near a Tohono O'Odham village called Ali-Shonak, "Place of the Small Springs." Spanish miners pronounced it "Arissona." A more recent theory posits that the name Arizona originated among the many Basque sheepherders living around Nogales in the 1800s, from the Basque words *aritz,* for "oak," and *ona,* meaning "good."

The first territorial capital was in Prescott, near the newly discovered gold diggings. Well-established Tucson was offended not to have been picked, but most politicians felt the Old Pueblo had too many Southerners and Mexicans. Three years later, Tucsonans garnered enough votes to move it to their town. It remained there until 1877, when Prescott won it back. By this time citizens had begun calling it the "capital on wheels." Finally, in 1889 the legislature chose a permanent site: the upstart, centrally located city on the Salt River, Phoenix.

The End of Apache Resistance

In 1872 Gen. Oliver O. Howard worked out a peace treaty with Cochise and his Chiricahua Apache. That same year, Gen. George Crook ordered a relentless winter campaign against the Tonto Apache and the Yavapai in the mountains of central Arizona. The federal government relocated the conquered tribes to reservations at Fort Apache and San Carlos. In 1874 Cochise died, and two years later the government moved his people to San Carlos.

Problems abounded for the people on the San Carlos Reservation, and disgruntled warriors began rallying around such leaders as Geronimo. War parties broke from the reservation to resume raiding, hiding out in the mountains of their former stomping grounds. In 1882 the government sent General Crook back to Arizona to stop the Apache breakouts. Several times during the next four years, Crook came close to securing Geronimo's surrender, but it was Crook's replacement, Gen. Nelson Miles, who finally succeeded. In 1886, Geronimo and his people were loaded into a train and shipped off to Florida. Eight years later, they were moved west again, but to Oklahoma, not to their Arizona home.

Mining Booms

Even as mining in the Bradshaw Mountains was peaking in the 1870s, prospectors discovered new, rich bodies of silver ore in the mineral belt that stretches diagonally, northwest to southeast, across Arizona. Thousands of newcomers added to the territory's population, and large capital investment from the East added to its prosperity.

The mining boom beginning in the 1870s gave rise to Arizona's Wild West days. For both better and worse, Arizona society was generally far less restricted than in the East, and the rough-and-ready mining towns attracted a wide gamut of frontier personalities. With the likes of Doc Holliday, Nellie Cashman, Big-Nosed Kate, and Wyatt Earp and his brothers, Tombstone alone still provides historians, pulp writers, and the silver screen with a nearly unlimited source of colorful material.

By the time the silver mines began to play out, vast deposits of copper brought Arizona a new source of wealth. America had entered the age of electricity, and World War I brought an enormous demand for the metal. Arizona was the king of the industry by the early 1900s. Twentieth-century boomtowns sprang up at Globe, Jerome, Bisbee, Morenci, Ajo, Clifton, and other former mining camps.

Whether their mines produced gold, silver, or copper, some towns lasted, in their entirety, only a few years. Other boomtowns held on to see second and even third booms. Jerome is a classic example. In the early 1900s Jerome's population peaked at 15,000. Soon after the mines closed in 1953, the town dwindled to fewer than 200 people. Picturesquely perched on the side of Cleopatra Hill and overlooking the Verde Valley, Jerome has made a comeback as a haven for artists and art lovers.

The Cattle Industry

The growth of mining towns created a demand for beef, and Arizona had some of the best grazing land in America. In earlier decades the Apache had discouraged attempts at ranching, but after the Indians' confinement on reservations in the 1870s and 1880s, ranching flourished once more in southern Arizona. Cowboys drove Texas cattle into the state by the thousands to meet market demands.

Ranching in northern Arizona opened up after the 1880s, when the railroads made shipping beef to market easier. By 1890 cattlemen had begun to fence their lands, provide permanent

Cowboys hamming it up for the camera (no date) —Arizona Historical Society

water supplies, and work on improving their breeds. Thus the era of the open-range cowboy—one of America's most enduring legends—drew to a close.

Iron Horse

In 1877, after many delays, construction on railroad lines began in southern Arizona, and in 1880, in northern Arizona. Building railways across the rugged Southwest was no easy task. With the perpendicular grades of canyons and gorges and other geographical challenges, it sometimes took thirty miles of track to go ten miles. In 1879 the Southern Pacific began extending its line from Yuma east through the rocky cuts and sandy desert arroyos toward Tucson, 250 miles away. Chinese laborers did most of the construction, laying more than a mile and a quarter of track a day for a dollar a day, from which they paid room and board. By August 1883 the Atlantic & Pacific (later the Atchison, Topeka & Santa Fe) had reached Needles, California, completing the transcontinental line across northern Arizona.

Once established, locomotives transformed Arizona's economy, quickly replacing mule-driven freight wagons as the best way to transport ore, merchandise, cattle, and humans. People affectionately dubbed the new machines "peanut roasters" and "coffee pots" because of their metal-canister appearance and the fire and steam that made them go. But the trains, while powerful and commodious, were not at first particularly speedy; it was said a reasonably sober fat lady could outdistance one in a downhill race.

More lines followed the A & P, and by 1895 Phoenix joined with main rail lines to the south and north. Historians usually mark this year as the end of the frontier in Arizona.

Statehood at Last

In 1912 Arizona was the last of the contiguous lower forty-eight states to be admitted to the Union. Since 1863, Arizonans had felt like second-class citizens. Their governors were appointed in Washington, and laws passed by the legislature were subject to review in Washington. Furthermore, Arizonans could not vote in national elections. The citizens made a bid for statehood in 1896, but Congress turned them down. In 1910, Congress passed the Enabling Act, allowing territories to apply for statehood after preparing a constitution. Arizona held a constitutional convention in October of that year in Phoenix. Congress and the president approved the petition. The celebration that occurred throughout Arizona on Statehood Day, February 14, 1912, was not surpassed until V-J Day in 1945.

Irrigation and Agriculture

Soon after the gold discoveries in the Bradshaws, Jack Swilling, an ex-Confederate soldier and Indian fighter, cleared out some old Hohokam irrigation canals in the Salt River Valley, and the city of Phoenix rose from the ashes of prehistoric Hohokam Indian settlements. As its population grew, so did its need for water. For a time the prospects for Phoenix's future growth looked uncertain. Then the National Reclamation Act (Newlands Act) of 1902 passed and the construction of Roosevelt Dam began. Its completion in 1911 guaranteed the prosperity of the Salt River Valley for years to come.

Arizona's sunny climate, mild winters, and now bountiful irrigation water made for abundant crops. The desert bloomed. During World War I, the demand for cotton, alfalfa, beef, and other agricultural products caused the market to soar. In the 1920s Arizona farmers also profited from a change in American eating habits—vegetables, fruits, and dairy products came into great demand. The market for Arizona lettuce was especially good, but farmers also grew cantaloupe, watermelon, carrots, cabbage, grapes, citrus, dates, pecans, and other specialty crops. Cotton remained the number one cash crop until late in the twentieth century, when head lettuce replaced it.

The Advent of the Automobile

Thirty years after the railroads came to Arizona, many people in the territory had still not ridden a train. Yet in the early 1900s another marvelous invention of the industrial revolution sputtered and jerked into the region: the gas buggy. Many saw the sturdy, durable machines as an improvement over horses. When cars broke down, monkey-wrench surgery and a little profanity were usually enough to get them running again. According to Will Rogers, "Only trouble with them is you get there quicker than you can think of a reason for going there."

Generally, people were divided into two camps regarding the horseless carriage: one saw the automobile as a plaything of the idle rich; the other proclaimed that a time would come when everybody owned one. Slowly but surely, the latter camp won out, and automobiles were integrated into the wide open spaces of the West. The great Apache war chief Geronimo rode in a tin lizzie several times. A few years later, Pancho Villa made a daring escape in a Model T. In "flivver [car] rodeos," cowboys bulldogged steers from running boards. One daring fellow even drove a car into the Grand Canyon.

With the popularization of the car in Arizona came the demand for better roads. Between 1908 and 1914, promoters of highway construction in the Southwest organized auto races across the desert between Los Angeles and Phoenix to bring attention to their cause. In 1916, the "Ocean to Ocean" excursion, a transcontinental auto caravan promoting the need for highway improvements, passed through Arizona.

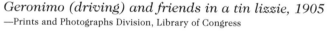

Geronimo (driving) and friends in a tin lizzie, 1905
—Prints and Photographs Division, Library of Congress

As late as 1926 the entire state of Arizona had only 140 miles of paved road. On several miles of road west of Yuma, drivers going to San Diego crossed the desert on wooden planks lashed together with cable. (Until recently portions of this road were still visible north of I-8.) The plank road was built with a steel frame to "float" on the shifting desert sands. For a long time service stations in Arizona reputedly sold more shovels than gas.

From the late 1910s through the 1980s, Arizona saw major highways spring up throughout the state. As the mines and railroads had earlier, the highways changed many towns in Arizona. Main Street shop owners picked up and reestablished along the new thoroughfares, leaving old business districts behind to become skid rows. With the completion of the interstate highway system of the 1980s, merchants relocated again, closer to off-ramps, and searched for ways to lure drivers

Yuma plank road, 1916-24
—Southwest Studies, Scottsdale Community College

off the fast-paced freeways. To attract tourists, some towns renovated their old buildings for a Wild West feel.

Postwar Boom

World War II transformed Arizona into a huge military-industrial complex as thousands of soldiers trained under the clear Arizona skies. After the war, other high-tech and manufacturing businesses set up shop. In 1949 Motorola opened a plant in Phoenix, and over the next few years, many more technology companies moved to the state. These developments, along with the advent of affordable air-conditioning, sparked unprecedented population growth. Some of the newcomers were veterans who returned to Arizona with their families when the war was over. Thus the 1950s marked a turning point in the history of the state.

Since the war, Arizona has become one of the top places to live in America. When the war began in 1941, the state had fewer than 500,000 residents. By the turn of the twenty-first century, Arizona had become home to 5.1 million. Future historians will probably divide the history of the state into two parts: the pioneer period, from 1540 to 1950, and the modern period, from 1950 to the present.

Most of these modern pioneers have settled in the greater Phoenix and Tucson areas—where over 75 percent of the state's population now resides. Arizona has become, unexpectedly, a state of urban dwellers. Phoenix grew from a city of 60,000 in 1940 to one of nearly a million in the mid-1980s. By 2000, it had become the fifth-largest city in the nation, with 3 million citizens. At the outset of World War II, sleepy little Scottsdale had some 400 residents; by 1989 it had 120,000. Arizona is outmoding the statistical facts faster than they are reported.

Tourism: Arizona's New Economic Base

Arizona is no longer developing through its traditional "five C's": cattle, copper, climate, cotton, and citrus. Today, computers, construction, cargo, and communication have taken the place of four of them. The only constant is climate, and that brings tourists.

Tourism is one of the state's largest and most important industries—second only to manufacturing in dollar earnings, and first in number of jobs. Tourism employs over 400,000 people and produces $30 billion annually, or some 25 percent of the state's economy. Domestically, Arizona is the fifth most popular state to visit; internationally, it's the seventh.

The Grand Canyon is the state's most obvious draw, as it has been since the turn of the twentieth century. Other attractions include Monument Valley, Canyon de Chelly, Sedona, Tombstone, and London Bridge at Lake Havasu City, as well as outdoor recreation such as river rafting, hiking, and backpacking. Arizona's professional sports teams also contribute to the state's appeal.

Changes in Indian Country

Before Indian gaming, the fate of Native Americans hung in the hands of the federal government. Over the years, failed government programs left the people with few ways to provide for themselves. Wisely, the tribes have put their earnings from gaming toward improvements in health care, housing, and education on the reservations. The economic growth is going a long way toward Indian self-determination.

Another recent development holds powerful potential for Arizona's Indian people. In September 2002, the Arizona Water Settlements Act was introduced to the U.S. Senate, giving 10 Arizona tribes control of 1.5 million acre-feet of water per year, enough to serve the residential needs of more than 5 million people, roughly the entire population of the state. The act gives control of huge amounts of water back to the tribes—a move that may someday make them major power brokers in allotting water to Arizona cities. Already the tiny Ak-Chin Indian community is providing water for a huge development north of Phoenix, and the Salt River Pima community leases water to both Phoenix and Scottsdale.

Professional Sports

As of the 1990s, Arizona can claim to be a full-fledged member of big-time sports. Home to the National Hockey League's Phoenix Coyotes, the National Football League's Arizona Cardinals, and the National Basketball Association's Phoenix Suns, Arizona was in 1995 awarded a Major League Baseball franchise to the Arizona Diamondbacks. Three years later, the team opened play in the

National League, and in 2001 the young franchise defeated the New York Yankees in the World Series, bringing the state its first professional sports world championship.

Beyond the Twentieth Century

In a survey conducted in 2000, Arizona historians and business and civic leaders were asked to pick the most important events of the twentieth century in Arizona history. Number one was the construction of the Roosevelt Dam on the Salt River in 1911. That, followed by other dams on the Salt and Verde Rivers, ensured a water supply for the Salt River Valley. Without it, life as we know it in Arizona would not exist. Second in importance was statehood in 1912. For third place, survey participants chose the nomination of Arizona native Barry Goldwater for the presidency in 1964. Fourth was the Central Arizona Project canal in the late 1980s, which brought water from the Colorado River. World War II—with the military personnel and new high-tech industry it brought to the state—was ranked fifth. All these events have contributed to Arizona's astonishing population growth.

With Arizona's population boom has come prosperity, but at a price. Like most major metropolitan areas, Phoenix and Tucson have serious transportation, pollution, and social problems, including overcrowded schools, crime, and social services stretched to the snapping point. More subtle, however, is the threat to Arizona's unique culture and the preservation of its history. Since man first walked upon the arid soil of this place, migrations by larger, more dominant groups have enveloped other cultures. Now the danger of that happening to "old Arizona" is real. Much of it has already been plowed under. Journalist Pat Murphy summed it up well when he noted:

> One of the greatest weaknesses in a state such as Arizona, where the growing population increasingly is made up of people with roots elsewhere, is that it tends to be a gathering place for strangers with not much sense of tradition or historic perspective on their new home. Without those values, newcomers tend to lack the spirit to preserve, to protect and to perpetuate qualities that attracted them here in the first place.

Why do people come? In a word, "lifestyle." Arizona is a great place to live, work, and play. The Salt River Project Economic Report of 1990 listed the state's positive factors in this order: healthy climate; open spaces; job opportunities; lower living costs; natural beauty; friendliness of the people; abundance of natural resources; good community colleges; and minimum danger of physical hazards such as earthquakes, tornadoes, fires, or floods. Not included in the report was the fact that, though it does get a little warm in the deserts during the summer, remember, it's a dry heat . . . and you don't have to shovel it.

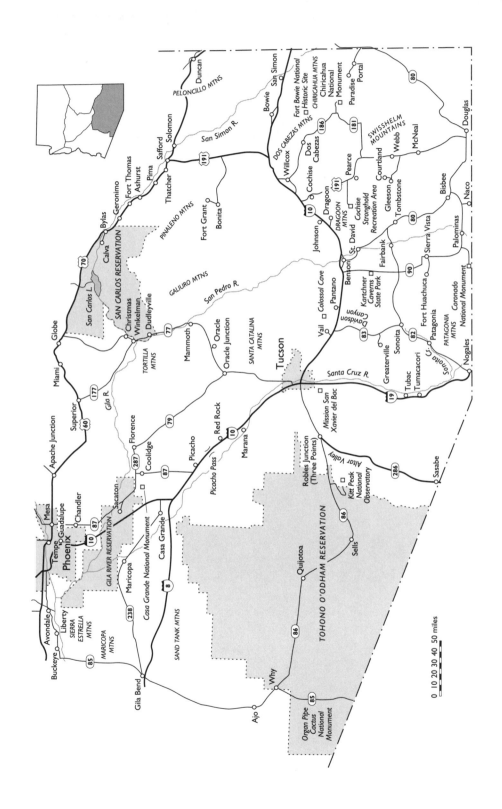

PELONCILLO MTNS

Duncan

San Simon R.

Bowie
San Simon

Fort Bowie National
Historic Site

DOS CABEZAS MTNS
CHIRICAHUA MTNS
Chiricahua
National
Monument

Paradise
Portal

80

Safford
Solomon
Thatcher

191

Pima
Ashurst
Fort Thomas
Geronimo
Bylas
Calva

Willcox
Dos
Cabezas

186

181

SWISSHELM
MOUNTAINS

McNeal
Webb

Douglas

10
Cochise
Pearce
Courtland
Gleeson
Tombstone

Bisbee

Naco

PINALENO MTNS

Fort Grant
Bonita

Dragoon

191

DRAGOON
MTNS

Cochise
Stronghold
Recreation Area

70

San Carlos L.

SAN CARLOS RESERVATION

Johnson

St. David

Fairbank

Sierra Vista

Palominas

90

Coronado
National Monument

Christmas
Winkelman
Dudleyville

GALIURO MTNS

San Pedro R.

Benson

Kartchner
Caverns
State Park

Fort Huachuca

Globe

77

Mammoth

Oracle
Oracle Junction

SANTA CATALINA
MTNS

Colossal Cave

Pantano

Davidson
Canyon

Patagonia

PATAGONIA
MTNS

Miami

TORTILLA
MTNS

Vail

83

Greaterville
Sonoita

82

Superior

177

Gila R.

Oracle Junction

Tucson

Santa Cruz R.

Tumacacori
Tubac

Nogales

60

Apache Junction

79

Red Rock

19

Sonoita Cr.

Florence

Picacho

10

Marana

Mission San
Xavier del Bac

Coolidge

287

Picacho Pass

Robles Junction
(Three Points)

Kitt Peak
National
Observatory

Sacaton

87

Casa Grande

86

GILA RIVER RESERVATION

Mesa
Chandler
Guadalupe
Tempe
Phoenix

10

87

Casa Grande National Monument

Altar Valley

Sells

Avondale
Liberty

238

Maricopa

SAND TANK MTNS

Quijotoa

TOHONO O'ODHAM RESERVATION

286

Sasabe

Buckeye

85

SIERRA
ESTRELLA
MTNS

MARICOPA
MTNS

8

86

Why

Gila Bend

Ajo

85

Organ Pipe
Cactus
National
Monument

0 10 20 30 40 50 miles

Part 1

The Old West

I-10
San Simon—Tucson
138 MILES

SAN SIMON

The town of San Simon, just off I-10 about twelve miles from the New Mexico border, lies in the valley of the San Simon River. During the 1840s some locals called the San Simon River the San Domingo. To others, it was the Rio de Suaz—"River of Willows"—after the trees along its banks. In fact, on some maps from the 1850s, it is Cienega de Suaz, or "Willow Swamps."

From the 1840s, people passing through the San Simon Valley described it as some of the richest cattle-grazing land in the entire West. Tall native grasses carpeted the area, which was crowded with antelope and deer. The San Simon River, a living stream, was full of Sonoran beaver.

In 1859 the government-subsidized stage line, the Butterfield Overland Mail Company (see also I-8, Gila Bend–Yuma, Part 5), built a relay station in the area, the first west of today's Arizona–New Mexico line. From 1858 to 1861 the Butterfield route crossed what is now southeastern Arizona from Mesilla, New Mexico Territory, to San Simon via Apache Pass, Ewell Springs, and Dragoon Springs. The coaches crossed the San Pedro River north of Benson and headed north to Tucson and on to Yuma, Los Angeles, and ultimately San Francisco. In all, the Butterfield route through Arizona spanned 437 miles. In 1881 the Southern Pacific Railroad arrived, followed quickly by a post office and the town

31

of San Simon. Wells, Fargo & Company express mail service also opened a station at San Simon in 1885.

San Simon was one of the remotest stops in Arizona. Here, just west of the New Mexico line, many travelers took either their first or their last glimpse of Arizona Territory. Working at San Simon was not for the timid. Already located in Apacheria—that area of southern Arizona and northern Mexico that the Chiricahua Apache called home—the settlement was also right in the middle of a major Apache raiding trail. (For more on the Apache, see San Carlos Indian Reservation.)

During the early 1890s ranchers moved some 50,000 head of Mexican cattle into the valley. The cattle grazed it down to the rocks. A three-year drought began in 1902, followed by heavy rains in 1905–6. With no grass to hold it, the rich, fertile soil washed into the Gila River, and stagecoach- and wagon-wheel ruts crisscrossing the valley turned into small arroyos. More drought and heavy rains in 1916 and 1920 continued the massive erosion, ultimately rendering the area useless for ranching. Since the 1930s ranchers, the federal government, and environmentalists have been working to restore the land to its former condition.

San Simon, 1939 —Arizona Historical Foundation

BOWIE

Capt. James Tevis homesteaded the town site of Bowie, about eighteen miles west of San Simon. Tevis first rode with William Walker's *filibusteros* in Central America (land pirates who invaded Hispanic lands for fortune and glory).

In 1857 Tevis joined a party of twenty-four adventurers bound for Arizona. Later that year he took a job as the Butterfield Overland stage agent at Apache Pass, about fifteen miles southeast of Bowie. Tevis made friends with some of the Chiricahua Apache, but others didn't like him.

During the Civil War, Tevis served as a Confederate officer. Mustering out in 1865, he settled in Austin, Texas, but returned to Apache Pass in 1880 to open a store at the site of the old Butterfield station. Tevis's book *Arizona in the Fifties,* written in 1886, reads like an action-packed novel. In the 1960s, Disney made a movie based on it called *The Tenderfoot.*

WILLCOX

Willcox lies in the heart of the Sulphur Springs Valley. About 15 miles wide and 100 miles long, the valley stretches from Douglas in the south to Fort Grant in the north. As with the San Simon Valley to the east, cattlemen in the early 1870s reported that the lush native grasses grew stirrup-high; it was some of the richest cattle country in the West. Sadly, that changed over the next twenty years due to drought and overgrazing. Historically, farming has been important to the economy of Willcox. Irrigation from deep wells has helped produce barley, alfalfa, maize, and cotton. But at heart, Willcox has always been a cattle town.

At times in the town's history, the lofty "island mountains" surrounding Willcox served as a refuge for cattle rustlers and outlaws. Now and then, any of these might descend into the valley and hire out as cowpunchers. The vast, dusty, windswept alkali sink southwest of town, Willcox Playa, is known for spectacular mirages (*playa* refers to a dry lake bed). Supposedly a World War II navy flying-boat pilot on a cross-country flight mistook it for a deep lake and decided to touch down. The landing proved mighty choppy.

The Southern Pacific finally reached the site of Willcox in August 1880. For the next quarter of a century the town enjoyed

Railroad Avenue, Willcox, 1880s —Southwest Studies, Scottsdale Community College

steady business growth. Before the railroads built branch lines to Bisbee and Globe, Willcox was second only to Tucson as the major shipping point in southern Arizona for cattle, ore, and other goods. Deep-bellied wagons crowded the town's dusty streets; from nearby smelters they hauled processed ore to be loaded onto the trains. Until 1935 trains shipped 40,000 to 50,000 head of cattle annually from Willcox. Since then the average has been about 30,000 a year. By 1891 a local brewery was turning out 1,000 bottles of beer a day to help wash the alkali dust down the parched throats of cowboys and freighters.

On January 30, 1895, a humorous train robbery took place five miles west of Willcox. Cowboys Grant Wheeler and Joe George decided to raise their station in life by holding up the Southern Pacific. Ready with a large box of dynamite purchased in Willcox, ostensibly for prospecting, they stopped the train, uncoupled the passenger cars, and ordered the engineer to take the mail and baggage cars several miles down the track. When they broke open the express car, the messenger, or guard, had already escaped out the opposite side.

Undaunted, the amateurs packed dynamite around the two safes. The first blast demolished the small safe, but the big, sturdy Wells Fargo safe remained intact. The cowpunchers tried again without success. Finally, frustrated, they placed the rest of the dynamite around the safe and piled eight sacks, each containing 1,000 Mexican silver pesos, on top for ballast. The ensuing blast shook the mountains, blowing apart not only the Wells Fargo safe, but the entire express car. Debris flew in all directions, including the 8,000 pesos, which penetrated and embedded in everything they hit, including telegraph poles. For the next thirty years, it was said, folks were picking up pesos in the surrounding desert.

The town's first ice plant, which opened in 1897, marked the beginning of the modernization of Willcox. Electricity arrived in Willcox in 1899 with a generating plant; for a time the boisterous cow town was literally lit up all night. However, three years later, when hard times hit and customers couldn't pay their light bills, the equipment was sold and Willcox went without electricity until 1926.

The business district of Willcox took a hit in the 1970s when I-10 was completed, bypassing downtown. Until then, AZ 86 brought tourists right into town, and the economy came to depend on them. Many of the old buildings still stand as a reminder of the town's bygone days. Among them is the Willcox Commercial Store, Arizona's oldest continuously operated mercantile store (since 1881).

Warren Earp, the youngest of the legendary Earp brothers, was shot and killed in Willcox on July 7, 1900, during an argument in the Headquarters Saloon on Railroad Avenue. For many years Warren Earp's body lay uncommemorated in the Willcox cemetery, but in 2002 a monument was dedicated to the youngest Earp. Willcox also hosts an annual event called Warren Earp Days.

Rex Allen, the last of Hollywood's "singing cowboys," was a native of Willcox. He grew up singing and playing guitar around the area. He gained national recognition when he sang for a radio broadcast in 1945. Famous for his version of "Streets of Laredo" and many other hits, Allen went on to act and narrate in film and television. He also appeared regularly with his horse Koko at rodeos across the continent. Allen's son, Rex Junior, wrote the state song, "I Love You Arizona."

Allen died at his home in Sonoita in 1999. His hometown of Willcox honors him with the Rex Allen Museum. Allen's faithful Koko is buried in the park across from the musuem. Each October the town celebrates Rex Allen Days.

Rex Allen —Rex Allen Museum

DRAGOON

Sixteen miles east of Benson, I-10 enters Dragoon Pass in the Little Dragoon Mountains. The mountains and the pass, a picturesque outcropping of reddish boulders, were named for the United States Dragoons, who camped in the range during the 1850s. Commissioned by Congress in 1833 to protect the Santa Fe Trail and patrol the frontier, the dragoons were forerunners of the U.S. cavalry.

Passing through on a railroad survey in 1856, Lt. John G. Parke of the Army Corps of Topographical Engineers called this place Railroad Pass. In a cemetery nearby, four soldiers from Capt. Sherod Hunter's Confederate cavalry are buried, killed by Apache on May 5, 1862.

It's accepted as historical fact that the cyanide method of extracting gold from ore-bearing rocks—a process with great impact on the history of Arizona—was developed by two Scottish chemists in the late 1890s. But one legend claims the discovery of the process came much earlier, by accident, near Dragoon.

Non-Assessable Smith, a well-known prodigy in the art of prevarication, had a prospecting partner named Bill Bolger. Bolger was powerfully addicted to ardent spirits. One hot summer day while Smith was out prospecting, a Mexican peddler came by the miners' camp and sold Bolger a hatful of fresh eggs. Tired of a diet of beans and jerky, and just drunk enough to be unsuspecting, Bolger decided to make himself an omelet. On a flat piece of granite, he solar-fried his eggs. Being considerate, he saved a few for Smith.

When Smith returned, Bolger had a severe stomachache. Smith loped his old mule to Benson to fetch a doctor, but by the time they returned, Bill was dead and getting stiff. Examining the corpse, the doctor declared, "This man's ossified."

Smith replied matter-of-factly, "He usually is by this time of day."

"No, I mean he's turned to stone."

Smith told the doctor about the eggs. The doctor examined them and declared, "Those are Gila monster eggs. They're full of cyanide."

As it happened, the flat rock Bolger used as a cookstove was full of gold. The cyanide absorbed the metal, which Bolger then consumed. You might say old Bill was transformed into a cyanide mill. By the time they put him in a pine box, his body weighed over 1,600 pounds. Out of curiosity, Smith hauled his late partner to Tombstone to have him assayed. Old Bill assayed out at 95 percent pure gold. Needless to say, they didn't bury the body. Non-Assessable inherited the remains and took early retirement. Anytime he needed a little spending money, he just sliced a piece off the carcass and cashed it in.

BENSON

About halfway between Willcox and Tucson on I-10 is Benson. In 1539, on an advance mission for the great Coronado Expedition, Fray Marcos de Niza and his Moorish guide, Esteban, passed this way. Later, Coronado himself did, and later still, Father Eusebio Kino.

In 1846, a few miles south of Benson, where the San Pedro River winds through cone-shaped hills called the Narrows, the Mormon Battalion (see historical overview) under Capt. Philip St. George Cooke encountered the only real opposition it had on its journey to California—a herd of wild cattle. A decade earlier Apache had driven some Mexican ranchers out of the valley, and their cattle, left behind, ran wild. The fierce bulls ran in herds, terrorizing anyone who invaded their lush river sanctuary, including Cooke and his battalion. The bulls stalked the battalion for a few days, then launched a ferocious attack. Fortunately, none of the battalion members or their mules were killed. Capt. Cooke dubbed the incident the Battle of Bull Run (in no way related to the Civil War battle of the same name, which occurred years later).

Because the usually placid San Pedro River went on an occasional rampaging flood, making the river impassable, a sturdy bridge was built about a mile north of present-day Benson in 1859. A stagecoach station at this site was first called San Pedro Station, and later, Ohnesorgen Station. In 1861 Cochise went on the warpath, effectively stopping stagecoach travel in southern Arizona for several years. During the Apache Wars of 1861 to 1886, the station doubled as a fort. Settlers drilled portholes through the thick adobe walls for guns. In 1883 a flood washed everything away, and by the time the railroad came to Benson, a mile south, the fort had already been abandoned.

VAIL AND COLOSSAL CAVE

Cattleman Walter Vail, along with Englishmen H. R. Hislop and John Harvey, owned the huge Empire Ranch near present-day Vail, just north of I-10 on Colossal Cave Road (still a working ranch; not open to the public). While the ranch's formal name came from Vail's dream of building an empire, informally people referred to it as the "English boys' outfit." In 1880, when the Southern Pacific laid track through the spread, the station was named after Vail.

During the 1890s drought and hard economic times hit the ranges of southern Arizona. To compound the problem, the railroad talked of raising shipping rates, which threatened to bankrupt cattlemen. Walter Vail stubbornly refused to be pushed around by the Southern Pacific. Along with his brother Ed, eight Mexican *vaqueros,* a trail boss, and a Chinese cook, Vail gathered his herd and drove it across the desert to California in one of the Old West's last great cattle drives. When other ranchers began to follow suit, the railroad reconsidered, and restored the old rates.

About five miles east of Vail is Colossal Cave, a huge cavern with connecting rooms and rock formations. First seen by whites in 1879, the cave shows evidence of occupation by prehistoric cultures. According to local legend, in 1887 four bandits stopped the Southern Pacific train at Pantano, robbed it of $60,000, then escaped from a posse by hiding in the cave. For three weeks, the posse patiently guarded the entrance, building fires to smoke the robbers out; however, the outlaws discovered another exit, stashed their loot, and vacated the premises. Soon after, three of the gang were killed in a gunfight at nearby Willcox. The fourth got twenty-eight years in the Yuma Territorial Prison. He was turned loose in 1912. Since the loot had never been recovered, Wells Fargo detectives trailed him, hoping he would lead them to the stolen money. They followed him to Tucson, then to Colossal Cave. But once again, he gave them the slip. All they found, supposedly, were some empty money sacks.

Today, Colossal Cave Mountain Park offers tours of the dry limestone cave, which stays at a constant seventy degrees. Guides recount the history and geology, but they don't reveal the whereabouts of the stolen loot.

TUCSON

Early History and Origins

Extending south from Tucson to the Mexican border, the Santa Cruz Valley could well be called Arizona's cradle of history. Long before the arrival of the whites, the prehistoric Hohokam people grew corn, beans, squash, wheat, and cotton in the fertile lands along the Santa Cruz River. Fragments of pottery uncovered in 1954 in the ruins of a pit house date back to A.D. 800–900.

The name Tucson comes from the Pima word *schookson,* which means "at the foot of the dark mountain." Most historians believe the name refers to the dark base of nearby Sentinel Mountain. Since 1916, Sentinel has been known as "A Mountain" thanks to a group of University of Arizona students who whitewashed that letter large upon the mountain's slope. Other scholars believe Tucson's "dark hill" to be a huge volcanic cinder cone near the original site of the village San Augustín de Oiaur, in the same area.

Missionaries: 1694–1821

It was in the Santa Cruz Valley that missionaries planted the first seeds of Spanish culture in the state. Soldiers and their families followed. The lyrical names applied to villages, missions, and geographical features in the valley—often combinations of Spanish and native words—are an enduring contribution of early settlers and exemplify the state's mixing of cultures.

Tucson traces its European roots to the legendary "padre on horseback," Eusebio Francisco Kino. The Jesuits couldn't have selected a gentler, kinder man to build a chain of missions among the Pima and Tohono O'Odham (Papago) along the Spanish frontier. Born in a small town in northern Italy, Kino was a brilliant student of mathematics who might have become one of the great scholars of Europe but for a serious illness while in college. He attributed his miraculous recovery to the divine intervention of St. Francis and decided to dedicate his life to missionary work. Joining the Jesuits, he completed fourteen years of study, then applied for duty in the Orient. Instead, he was assigned to Mexico. Arriving there in 1681, he was sent six years later, at the age of forty-two, to the Pimeria Alta—in Spanish, the "Upper Land of

Father Kino in Arizona, diorama (artist unknown)
—Arizona Historial Society Library/Tucson

the Pima." Generally, Pimeria Alta stretched from Yuma Crossing
to the San Pedro River, south of the Gila River. In Italy, Kino's
family name had been Chinus, pronounced "Chino." However,
Chino in Spanish referred either to a Chinese person or someone
of low caste. To avoid any misunderstanding, Eusebio changed
his last name to Kino.

In January 1691, Kino first set foot in what is Arizona today.
For the next twenty-four years he crisscrossed Arizona, covering
some 75,000 miles in all. Kino was truly a man for all seasons—
humanitarian, explorer, cartographer, mathematician, geographer,
cattleman, and farmer.

Kino's greatest gift was his manner with the native people.
Merciful, kind, sensitive, and humble, he always defended the
Indians in his charge. They in turn worshipped him and, in
troubled times, saw that no harm came his way. Kino firmly
believed that Christianity was easier to swallow on a full stomach

than on an empty one. He introduced animal husbandry and new fruits and vegetables to his converts, ensuring them a regular food supply. During a Pima rebellion in 1694, many Spaniards, including another priest, were killed. Alone in his mission at Dolores, Kino stoically awaited martyrdom, but the natives refused to harm him. Later Kino was able to bring the rebels and Spanish authorities to a parley, ending further slaughter. When the shooting stopped, Kino resumed his missionary work. Historians generally agree that if Spanish authorities had allowed Kino to intervene at the outset of the revolt, he could have prevented the bloodshed altogether.

In November 1694, this tireless Jesuit chose a Pima village on the banks of the Santa Cruz River for the site of a visita, christening it San Augustín de Oiaur. The site lies near today's Miracle Mile overpass of I-10. Kino named another village a few miles south San Cosme de Tucson. The whole area came to be known as Tucson.

For more than half a century, the natives of Tucson flourished unencumbered by the restraints of mission life. Finally, in 1757 a German-born Jesuit named Bernardo Middendorf was ordered to build a head mission near the rancheria of Tucson. However, Tucson's first and only cabecera had a short history. Just four months after it was completed, 500 Apache came down from the mountains and destroyed it. Tucson reverted back to visita status, with only occasional visits from the padres.

In Apacheria, native resistance to the colonial presence was one of the toughest issues facing the Spanish government. In 1762 the government tried to reinforce Tucson against the Apache by relocating the Sobaipuri Indians, relatives of the Pima, there. In their former home along the San Pedro River, the Sobaipuri were used to fighting the Apache. To welcome and honor the Sobaipuri, residents renamed the rancheria San José del Tucson. However, the relocation backfired. Removing the intrepid Sobaipuri from the San Pedro Valley simply allowed the Apache to raid further west into the Santa Cruz Valley.

At Tucson, native people resisted missionaries' attempts to change their ways. *The hechiceros* (medicine men) resented the competition from the black-robed padres. By the time Spain's rulers finally expelled the Jesuits from the Spanish

Empire in 1767, Tucson had only about 250 native inhabitants. When the Franciscan order replaced the Jesuits in 1768, they renamed the visita San Augustín del Tucson. San Augustín continued to be a visita for San Xavier del Bac.

Military Presence (1772–1821) and the Royal Presidio

To fit into the new arc of presidios being constructed across the Spanish Empire's northern frontier, to be closer to Apache strongholds, and at the same time to protect the new overland road to California, the existing presidio at Tubac was to be moved north. The military chose a durable red-headed Irish mercenary, Col. Hugo O'Conor, to implement this. On August 20, 1775, accompanied by Kino's equally kind and notable Franciscan successor, Father Francisco Garcés, O'Conor selected a site on the east bank of the Santa Cruz River opposite San Augustín del Tucson, near today's Pima County Courthouse.

The Royal Spanish Presidio of Tucson, circa 1795; view to the southeast (drawing by Cal Peters) —Arizona Historical Society/Tucson

On November 6, 1779, a large force of about 350 Apache attacked the tiny half-built presidio, but soldiers under the new commandant, Capt. Pedro Allande y Saabedra, fended them off. Reportedly Allande beheaded the Apache leader and impaled his trophy on the tip of his lance, effectively driving the remaining warriors away. On May 1, 1782, an estimated 600 warriors swarmed through Tucson again. But for the stubborn defense of Allande's well-disciplined soldiers, the Spanish and their Pima allies would have been annihilated. A seasoned veteran of European wars when he first set foot in the New World in his thirties, Allande would become one of Spain's greatest combat commanders. His relentless pursuit of Apache bands around Tucson in the 1780s resulted in forty years of peace.

Gálvez Plan, 1786

Captain Allande led several successful campaigns into Apacheria. His hard-riding sorties proved that tough, well-disciplined soldiers could defeat the nomadic warriors in the field. Spurred by these successes and by the belief that the Apache might succumb to bribery, Viceroy Bernardo de Gálvez conceived a culture-weakening strategy calculated to bring about unconditional surrender or extermination of the Apache tribes.

The Gálvez Plan of 1786 called for the establishment of trading posts among tribes after the signing of treaties. These *establecimientos de paz* or "establishments for peace" would appease the Apache with alcohol, food, and inferior guns. Post traders were trained to gather information by gaining the Indians' confidence. Warfare within and between tribes was encouraged and rewarded. At the same time, elite light horse or "flying" companies in the field kept pressure on harried warriors.

By the early 1790s, a number of settled Apache living peacefully at Tucson demonstrated the success of the Gálvez Plan. So did the group of so-called "Apache de Paz," also called *mansos* or "tame ones," who rode with Spanish soldiers on forays against other Apache. The next few years around Tucson were relatively peaceful and prosperous. By 1804 thirty-six Spanish settlers had taken up residence. Fifteen years later, the number had increased to sixty-two.

*Chiricahua
Apache man
(no date)*
—Southwest
Studies, Scottsdale
Community College

Life was simple for the frontier people. Farming and tending sheep and cattle, they were self-sufficient and had limited contact with the outside world, including their own government of Mexico. Similarly, the Mexican Revolution in 1821 had little effect on Tucson. However, in the 1830s, the Mexican government discontinued the amenities offered under the Gálvez Plan, and those Apache who had never settled down resumed their warfare. In the capital of the new Mexican Republic, officials were too busy dodging local bullets to worry about far-flung frontier settlements. So, the stubborn natives of Tucson were left to fend for themselves.

From Mexican Pueblo to American Town

At this time, with the exception of some mountain men in the 1820s, few Americans had seen Tucson, or the Old Pueblo, as it has long been called. Tucson was still a small village on December 17, 1846, when the road-building Mormon Battalion stopped for supplies on its way to California. The Old Pueblo was under the command of Lt. Antonio Comaduran of the Mexican army. Since their two countries were currently at war (the Mexican-American War, April 1846 to February 1848), Comaduran warned that the American army unit risked total annihilation if they entered the town.

Returning warmest greetings, battalion leader Capt. Philip St. George Cooke said his war was with the despotic government in Mexico City, not with the Sonorans; he wished only to get supplies and move on to California. Discreetly, the Mexican troops withdrew a few miles south to San Xavier while the Mormons temporarily occupied the town. During the two-day occupation, the American flag flew for the first time over what would become Arizona. With approximately 100 curious residents looking on, a young soldier attached the Stars and Stripes to a tent pole and climbed a rampart to plant the flagstaff in the barrel of a four-pound brass cannon.

The Treaty of Guadalupe Hidalgo in 1848 ended the Mexican-American War. Through miscalculation, the boundary between the two countries became the Gila River, eighty miles north of Tucson. Thus Tucson remained part of Mexico until 1853, when James Gadsden negotiated the purchase of an additional 29,670 square miles. Even then, Tucson was a Mexican garrison until March 10, 1856. On that day, Capt. Hilaron Garcia lowered the Mexican flag, gathered his soldiers and their families, and headed slowly down the road to Sonora.

At the same time, a small group of Americans led by Virginian Bill Kirkland hoisted the Stars and Stripes atop the roof of the Edward Miles Mercantile Store. Kirkland, a rancher, was one of only seventeen Americans in Tucson at the time. A few years later he married "Missouri Ann" Bacon in what was said to be the first Anglo American wedding in Tucson.

Tucson went without military protection from March to November of 1856. In Apacheria, that always meant a great deal of nervousness among the locals. So when the American First Dragoons—America's first cavalry units—arrived to occupy the newly acquired American lands, they were a welcome sight. Just as welcome a sight to the soldiers were the pretty dark-eyed ladies of Sonora, who coated their delicate faces with flour paste to screen out the sun's skin-damaging rays. Anglo-Mexican marriages formed the foundation for the rich cultural background of Tucson.

Life in the Old Pueblo, 1850–1880

In 1858 the first of John Butterfield's famous leather-slung stagecoaches rumbled into town. Tucson was one of sixteen stations across Arizona that linked the area with the rest of the country. A year earlier the San Antonio & San Diego Mail Line had been organized to haul mail and passengers. It was nicknamed the "Jackass Mail" since, in one section of the trip, passengers actually had to climb on board the mules.

Some of these travelers recorded their impressions of the adobe village of Tucson. They weren't always favorable. Phocion R. Way, who arrived with the Jackass Mail on June 11, 1858, wrote, ". . . a small creek runs through town. The water is alkaline and warm. The hogs wallow in the creek, the Mexicans water their asses and cattle and wash themselves and their clothes and drink water out of the same creek."

By 1860 Tucson's 650 American citizens made up the bulk of Arizona's non-Indian population. Among these were not a few nefarious rascals chased out of California. World-traveling journalist J. Ross Browne wrote of his visit in 1864: "If the world were searched over I suppose there could not be found so degraded a set of villains as then formed in the principal society of Tucson. Every man went armed to the teeth, and street fights and bloody affrays were of daily occurrence." Capt. John C. Cremony was even less complimentary:

> Innocent and unoffending men were shot down or bowie-knifed merely for the pleasure of witnessing their death agonies. Men walked the streets and public squares with double-barreled shotguns and hunted each other as sportsmen hunt for game. In the graveyard of Tucson there were forty-seven graves of white men in 1860 . . . of that number only two had died natural deaths, all the rest being murdered in brawls and barroom quarrels.

As hazardous as Tucson may have been, it was safer than being outside its walls, prey to relentless Apache attacks. That was especially true after the Civil War broke out and federal troops, needed elsewhere, were withdrawn. Ranchers, miners, and settlers gathered inside the thick adobe walls of the Old Pueblo, one of the few refuges in the territory, to await the army's return. When fifty-four mounted riflemen under Capt. Sherod Hunter rode into town on February 28, 1862, the residents raised a cheer. It mattered little that the uniforms were gray, or that the flag bore the stars and bars of the Confederacy. Besieged Tucsonans were simply happy for military protection.

The Confederate occupation of Tucson was short-lived. On May 20, 1862, Union colonel James Carleton's 2,300 California Volunteers planted the Stars and Stripes once more. No battle took place; the Confederates had already retreated to Texas in anticipation of Carleton's coming.

While Tucson remained a rowdy frontier town of which many observers disapproved, it enchanted John G. Bourke, a young army lieutenant, who wrote in 1869, "Tucson was as foreign a town as if it were in Hayti instead of within our own boundaries." He went on to describe the typical Mexican pueblo village in the border country of that time. Stately cottonwood trees lined the banks of the Rio Santa Cruz. Low adobe homes with colorful *ristras* of red chiles hanging from beams clustered around the plaza. Narrow, dusty streets led away from the center of the village. Children played noisily. Women of all ages went about with their heads covered with scarves, or *rebozos*. Men in cotton serapes and wide-brimmed sombreros gazed curiously at passing soldiers. Mule-drawn wagons and carts bounced through the narrow streets, scattering meandering dogs, chickens, and pigs.

In 1869, the Shoo Fly was a popular place to dine. A long, low room of adobe, it had a floor of rammed earth, white muslin ceilings, and crude pine tables, benches, and chairs held together with rawhide. Ignoring the dust and flies, diners enjoyed meals of jerked beef and the ubiquitous *chile colorado,* made with red chile sauce. Fresh vegetables and fruits came by burro train from Sonora, if Apache raiding didn't interfere, and on rare occasions, honey and dried shrimp were hauled up from Baja California. The restaurant's name came from the fact that, despite the best efforts of two energetic young Mexican waiters in white cotton jackets, there were some flies that just refused to "shoo."

A Tucson wedding (no date) – Southwest Studies, Scottsdale Community College

Old Tucson offered many other delights. Its gambling casinos ran twenty-four hours a day. Here one could read the latest newspaper from New York or San Francisco. Playhouses were a favorite social gathering place. Admission was fifty cents for Mexicans and a dollar for Americans—*yanquis,* it was generally conceded, had more money. *Bailes,* or dances, also drew crowds. Of these events, rich with Spanish-Mexican traditions, John Bourke wrote, "The rooms were wanting in splendor, perhaps in comfort but the music was on hand, and so were the ladies, young and old, and their cavaliers, and all hands would manage to have the best sort of time." Afterward, young musicians traveled from one senorita's home to the next, rendering serenades at their windows. The gentle nature and social graces of the Mexican people left a lasting impression on Bourke.

Into Modern Times

By the 1870s, Tucson was fast becoming "civilized." In 1873, the telegraph linked the Old Pueblo to the outside world. Eight years later, Alexander Graham Bell's magic talking-box telephone arrived. On March 20, 1882, the city came ablaze with gas streetlights. That same night, down at the railroad depot, in the train yards, a vengeful Wyatt Earp shot and killed Frank Stilwell for his part in the murder of Earp's brother Morgan two nights earlier at Tombstone.

Martha Summerhayes, originally Martha Dunham of Nantucket, married an army man and lived with him at rough outposts in Arizona between 1874 and 1878. The diaries she kept provide a wealth of information about the Arizona frontier and served as the basis for the book she wrote later, *Vanished Arizona*. Revisiting Tucson in 1886, six years after the railroad had connected it with the rest of the world, she wrote, "Everything seemed changed. Iced cantaloupe was served by a spic-and-span alert waiter; then quail on toast. 'Ice in Arizona?' It was like a dream, and I remarked to Jack, 'This isn't the same Arizona we knew in '74 and then I don't believe I like it as well either; all this luxury doesn't seem to belong to the place.'"

The University

In 1867, Tucson had garnered enough votes and political clout to take the territorial capital away from Prescott—at least until 1877, when the honor returned to that city. In early 1885, when Tucson's representatives went to Prescott for the Thirteenth Territorial Legislature, they left with a strong mandate from their constituents to bring the capital back to Tucson, and nothing less. However, bad weather delayed the delegates, and by the time they arrived at the assembly, Prescott had rallied enough votes to keep the capital there. Legislators tossed Tucson a consolation prize, however: the university. Back home, the ill-starred delegates were met with a barrage of rotten vegetables. One saloon keeper's lament indicated a different breed of youth back then. "What do we want with college students?" he reportedly said. "They don't drink!"

The legislature had given Tucson $25,000 to build a university. The city was required to match that amount with forty acres of land. Civic leaders persuaded a saloon keeper and two gamblers to deed some land east of town for the new institution. In 1891, Arizona's first university opened its doors with six faculty and thirty-six students. Since there were no high schools in the entire territory at that time, university faculty did double duty, teaching students their prerequisites before they commenced their college

Old Main, first building on the University of Arizona campus, circa 1900 —Arizona Historical Foundation

work. Since then, the University of Arizona has brought prestige and economic prosperity to the Old Pueblo.

City of Modern Transportation

A monumental event occurred in 1880 when at long last the Southern Pacific Railroad stretched its steel ribbons eastward to Tucson. On March 20, Tucsonans nailed down the last steel rail with a silver spike presented by the citizens of Tombstone. Speech making, socializing, and imbibing of spiritous beverages followed. Self-congratulatory telegrams flew to distant American cities. Some wag even conceived the brilliant notion of notifying the pope. Mayor Bob Leatherwood quickly penned the following:

> To His Holiness, the Pope of Rome, Italy:
>
> The mayor of Tucson begs the honor of reminding Your Holiness that this ancient and honorable pueblo was founded by the Spaniards under the sanction of the Church more than three centuries ago, and to inform Your Holiness that a railroad from San Francisco, California, now connects us with the entire Christian World.
>
> R. N. Leatherwood, Mayor

A few minutes later a young telegrapher handed Mayor Leatherwood a telegram. The mayor read out "The Pope's Reply":

> His Holiness the Pope acknowledges with appreciation receipt of your telegram informing him that the ancient city of Tucson at last has been connected by rail with the outside world and sends his benediction, but for his own satisfaction would ask, where the hell is Tucson?

> Antonelli

The message, undoubtedly created by celebrants, added considerable merriment to the festivities. As a matter of historical record, on March 20, 1955—the seventy-fifth anniversary of the railroad's arrival—the pope did send a congratulatory message to all of Tucson.

Beginning in 1896, mule-driven streetcars provided public transportation in Tucson. At night, after the mules were corralled, university students delighted in lifting the trolley cars off their tracks and depositing them elsewhere—to the consternation of the conductors the next morning. In 1906 newfangled electric cars replaced the little trolleys.

Bird's-eye view of Tucson from the courthouse in the 1880s —Southwest Studies, Scottsdale Community College

On February 17, 1910, local promoters raised $2,000 to bring barnstorming pilot Charles Hamilton and his eight-cylinder biplane to town. The whole town turned out to see Hamilton reach an unbelievable height of 900 feet. Unfortunately, the landing was not as smooth as the flight. The biplane overran the baseball park landing field, coming to rest ingloriously against a fence post. Nineteen-year-old Katharine Stinson, a daredevil aviatrix who also drove race cars, had better success when she delivered the city's first air mail in 1915. Tucson continued to pioneer in aviation, building the nation's first municipally owned airport in 1919.

The horseless carriage arrived in Tucson in 1899. In 1903, the city council set the speed limit at seven miles an hour, grudgingly increasing it to ten in 1913. Racing enthusiasts who called themselves "scorchers" made use of an old dirt road on the outskirts of town. The roadway became popular and folks started to call it "the speedway." Today, Speedway is one of the main thoroughfares across town.

Rillito Creek and Fort Lowell

The name Rillito Creek belongs in a redundancy file along with some other Arizona place names—Table Mesa, for example, and Picacho Peak. *Rillito* is Spanish for "little river." However, when heavy rains fall in the lofty Santa Catalina Mountains to the east, the Rillito swells into a raging torrent. A tributary of the Santa Cruz River, the creek runs through northern Tucson along River Road.

Fort Lowell was one of Arizona's major military posts during the Apache Wars. In 1872 the army moved the fort from its original site in downtown Tucson to the banks of Rillito Creek. There, the cavalry mounts had more water and alfalfa, and soldiers and civilians had less contact and thus less friction. After the Apache leader Geronimo surrendered in 1886, Fort Lowell diminished in importance. It was abandoned in 1891 and quickly took on a ghost-town appearance as the stately rows of trees died and buildings deteriorated. Eventually, the city of Tucson expanded into the desert, enveloping the ruins of old Fort Lowell. In the 1980s civic-minded Tucsonans restored the old post and built a museum at the site.

US 191
Douglas—Cochise
64 MILES

DOUGLAS

The area around Douglas, on the Mexican border, has always been some of the most remote country in Arizona, well off the beaten path for most travelers. Douglas lies in the flat, open plain of the Sulphur Springs Valley, at an elevation of 4,000 feet. Uncultivated land there is high desert, with mostly chaparral and mesquite. Across the plain, long before spotting the town, one used to be able to see the smoke billowing from the chimneys of the Phelps-Dodge smelter. However, the chimneys puffed their last in 1987.

Originally Douglas was called Black Water. Apparently the water there was so rank, people had to shut their eyes and hold their noses to drink it. Yet water was so scarce, no one complained too much. On the Mexican side of the border, the city of Agua Prieta has kept the old name, which means "black water."

In the 1880s and 1890s this area was mostly rangeland. Thousands of cattle grazed on the rich native grasses. In the spring and fall ranchers held roundups, gathering their cattle to mark their ears, brand them, and move them to a shipping point on the railroad.

In 1901 Phelps-Dodge mining company built the smelter here, and the town grew up around the smelter. The company named the town after James Douglas, who was prominent in the history of this area. Dr. Douglas's El Paso & Southwestern Railroad from Bisbee to El Paso passed through Douglas, bringing ore from both Bisbee and Nacozari, Sonora, for smelting. At the smelter, the company built a hospital and residences for employees.

At the same time, the town was gaining a reputation for lawlessness. When the Arizona Rangers were organized in 1901, they had orders to headquarter where crime was heaviest. They moved to Douglas. Tom Rynning, formerly one of Teddy Roosevelt's Rough Riders and a captain of the Arizona Rangers, said of Douglas: "I've been in many a rough town in my day, but

James Douglas
—Arizona State Library

from Deadwood to Tombstone I've never met up with a harder formation than Douglas was when we made the Arizona Rangers' home corral there in 1902." Hard-core border ruffians gathered in the row of saloons on Sixth and Tenth Streets. The Cowboy's Home was a particular favorite.

Gadsden Hotel

The most famous landmark in Douglas is the fabulous Gadsden Hotel, still thriving today. The stately five-story, 160-room structure was built in 1907, with no expense spared to make it the "best hotel in the West." The spacious lobby features four towering marble columns, a winding marble staircase, an exquisite stained glass skylight, and a gold-leaf ceiling.

The Gadsden became a social and financial center for cattle barons and mining magnates. Million-dollar deals have been made there with nothing more than a handshake. In the Saddle and Spur Saloon next to the lobby, for a fee, cattlemen could have their ranch brands painted on the walls.

During the Mexican Revolution, from the roof of the Gadsden, Douglas residents had a ringside view of Gen. Francisco "Pancho" Villa's army battling *federales* at Agua Prieta. Occasional stray bullets sent spectators scurrying for cover. In the streets of town, residents piled bales of hay or sandbags around their homes to stop the bullets, but not always with success. One bullet shattered the window of a house, went through a birdcage, and knocked the tail feathers off a parakeet.

The Gadsden Hotel burned down in 1927, and Douglas wasn't the same without it. The owner decided to build an exact replica with one exception—steel and concrete replaced the wood. At 1929 gold prices, the new gold-leaf ceiling cost $20,000. In 1929 the Gadsden, billed as "the last of the Grand Hotels," resumed its role as the key attraction in Douglas.

Arizona ranch girl (no date) —Arizona Historical Society

SAN BERNARDINO RANCH AND
SLAUGHTER RANCH MUSEUM

East of Douglas, heading for the New Mexico line, AZ 80 bends its way around the southern end of the Chiricahua Mountains. Seventeen miles east of Douglas is the San Bernardino Ranch. A natural spring there provided water. In the early 1700s, Father Eusebio Kino had a visita at the springs. In 1773 Juan Bautista de Anza, out scouting for Apache, had a military camp there, and two years later, Capt. Hugo O'Conor proposed a presidio at the site, but it was never built.

In 1879 John Slaughter, a former Texas Ranger, drove a large herd of longhorns from Texas to Arizona. On the way, in New Mexico, forty-year-old Slaughter met nineteen-year-old Viola Howell, who was helping her father move cattle along the same

John Slaughter —Brandes Collection, Arizona Historical Foundation

trail. It was love at first sight, and the couple married at a small church along the way. The Slaughters founded the San Bernardino Ranch in 1884.

The San Bernardino became one of the largest ranches in Arizona history. Mrs. Slaughter worked cattle with the best of men, and her husband's small army of cowboys could handle a Winchester as well as a lariat. Rustlers in southeast Arizona soon knew to stay away from the Slaughters' Z, one of the first brands registered in Cochise County. In 1886 John Slaughter's neighbors persuaded him to run for sheriff, and he was easily elected. A short, quiet man with piercing black eyes, Slaughter didn't care much for lawyers or trials, and he usually acted alone—as judge, jury, and executioner.

Slaughter ran thousands of cattle on the high plains, and his ranch extended deep into Mexico. The San Bernardino became a veritable feudal barony complete with store, school, blacksmith shop, and post office. Slaughter died in 1922. Today, the ranch operates as the Slaughter Ranch Museum.

GHOST TOWN TRAIL:
GLEESON, COURTLAND, AND PEARCE

North of Elfrida, Gleeson Road, a dirt road, heads west off US 191 into the Dragoon Mountains to Gleeson. The area around Gleeson, Courtland, and Pearce is the Turquoise Mining District, so called for the turquoise people have mined there since prehistoric times. In addition to turquoise, prospectors found copper, lead, and silver in this area during the late 1870s, at about the same time as discoveries around Tombstone, sixteen miles west.

In the 1890s, John Gleeson, a native of Ireland, was working as a hard-rock miner in Pearce and doing some prospecting on the side when he located a rich copper deposit. Gleeson called his strike the Copper Belle. Between 1896 and 1901 the mine produced $300,000 in copper. A town grew up around the strike, named after Gleeson. By 1909 it had 500 residents and a hospital. Three years later, the town of Gleeson burned—a common occurrence in Arizona mining camps. The industrious citizens were out rebuilding before the last embers died, but a depression in the copper industry after World War I sounded the death knell for the little mining town. Today, it's a ghost town, though a few people still live there.

The Gleeson-Pearce Road heads north from Gleeson to Pearce, stopping first in Courtland. Six weeks after several large copper companies began operations in the Courtland area in 1909, the local newspaper boasted of a population of 2,000 living in tents and shacks. "No other camp in Arizona ever made such a showing in so short a time," the local paper proclaimed with civic pride. It was estimated the mines would produce 2 million pounds of copper per month. During its heyday, Courtland had telephones, movie theaters, an ice cream parlor, an automobile dealership, and five miles of underground water pipes. A branch line of the Southern Pacific linked the town with the rest of the world. However, the miners never did construct a jail; a tunnel with a wooden door sufficed.

Courtland boomed for about ten years until the end of World War I, when the copper market declined. However, the town held on for twenty-three more years before most of its citizens drifted on to other places. All that remains today are a few ghosts, dangerous open mine shafts, and numerous foundations.

The Gleeson-Pearce Road goes to Pearce; one can also get there just off US 191. A prospector's dream came true for Jimmy Pearce the day in 1894 he picked up some rich ore specimens. Working as a hard-rock miner in Tombstone, the young Cornishman and his industrious wife had saved money and bought a small cattle ranch in the Sulphur Springs Valley. One day, moving cattle, Jimmy stopped to rest on the side of a hill. Like any hard-rock miner, he couldn't resist examining the rocks around him—despite the fact that, for twenty years, prospectors had been scouring every inch of those hills. One piece of ore he shattered had a gold interior. Pearce's ore specimens assayed out at $22,000 to the ton in silver and $5,000 to the ton in gold. Pearce quickly staked a claim for each member of his family and named the mine Commonwealth. Almost overnight the town of Pearce materialized at the foot of the slope.

A short time after the Commonwealth went into operation, a banker from New Mexico named John Brockman talked Pearce into selling out for $250,000. Most prospectors lacked the capital

Pearce, 1912; Commonwealth Mine in foreground —Arizona Historical Foundation

to develop their claims and often sold a rich prospect for a few dollars, but Pearce held out for more. In addition, since many considered the hotel business a more reliable profit maker than the mines, Mrs. Pearce demanded and received the lucrative exclusive on the hostelry business in the town.

It wasn't long before people began drifting in, looking for employment and get-rich-quick opportunities. Some residents of Tombstone even dismantled their homes and businesses, packed them to the east side of the Dragoon Mountains, and reconstructed them in the new town.

The boom times in Pearce lasted several years, peaking in 1919 at a population of 1,500. Pearce had the usual assortment of stores, saloons, and restaurants, and it even had a movie theater. However, as the Great Depression took its toll and the railroad pulled up tracks in the 1930s, Pearce declined. At the same time, the seemingly inexhaustible Commonwealth Mine played out. Today, Pearce has only a handful of residents.

COCHISE STRONGHOLD

West of Pearce is Cochise Stronghold, now a recreation area in the Coronado National Forest, accessible via local roads from Sunsites. The area was one of several frequented by its namesake, the Chiricahua leader Cochise.

Born around 1805, Cochise became a prominent leader among his people at an early age. By 1858 he was chief of the entire Central Chiricahua Apache group. Although he waged fierce war with the Mexicans, Cochise acted moderately toward the newly arrived Americans and kept his people at peace with them—until 1861. Then, the army accused him of kidnapping a child and hanged some of his family members. Outraged, Cochise warred against the Americans for the next ten years. Ultimately, Cochise was proven innocent of the crime that started it all.

In 1867, a legendary friendship began when Thomas Jefferson Jeffords, the superintendent of a mail route between Lordsburg, New Mexico, and Tucson, boldly rode into Cochise's stronghold to ask the leader for safe passage for his mail riders. Cochise agreed and kept his word, and the mail went through. From that time on, Jeffords and Cochise were friends for life—even through the difficult time of the war. Finally, Gen. Oliver Howard asked Jeffords to help end the Apache Wars. In 1872 Jeffords brought the two leaders together to negotiate a treaty. Cochise asked for two things: that the reservation the government wanted his people to live on be in his beloved mountains; and that Jeffords be the Indians' agent. Howard agreed to both. Cochise had won his war; he died two years later. In 1875, despite the stability of the Chiricahua under his supervision, Jeffords was removed as Indian agent, and the Chiricahua were relocated to the San Carlos Reservation. Under these circumstances, a new generation of leaders less moderate than Cochise—among them, Geronimo—rose, and soon reignited the war.

When Cochise died in 1874, mourners took his body to a secret place in these mountains and buried it according to the traditional custom of the Apache, with all traces of the grave eradicated. Cochise's friend Tom Jeffords far outlived him, but not necessarily happily. Whites had launched the campaign to remove Jeffords as Indian agent, and according to some sources, never forgave him for being an "Indian lover." Jeffords eked out a hermit's

Cochise (artist unknown). No known photographs exist of the great Chiricahua leader, but several artists have made pictures from descriptions of him. —Southwest Studies, Scottsdale Community College

existence homesteading and mining in the Tortolita Mountains until his death in 1914.

COCHISE

Four miles south of I-10, off US 191, Cochise was a thriving community around the turn of the century. It was named for the noted Chiricahua Apache leader, whom whites had respected as a peace-loving chief (until the Bascom Affair—see Sonoita Creek); as a man who, once he gave his word, always kept it; and as a great military tactician.

During the heyday of the boomtowns of the Turquoise Mining District, Cochise was the shipping point for the Arizona Eastern Railroad. As late as the 1920s, the Arizona Eastern was running three trains a week to Courtland and Gleeson. Hard times came with the Great Depression, however, and in 1933 the railroad abandoned its lines between Cochise and Douglas. The most notable reminder of the town's early days is the historic adobe-walled Cochise Hotel.

A train robbery with a twist took place in Cochise on the evening of September 11, 1899. At about 11:30, two men climbed aboard the westbound Southern Pacific and hijacked it to a prearranged point, where some accomplices waited with a box of dynamite and some horses. The outlaws blasted open the safe and quickly emptied its contents—probably about $30,000 in gold. They loaded the loot on horses and rode off.

The engineer alerted the Willcox town marshal, Burt Alvord, who was playing poker in the back room of Schwertner's Saloon. He deputized his pal Bill Downing and they rode toward Cochise, but the robbers' tracks were lost. Exhibiting great frustration, the two returned to their poker game.

The robbers' identities might never have been discovered but for persistent lawman Bert Grover. Grover suspected Marshal Alvord himself. Alvord was a "good ole boy" raised in Tombstone, liked by everyone from judges to merchants to cattle rustlers. Recently, he had befriended an ornery bunch of outlaws.

Grover cajoled the porter at Schwertner's into confessing that, on the night of the robbery, he had been bribed to take drinks to the back room every few minutes and return with empty glasses. Meanwhile, Alvord and gang exited through a window and pulled their caper. By the time the robbery was reported, the outlaws had returned to the bar and resumed their poker game. Later Alvord buried the gold in a secret cache.

Before Grover could bring charges against his suspects, his star witness got cold feet and left the territory. But after a later, botched train heist, Alvord and his gang were convicted and jailed. Over the next few years, Alvord was in and out of jail in Arizona, finally serving his full time at the prison in Yuma. Upon his release, Alvord returned to Willcox for a few days, said howdy to all his old cronies, then skipped town for Panama, Brazil, and Barbados, where he died in 1909. The loot is probably still out there.

AZ 181 and AZ 186
US 191—Willcox
45 MILES

AZ 186 becomes AZ 181 after the junction at the Chiricahua National Monument. To the east, the imposing Chiricahua Mountains separate Sulphur Springs Valley from San Simon Valley. In 1872 a large part of this area was designated a Chiricahua Apache reservation after a treaty between Chief Cochise and Gen. Oliver O. Howard ended the bloody ten-year Apache Wars, which had made the area uninhabitable for settlers, miners, and ranchers. Four years later, the Chiricahua were moved to the San Carlos Reservation east of Phoenix, near Globe. The government closed the reservation here, and soon the grassy valley swarmed with Texas cattle.

Where AZ 181 turns and heads north toward the junction of AZ 181 and AZ 186, a dirt road takes off to the east through West Turkey Creek Canyon. Four and a half miles along this road is the gravesite of Tombstone gunfighter Johnny Ringo.

APACHE PASS

Unpaved but signed, Apache Pass Road takes off from AZ 186 near milepost 351 and travels northeast to the town of Bowie on I-10. Fort Bowie is about eight miles up Apache Pass Road from AZ 186. Twisting and narrow, Apache Pass separates the Dos Cabezas and Chiricahua Mountains. Here desert grasslands merge with mountain piñon and juniper. Sandy washes lined with oak, hackberry, willow, and black walnut streak the rough-hewn mountains. This area is a biotic transition zone: to the east is the Chihuahuan Desert; to the west, the Sonoran Desert.

An ancient, well-traveled Indian trail through the pass connected Sulphur Springs Valley with San Simon Valley. Spanish soldiers used the trail during early campaigns against the Apache. Lt. John G. Parke camped near Siphon Canyon in 1854 while surveying a proposed railroad route. He determined that the grade there was too steep, so a new route was surveyed north of the Dos Cabezas Mountains—the route of I-10 in this area today.

Eastbound from Dos Cabezas, the stage line crossed the summit at 5,115 feet and descended two miles along arroyos and rocky slopes to the entrance to Siphon Canyon, the site of an old Butterfield station. East of the station, a narrow defile led north to the San Simon Valley.

During the mid-1850s, a bloody massacre took place in Apache Pass. Nachi, the father of Cochise, ambushed a westbound wagon train in Siphon Canyon. More than thirty emigrants, including women and children, were murdered and mutilated. In addition, the Indians took several women captive. They sold two in Mexico and put the others to death.

The Butterfield Overland Mail stage line opened its station in Apache Pass in July 1858. At that time about 1,500 Chiricahua Apache warriors and their families living under the leadership of Cochise, Jack, and Esconolea occupied rancherias in the area. Relations between the Butterfield employees and the Apache were relatively serene, but the close proximity of so many warriors kept the ten station employees in a state of constant wariness. Until the time of the Bascom Affair (see Sonoita Creek), the Apache who lived around the station allowed the stages to pass through twice a week and tolerated the presence of the employees.

In the Bascom Affair, in October 1860, Cochise's band was blamed for a kidnapping its members did not commit. Here at the pass, tragic misaccusation and misunderstanding led to the deaths of innocent Apache and whites. The ensuing hostilities would last ten years.

After the tide of relations between whites and Apache at the pass had turned, both the eastbound and westbound stagecoaches narrowly made it through attacks. In one instance, as a coach reached a small bridge across a deep arroyo, the driver saw that the Apache had removed the side planks. Cracking his long whip, he forged ahead; the belly of the coach literally slid across the center of the structure and up the other side to the safety of the station. On March 2, 1861, the Butterfield stagecoach line through Arizona was closed, and would remain that way for several years.

Battle of Apache Pass

The Battle of Apache Pass was fought here on July 15 and 16, 1862. Some 700 Apache fought 126 Union army soldiers from the California Column who had come to rid the area of both Apache and Confederates. It would be the largest battle between army troops and Indians on Arizona soil.

Earlier in the year, threatened with an invasion by Confederate Texans, the federal command had abandoned both Forts Breckenridge and Buchanan. The soldiers went east to the Rio Grande, leaving citizens in the area vulnerable to Apache attacks. In February 1862 fifty-four men under Capt. Sherod Hunter rode through Apache Pass on their way to occupy Tucson for the Confederacy. In late April, withdrawing to Texas after Confederate defeats in New Mexico and with 2,000 California Union volunteers on their way, Hunter passed through the pass again with only minor opposition from the Apache.

Meanwhile, the California Column reached Tucson and raised the Stars and Stripes over the city. Column commander James Carleton dispatched an advance force to Apache Pass to fortify the station and protect supply trains for the main column. On July 8, 1862, Capt. Tom Roberts and 126 men left for the abandoned Butterfield station at San Simon, just east of Apache Pass. Behind them trundled the supply wagons with a small detachment of men.

At the same time, the Chiricahua at Apache Pass were joining forces with the Mimbreño, another Apache band, under their great chief Mangas Coloradas. At six-foot-six and over 200 pounds, Mangas Coloradas—soldier, statesman, and diplomat—was considered the greatest of all Apache chiefs. In one example of his shrewd statesmanship, Mangas, like European feudal lords of old, married his several daughters off to leaders of nearby bands, including Cochise. Usually, Apache groups lived independently of each other, but Apache society was also matrilineal, so husbands became obligated to their wives' clans. When Mangas called upon his sons-in-law for help, they were compelled to go. So it was, that summer of 1862, that such a high number of warriors met the soldiers at the pass.

At about noon on July 15, Roberts arrived at the entrance to the pass with sixty infantry soldiers, seven cavalrymen, and a battery of two twelve-pound prairie howitzers. A half mile from the abandoned stage station, Apache began firing down on the rear of the column from the surrounding hills. The soldiers

Mangus, son of Mangas Coloradas
—Southwest Studies, Scottsdale Community College

returned fire, spurred on by desperation: they were thirsty, and unless they took the spring by the station, they would not drink. That night, surprising the Apache with their howitzers, they won the spring. Thirsty troopers filled canteens and drank heartily.

The same evening, Roberts dispatched a handful of cavalrymen to rejoin the supply train and escort it to the pass. In the Sulphur Springs Valley, Apache attacked them. Most of the soldiers escaped and reached the supply train, but Pvt. John Teal fell behind and soon found himself cut off. When the warriors shot his horse, Teal sheltered behind the animal and kept his attackers off for an hour with his breech-loading carbine. Then, when Teal managed to wound one warrior, the Apache suddenly lost interest and rode away with the wounded man. Teal walked eight miles to the supply train, surprising his friends, who thought he was dead.

It turned out that the man Private Teal shot was Mangas Coloradas. The old chief recovered, but never fully. About one year later he was captured by prospectors and turned over to U.S. soldiers, who tortured and brutally murdered him.

The next day, the Apache regained control of the spring and surrounding high ground, but the howitzers triumphed again after another round of battle.

A few days later, Colonel Carleton arrived at the pass. On July 28, 1862, Fort Bowie was established there; in 1868 it was moved a half mile east. During the 1880s the fort became one of the most important posts in the Southwest, from which, until Geronimo's final surrender in 1886, search and destroy missions

Fort Bowie at the time of Geronimo's surrender in 1886 —Arizona State Library

Ruins and cemetery at Fort Bowie —Author photo

against the Apache were launched into Mexico. The military abandoned the post in 1894. In 1964 the crumbling fort was designated a national historic site. To see the ruins, walk three miles round-trip from the trailhead on Apache Pass Road.

DOS CABEZAS

Dos Cabezas, a dot on the map on AZ 186 seven miles northwest of the Apache Pass Turnoff, is in an active mining area. Dos Cabezas means "Two Heads" in Spanish. It refers to the two distinctive bald knolls that characterize the nearby range of mountains with the same name.

When prospectors filed gold and silver claims near the two bald summits in the late 1870s, a town of about 300 sprang up nearby. According to a reporter in 1881, Dos Cabezas had about fifty buildings, mostly of adobe; one hotel—"not first class"; three saloons; a blacksmith shop, a post office, and a stamp mill.

US 191
I-10—Safford
36 MILES

BONITA

About seventeen miles north of I-10, AZ 266 branches off from US 191. It travels west about eighteen miles, crossing the Pinaleno Mountains to the little community of Bonita, which means "pretty" in Spanish.

Bonita was a rough place in the 1880s when the military post at Fort Grant, three miles north, was in its heyday. It was here in 1871 that Billy the Kid killed his first man. Every four months when the soldiers were paid, they came to Bonita to whoop it up. On that day, ladies of easy virtue gathered from miles around to help them spend their wages in the town's ten saloons. However, on most days, the population of the town was around 1,000, including the families of soldiers stationed at the fort.

Class-conscious officers and their wives preferred to do their genteel socializing at Henry Clay Hooker's famous Sierra Bonita Ranch, at the northern end of the Sulphur Springs Valley. The ranch, covering about 800 square miles, was the largest in Arizona at the time. With hospitality and cuisine that was already an

Sierra Bonita Ranch (no date) —Arizona Historical Society

*Colonel Hooker on
the patio of Sierra
Bonita Ranch*
—Arizona Historical
Society Library

Arizona legend, the Sierra Bonita made a happy stopover for weary travelers, and many famous personalities visited there. At an elevation of 4,000 feet, the ranch was blessed with an abundance of water and lush grass. It was known throughout the West for its purebred cattle and fine racing horses.

In addition, the Sierra Bonita had hot springs. Before the white man came, the 115-degree mineral water had cured the aches and pains of many an Apache after a long raid into Mexico. When Hooker started his ranch, he went to work developing "Hooker's Hot Springs," claiming far and wide that the water cured everything from rheumatism to acne. By 1889 there were so many guests at the hot springs it had to have its own post office. Playwright Augustus Thomas, a guest at the Sierra Bonita, wrote an 1889 Broadway hit called *Arizona* after staying at the ranch. During the 1930s the play was made into a movie, *'Neath Arizona Skies,* starring John Wayne.

Hooker started in the livestock business during the silver rush to Nevada, when he bought a flock of 500 turkeys in California and drove them over the Sierra Nevada to sell them in Virginia City, Nevada. When his less-than-bright birds stampeded over a cliff, it looked like his investment had been lost. However, when Hooker reached the valley below, he found his flock had soared free and were waiting for him. At the silver camp, he sold the birds for five dollars apiece and bought his ranch in Arizona. Hooker is one of the few Arizona ranchers to have been inducted into the National Cowboy Hall of Fame at Oklahoma City. The Sierra Bonita, still a working ranch, is not open to the public.

FORT GRANT

Three miles north of Bonita at the end of AZ 266, on the southern slopes of the lofty Pinaleno Mountains, Fort Grant was established in 1873. Old Camp Grant had been situated at the junction of Aravaipa Creek and the San Pedro River. However, following the massacre of peaceful Apache there in 1871, and due to problems with malaria, the army decided to move the post. Soldiers developed a different health problem at the new Fort Grant: venereal disease. Two notorious bawdy houses posing as whiskey mills beckoned just outside the post. Fort Grant was abandoned in 1895. Years later it was used as a state reform school.

The Galiuro Mountains, a spectacular range west of Safford and Fort Grant, are in one of the most remote regions of the Southwest.

SAFFORD

Safford, at US 191 and US 70, is a town of about 7,000 on the Gila River. In 1872 a group of farmers from Gila Bend relocated here after several devastating floods downstream. They named the town for the territorial governor at the time, Anson P. K. Safford.

Known as the "little governor" because of his diminutive size, Safford is probably the only governor to be granted a divorce by an act of legislature. At the time, the territory had no divorce law, so he asked legislators to pass an act dissolving his marriage. They did, and he gladly signed it.

As governor, Safford promoted Arizona's mines to eastern investors and pushed hard for more schools in the territory. On one occasion he rode at the head of a punitive expedition in pursuit of raiding Apache. In 1877 poor health kept him from accepting a second appointment as governor.

AZ 80
New Mexico Border—Benson
121 MILES

PORTAL

AZ 80 leaves Rodeo, New Mexico, crosses the state line in just a few miles, and heads down toward Douglas. To see the east side of the beautiful Chiricahua Mountains, take a road that leaves AZ 80 about three miles north of Rodeo and leads northwest, back into Arizona, to the sleepy hamlet of Portal. Portal, at the base of Cave Creek Canyon, has a tiny store, some lodging, and several campgrounds. It's also home to the Southwest Research Station of the American Museum of Natural History.

GERONIMO MONUMENT

North of AZ 80, rising to nearly 10,000 feet, the Chiricahua Mountains bear the name of the Apache band that made them their home for hundreds of years. Independent of all authority but their own, the Chiricahua were the scourge of Mexico, Spain, and the United States before they finally surrendered in 1886. Commemorating this surrender, a monument to Geronimo stands at the side of AZ 80 at Apache, thirty-nine miles northeast of Douglas. Dedicated in 1934, the monument is a sixteen-foot-high pyramid. Skeleton Canyon, where the surrender took place, is a few miles to the southeast on a dirt road off AZ 80. The canyon is

Geronimo (right) at the time of his surrender in September 1886 (photo by C. S. Fly) —Southwest Studies, Scottsdale Community College

named after a massacre of Mexican smugglers perpetrated there by the American outlaws Curly Bill Brocius and N. H. "Old Man" Clanton, five years before the surrender.

Born in 1823 into the Bedonkohe Apache near the headwaters of the Gila River, Geronimo was an Apache warrior and medicine man. At the peak of his glory in 1886, with fewer than two dozen warriors, he was the subject of a massive manhunt by 5,000 soldiers—one-fifth of the U.S. Army. Geronimo began his life as a warrior by following such Apache leaders as Mangas Coloradas, Cochise, Juh, and Victorio. In 1850 he journeyed with the men of his family to Janos in Chihuahua. While they were away, Mexicans raided the camp and murdered his wife and three children. From that day forward he killed Mexicans blindly and with passion. It is said his name came from Mexicans in terror calling on their patron saint Geronimo for protection. Geronimo was never a chief. While his skill as a leader gained him many followers, he always deferred to the true chiefs of his tribe. He was probably at the Battle of Apache Pass in 1862 with Cochise and Mangas Coloradas.

After the conclusion of the Apache Wars in 1872, the Chiricahua, including Geronimo, were allowed to remain in the Chiricahua Mountains until the mid-1870s, when the U.S. government decided to consolidate the various Apache groups at the San Carlos and White Mountain Agencies. However, this proved unwise; some of the tribes disliked each other as vehemently as they disliked whites.

The restive Apache, especially the Chiricahua, detested reservation life with its meager rations, atrocious conditions, and boredom. However, probably even ideal conditions would not have kept the Chiricahua, the most independent and warlike of the southwestern tribes, happy for long. Soon adding to their unhappiness was the discovery of rich minerals in their homeland, with resulting encroachment by whites. Finally, rumors that all Apache would be moved to Oklahoma made the Indians ripe for revolt. It was from this context, around 1881, that Geronimo emerged as a prominent leader among the Apache.

That fall, Geronimo left the reservation with several warriors, making a terrorizing series of raids on the way to Mexico. On September 4, 1882, the army recalled Gen. George Crook to Arizona to find and stop Geronimo. During his 1872–73 campaign in Arizona's central mountains, Crook had won the respect of both Indians and whites when, in hard winter warfare, he subjugated the Yavapai and Tonto Apache. Unlike many of his peers, quiet, unpretentious Crook respected and sympathized with the Apache, but he firmly believed they must trade in their nomadic ways for agriculture.

Crook employed several key tactics in his campaigns. One was to use Apache scouts; another was to carry supplies on mules instead of in less mobile wagons. In 1883 Crook's force of a cavalry troop and 193 Apache scouts left San Bernardino Springs with enough supplies and ammunition for sixty days. Their invasion of the Chiricahuas' natural fortress dealt the Indians a huge psychological blow, and the Apache called for a truce. Crook's

Apache scouts (no date) —Southwest Studies, Scottsdale Community College

Historic parley between Geronimo and Crook,
1886 —Southwest Studies, Scottsdale Community College

Gen. George Crook
—Southwest Studies,
Scottsdale Community College

terms were terse: Return to the reservation at once. Within a few months Geronimo and his people were back at San Carlos.

The uneasy truce lasted until early 1885 when Geronimo led a disgruntled group to protest Crook's policy against wife-beating and alcohol. The situation became tense, and in May Geronimo bolted again with forty-two warriors and ninety-two women and children. For the rest of the year, the army campaigned against the elusive Chiricahua band in the Sierra Madre.

Finally, in early 1886 Geronimo agreed to meet with General Crook at Canyon de los Embudos, about twelve miles south of the border. Officials in Washington had authorized Crook to set the terms for surrender, and he decided on two years of confinement for the Apache with their families in Florida before returning to the reservation. At Los Embudos, Crook, Geronimo, and other leaders agreed to the terms. The general headed back to Fort Bowie to wire Washington.

In the meantime, a whiskey peddler visited Geronimo's camp,

got Geronimo well-oiled, and told him that the soldiers planned to kill him. The next morning Geronimo and his party were missing. General Crook, knowing he was blamed for putting too much trust in Geronimo, asked to be relieved of his command and was replaced by Gen. Nelson Miles.

Miles, a successful Indian fighter like Crook but also vain and ambitious, recognized what capturing Geronimo could do for his career. He continued the campaign against the Chiricahua using Crook's tactics. He too used Apache scouts, though he gave major credit to his white troops. However, the most effective tactic turned out to be the rounding up, on August 29, 1886, of the remaining, peaceful Chiricahua from the reservation, who were marched to Holbrook, loaded on trains, and shipped to Florida.

When Geronimo was informed that Apache families were already in Florida, he agreed to come in. The surrender took

Geronimo (front row, third from right) and his band of Chiricahua Apache prior to their departure for Florida in 1886 —Arizona State Library

place on September 4, 1886, at Skeleton Canyon. However, the government did not honor the terms. In Florida, prisoners were separated from their families. Many died in the fierce tropical climate. Two years of confinement stretched into eight. Finally the Apache were moved in 1894 to a more suitable climate at Fort Sill, Oklahoma. A proposal that they settle permanently on Catalina Island, California, never jelled. In 1913, fewer than 200 Apache were allowed to move to the Mescalero Reservation in New Mexico. The rest remained in Oklahoma.

The results of the Geronimo campaign were surprisingly mixed. The dominance of the intractable Chiricahua Apache ended, but the military's pullout soon thereafter caused severe economic loss in the state. Some merchants not directly in harm's way actually wished the wars could continue indefinitely. The many loyal Chiricahua scouts the army had relied on to gain the upper hand were shipped east along with the renegades and kept in the same prisons.

General Crook died in 1890. He spent his last years lobbying his government to honor the terms of Geronimo's surrender. General Miles rose to the rank of army chief of staff, but in 1898 so bungled his part in the Spanish-American War that his hopes for the presidency were dashed forever. His nemesis, Teddy Roosevelt, unceremoniously retired the general once he secured the oval office.

Geronimo converted to Christianity, dictated his auto-biography, became a skilled poker player, visited fairs and expositions as a celebrity, and rode in an automobile in Teddy Roosevelt's inaugural parade in 1905. He died on February 17, 1909, and was buried at Fort Sill. He remains a controversial and colorful figure. While he was never more than a partisan leader—never attained the stature of Cochise, Juh, Victorio, or Mangas Coloradas—his name remains fixed in American mythology.

BISBEE

Twenty-four miles west of Douglas on AZ 80, Bisbee lies nestled in the heart of the Mule Mountains. Beneath these granite mountains, the wealth of gold, silver, and copper would defy a prospector's wildest imagination. But for years the mountains guarded their secrets well. It was late in the nineteenth century before a cavalry scout named Jack Dunn stumbled across some rocks of unusual interest. In the midst of chasing hostile Apache in the spring of 1877, Dunn stopped to camp in Mule Pass. Searching for water in the vicinity of today's Castle Rock, he found rich outcroppings of ore.

Back at Fort Bowie, Dunn met prospector George Warren. Knowing that the Apache campaigns would keep him on the trail for the next several months, Dunn and some partners chose to back or "grubstake" Warren to mine what Dunn had found, as long as they were included on the claims. On his way to the Mule Mountains, Warren got sidetracked in a saloon, where he lost his

George Warren —Southwest Studies, Scottsdale Community College

grubstake money. After revealing his mission to some of the saloon's denizens, however, he was quickly reequipped by some new partners. When Warren eventually filed claims in Mule Pass, Dunn and his partners were not listed.

Two years after the discovery of the ore, a drunken George Warren wagered his share of what would become the legendary Copper Queen Mine on a footrace. Firmly believing he could outrun a man on horseback, he lost the race and with it millions of dollars. Warren died in poverty, alone and forgotten. Years later he was reburied with a headstone honoring him as "Father of the Camp." A more lasting memorial is the nearby town of Warren, named in his honor.

Early Bisbee

Soon after prospectors' picks struck pay dirt, a town sprang up nearby, called Bisbee after Judge DeWitt Bisbee of San Francisco, a financial backer. Despite the fact that mile-high Bisbee became known as the most cultured and gracious city between San Francisco and New Orleans, Judge Bisbee never visited.

In the early days of the 1880s Bisbee was rough around the edges. Wood-framed homes perched precariously on the steep, terraced hillsides; it was said you couldn't spit tobacco juice off your front porch without hitting your neighbor below; small children had to be tethered to fence posts lest they fall onto neighboring rooftops.

Bisbee was a two-canyon city. The main thoroughfare was Tombstone Canyon, later called Main Street. Another canyon, Brewery Gulch, came in from the north. Tombstone Canyon became the central business district, while Brewery Gulch gained notoriety for its saloons and shady ladies. Supposedly Brewery Gulch got its name when Gen. George Crook's legendary scout Al Sieber dug a hole in one side of the gulch and opened a brewery. Brewery Gulch went down in western history as one of America's rowdiest avenues of pleasures. Old-timers used to say the farther up the gulch you went, the rougher the saloons and the wilder the women. However, action slowed in Brewery Gulch in 1910 when prostitution was outlawed, and five years later, Prohibition became law. After that, anyone with wild oats to sow had to cross the Mexican border at Naco.

Bisbee, looking west up Tombstone Canyon (no date) —Arizona Historical Foundation

Bisbee's Brewery Gulch in the 1880s; Orpheum Theatre in forefront —Arizona Historical Foundation

Like all mining towns, Bisbee had its share of violence. The notorious Bisbee Massacre occurred during the Christmas season of 1883, when five men held up the Goldwater-Casteneda Store on Main Street. During the robbery, the men stationed outside the store opened fire, killing five people, including a pregnant woman. After a lengthy manhunt, the outlaws—Red Sample, Bill Delaney, Tex Howard, Dan Dowd, and Dan Kelley—were captured and sentenced to hang. A sixth man, John Heith, who owned a dance hall in Bisbee, was charged with planning the robbery and sentenced to prison. While jailed in Tombstone, Heith was killed at the hands of a lynch mob.

Mining in Bisbee

During the Copper Queen's peak years (1890–1920), 10,000 people occupied the 640 acres of livable hillside land near Bisbee; the greater Bisbee area supported a population of 20,000. Officially, this area was known as the Warren Mining District and included Bisbee, Warren, Lowell, San Jose, and a humble Mexican community called Tintown. Amazingly, the district's ore-bearing land encompassed an area only 2 miles by 3 miles on the

Bisbee, looking east, 1888. The cone-shaped mountain in the center no longer exists; it is a huge open pit today. —Southwest Studies, Scottsdale Community College

surface, running to a depth of 4,000 feet. The Copper Queen ran day and night. In 1880, a smelter was erected in Bisbee. Before, the ore had to be shipped all the way to Pennsylvania for smelting.

In early 1881 metallurgist and geologist Dr. James Douglas paid a visit to the boom camp. Some eastern speculators had commissioned him to examine mining properties between Prescott and Flagstaff. Douglas also decided to check out Bisbee and was so impressed he convinced the New York–based import-export company Phelps-Dodge to go into mining. They purchased 51 percent of the Copper Queen Mine and adjacent properties. Dr. Douglas was given a choice of taking a commission in cash or a piece of the action, and wisely chose the latter. From 1885 to 1908 he was president of Copper Queen Consolidated. Mine workers and investors alike trusted and respected him for his honesty, integrity, and loyalty. When he died in 1918, Douglas had accumulated more than $20 million.

In 1901 the Calumet & Arizona Mining Company (named for investors in Calumet, Michigan) hit an immense body of high-grade ore in Bisbee that became one of the richest mines in the world, paying out $47 million in dividends. The Calumet and the Phelps-Dodge thrived in friendly competition until the Great Depression, when Phelps-Dodge bought out the Calumet & Arizona.

During World War I, new techniques for reducing low-grade ore at a profit and the advent of large trucks and earthmoving equipment made open-pit mining feasible. Mountains became terraced canyons. Sacramento Hill, just east of Buckey O'Neill Hill and southeast of Bisbee, was a classic example. In 1917, destruction of the cone-shaped mountain began when tons of explosives literally blew its top off.

The Bisbee Deportation

In 1917, one of the most traumatic events in Arizona history took place: the infamous Bisbee Deportation. For years the unions and the copper companies had struggled bitterly. With the advent of World War I and the allies' desperate need for copper, the price of the metal skyrocketed, and the unions judged the time was ripe for a strike. Mining towns throughout the state felt the rumblings. One union, the Industrial Workers of the World (IWW), or Wobblies, was more vocal than the rest and gained a reputation for troublemaking. To fight the IWW, the copper companies, led by Phelps-Dodge, began a clever propaganda war against the IWW. Since Phelps-Dodge controlled several newspapers, not to mention a number of legislators, it wasn't hard to arouse the public's ire against a group preaching for strikes during critical times.

The situation climaxed on July 12, 1917. At 6:30 A.M. 2,000 armed, deputized citizens loyal to the copper companies took to the streets of the Warren Mining District. Wearing white handkerchiefs tied around their arms, they rounded up more than 2,000 suspected IWW members and sympathizers and herded them to the baseball park at Warren. By day's end, nearly 1,200 of them had been loaded into boxcars and shipped to a military post in Columbus, New Mexico. Considering the intensity of emotions on both sides, it is miraculous that only two men died during these proceedings; one was a suspected Wobbly, the other a vigilante. In Columbus, the deported miners were warned that if they returned to Bisbee, they would be killed. The deportees stayed for a time at the post, then drifted to other mining camps far from Bisbee.

Back in Bisbee, vigilantes belonging to the so-called "Loyalty League" patrolled the town for a month, continuing their purge of anarchistic Wobblies. Most Arizona citizens supported their actions; those who sought justice for the miners met with frustration. Charge after charge failed in the courts. President Woodrow Wilson ordered Judge Felix Frankfurter to investigate, but Frankfurter found no federal offense. The Supreme Court concluded that the Loyalty League had been enforcing the "law of necessity." Though the president rebuked the mine owners, they had succeeded in dealing the unions a crushing blow. It would be decades before the unions regained the ground they had lost.

Modern Times

In the mid-1950s, a new operation was begun that overwhelmed the Sacramento Pit. Called the Lavender Pit in honor of Harrison Lavender, manager of the Copper Queen branch of Phelps-Dodge, the huge pit reached more than 900 feet deep before it

Copper Queen Hotel in Bisbee, circa 1900 —Arizona Historical Foundation

shut down in 1974. By the time underground operations ended a year later, the Bisbee area, one of the richest mineral sites ever known, had produced a staggering $6.1 billion from approximately 3 million ounces of gold, 97 million ounces of silver, 8 billion pounds of copper, 304 million pounds of lead, and 273 million pounds of zinc.

Like so many Arizona mining towns, Bisbee exudes a rich sense of the turn of the twentieth century. The Copper Queen Hotel, built in 1902, was as opulent as any big-city hostelry. Celebrities who spent the night there and dined in its elegant restaurant include President Teddy Roosevelt and Gen. John "Blackjack" Pershing. Other old buildings and landmarks include the elaborate Phelps-Dodge general offices, now the Bisbee Mining Museum; Mulheim's Brewery; the Pythian Castle, with its magnificent green dome; and Castle Rock, a natural landmark. Today, tourism is a mainstay of Bisbee's survival. Art is part of the town's attraction; artists occupy many of the old houses and buildings.

TOMBSTONE

From Bisbee, AZ 80 heads north twenty-four miles to the legendary and historic town of Tombstone. When prospector Ed Schieffelin set out to explore the mountains of southeast Arizona, an Apache stronghold, people warned him that all he would find was his own tombstone. Instead, a few miles east of the San Pedro River, he succeeded in locating a veritable mountain of rich silver. It was only fitting that the town that sprang up nearby be named Tombstone.

Originally, Tombstone was about two miles west of its current location, but in 1879 setters established a new town site on Goose Flats. There they set up housekeeping in canvas tents, brush wickiups (teepeelike huts), and flat-board shanties. Within a year the town boasted telegraph service and gas lighting.

Ed Schieffelin

When prospector Ed Schieffelin heard about the gold and silver strikes in Arizona Territory, he set off in search of the illusive rainbow's end. His quest led him into the San Pedro Valley, to a geologic upheaval north of the Mule Mountains. There, combinations of igneous rock and limestone led him to suspect that beneath the drab mantle of gray stone on the surface, great treasure lay.

Schieffelin spent the summer of 1877 scouring the hills, gathering ore specimens and staking two claims, which he called the Tombstone and the Graveyard. When supplies ran low, he headed west to Tucson. People around Tucson came to look on the shaggy prospector as an eccentric; therefore, even though his ore samples looked promising, nobody would grubstake him.

Undaunted, he took his specimens and headed for Globe, where his younger brother Al was hard-rock mining. When he got there, Schieffelin learned that Al had moved on to McCracken, Arizona, 250 miles to the west, near the Colorado River. With his last thirty cents, Schieffelin bought a plug of chewing tobacco—his only vice—and set out on foot. When he got to McCracken, his brother wasn't impressed with his ore samples either. Instead, Al suggested his brother throw away his rocks and take a regular job in the mines.

Ed Schieffelin
—Southwest Studies,
Scottsdale Community
College

Fortunately for Schieffelin, renowned assayer Richard Gird also lived in McCracken. Gird assayed some of the specimens at $2,000 to the ton. Although Al remained skeptical, the three of them formed a partnership. Fearing Gird's absence would arouse unwanted attention, the threesome snuck out of camp. Traveling southeast, the men passed evidence of a recent Apache attack: bullet-scarred walls at Pantano stage station, and, a few miles on, the shallow graves of two unlucky travelers. Undaunted, they followed the San Pedro River twenty miles upstream to the Narrows. There, in an abandoned adobe cabin, the resourceful Gird transformed the fireplace into an assaying furnace.

Unfortunately, Schieffelin's ore specimens had come from a rich but shallow pocket that soon played out. For a time it looked like the Graveyard claim was well named. Then Schieffelin uncovered a ledge of ore-bearing granite that assayed out at $15,000 to the ton of silver and $1,500 to the ton of gold. "Ed,"

Gird is said to have exclaimed, "you are a lucky cuss—you have hit it!" Thus was born the fabulous Lucky Cuss Mine.

In the meantime, other prospectors were staking claims. Hank Williams struck a deal with Gird to split everything fifty-fifty if Gird did his assaying for free. When Williams struck pay dirt, he conveniently forgot Gird's name on the claim. Confronting Williams, the two Schieffelins and Gird jogged his memory. Williams agreed to keep his end of the bargain, and physical violence was averted. Named in honor of the confrontation, the Contention Mine turned out to be one of the richest in the area.

In 1880 Schieffelin sold his interests in the Contention Mine for $10,000. Three years later it produced $5 million in ore. Soon after, Schieffelin sold all his interests in the Tombstone area. Now, when Ed Schieffelin walked down the street, people no longer snickered; his words, once the object of ridicule, were considered prophetic. From Wall Street to San Francisco, everyone had heard of the man who made the biggest silver strike in Arizona history.

Schieffelin died in the wilds of Oregon on May 12, 1897. Just before he died he wrote, "I am getting restless here in Oregon and wish to go somewhere that has wealth for the digging of it. I

Ed Schieffelin Monument, Tombstone; Dragoon Mountains in background —Southwest Studies, Scottsdale Community College

like the excitement of being right up against the earth, trying to coax her gold away and scatter it."

Ed Schieffelin's final wishes were to be dressed in prospector's clothing, equipped with pick and canteen, and buried in Tombstone at the place he had camped just before the fabulous strike. At the west end of town, a narrow dirt road meanders past the old cemetery. Down this road about two and a half miles, on a gentle rock-strewn slope, a monument marks the final resting place of the discoverer of the Tombstone treasure.

1880s Boomtown

At one time larger than San Francisco, Tombstone in the 1880s was the most notorious boomtown in the West. Hollywood has portrayed it as a frontier Sodom and Gomorrah that each day claimed "a man before breakfast," but actually Tombstone was less violent than some other mining towns. Everyone pitched in to build churches and schools. Miners labored ten hours a day in the mines and raised families. However, like all boomtowns, Tombstone had its share of growing pains. The vast riches uncovered by the Schieffelins and others attracted a wide gamut of frontier society, including gamblers, lawyers, ladies of easy virtue, merchants, real estate dealers, stock swindlers, and con artists.

The two sides of Allen Street were quite distinct. On the south side, stores, cafes, and similar enterprises conducted business, while the north side was a Barbary Coast, Old West style, known

Tombstone in the 1880s —Southwest Studies, Scottsdale Community College

affectionately as Rotten Row. Bars and casinos with their faro tables and spinning roulette wheels, boisterous laughter, and rinky-tink pianos operated twenty-four hours a day. No self-respecting lady would be caught dead strolling down the boardwalk on the north side lest she be mistaken for such boomtown belles as Dutch Annie, Crazy Horse Lil, Lizzette the Flying Nymph, or Little Gertie the Gold Dollar. Both dingy crib houses and fancy brothels were located in the vicinity of Sixth Street and Allen. Two blocks west at Fourth Street between Allen and Tough Nut, lawyers' offices were conveniently situated near both the courthouse and the local watering holes.

Two major fires destroyed the Tombstone business district. The first, on June 22, 1881, ignited when a bartender tried to measure the contents of a whiskey barrel with a cigar in his mouth. Flames soon engulfed more than sixty saloons, restaurants, and businesses. The industrious citizens went to work immediately rebuilding the town, and within two weeks business was booming again. Less than a year later, however, a second fire started in the Tivoli Saloon. Once again it burned down the business district, causing $500,000 in damage.

Since the lack of water made even herculean fire-fighting efforts futile, this time, wisely, the city decided to rebuild in brick and adobe. Eventually the Huachuca Water Company was successfully organized. An iron pipeline brought water from the Huachuca Mountains, twenty-one miles to the southwest.

In silver-rich Tombstone, wealthy citizens imported the best culture and entertainment money could buy. An endless array of acting troupes and other performers played such theaters as the Bird Cage and Schieffelin Hall. The Bird Cage, built in 1881, was a saloon, brothel, burlesque theater, and dance hall rolled into one. Schieffelin Hall, built in 1881 by Al Schieffelin in honor of brother Ed, was the civic, social, and cultural center of Tombstone. It still stands and is open to visitors.

Boomtown Tombstone attracted many colorful characters. Doctor George Goodfellow, the famous "gunshot physician," was one. Doc Goodfellow opened an office over the Crystal Palace Saloon in the early 1880s. He quickly established a reputation as an expert in treating gunshot wounds and even published on the subject. But whatever the situation, whether it was commandeering and driving a steam locomotive to rush a gunshot victim to a hospital in Tucson, riding to some remote hideaway to treat a cattle rustler suffering from lead poisoning, or crawling into a smoke-filled mine shaft to rescue hard-rock miners, Doc Goodfellow was the man of the hour. During the great earthquake in northern Sonora in 1887, he was one of the first to rush to the stricken area. Mexican President Porfirio Diaz rewarded him with a special medal.

Goodfellow's greatest notoriety may be in connection with the lynching of John Heith after the Bisbee Massacre in 1883, in which five citizens, including a pregnant woman, were killed during a robbery. While most of the perpetrators were captured and hanged for their crime, Heith received only a prison sentence. Outraged citizens wrested Heith, sequestered in the Cochise County Jail in Tombstone, and strung him up to a telegraph pole on Tough Nut Street, effectively administering the Old West's version of a suspended sentence. (Surprisingly, considering Tombstone's reputation, this was the town's only lynching.) Charges were brought against the vigilantes, pending a report by the county coroner—Doc George Goodfellow. With all the aplomb of a frontier Solomon, Goodfellow ruled that John Heith had come to his end due to emphysema—shortness of breath at a high altitude.

Nellie Cashman was another unforgettable Tombstone character—and an incurable argonaut if there ever was one. With her sister, she immigrated to San Francisco from Ireland during the California gold rush. Nellie never succeeded at clearing gold fever from her system; gold seeking would eventually take her from Mexico to the Arctic Circle. Too adventuresome to be tied down, there's no record of the number of marriage proposals she turned down. During her time in Tombstone, Nellie ran the Russ House rooming house and cafe at Tough Nut and Fifth Streets. Most of her boarders were hard-rock miners.

Kindhearted and generous, she never refused to help someone down on his luck. As the date approached for the legal hanging of the infamous Bisbee Massacre outlaws at the county courthouse, an enterprising but ghoulish carpenter erected a grandstand overlooking the walls and planned to charge admission. The condemned men called on Nellie to prevent their deaths from becoming a public spectacle. She obliged, rounding

Nellie Cashman, "Angel of the Mining Camp"
—Southwest Studies, Scottsdale Community College

up a few friends who destroyed the structure the night before the execution—the largest mass hanging in Arizona history.

The Gunfight and Its Aftermath

Most of Tombstone's notoriety stems from the "Gunfight at the OK Corral," although the shoot-out actually took place near the corner of Fremont and Third Streets. The fight, which happened on October 26, 1881, grew out of a long and bitter struggle for power among three parties in Cochise County: the Earp brothers and their allies, including Doc Holliday, Mayor John Clum, and leading businessmen; Sheriff Johnny Behan, leader of the Democratic Party machine; and the Clanton gang, cattle rustlers who portrayed themselves as honest ranchers. Behan sided with the Clantons, probably in part because a woman he loved, Josephine Sarah Marcus, loved Wyatt Earp instead.

Wyatt Earp
—Courtesy author

The night before the shootout, Ike Clanton and Doc Holliday had a verbal confrontation. The next morning, October 26, Clanton went gunning for Holliday and was arrested for carrying firearms. Soon the other Clantons and the Earps faced off. Some of the Clanton gang turned tail and ran before the shooting started; the three who didn't soon lay dead in the street. Two of the Earps, Virgil and Morgan, and Holliday were also wounded.

Severely whipped in the stand-up gunfight, the Clanton gang turned to ambush tactics. On December 14, an unknown assailant fired at Mayor John Clum. Two weeks later, a full load of buckshot crippled Virgil Earp. The final blow came on March 18, 1882, when someone shot Morgan Earp to death in an Allen Street pool hall. Since Wyatt Earp could expect no justice from Sheriff Behan, he went on a personal vendetta outside the law, and within a week, suspects Frank Stilwell, Florentino Cruz, and outlaw leader Curly Bill Brocius were dead. The turmoil in Cochise County was so great, President Chester A. Arthur threatened to proclaim martial law there.

With his life in danger as long as he remained in Arizona, Wyatt Earp left for Colorado. Some say he never returned. Others believe he came back in July and gunned down another old nemesis, Johnny Ringo, up at Turkey Creek.

With Wyatt Earp's departure from Tombstone, the Cochise County War came to an end. But cattle rustling and associated crimes continued to rise. By 1901, the territorial assembly and the governor decided to organize a new force: the Arizona Rangers. The rangers were empowered to cross county lines in pursuit of outlaws; a few bold ones even crossed the international boundary to get their man. Until their discharge in 1909, the Arizona Rangers were an effective force against rustling.

Demise of Tombstone

Almost from the beginning, Tombstone's days were numbered. At 500 feet down, mine workers hit water. The companies installed pumps to lift it out, but in 1886 fires destroyed the pumps at the Contention and Grand Central, flooding the mines. By 1890 the town was nearly dead. The Panic of 1893 and the demonetization of silver struck further blows. For a time in the early 1900s, when the Tombstone Consolidated Mines Company installed new pumps and a spur line came through from Fairbank, it looked like Tombstone might prosper once more. But in 1909 the pumps failed again, and two years later, Tombstone Consolidated was bankrupt.

Tombstone, the town too tough to die, was barely hanging on when the final humiliation came in 1929: Bisbee took the county seat away. Today, the venerable old red brick Tombstone County Courthouse, built in 1882, still stands at the corner of Tough Nut and Third Streets. Now in the capable hands of the State Park Commission, the courthouse remains a reservoir of Tombstone's rich and illustrious history—with the added distinction of being the smallest state park and museum in Arizona. Today, tourism is an important industry in Tombstone.

From Tombstone to Benson, AZ 80 roughly parallels the old stagecoach road linking the two communities before the railroad reached Fairbank in 1881. Some adobe ruins remain on private land.

AZ 92 and AZ 90
Bisbee—I-10
48 MILES

NACO

Ten miles south of Bisbee and a few miles west of Bisbee Junction is the border town of Naco, established in the 1890s on the rail line to the mines at Nacozari, Sonora. Naco, a Ute-Aztecan word, refers to the fruit of the barrel cactus—the source of a tasty jelly and, from the fermented juices, an alcoholic beverage. The short, round cactus grows throughout this area.

Few people outside of Cochise County have heard of Naco. Actually, there are two Nacos, one on each side of the Mexico-U.S. border. During Prohibition (1915–33), in daytime, these two communities seemed like sleepy, quiet villages basking in the desert sun. After dark, however, Naco, Sonora, transformed into a bibulous Babylon, its cantinas lit up like Christmas trees and beckoning to pleasure seekers from Bisbee and Fort Huachuca as seductively as the Sirens called to Ulysses.

Mexican Naco was a favorite haunt of Mexican guerrilla leader Pancho Villa and other revolutionaries. Around 1915, Mexican government troops occupied Naco, and Villa's army tried to retake it. To the west, near Palominas, the *Villistas* hauled an antique cannon up a cone-shaped mountain to lob shots down onto the Mexican government troops, or *federales.* However, each time the cannon fired, the recoil jarred it loose and sent it careening down the mountain. It took hours to get it in place for another shot, allowing the Villistas only a few sporadic rounds a day.

Mexican Naco was again the site of fighting in a rebellion in 1929. Often there was no major plan of attack in these battles—or any plan at all. This time, the federales were entrenched on three sides of Naco, Sonora, with their backs to the American border. The rebels occupied the surrounding countryside. Waiting until the gambling houses closed and Bisbee residents had gone home, the rebels loaded a freight car with gunpowder and sent it hurtling toward the center of town. It picked up so much speed, however, that it derailed and blew up before reaching its target.

*Mexican
revolutionary
Pancho Villa*
—Arizona Historical
Society Library/Tucson

It is said that, during days this battle was being waged, the armies engaged in combat only during daylight hours. Nights were reserved for revelry, when combatants from both sides converged on the bistros and bawdy houses of Naco. There, wandering minstrels filled the air with spirited *corridos*—traditional Mexican ballads of love and heros—and fraternizing between soldiers lasted far into the night. At dawn, it was business as usual, and the revolution continued.

Norteamericanos from Bisbee and the surrounding area couldn't stay away from the fighting. Schoolchildren ditched classes, housewives abandoned their kitchens, and businessmen locked up their shops to head to the border at Naco. A railroad track ran parallel to the border, and spectators climbed up on the cars for a good view of the fighting. Occasional stray bullets sent them dropping for cover, but for the most part, revolutionaries and federales alike avoided firing toward American Naco lest they incur the wrath of the U.S. Army.

During this 1929 revolt, a rogue American pilot named Patrick Murphy offered his services to the rebel forces, boasting that he could blow the federales out of their trenches. Revolutionary leaders seized the opportunity, and the soldier of fortune and his nondescript biplane became the Rebel Air Force. The bombs were primitive affairs, leather pouches loaded with explosives and scrap metal with a fuse. The bombardier simply lit the fuse with his cigarette and tossed the suitcase-sized pouch over the side. Several of Murphy's bombs landed in Arizona. One went through the roof of a local garage, destroying an automobile; another landed in the Phelps-Dodge store. Finally, a federale with a 30.06 Springfield rifle shot down Murphy's plane. The pilot crash-landed and was jailed in Nogales, but soon escaped and was never heard from again.

Today, both Nacos are truly quiet. On the Arizona side, two buildings remain as evidence of the turbulent past. The "Bulletproof Hotel" was a rooming house a few blocks north of the border. Its owners armor plated it with corrugated tin for the supposed safety of their guests. Most recently, it was in operation as the Two Owls Inn. The Phelps-Dodge store, a run-down red brick building just north of the customs station, is still standing, but is mostly in ruins.

CORONADO NATIONAL MEMORIAL

The Coronado National Memorial is five miles south and west of AZ 92's junction with AZ 83. It commemorates the approximate site of the *entrada conquista* (entrance of the expedition of conquest) into Arizona of the Spanish conquistador Francisco Vasquez de Coronado (see also Coronado Trail). Between the memorial and Fort Huachuca, AZ 92 hugs the eastern slope of the Huachuca Mountains.

American historian Samuel Elliot Morrison wrote of Coronado's expedition in *The Growth of the American Republic:* "There is no other conquest like this one in the annals of the human race. In one generation the Spaniards acquired more new territory than Rome conquered in five centuries."

Spanish and Aztec tales of fabulous cities of gold inspired this epic 4,000-mile journey from 1540 to 1542. The legends were easy to believe: the Spanish had already found vast, previously unimaginable treasures of gold and silver in Central and South America. In addition, in 1536 four survivors of a Spanish expeditionary force that had shipwrecked off the west coast of Florida and traveled through the wilderness for eight years to Mexico's west coast, returned to civilization. The castaways, including a Moorish slave named Esteban, claimed to have evidence of seven large cities of gold to the north.

Viceroy Antonio Mendoza began making plans for a grand expedition to locate and claim the legendary seven cities and/or the mythical Northwest Passage to the Orient. But first he sent a small party to verify the cities' existence. Because none of the Spanish survivors wanted to venture north again, Mendoza sent the slave Esteban and a Franciscan priest, Fray Marcos de Niza. Traveling down the San Pedro River, the two men reached present-day Arizona in 1539. In early July at the Zuni pueblo Hawikuh near today's Arizona–New Mexico border, south of Zuni, New Mexico, Esteban was killed. Father Marcos returned to Mexico, where he confirmed the existence of the mythical cities and thousands of heathen souls waiting to be saved.

Viceroy Mendoza moved ahead with his plans. Mexico City abounded with young adventurers eager to conquer new lands and take treasure for the Crown. To lead them, Mendoza chose Francisco Vasquez de Coronado, a handsome young man whose wealthy wife financed the trip with the equivalent of a million dollars. Decked out in splendorous regalia, 225 *caballeros* (horsemen), 60 infantry, 2 white women (Spanish officers' wives), 1,000 native allies (men and women), and several black slaves left Compostela, Mexico, in February 1540.

The large party crawled northward along the west coast of Mexico, with the shimmering blue Pacific Ocean to the west and the towering Sierra Madre to the east. They crossed 150 miles of desert and ran short of food. A few miles west of Bisbee, they entered present-day Arizona and headed north through the San Pedro Valley. Bearing east and north, come summer they began encountering disappointingly realistic villages with no gold, as well as hostile inhabitants. Coronado's forces and the Zuni briefly battled on July 7 at Hawikuh Pueblo.

Finally, in parleys after fighting Hopi Indians, the Spaniards learned of a great river to the west and a tall race of people (the Quechan, or Yuma) who lived there. Coronado was optimistic and sent another expedition to locate this "river of giants," which, he believed, might be the Northwest Passage. Hopi guides led García López de Cárdenas and twenty-five men northwest of the mesas and down a twisting, 100-mile trail into the Grand Canyon. Far below, between almost vertical walls, a thin rivulet wound its way through the abyss. The soldiers tried to reach it but gave up. When Cárdenas returned with the discouraging news, Coronado decided to mount no future expeditions to the west. His dream of finding the cities of gold or the Northwest Passage never materialized, and in 1542 the expedition returned to Mexico City in disgrace.

Coronado died a few years later, having opened the vast terra incognita of Arizona for future exploration and settlement. Ironically, the riches he sought were there all the time; he came within a stone's throw of the rich mining regions of Bisbee, Tombstone, and Clifton-Morenci. Writing later, Pedro de Casteñeda, the expedition chronicler, recognized the real significance of Coronado's quest: "Granted they did not find the gold, [but] at least they found a place in which to search."

SIERRA VISTA AND FORT HUACHUCA

Sierra Vista is situated where AZ 92 meets AZ 90, and Fort Huachuca is a few miles west of there. The name of the small community of Sierra Vista changed from Garden Canyon to Fry in 1937 to honor Oliver Fry, an early settler. During World War II the black soldiers at Fort Huachuca nicknamed the town "Hook" because of its numerous prostitutes. Apparently the name Fry, Arizona, and its connotations of suffocating heat did not sit well with the new wave of post–World War II settlers and the tourist-oriented Chamber of Commerce. In 1955 the town was incorporated with the more poetic—and marketable—name of Sierra Vista.

Fort Huachuca is the only active military post in Arizona that traces its roots back to the Apache Wars. After Cochise died in

Fort Huachuca, 1886 —Arizona Historical Society/Tucson

1874, and his people, the Chiricahua Apache, were moved to the San Carlos Reservation, many of the men left the reservation to resume raiding into Mexico. As part of its response, the U.S. established Fort Huachuca a few miles north of the border.

The climate around Fort Huachuca is mild, and the scenery some of the best in southern Arizona. However, early visitors to the fort reported dreary, primitive living conditions. Steady rains from early July through September were followed by prolonged drought. It is still true that the wind begins howling there on the first day of January and doesn't stop until the last day of December.

In 1882, during a resurgence of Apache warfare, Fort Huachuca was upgraded to a permanent military post. Living conditions improved as buildings were constructed. Gen. William Tecumseh Sherman visited the post and selected it for a new parade field— still the center for ceremonies and activities today. Early military activity at the fort peaked in 1885–86. In 1886, after Gen. Nelson Miles replaced Gen. George Crook at the head of the campaigns against the Apache, Miles designated Fort Huachuca as the advance base for expeditions into Mexico.

Miles chose Capt. Henry Lawton, a Civil War recipient of the Medal of Honor and commander of B Troop, 4th Cavalry, Fort Huachuca, to lead a summer campaign into the mountains and deserts of Mexico. On May 5, 1886, while the band played "The Girl I Left behind Me," Lawton led his troops and Apache scouts out the fort's gates and turned south toward Mexico.

The exhausting campaign took its toll. Two-thirds of the officers and men, worn out or ill, failed to finish the campaign. On trails leading up and down the jagged mountains, through steep canyons and gorges, Geronimo and his band evaded their pursuers with relative ease.

Assisting Lawton in the campaign was surgeon Leonard Wood, also of Fort Huachuca. Wood, a graduate of Harvard, put aside his medical bag to hit the campaign trail with the troops. He was awarded the Medal of Honor for bravery and deserves some recognition for common sense when it came to proper desert attire. To combat the hot desert weather, he ordered his troops to strip to their underwear and don straw hats.

During World War II, Fort Huachuca swelled in both importance and size, with more than 30,000 soldiers and civilians stationed there. After the war, however, the army turned the fort over to the Arizona National Guard. Around 1950 the post was abandoned, but the outbreak of the Korean War brought life back to the fort. Today it functions as an Army Intelligence School and a center for testing electronics and communications equipment.

KARTCHNER CAVERNS STATE PARK

In November 1999, a unique state park in the Whetstone Mountains opened ten miles south of Benson. Kartchner Caverns consists of two large rooms, each 100 feet high, connected by two and a half miles of passageway. The caverns host a rare and fragile underground ecosystem—a veritable wonderland of rock formations, colorful limestone columns, calcite shields, rain-fed pools, and dripping stalactites, helictites, and stalagmites. Special attractions include "bird's nest" needle quartz; the longest measured soda straw (tubular stalactite) in the United States; and a fifty-eight-foot "Kubla Khan" column. The temperature in the caves stays a constant sixty-eight degrees and the humidity is 99 percent.

Cavers and friends Randy Tufts and Gary Tenen discovered the caves in 1974. Tufts came close in 1967, at age eighteen, when he keyed in on an unusual sinkhole, but it took him seven years to come back and try again. For fourteen years, the two men kept their discovery a secret until the caves' protection was ensured. The caves are named for the Kartchner family, who owned the land surrounding the caves and helped keep them secret.

AZ 82
AZ 80—Nogales
68 MILES

FAIRBANK

Most of the surrounding country along AZ 82 around Fairbank is rangeland for the famous Boquillas Cattle Ranch, once owned by William Randolph Hearst. The San Juan de las Boquillas y Nogales grant was issued in 1833 for $250. Years of overgrazing, drought, and soil erosion turned sacaton grass and trees into scrubby mesquite and deep-cutting arroyos.

Across the San Pedro River from Fairbank is the site of an old Sobaipuri Indian village called Santa Cruz that dates back to the 1600s. Another village called Quiburi lay about two and a half miles farther north. Father Eusebio Kino, the legendary Jesuit missionary, first visited these villages in 1692. The Sobaipuri, related mainly by language to the Pima, were renowned fighters. Kino established a visita (part-time mission) among the natives, but the Apache forced its abandonment in 1698. The Apache helped extinguish the already small population of Sobaipuri by both killing them and driving them out to take refuge with the Akimel O'Odham, or Pima, with whom they eventually merged.

From 1775 to 1780, the Spanish had a presidio, or fort, at Quiburi called Santa Cruz de Terrenate, constructed by the storied Irish mercenary Col. Hugo O'Conor. But the Apache succeeded in driving the soldiers out, too. Visitors can hike to the site. To get to the trailhead, go west on AZ 82 1.2 miles out of Fairbank, to milepost 60. Turn north for 1.8 miles on Kellar Ranch Road. The ruins are a 1.2-mile hike to the east, overlooking the San Pedro River.

BABOCOMARI RANCH

Traveling west from Fairbank toward Sonoita, the sprawling, grassy rangelands are part of the old San Ignacio del Babocomari grant. In 1827 Don Ignacio Elías Gonzales and his wife Doña Eulalia paid $380 for over fifty-four square miles stretching along both sides of Babocomari Creek. At an elevation of 4,000 feet, it enjoys abundant rainfall, making it one of the best places to raise cattle in southern Arizona. For almost twenty years the Elías family ran over 40,000 head from the Santa Rita Mountains on the west to the San Pedro River on the east. Their home was an adobe fort surrounded by a fifteen-foot wall.

After Apache attacks killed two Elías brothers, the Babocomari Ranch was abandoned during the 1840s. A troop of U.S. Cavalry occupied the old adobe fort in 1864, renaming it Camp Wallen, and from it launching campaigns against Cochise and his Chiricahua Apache. During the 1870s Dr. Edward Perrin, a former Confederate soldier from Alabama, began buying up the rights to the Babocomari. Perrin would become one of the largest landowners in Arizona.

Like other area ranches, the Babocomari suffered from drought and ersion from overgrazing. In the 1930s the Brophy family acquired the land and commenced a thirty-year effort to reclaim and restore the ranch. They dug wells and reseeded ranges, and gradually the land began returning to its natural state.

SONOITA AND SONOITA CREEK

Sonoita Creek is the major tributary of the Santa Cruz River. Almost completely surrounded by mountains, the rolling grassy hills around the creek are studded with groves of live oak, ash, sycamore, black walnut, and cottonwood. During the 1950s location scouts chose the area for the filming of Rogers and Hammerstein's *Oklahoma*. The land had all the natural beauty of turn-of-the-century Oklahoma except for golden fruit and corn as "high as an elephant's eye." However, special projects personnel were able to fix that; they created cornfields and orchards with simulated fruit made out of wax. During filming, a steady supply of wax was needed as the fruit kept melting in the Arizona sun.

However, it seems that real corn did grow here at one time: in Tohono O'Odham, Sonoita means "Place Where Corn Will Grow." Father Kino first mentioned the place in 1700. The Sobaipuri Indians had settled along Sonoita Creek after they abandoned their villages at Quiburi and Santa Cruz to the east in 1698. Earlier they had whipped the Apache; fearing retaliation, Chief Coro moved his people farther west, about two or three miles southwest of Patagonia. He called their new village Sonoita. The present-day town is not on the same site as the old one, but it is named after it.

Bascom Affair

The Bascom Affair, the event cited as igniting ten years of warfare between the United States and the Apache, started at Sonoita Creek. In October 1860 a band of Apache swooped down on the ranch of an Irish settler, John Ward, and kidnapped Ward's stepson, Felix Teliz. The military decided the most noteworthy chief in the area, Cochise, must be the culprit. Early in 1861, a small force under Lt. George Bascom went to Cochise's camp in Apache Pass, at the north end of the Chiricahua Mountains, to parley.

Despite the chief's denial of involvement with the kidnapping, the soldiers tried to take him prisoner, but the wily Chiricahua chief escaped into the brush. The soldiers seized three of his relatives and held them hostage. Cochise retaliated by attacking the Butterfield Overland stage station in Apache Pass and capturing three employees.

Reinforcements from Fort Buchanan arrived. On the way, they captured three more Apache hostages. When he heard the news, Cochise also took three more hostages; each side now held six. The white captives pleaded with the officers to relinquish the Apache captives, but Bascom stubbornly refused to do so until the kidnapped youngster was returned.

Finally, growing tired of the stalemate, Cochise killed his captives. In turn, the military hung its six Apache hostages, all from the same tree limb. Outraged, Cochise commenced a bloody ten-year war. Along Sonoita Creek, the situation intensified a few months later when the Civil War broke out and the army was called away from Fort Buchanan, leaving settlers at the mercy of Cochise's raiders.

In the end, Cochise was proven innocent in the Bascom Affair. It turned out an unrelated band of Apache, Coyoteros, had taken the youngster. Interestingly, the child remained among his captors, acquiring the name Mickey Free. During the Geronimo Campaign of the 1880s, Free served as one of General Crook's most valuable scouts.

The army returned to Sonoita Creek after the Civil War. In 1867 they established a new military post, Fort Crittenden, on a hill overlooking the ruins of abandoned Fort Buchanan. Fort Crittenden closed in 1872.

Mickey Free
—Southwest Studies,
Scottsdale Community
College

PATAGONIA MOUNTAINS AND PATAGONIA

In the 1860s the Patagonia Mountains, southeast of AZ 82, were the site of several rich mining ventures. One of the most famous was the old Patagonia Mine, dating back to Spanish times. Lt. Sylvester Mowry, a flamboyant officer stationed at Fort Buchanan, purchased the mine in 1859, changing its name to the Mowry. Under Mowry's ownership the mine employed over 100 workers and produced $1.5 million in silver and lead ore; in the early 1860s it was one of the nation's richest mines. However, during the Civil War, Mowry was arrested as a Confederate sympathizer. In his absence, high-graders—miners who pocket ore while they work—gutted his mine, and in a few decades, the Mowry mining camp joined the list of ghost towns in the area. Others included Harshaw, Washington Camp, and Duquesne.

At the feet of the Patagonias, on AZ 82, the town of Patagonia remains. *Patagon* is Spanish for "big paw." It's believed that in 1855 American boundary surveyors named the place after a paw print of a large grizzly bear they found there. Between 1867 and 1873, Patagonia was closely connected to nearby, short-lived Fort Crittenden. In 1883 Rollen Richardson bought squatters' rights to the abandoned fort and named it the Pennsylvania Ranch after his home state. In 1896, Richardson moved the town to its current location. He wanted to change the name to Rollen or Rollentown, but residents held firm to Patagonia.

NOGALES

Some old-timers say the diagonal line running between Nogales and Yuma is due to some thirsty surveyors. Supposedly they reached the desert west of Nogales before realizing that the nearest saloon was northwest at Yuma. Aware of their priorities, they turned and headed in that direction—depriving Arizona of its sea coast in the process.

Long before that time, bordertown Nogales and the surrounding area were Arizona's cradle of civilization. Before recorded history, the Pima, the Tohono O'Odham or Papago, and the Apache all lived there. The European presence arrived in 1691 with Father Eusebio Kino on his first trip into Arizona. Invited by the Sobaipuri who lived along the Santa Cruz River, the Italian Jesuit stopped at Guévavi, two miles south of Sonoita Creek and ten miles north of Nogales.

By 1843, the Los Nogales land grant, nearly 33,000 acres, had been awarded to Don José Elías. The Elíases were ranchers, and the grass-carpeted hills provided feed for as many as 4,000 head of cattle. Los Nogales, "the walnut trees" in Spanish, refers to trees in the area. In the early 1850s Maj. William Emory of the Army Corps of Topographical Engineers, who camped on the site of the future town while surveying the Gadsden Purchase, noticed two big walnut trees straddling the border with Mexico, inspiring the camp name, Dos Nogales.

The actual city of Nogales dates from 1882, the year the Arizona & Southwestern Railroad between Benson and Guaymas, Sonora, came through town. At the same time, Jacob Isaacson, a traveling salesman, arrived in the small community and started a store near the railroad. The store straddled the international boundary. On May 31, 1882, a post office opened in the store and the place became known as Isaacson. A respected community leader, entrepreneur, and musician, Isaacson accepted the honor in September 1882 of driving the last ceremonial railroad spike into the Guaymas-Benson line. After a year, the town decided on a name change, and Nogales prevailed.

By 1898 Nogales, population 1,500, had grown into the fifth largest city in the territory. In 1916, during the Mexican Revolution, Pancho Villa's army captured Nogales, Sonora. When his troops threatened to cross into Arizona, American gunfire drove them back. American infantry were deployed along International Street, and American sharpshooters killed several *Villistas* in a tense thirty-minute shootout. The incident brought about the establishment of a military post, Camp Little, on the edge of town.

Two years later, relations between the two Nogales deteriorated into the so-called Battle of Ambos ("both") Nogales. That summer, U.S. intelligence noted the presence of well-armed Mexicans and a number of Germans around the border near Nogales. An anonymous letter warned the Americans to expect action from the Mexicans sometime in August. On the afternoon of August 27, a Mexican national crossed the border despite warnings to halt. When Americans went in pursuit, a Mexican customs agent opened fire on them. Other Mexicans rushed to join the shooting, as did American soldiers from the 10th Cavalry. Soldiers were killed on both sides.

Three troops of black cavalry from Camp Little galloped into Nogales, followed by three companies of infantry. By 6:00 P.M. the Americans held several strategic points on the Mexican side. Mexican losses were high and the commander ran up a white flag, though in the ensuing talk, he called on the Americans to throw down their guns and surrender. Four days of fighting passed before Arizona governor George W. P. Hunt and Sonoran governor Plutarco Calles arranged an armistice. Five Americans had been killed and 29 wounded. The Mexicans lost 129 men, including the mayor of Sonoran Nogales.

Since that time, relations between the two Nogales have generally been good. Camp Little closed in 1933. Tourists discovered the towns in the 1940s. Today, Nogales's main claim to fame is as the major port of entry and processing for produce heading to U.S. and Canadian markets. Since the North American Free Trade Agreement, or NAFTA, the Nogales area has become

Nogales in the 1920s —Arizona Historical Foundation

home to numerous maquiladoras, U.S.-owned factories located just across the border. The factories have boosted local economies, but also have created new problems and challenges.

Two renowned musicians hail from Nogales. American jazz bassist Charles Mingus was born at a military base there, and Travis Edmonson, known for introducing Mexican folk music to mainstream America, grew up in Nogales. The Pimeria Alta Historical Society Museum, housed in the old town hall, is a good source of information about the area's history.

AZ 83
Sonoita—I-10
26 MILES

TOTAL WRECK

Total Wreck is in the Empire Mountains east of AZ 83, about nine miles south of Pantano and twenty miles northeast of Greaterville. It's a ghost town now. Supposedly, after John Dillon discovered the silver and lead mine, someone asked him what he planned to call it. He replied he didn't know, but the ledge the claim was on looked like a total wreck. The unusual name stuck.

Two years after Dillon's discovery in 1879, the Southern Pacific reached Pantano, and a seventy-ton mill was built at Total Wreck. By 1883 the population had reached 200; there were four saloons, a barber shop, a lumberyard, three stores, and three hotels.

In Total Wreck's most memorable gunfight, one man drew his revolver during an argument and shot another in the chest. The bullet lodged in a packet of love letters the fellow had in his breast pocket, and he lived. The lucky man went home and married the girl—whether out of love or gratitude, it is not known.

DAVIDSON CANYON

AZ 83 crosses and runs near Davidson Canyon. The canyon—between the Santa Rita and Empire Mountains—was named for

Total Wreck, circa 1883 —Arizona Historical Society Library, Tucson

an Indian agent headquartered at Tubac, later killed by Apache. This area was a dangerous place to travel in the 1860s and 1870s. Several freighters and prospectors died at the hands of Apache during those years.

Cpl. Joe Black, a mail carrier between Fort Crittenden and Tucson, had made the trip safely many times, but always at night, when by custom the Apache didn't fight. On August 27, 1872, he was escorting Lt. Reid Stewart and a party of troops to Tucson. Stewart and Black were in a buckboard; the others rode behind. Near Davidson Canyon, Black urged the lieutenant to wait until dark before proceeding, but the officer wouldn't listen; he had to get to Tucson to testify in a court-martial case. Before long the faster-paced buckboard was an hour ahead of the escort.

When the escort reached the top of the divide, they discovered Stewart's body with a bullet through the head and five other body wounds. Mailbag contents were scattered on the ground; mules, harness, and Corporal Black were missing. Picking up the trail, the soldiers soon came upon a horrifying scene: the Apache had tied the corporal to a dead tree and set it ablaze. The soldiers rushed forward but were too late to save Black. When they recovered the body, it had more than 100 wounds from lances, knives, and firebrands.

I-19
Nogales—Tucson
65 MILES

PETE KITCHEN'S RANCH

Near exit 12 about four miles north of Nogales, at the junction of Potrero Creek and the Santa Cruz River, Pete Kitchen, one of Arizona's most illustrious pioneers, had his ranch headquarters. Born in Kentucky in 1822, Kitchen arrived in Arizona in 1855. His first ranch was at Canoa, a few miles farther down the Santa Cruz, but he left it when federal troops went east for the Civil War, leaving settlers at the mercy of the Apache. When the war was over, Kitchen found the unclaimed land south of Calabazas to his liking and built El Potrero, a fortified ranchhouse on a hill with a commanding view on all four sides. The five-room main building had adobe walls twenty-five inches wide—thick enough to stop any assailant's bullets—and a twelve-foot-high ceiling. A

Pete Kitchen
—Arizona State Library

trapdoor and stairs provided quick access to a flat roof surrounded by a parapet with portholes—in other words, a safe fort from which to fend off Apache attacks. "Pete's Stronghold," as he called it, became a refuge for many a harried rider between Tucson and Magdalena. Pete coined a phrase during those years—"Tucson, Tubac, Tumacacori, to hell."

Kitchen's vaqueros had to be as handy with a rifle as they were with a lariat. Manuel Ronquillo, his trusty *caporal* (foreman), and Francisco "Pancho" Verdugo were his most dependable defenders. Manuel, Pancho, and Don Pedro, as Pete's Mexican friends called him, used to practice quick-shooting at targets while blindfolded. All three were expert shots with or without the blinds. Kitchen ended up marrying Verdugo's beautiful sister Rosa. Her ability to ride an outlaw horse and her marksmanship were almost as legendary as her husband's.

Apache bands on the prowl probed constantly for some weakness in the defense. They killed so many of Kitchen's ranch hands that a cemetery was established on the property. In one blitz, Apache slit the throat of Kitchen's twelve-year-old stepson. Another time, they attacked the ranch three times in twelve hours. But Kitchen stubbornly refused to be driven out. At long last, their own high casualties convinced the Apache to avoid El Potrero.

GUÉVAVI AND TUMACACORI MISSIONS AND CALABAZAS

Originally, the area encompassing the sites of Guévavi Mission and the town of Calabazas, as well as present-day Tumacacori, was populated by 1,000 or more Pima Indians settled in villages along the Santa Cruz River. Jesuit father Eusebio Kino arrived in 1691. He stopped at the Sobaipuri village of Guévavi, ten miles north of Nogales near Calabazas (now on private land), then continued five miles north to Tumacacori. Nine years later, in 1701, he established the Mission San Gabriel de Guévavi. During the Jesuit period in Arizona (1691–1767), Guévavi retained its mission status, while Tumacacori ("Curved Peak" in the Piman language) and Calabazas were visitas.

Kino's converts loved him for several reasons. In addition to establishing a regular food supply for them, he also made no

Tumacacori National Monument —Southwest Studies, Scottsdale Community College

attempt to restrict such age-old cultural practices as plural marriages and the wild drinking that took place during the cactus fruit harvest. Whether this was from a spirit of tolerance or because he seldom stayed in one place long enough to observe the indiscretions is not clear.

After the good father's death in 1711, a succession of German Jesuits tried to continue Kino's work in the area. However, unlike their predecessor, they could not help but look askance, for example, at the Pima method of bride selection—after an all-night dance, the man took home the woman who had endured the longest; or Piman divorce, in which the couple simply separated; or the plural marriages, despite explanations that the rooster keeps several hens, and the stallion satisfies a brood of mares. The padres did not conceal their feelings from the Pima, and the Pima resented the priests' meddling. One young Austrian's fate was not unique. He disapproved of what he perceived to be the Indians' boozing and wenching, and the Pima took exception to his piety. He died one night after consuming a poisoned dinner.

At Guévavi the downhill spiral after Kino's death continued when, in 1762, the Spanish decided to relocate the fierce Sobaipuri Pima, veteran fighters of the Apache. Their absence made both Guévavi and Tumacacori more vulnerable to Apache attack, and by 1766 the native population at Guévavi had dropped to fifty. In 1768, Franciscans replaced Jesuits at Guévavi. The newcomers transferred Guévavi's mission status to Tumacacori in 1771, and, two years later, in the face of Apache depredations, they abandoned beleaguered Guévavi for good. Ironically, a thirty-year peace with the Apache lay just ahead, but it would come too late for Guévavi. Today, only remnants of a few walls remain.

During the golden years from 1786 to 1821, when peace with the Apache prevailed, the Tumacacori and San Xavier Missions underwent great construction. But when Mexico gained independence from Spain in 1821, the new republic expelled the Franciscans, and the years of prosperity ended. For a time, local Indian people maintained Tumacacori. However, in 1831, when Mexico repudiated the peaceful coexistence treaty with the Apache, the warriors resumed the warpath. The last mission guardians, driven out in 1848, packed up the church furnishings and moved north to San Xavier del Bac. In 1990, the well-preserved ruins at Tumacacori became a national historic park.

During Tumacacori's prosperous years in the early 1800s, the visita Calabazas on the Santa Cruz River, near today's Rio Rico, served as a stock farm for Tumacacori. In 1844 Manuel María Gándara, governor of Sonora, bought Calabazas at auction. He converted the old church into a ranch headquarters and ran thousands of goats and sheep on the ranges. However, persistent Apache attacks forced Gándara to abandon the place in 1856, and in 1869 he sold the Tumacacori-Calabazas mission ranch to a Californian named Charlie Sykes.

Sykes knew something about promotion. He sold the land at great profit to an eastern company called the Calabazas Land & Mining Company, which turned around and hired him to sell lots for homes. One of his brochures depicts steamers hauling ore on what was in reality the tiny and often dry Santa Cruz River. Sykes established a town and built a fancy two-story brick hotel called the Santa Rita. By 1882, 2,500 of 2,800 lots at

Calabazas had been sold—though not built on, since the town had only 150 residents.

The notoriety was short-lived. Despite great expectations that the railroad would make Calabazas a port of entry into Mexico, Nogales was chosen instead. By the time it burned down with the rest of the town in 1927, the once opulent Santa Rita Hotel had become a place to store hay. Plowed under in the 1930s, the town site became a cotton field.

TUBAC

The origin of Tubac's name is disputed. Some say Tubac, a Ute-Aztecan word, means "Place of Brackish Water," while others insist it means "Low Ruins" or "Low House." The towering Santa Rita Mountains give Tubac, twenty miles north of Nogales on I-19, one of Arizona's most spectacular settings. Tubac's history after 1752 was often violent and bloody; written off as dead several times, it is a city with nine lives. Interestingly, a third of the original settlers of San Francisco, California, came from Tubac, and Arizona's first newspaper was published here.

Spanish Roots

Under the Jesuits, from 1691 to 1767, Tubac started out as a visita for the mission at Guévavi. Here, as in the other missions, the judgmental Jesuit padres who came after the beloved Eusebio Kino did not fare well with the natives. In 1736 a great silver strike at a place called "Arissona" brought a large number of Europeans into the Pimeria Alta. Over the next several years, the inevitable conflicts among civilians, military, church, and native peoples gradually set the stage for the great Pima Revolt in 1751, fueled by the native desire to expel the Europeans for unjust and capricious behavior. The revolt began in Sonora and spread quickly to the Santa Cruz Valley. The church at Tubac was burned and ransacked. By the time Spanish troops quelled the four-month-long revolt, more than 100 settlers and miners had been killed, along with 2 priests.

The first presidio in Arizona was established at Tubac the year after the revolt, in 1752. The soldiers who came with their families to serve at the fort constituted the first European community in Arizona, including Arizona's first white woman. Rich minerals

Se fueron con Dios (by Theresa Potter). Father Garcés and Juan Bautista de Anza on the way to San Francisco.
—Southwest Studies, Scottsdale Community College

in the nearby mountains and a fertile valley with abundant water also soon brought a rush of miners and farmers.

It was from Tubac that one of Spain's greatest soldiers, Capt. Juan Bautista de Anza, launched his expedition to find an overland road to California. In January 1774, Father Garcés had convinced Anza to accompany him west along the dreaded El Camino del Diablo (today's U.S.-Mexico border) to Yuma and thence to California. In October 1775, Anza and Garcés led a second expedition of 240 colonists, this time along the less forbidding Gila Trail, to Yuma, and from there to the Pacific coast and San Francisco to found a colony. In the earliest census of the city by the bay, one-third of the population listed Tubac as their birthplace. For his great work, Anza was promoted to Governor of New Mexico.

In 1775, the Spanish made Tucson the new site of the presidio, leaving the remaining citizens of Tubac without military protection. Eventually some soldiers were stationed at Tubac, and during the golden years of peace with the Apache, the community prospered. During the unstable early years of the Mexican Republic, however, Tubac once again fell on hard times.

The Americanization of Tubac

The first recorded American immigration to the city occurred during the gold rush to California in 1849. A well-traveled route across Sonora and down the Santa Cruz River to Tucson brought thriving business to the community, but roving bands of Apache warriors were still a constant threat. In October 1849, an emigrant party from Missouri experienced a sense of foreboding as they approached Tubac. It seemed unusually still. Indeed, the party found the village in smoldering ruins, and all the inhabitants murdered.

Tubac remained deserted until 1854 when two prospectors, Charles Poston and Herman Ehrenberg, came looking for gold and silver. When they found rich ore specimens in the mountains, Poston, who became known as the "Father of Arizona," went east to raise capital for a mining venture. He founded the Sonora Mining & Exploring Company and set up residence in the old Tubac presidio. The town came back to life. Charles Poston became the *alcalde,* or mayor, as well as a magistrate, patron, and self-styled "Marrying Sam."

Arizona's first newspaper, the *Weekly Arizonan,* came out in Tubac in 1859. In those raw, untamed days a journalist had to be as good with a six-gun as he was with a type case. Soon after the paper opened, local mining magnate and promoter Sylvester Mowry took exception to some of editor Ed Cross's written comments and challenged him to a duel. People came from as far as Tucson to watch two of Arizona's best-known citizens shoot it out. Bets piled high as the two men, armed with Burnside rifles, squared off at forty paces. Three times they fired, and three times they missed. At that point, Cross folded his arms and grimly faced his adversary; but Mowry, feeling his honor vindicated, gallantly fired over the editor's head. With their spectators, the duelists consummated the affair with the contents of a forty-two-gallon barrel of whiskey. Afterward, Mowry purchased the newspaper and moved it to Tucson.

The Civil War ended these tranquil times in Tubac under the benevolent dictatorship of Poston. In need of soldiers, the government abandoned its far-flung military posts. Consequently,

Apache bands became even bolder, forcing settlers to flee the area. During Apache depredations, Poston closed his mining company and barely escaped with his life. About forty residents who stubbornly refused to leave Tubac soon found themselves with 200 Apache on one side and 75 Sonoran bandits on the other. Only the timely arrival of a rescue party from Tucson prevented another massacre. After the war, when the army returned, settlers moved back into the fertile valley. Still, Apache war parties kept up attacks. During one month in 1869, they raided Tubac five times. By 1871, once more, the town was abandoned.

The building of a railroad from Tucson to Nogales and the end of the Apache Wars in 1886 revived Tubac, but it never regained its stature as one of Arizona's largest communities. In the 1950s Tubac seemed on the verge of becoming a ghost town again— this time because of the exodus of its young people to Tucson, Nogales, Phoenix, and beyond. Fortunately, a community of artists and art fanciers took up residence, and the town with nine lives lived on.

SAN XAVIER DEL BAC

The easiest way to get to San Xavier, a small town south of the San Xavier Indian Reservation—part of the Tohono O'Odham Reservation—is to take exit 75 from I-19 and follow Helmet Peak Road west five miles to Mission Road, then turn north to the mission.

San Xavier was the site of Arizona's first and principal mission, which Father Eusebio Kino founded in 1700. The legendary "padre on horseback" first stopped at the site in 1692 when native people invited him to visit their rancheria. The mission, named for Kino's patron saint, would remain one of the priest's favorites.

Father Francisco Garcés arrived at San Xavier on June 30, 1768. The humble, quiet Franciscan lacked Kino's administrative ability and scientific background, but more than made up for this with his stamina and zeal. He had deep feelings of affection for those in his charge. Sitting on the ground among the Indians, eating their food and socializing, Garcés was in his glory. Another priest wrote: "God, in his infinite wisdom, must have created Garcés for the place in which he served."

San Xavier del Bac in 1890 —Arizona Historical Foundation

When he wasn't out in the wilderness "harvesting souls," Garcés was happiest at San Xavier, where there were no other Spaniards. He expressed these feelings when he wrote simply, "I am very content. There are plenty of Indians. I like them and they like me." Sadly, in 1781, this great missionary would be murdered in an Indian uprising at two other missions on the Colorado River (see Yuma, "Quechan uprising").

The Mission San Xavier, also called the "White Dove of the Desert," is a beautiful blend of baroque, Moorish, and Byzantine architecture. Begun in 1783, construction took fourteen years to complete. The mission's uncapped tower has inspired many stories and legends. According to one, when the Crown placed a tax on finished buildings, the Franciscans purposely left the tower incomplete.

Like all of the missions in the area, San Xavier flourished during Spain's golden years of peace with the Apache (1786–1821) but suffered after the Mexican Revolution. In 1831 the mission was abandoned, and it stood neglected for years. Then, in the mid-1800s, the Catholic Church reopened it and began renovation. Still, by the early 1900s, the ancient adobe walls were deteriorating so badly, the government threatened to close the church school. Bishop Henri Granjon completed the renovation, thus preserving one of Arizona's greatest historic and cultural treasures. Today, San Xavier is a "living" mission, where services are still held.

AZ 77
Tucson—Globe
106 MILES

CAÑADA DEL ORO

Cañada del Oro is the name of both a canyon and the stream that flows through it, both of which cross AZ 77 at Oro Valley, just north of Tucson. The stream flows down from up around Oracle, many miles to the northeast. Placer gold found in the canyon before the 1850s gave it its name, which means, in Spanish, "Gold Ravine." The military built a road along the Cañada del Oro from Tucson to Camp Grant, which was at the junction of Aravaipa Creek and the San Pedro River. For Apache war parties, the twisting canyon was ideal for ambushes.

BIOSPHERE 2

Past mile marker 96 north of Oracle Junction, a blue flag by the side of the road signals the turnoff to Columbia University's Biosphere 2 Center. The world's largest greenhouse (ninety-one feet high, covering about three acres), Biosphere 2 is dedicated to better understanding of Biosphere 1—planet earth. Biosphere 2 was the brainchild of engineering visionary John Allen in the 1970s. Allen wanted to build a giant self-sustaining greenhouse sealed off from the outside atmosphere. Inside would be a microcosm of earth and all its ecosystems, complete with tropical rain forest, desert, farmland, marsh, savanna, ocean, and more. Colonists would live there, and everything, including food, water, and air, would be recycled or produced within the structure.

Construction begun in 1986 was completed in 1991. At that point the first Biosphere 2 crew of four men and four women stepped into their new mini-world for two years. However, all did not go according to plan. One member had to leave for medical treatment. Insects became a menace, and declining oxygen levels increased fatigue. Critics lampooned the project, calling it a new age cult rather than a scientific experiment. In short, chaos ruled until Columbia University scientists took over the project. To date, over 200 scientists and researchers have worked on the $200 million project.

Biosphere 2 is open to visitors. Tours start with a short film, then visitors explore a series of greenhouses with varying climates.

ORACLE

Eight miles east of Oracle Junction, American Avenue branches off to the south from AZ 77, leading to downtown Oracle.

Black pioneer Bill Neal, better known as "Curly Bill," settled in Oracle in the late nineteenth century. Neal was born in Oklahoma Territory to an African American father and a Cherokee mother. Although his Indian name was "Bear Sitting Down," the energetic young man spent little time in that position, unless it was on the back of a horse. Neal rode with "Buffalo Bill" Cody during the Indian Wars on the plains. After the wars, he moved to Tucson and worked as a cook, learning the hospitality business from the ground up. Next, in 1878, he opened a prosperous freight business, supplying charcoal smelters at nearby mines with fuel, and hauling ore on the return trip. In his spare time, Neal took up ranching; within a few years his 3-N outfit at Oracle was running thousands of cattle over the ranges on the north slopes of the Santa Catalinas.

Bill Neal in Oracle, 1890s —Arizona Historical Society, Tucson

During those years, Neal also found time to marry his sweetheart, Ann. In 1895 they opened the Mountain View Hotel in Oracle. The cool, scenic Santa Catalina Mountains were a favorite summer tourist attraction, and the hotel quickly gained a lofty reputation. On the stage lines he also owned, he hauled winter visitors to Oracle. Then Ann took over and organized outings, parties, and picnics for them. Curly Bill died in 1936. Ann Neal operated the hotel by herself until her death in 1950.

DUDLEYVILLE

From Mammoth—supposedly named for gold deposits of mammoth proportions—AZ 77 follows the San Pedro River to Dudleyville, about fifteen miles north. William Dudley Harrington, native to Ireland, was one of the first settlers in this area in 1877. Dudleyville is notable mainly for its proximity to the site of Camp Grant, a primitive military post described by Lt. John G. Bourke in 1870 as "the most thoroughly God-forsaken post of all."

On April 30, 1871, one of the most brutal massacres in Arizona history took place near this desolate outpost. At the time, Gen. George Stoneman was the commander of the army's Department of California, of which Arizona was a part. Perhaps spurred on by remarks Stoneman made encouraging settlers to adopt a do-it-yourself policy toward Apache depredations, a group of Tucsonans and their Papago allies rode into an Apache village near Camp Grant and slaughtered eighty-five Aravaipa Apache. Horrified, President Ulysses S. Grant ordered the leaders brought to trial. The jury immediately found them innocent; in the 1870s it would have been difficult to find one white Arizonan who would prosecute another for killing Apache.

WINKELMAN

At the confluence of the Gila and San Pedro Rivers a few miles north of Dudleyville, Winkelman rests on the site of an old Sobaipuri Indian village. Father Francisco Eusebio Kino and his mission party visited the village in 1697. They called the place La Victoria in thanks and celebration for making it safely through a region they believed was inhabited by cannibals.

A town of fewer than 700 people today, Winkelman is the hometown of Arizona's "grand dame of the state legislature," Polly

Rosenbaum. Born in Iowa and raised in Colorado, Edwynne "Polly" Pendergast came to Hayden, Arizona, in the 1920s to teach after college. There she met and married George Rosenbaum, who served many years as house majority leader in the state legislature. Following his sudden death in 1949, Rosenbaum was appointed to fill out her husband's term—a position she held until 1995. During her long, productive tenure, she served on nearly every house committee—including a stint as the only Democratic committee chair in a Republican administration.

A tireless advocate for education and the expansion of libraries in rural areas, Rosenbaum also helped found numerous programs and institutions aimed at preserving Arizona's history. After retirement, the energetic, wiry woman continued her state historic preservation efforts. In the year 2002, at age 103, Polly Rosenbaum was still going strong.

CHRISTMAS

Seven miles north of Winkelman, just off AZ 77, is the ghost town of Christmas. Despite the discovery of rich deposits of copper in the early 1880s, prospectors could not stake claims because the land was part of the San Carlos Apache Indian Reservation. In Washington, certain congressmen tried to get the reservation boundaries redrawn so mining could proceed; finally, George B. Crittenden, a lobbyist, was able to push a bill through accomplishing this. Crittenden learned of his bill's success on Christmas Day, 1902. Immediately he staked a claim, naming the mine and town Christmas.

Crittenden's claim was a jump, however. Dr. James Douglas, president of the mining company Phelps-Dodge, had hired an Irishman to squat on the property until the bill that changed the boundaries passed, then he was to file on the land for the company. On Christmas, however, being a good Irishman, the squatter felt he needed to ride into Globe to celebrate the holiday properly. While he was away, Crittenden came in and staked his claims.

A boomtown during World War I, Christmas went into decline in the years after. The post office closed for good in 1935.

GLOBE

With the majestic backdrop of the Pinal Mountains on one side and the Apache Range on the other, the town of Globe perches on the banks of Pinal Creek, its old buildings huddled on steep slopes. Globe was one of the great mining camps of old Arizona. Braving everything from isolation to frequent, unwelcome visits from Apache war parties, the town's intrepid citizens carved out a community in the rugged, mineral-laden mountains.

A party of prospectors established the first mine of importance near Globe in 1873. Two years later they formed the Globe Mining District. Colorful legends about how the town got its name include the discovery of a spherical silver boulder, or alternately of a large round chunk of silver with lines resembling the continents.

In 1878 settlers moved a short distance from the original town site to the banks of Pinal Creek to be closer to their water source. Originally called Globe City, the "City" soon dropped away. In 1880 Globe incorporated, but city fathers either had short

Globe in the 1880s —Southwest Studies, Scottsdale Community College

memories or liked celebrations, for they reincorporated in 1905 and again in 1907. The main street, Broad Street, meanders along, following the curves of Pinal Creek. Old-timers attribute the crookedness of the road to local miners and prospectors' stubborn refusal to move their shanties for surveyors to lay out a straight road.

Globe's early history was one of physical isolation. During its first twenty-two years, the nearest railroad was 120 miles away. In the 1870s supplies were hauled in by wagon from Silver City, New Mexico, 150 miles to the east. By 1878 the new town of Florence, only sixty miles away, was supplying Globe, but the trip through that rough mountainous country took five days. By 1898 the Gila Valley, Globe & Northern Railroad finally reached Globe, enabling mining companies to get down to serious business in the area.

The granddaddy of all the mines in the Globe district was the Old Dominion, on the north side of town. In the early days, a persistent water problem plagued it. In 1903, however, Phelps-Dodge acquired the property on the sage advice of James Douglas and overhauled its equipment, after which the mine started

Globe after 1900 —Clara T. Woody Collection, Arizona Historical Society Library/Tucson

turning a profit. For the next twenty years the Old Dominion was one of the greatest copper mines in the world. Phelps-Dodge shut down its smelter in 1924 and closed the mine itself during the Great Depression. By that time the Old Dominion had produced $134 million in gold, silver, and copper.

Globe's silver boom lasted only four years. Fortunately, before it played out, copper came into great demand, so the silver camp slid right into a prosperous copper mining town. By 1886, the boast was that all U.S. copper coins were minted from Globe copper.

Though Globe's mines continued producing through the 1920s, the town's demise began in 1909 when richer deposits of low-grade copper ore were discovered seven miles west at the upstart town of Miami. Many Globe merchants rushed to establish stores in the new community. The Great Depression really shut Globe down in 1931. However, in recent times, the former silver camp has made a comeback. Self-guided tours through the historic community are available.

People of Spirit

Globe's residents could always be counted on to display a spirit of independence in the face of bureaucracy. Maggie Wilson, author and Globe native, told about the time residents realized the new Central School had been rebuilt near a house of ill repute. Prostitution was legal in the 1800s and openly tolerated up until the 1960s, but in Globe the law did require parlor houses to be at least 400 feet from a school. Citizens requested that the sheriff close the house. Another group of equally concerned citizens petitioned the sheriff to move the school. The lawman ended up measuring the distance between the structures. Finding that the 400-foot limit extended 4 feet into the parlor house, he simply instructed the madam to confine all business activities to the back rooms, which were in the legal zone.

The Globe area has produced successful people in all walks of life. Among them is Rose Perica Mofford, the first woman governor of Arizona and one of Arizona's most popular and colorful personalities. A former softball player, Mofford starred for the Arizona Cantaloupe Queens during the early heyday of women's softball. Jack Elam, a well-known Hollywood character actor, hails from Globe. Marine sergeant James Lopez, hostage and hero during the 1980 Iranian hostage crisis, was also a native.

Globe had always had its Mexican, Italian, Irish, and Slavic sections. After sundown, it was said, nobody dared venture into another ethnic area. However, high school sports eventually improved long-standing tensions and rivalries between ethnic groups. On the playing fields of the 1940s and 1950s, with starting lineups that often included a Martinez, a Battina, an O'Leary, and an Ivanovich, Globe kids—and their community—began learning new ways.

AZ 177
Winkelman—Superior
34 MILES

KEARNY, RAY, AND SONORA

All that's left of the mining towns of Ray and Sonora is a huge, open-pit operation started by the Kennecott Copper Corporation in 1947 and currently owned and operated by ASARCO. The Ray Copper Company founded Ray near its mine in 1884. Initial returns on the mine were disappointing, but in 1906 things turned around when D. C. Jackling, a Utahan who knew how to work large tonnages of low-grade copper ore profitably, bought it. Since then the mine has operated and shut down according to the whims of the copper market.

In the old days, some mining companies segregated workers by race and culture. In this area, Ray was for white workers, Sonora for Mexicans, and a third small town, Barcelona (also swallowed by the mine), was for the Spanish. Like many mining communities, Ray-Sonora became known for its sports teams.

One of Arizona's historic grocery chains, Basha's, started in Ray-Sonora. Najeeb Basha immigrated to America from Lebanon at age sixteen. In 1901 he married Najeeby "Jeeby" Srour, another Lebanese immigrant. Najeeb and Jeeby came to Ray in 1910 to join her family's mercantile business. They opened a store in Sonora and, during the 1920s, another in Chandler. Their two sons, Ike and Eddie, founded the Basha's company in 1932. Today, Basha's has stores throughout the state.

In 1958 the Kennecott Company included the community of Kearny in its plans for a new installation, and when the open-pit mine at Ray engulfed Ray and Sonora in the 1960s, residents were relocated to the new town.

SUPERIOR

The towering, red-streaked cliff that hovers above the town of Superior is known as Apache Leap. The story is told that one day in the 1870s a picket spotted an Apache raiding party heading up a precipitous mountain trail to a secret hideout. An expedition of soldiers from Camp Pinal, sent in pursuit, cornered the Indians at the edge of the cliff. Rather than surrender, the Apaches plunged over the edge to their deaths on the rocks below.

Main Street, Superior, in the 1920s —Superior Historical Society

During the 1870s, a rich lode was found and lost by a man named Sullivan. Found again, it became the fabulous Silver King. In the meantime, prospectors found another silver outcropping where Superior is today. The ore wasn't as rich as the Silver King's, so they named the mine the Silver Queen. The Silver Queen Mining Company was founded in New York in 1880. The lode was inconsistent, however, and the Queen never reached the expectations of its developers.

By 1879 the town—known as Hastings until 1900—had some 2,000 residents and boasted of "21 saloons and world-famous bordellos." However, the bottom fell out of the silver market and by 1891 only ten residents were left. In 1900 the town's name was changed to honor the nearby Lake Superior & Arizona Mining Company, which ran the mine for a time. Ten years later, the Magma Copper Company took over the Silver Queen properties after an incredibly rich deposit of copper was discovered beneath the silver capping—the old Queen came up a winner after all. The Magma Mine, founded by W. Boyce Thompson, went on to become one of Arizona's greatest copper bonanzas.

In 1925 scenic US 60 was built through Queen Creek Canyon, linking Phoenix to Globe. Booms and busts followed in Superior, but in 1981 a smelter built in the early days closed and so, eventually, did the mines. In that familiar story of western mining towns, business closings followed. Buildings decayed and paint peeled.

While towns like Bisbee and Jerome turned to tourism, Superior took another path: it invited Hollywood. The run-down, boarded-up downtown is desired by some directors, and a sign outside town now reads, "From Mining to Motion Pictures." Films set in Superior include *How the West Was Won, The Gauntlet, Used Cars, U-Turn,* and *Eight-Legged Freaks.* Television productions have included an episode of the PBS series *Mystery* and a Hallmark Hall of Fame presentation, "Lost Child." But this success creates a dilemma for the citizens. If new businesses open on Magma Avenue, will Hollywood still want to use the town as a backdrop? Fake towns are a dime a dozen, while the decrepitude of Superior is real. Meanwhile Superior, and small western towns in general, have gained a new image. In his review of Oliver Stone's movie *U-Turn,* movie critic Roger Ebert describes the town as "one of those backwater hells much beloved in movies where everyone is malevolent, over-sexed, narrow-eyed and hateful."

Superior, one of the best-kept secrets in the state, sits in some of the most picturesque country in Arizona, quietly surviving. It's questionable, however, whether it can stay that way. The spread of Salt River Valley development may make Superior an upscale community one day. In that case Hollywood—and the residents who enjoy Superior's backwater peace—would have to find some other place to go.

AZ 79
AZ 77—Florence
42 MILES

TOM MIX MEMORIAL

In October 1940, at the age of sixty, cowboy movie idol Tom Mix fatally crashed his Cord automobile in a shallow arroyo near Florence. Before becoming one of Hollywood's greatest movie stars in the 1920s, Mix was a horse wrangler and rodeo performer. His amazing stunts and horsemanship gave him an edge over other Hollywood cowboys and made him one of the brightest "shooting stars" of the Roaring Twenties. During his early film career, Mix spent plenty of time in Arizona; many of his movies were filmed at the Selig Polyscope Ranch near Prescott and at other locations around the state.

Mix's legend encompassed many of the heroic adventures of his day. He was said to have ridden as a Texas Ranger and with Pancho Villa, charged up San Juan Hill with Teddy Roosevelt's Rough Riders, and battled Boers in South Africa. While these bigger-than-life adventures made great fodder for his hero-worshippers, his biography was obviously embellished. As a matter of record, Mix had an unglamorous military career before deserting his post at Fort Hancock, New Jersey, in 1902. In 1910 he was arrested in Knoxville, Tennessee, for stealing a horse.

Tom Mix Memorial —Jeff Kida photo

While these revelations tarnish Mix's reputation, no one can deny that he loved horses, knew how to ride, and was a marvelous showman.

FLORENCE

Florence was an important freighting and supply center for the gold, silver, and copper mines in the mountains to the northeast. With the exception of pavement and a few modern fixtures, the place hasn't changed much since 1880, when the population was about 900. Now it's about 7,500.

In its earlier days, Florence was a modest agricultural area, but with the completion of the Ashurst-Hayden Diversion Dam near town in 1921, it became the agricultural center of Pinal County. Irrigation water provided by Coolidge Dam, constructed in the late 1920s on the upper Gila fifty miles east of Florence, reinforced the town's agricultural position.

In 1866, looking for a safe place to cross the Gila River, Levi Ruggles found it in what would become the town of Florence. An Indian agent, he laid claim to some land there, then transferred the title over to the town in 1875. The same year, Florence, named for one of Ruggles's daughters, became the Pinal County seat. The old courthouse, completed in 1891 for $29,000, still serves its original purpose. Crowning the courthouse, the town's clock stands frozen at 9 o'clock. In fact, it never ran even from the

Pinal County Courthouse in 1895 —Arizona State Library

beginning; funds for a working clock were diverted to construct what citizens felt was more necessary—a jail.

Pauline Cushman, the notorious Union Army spy during the Civil War, called Florence home for a spell. Captured by Confederates, she was supposed to hang, but Southern troops abandoned her during a hasty retreat. For her service to the Union, President Abraham Lincoln praised her as a bona fide American heroine. Billed as "Major Cushman," she sustained a good living on the lecture circuit. She headed west and in California met Jere Fryer. They married, moved to Casa Grande, Arizona, and opened a hotel and livery stable. In the mid-1880s Fryer was elected Pinal County sheriff, and the couple moved to Florence. However, the pressures of Fryer's philandering and the couple's inability to have a child broke the marriage apart. Cushman moved to San Francisco, where her life spiraled downward, ending in death from an overdose of morphine. Her body was headed to a pauper's grave when an enterprising newspaperman discovered her identity, and in the end she was buried with full military honors.

In 1885, the citizens of Florence petitioned the territorial assembly for a bridge across the erratic Gila River. The stream was usually dry, but on those occasions when water did materialize, the river became impossible to cross. Sympathetic legislators granted $1,200 for the bridge. Soon after its completion, however, the river changed its course, meandering around the bridge and continuing merrily on its way to Yuma. It is still flowing generally along the same course. There's a new bridge over the Gila today.

Today, Florence is best known as the site of the state prison, which, when the town was chosen in the early 1900s, was a political plum. The old territorial prison at Yuma, which dated from 1876, closed in 1909, and the prisoners were transferred to the new facility. The prison is one of the main employers in town.

Ernest W. McFarland State Park, on the north end of Main Street, honors one of Arizona's most distinguished politicians. McFarland, an Oklahoma native, moved to Arizona after serving in World War I, and settled in Florence in 1925. A lawyer, Democrat McFarland served as U.S. senator from Arizona from 1941 to 1953, and as Senate majority leader for the last two years

Crossing the Gila River at Florence (not date) —Arizona Historical Foundation

of his term until Republican and fellow Arizonan Barry Goldwater helped unseat him. McFarland went home to serve as governor of Arizona from 1955 to 1959, then on the state supreme court from 1964 to 1970—as chief justice for the last two years. Arizona legislator Polly Rosenbaum said of McFarland, "He was at ease talking with a farmer about crops or with the president of the United States about foreign policy." McFarland died in 1984.

Picturesque downtown Florence has been the setting for several movies, including *Murphy's Romance* with James Garner and Sally Field.

Poston's Butte

Just across the Gila River from Florence is a cone-shaped mountain known as Poston's Butte. The entrepreneur and promoter Charles Poston spent many of his twilight years here. During his world travels Poston became a worshipper of the sun. He planned to erect a temple to the sun on top of this butte; instead, he spent his final days in poverty in Phoenix. Poston died on June 24, 1902, and was buried in the capital city. Originally, he had requested to be buried on top of this butte; in 1925 a group of citizens granted his wish.

AZ 287 and AZ 87
Florence—Chandler
41 MILES

CASA GRANDE NATIONAL MONUMENT

Just north of Coolidge, named for the dam, is Casa Grande National Monument, designated in 1918 and considered one of the best-preserved prehistoric dwellings in southern Arizona. Several notable travelers came across the structure on their journeys. Father Kino visited and named Casa Grande in 1694. Lt. Juan Mateo Manje, traveling with him, described it as a "large edifice whose principal room in the middle is of four stories, those adjoining being of three. Its walls are two veras [about five feet] thick, made of strong cement and clay and are so smooth on the inside that they resemble planed boards and are so polished that they shine like pueblo pottery."

Nearly 100 years later, in 1775, Father Garcés described Casa Grande as being in a state of near ruin. Some of the famous mountain men were familiar with the place: James Ohio Pattie reported passing by during the 1820s, and during the next decade, Pauline Weaver's name was carved on one of the walls. In 1846, crossing Arizona with the Army of the West, Maj. William Emory mentioned the site in his notes. Dr. J. Walter Fewkes of the Smithsonian Institution initiated scientific study and excavation of the site in 1892.

Hohokam Indians built the eleven-room structure sometime around A.D. 1300. Its facade is of mud and caliche (chalky rock), and the upper floors are made of logs floated down the Gila from the high country. Two small openings in the east and center rooms, called "calendar holes," let the sun's rays through. At the spring and fall equinoxes, a streak of light comes through both holes and lines up on a target.

Used as a calendar, Casa Grande may have helped the Hohokam determine times for planting and harvesting ceremonies. Since nomadic tribes frequently raided the Hohokam after the harvest, the structure may have served as a watchtower. Or perhaps it was the temple of some great leader. Whatever the case, by 1450,

Tourists at Casa Grande, 1880s —Southwest Studies, Scottsdale Community College

the building had been abandoned. Perhaps the soil became saturated with alkali or waterlogged, and the people moved on. Or, if the building was the temple of a leader, he may have died. Pima custom called for the abandonment and burning of a dwelling after the death of its inhabitant; Kino reported that the interior of Casa Grande had been burned. In sum, Casa Grande remains an enigma.

SACATON AND THE GILA RIVER INDIAN RESERVATION

A few miles west of Coolidge, AZ 87 passes through the Gila River Indian Reservation, just south of Phoenix. Sacaton is the headquarters of the 12,000-member reservation, home to members of the Pima and Maricopa tribes. In Ute-Aztecan language, *sacaton* means "tall, rank herbage, unfit for forage"; it is also the name of a type of grass. Contrary to its name, the

Dwelling reconstructions at the Gila River Cultural Center near Sacaton. Top: *A desert brush dwelling.* Bottom: *Earthen desert dwellings. The dark doorways are open and reinforced.*
—Author photos

sacaton grass in Arizona is good forage for grazing animals. The word also refers to broad, flat land—a suitable description of this area. The Gila River Cultural Center near Bapchule, northwest of Sacaton, provides an excellent introduction to the history and culture of the region.

The reservation's 372,000 acres straddles the Gila River. Organized in 1859, Gila River is the oldest reservation in Arizona. For hundreds of years these lands have been the home of the Akimel O'Odham—the "People of the River"—also called the Pima. The name Pima may have come from a corruption of *pinyi-match,* or, "I don't understand you," the native response to early Spanish explorers' attempted communication. Rolling off the Spanish tongue, the phrase came out sounding like "peema."

The Pimeria Alta of the Spanish period was the homeland of the Pima. Piman ancestry, many anthropologists believe, traces back to the Hohokam, who lived here as early as 300 B.C. The Pima are closely related to the Tohono O'Odham or Papago. Since the northern reaches of Pimeria Alta were too close to Apacheland for safety, no missions were built in this region. Thus the Pima remained relatively free from Spanish and, later, Mexican influence. However, the Spanish did contribute to Pima agriculture with the introduction of winter wheat and barley. Up until then, the natives grew summer crops such as melons, squash, maize, and cotton. Now they could farm year-round. The Spanish also introduced livestock to the Pima.

Allied with the Pima, the Maricopa, a branch of the Quechan, often fought their Quechan relatives along the Colorado River to the west. Finally, in the mid-1800s the Maricopa moved farther up the Gila River to the Sacaton area to escape the warfare with their cousins. Immigrants and military alike remembered the Pima and the Maricopa as the most hospitable and helpful of all the tribes encountered in the great mid-nineteenth-century movement west. They lived on the eastern edge of the most torturous part of the southern route to California. Here travelers could rest, recoup, and resupply among the friendly native people at the "Pima Villages," as the place was called, before or after the long desert trip.

The Pima first met Anglo Americans in the 1820s when the likes of Pauline Weaver, Bill Williams, Joe Walker, Ewing Young, and James O. Pattie came to trap beaver on the Gila River. Relations between the two groups were cordial. The next major contact with Anglos came in 1846, when Gen. Stephen Kearny's hard-riding dragoons and their guide Kit Carson passed through on the way to California. Traveling with Kearny, Lt. William Emory of the Army Corps of Topographical Engineers was conducting the first scientific study of the land and its people. The notes he took reveal deep admiration for the Pima:

> We came in at the back of the settlement of Pimos [sic] Indians, and found our troops encamped in a corn field, from which the grain had been gathered. We were at once impressed with the beauty, order, and disposition of the arrangements for irrigating and draining the land. Corn, wheat, and cotton are the crops of this peaceful and intelligent race of people. . . . To us it was a rare sight to be thrown in the midst of a large nation of what is termed wild Indians, surpassing many of the Christian nations in agriculture, little behind them in the useful arts, and immeasurably before them in honesty and virtue. During the whole of yesterday, our camp was full of men, women, and children, who sauntered amongst our packs, unwatched, and not a single instance of theft was reported.

Pima woman (no date)
—Arizona Historical Society

   Despite their renowned friendliness, the Pima were also brave warriors who feared neither Mexican nomadic bands nor Americans. They fought long, sometimes bloody wars against the various Apache and Yavapai bands to the east and north, and the Quechan and Mojave to the west. During the 1860s and 1870s, rugged Pima rode with American troops against some of these tribes. In fact, some of Arizona's first national guard units, formed at the old Butterfield station at Maricopa Wells in 1865, consisted of Pima and Maricopa warriors. Company C, under Lt. Antonio Azul, a Pima chief, and Company D, led by Lt. Juan Chivaria, a Maricopa chief, campaigned against the Apache and the Yavapai.

However, whites forgot the military assistance and gracious hospitality of the Pima after the subjugation in the 1880s of the Yavapai and Apache. Settlers who poured into the Gila River area above the Pima villages cut off the Indians' water. Despite pleas from both the Pima and friendly whites, the bureaucracy in Washington responded incredibly slowly to the tribe's needs. For a time the federal government planned to move the tribe to Oklahoma—a plan the Pima fiercely resisted. From the 1860s into the 1870s, some Pima moved to the Salt River Valley, where there was more water. They are the ancestors of the people of the Salt River Indian Reservation east of Scottsdale.

In fall 2002, the $125-million, 500-room Sheraton Wild Horse Pass Resort & Spa and the eighteen-hole Whirlwind Golf Course opened for business in the Gila River Indian community.

Pima Notables

The Pima contributed at least two notable modern-day warriors to American causes. In World War I, Mathew B. Juan of Sacaton became the first Arizonan and the first Native American to give his life for his country; a monument near the center of town honors him.

Ira Hayes
—Southwest
Studies, Scottsdale
Community College

Ira Hayes of Bapchule became one of the most famous fighting men of World War II. Enlisting as a Marine in 1942, Hayes participated in landings at Vella Lavella, New Caledonia, Bougainville, and Iwo Jima. At the latter on February 23, 1945, Hayes gained immortality when he and four other Marines were photographed raising the flag atop Mount Suribachi. The picture captured the imagination of Americans and became one of the most celebrated wartime photographs ever taken. Two days after the photo's release, U.S. senators called for a national monument modeled after the picture. The result was the Marine Corps War Memorial statue, dedicated in Arlington, Virginia, in 1954.

The famous Iwo Jima photograph (by Joe Rosenthal) —Southwest Studies, Scottsdale Community College

Hayes returned home to a hero's welcome. Sadly, in postwar Arizona, he faced a difficult adjustment, and newspapers made much of his personal battles with alcohol. His death in 1955 at age thirty-three recalls the words of F. Scott Fitzgerald: "You show me a hero and I'll write you a tragedy."

CHANDLER

Chandler lies southeast of Phoenix on AZ 87. During the latter part of the nineteenth century, Dr. A. J. Chandler was Arizona's first veterinarian surgeon. In the 1890s he established the Chandler Ranch in the eastern Salt River Valley, and in 1911 subdivided the land, offering irrigated plots for sale. He also built the elaborate San Marcos Hotel in 1913 to lure buyers to his Chandler Ranch properties. At first, the response was great, and the town of Chandler was born. But growth was slow; by 1940 the population was only 1,300. The San Marcos Hotel is still going strong today.

Chandler remained a quiet agricultural community until World War II, when Williams Air Force Base was established east of town. By the 1980s high-tech industry had come to Chandler, resulting in a phenomenal boom. Williams Air Force Base closed in the early 1990s, but was transformed into Williams Gateway Park, home to Arizona State University East and an industrial park. Chandler's population is up to approximately 200,000.

I-10
Tucson—Phoenix
111 MILES

RED ROCK

Named for a red butte nearby, Red Rock, like many Arizona towns, originated with the railroad. The Southern Pacific built a station here in the 1880s along with a spur line to the Silver Bell Mine smelter twenty miles south.

South of Red Rock, in the Avra Valley, was the home of one of Arizona's greatest ranching families. Until 1852, Don Pedro Aguirre was a prosperous freighter and *ranchero* in Chihuahua, Mexico. Then, when he let some American troops in pursuit of Apache stay overnight at his ranch, he was accused of being a traitor. Given the choice of being shot or moving to the United States, he chose the latter.

Don Pedro first moved to New Mexico, then established the Buenos Aires Ranch in the Altar Valley. During the 1880s one of Don Pedro's sons, Don Yjinio Aguirre, began a successful freighting operation around Willcox. In 1892 the family moved the freight business and cattle operation to Red Rock, and established El Rancho de San Francisco. During the prosperous days of the Aguirre Cattle Company, Don Yjinio and his son Higinio ran thousands of head of cattle in southern Arizona while the family's freight wagons hauled ore from the Silver Bell Mine to the railroad spur at Red Rock. Today, younger generations of Aguirres carry on the family traditions. Among them, Yjinio Aguirre became a well-respected author and expert on the history and culture of early ranching in Arizona.

PICACHO AND PICACHO PEAK

I-10 and the Southern Pacific Railroad, both of which connect Phoenix and Tucson with the outside world, run through Picacho Pass, about forty miles northwest of Tucson. The town of Picacho is a few miles north. Lengthy winter rains transform the harsh gray-buff foothills near Picacho into a tapestry of variegated color, with galaxies of wildflowers heralding spring.

In the 1850s the Butterfield Overland Mail stage line had a station in the pass, to the north of the peak. Picacho Peak, which is west of the highway, is a huge pile of volcanic remnants rising 3,374 feet into the air.

At the base of the volcanic Picacho Mountains, several springs provided water and a good place to rest or camp for travelers. Prehistoric Hohokam stopped at Picacho on their way to commercial dealings farther south. So did their descendants, the Pima and Papago, and the Spanish missionaries. When the Mormon Battalion built the first wagon road across the Southwest in 1846, they, too, rested at Picacho. To emigrants on the Gila Trail, the

Picacho, during a reenactment of the Civil War battle of 1862 (Picacho Peak in background) —Author photo

towering peak was a beacon in much the same way Chimney Rock and Independence Rock were on the Overland Trail.

In the spring of 1862, small Confederate and Union forces clashed briefly at the foot of the ancient *picacho* (peak) in what is generally referred to as the westernmost battle of the Civil War. The Battle of Picacho was really only a skirmish, although three Union soldiers lost their lives before the Confederates retreated. Monuments dedicated to the battle and to the Mormon Battalion are located south of I-10 in Picacho State Park.

ARIZOLA

Southwest of the town of Casa Grande, Arizola was the headquarters during the 1880s of James Addison Reavis, also known as the "Baron of Arizona." Reavis had a home there. In the Confederate army, the former Missouri streetcar conductor learned the dubious art of forgery. Ultimately he forged his own discharge papers and went home to Missouri, where his ability to forge documents came in handy once again in selling real estate. He got rich, and the idea of building on this success by creating a phony Spanish land grant in Arizona blossomed.

The Treaty of Guadalupe Hidalgo in 1848 stipulated that the United States recognize prior ownership of land under the Spanish and Mexican governments. Landowners simply had to "locate and duly record" their ownership claims in the archives of Mexico. Reavis traveled to archives in Mexico and Spain, removed legitimate documents, and inserted forgeries that would substantiate his claims. Then, in 1885, he filed on about 12 million acres of rich agricultural and mineral lands smack in the center of Arizona, extending from today's Sun City near Phoenix to Silver City, New Mexico. The title, Reavis said, had come to him from an impoverished member of the former nobility, Miguel Peralta. To solidify his claim, Reavis found a sixteen-year-old Mexican orphan, convinced her that she was a baroness, and married her.

James Addison Reavis, the "Baron" of Arizona, and the "Baroness" Sofia —Southwest Studies, Scottsdale Community College

"Baron" Reavis did not plan to evict the settlers and farmers on the lands in question. He would graciously accept rent and other fees. The owners of large mines and the railroad nabobs decided it was cheaper to pay the Baron his fees than to fight him and risk losing their valuable properties. Besides, the tall, rangy Missourian with the muttonchops charmed them. The railroad paid him $50,000; the Silver King Mine handed over $25,000. Soon Reavis and his family were touring Europe in style and maintaining homes around the world.

Senator Roscoe Conkling, a Republican Party stalwart, and Robert Ingersoll, a prominent attorney, pronounced the Baron's documents authentic, but small landowners, outraged at the idea of becoming vassals, talked of lynching. The federal government considered paying Reavis millions of dollars to settle the claim. Finally, a printer at the newspaper in nearby Florence, William "Stammering Bill" Truman, whose hobby was calligraphy, found proof of the recent application of some of the documents' supposedly "ancient" print.

In a bold move, backed by lawyers Conkling and Ingersoll, Reavis sued the U.S. government. The case went to trial in Santa Fe in 1893. Reavis lost. He was soon found guilty himself and sentenced to two years in the penitentiary in Santa Fe and a fine of $5,000—a light sentence, proving once again that Americans love a creative con man. Abandoning his wife and two sons, Reavis became a drifter, occasionally appearing on the streets of Phoenix to promote some new scheme. He died in 1914 and was buried in a pauper's grave in Denver. Until her death in the 1930s, Reavis's wife Sofia believed she was a baroness.

CASA GRANDE

People have lived in the area around the town of Casa Grande for a long time. Evidence at nearby Ventana Cave points to 10,000 years of human habitation. Hohokam Indians farmed the valleys along the Gila River from about A.D. 300 to 1400. At some point during that time, the Apache migrated into the area, subsisting by raiding the farmers.

Mines and the railroad brought Casa Grande into more modern times. Casa Grande, then called Bluewater, became a distribution center for area mines and a transfer point for passengers and freight on stagecoaches, wagons, and trains heading to Florence and Tucson. Later the Southern Pacific changed the town's name to Casa Grande because of its proximity to the famous ruins.

Construction of Coolidge Dam in the late 1920s provided a reliable source of water and made Casa Grande into a farm center. Due to high demand during both world wars, cotton became the staple crop in the Gila Valley. Following World War II, Casa Grande's close proximity to railroads and highways made it an ideal location for fattening cattle. With its mild climate, the area also became a mecca for winter visitors and retirees.

On the northern outskirts of Casa Grande, at AZ 387, exit 185, is a simple concrete monument honoring the Mormon Battalion—in particular, a harrowing three-day desert crossing that ended at a campsite here on December 20, 1846.

GUADALUPE

As one approaches the Phoenix metro area from the south, I-10 crosses from the Gila River Valley into the Salt River Valley. Guadalupe is a small Pascua Yaqui Indian community off I-10 in Phoenix's southern suburbs, just south of Tempe. The Yaqui have been called the "fighting farmers of Mexico." Their history in their native country parallels that of the Apache in the United States. Both waged long, bitter wars against domineering invaders. The Yaqui first fought the Spaniards, and later, in the 1800s, the Mexicans, who coveted their fertile farms along the Yaqui River in Sonora. Just as the U.S. government moved the Apache to Florida during the nineteenth century, many Yaqui were rounded up and exiled to the alien jungle climate of Yucatán.

During the Mexican Revolution the Yaqui sided with Gen. Francisco "Pancho" Villa; when Villa's army was defeated, many Yaqui sought refuge in the United States. The Mexican government tried to extradite them, but because of their probable extermination in their homeland, the United States refused. A large number of Yaqui moved to the Salt River Valley. Many hired out as laborers on canal-building projects and settled in Scottsdale and Guadalupe.

In Mexico, Catholic priests befriended the Yaqui and staunchly defended them against Spanish oppression and landgrabbing. The Catholics left a deep impression on the native religion, resulting

Yaqui ceremonial figures —*Arizona Highways*

in an interesting blend of the two religions. The blend is most beautifully and memorably apparent in the annual Yaqui Easter ceremonies. Started in Arizona in 1909, the ceremonies are based on the Jesuits' miracle plays, which dramatized the life of Jesus. To these the Yaqui added their own beliefs and rituals. Reenacted with great devotion, the processions, dancing, and pantomime continue through several days and nights. Flowers—what Christ's blood turned into when it hit the earth—are a constant theme in the ceremonies and in Yaqui beliefs in general. Townspeople act out the carrying of the cross and the crucifixion.

On Easter Sunday, melodious bells and cocoon ankle rattles herald the arrival of the *Pascolas,* the old men of the fiesta, who dance to flutes, drums, violins, or harps. When they're not dancing, the Pascolas entertain the crowd with nonsense, double-talk, jokes, and stories. During the ceremonies, masks, costumes, ribbons, flowers, songs, and dances abound. At the climax, evil is driven away and good prevails.

Phoenix: See Part 2

AZ 86
Tucson—Why
131 MILES

THREE POINTS AND ROBLES JUNCTION

Twenty-two miles west of Tucson on AZ 86 is the turnoff for AZ 286. The junction is called Three Points, also known as Robles Junction. The alternate name is for pioneer Bernabé Roblés, who had a ranch in this area around the turn of the twentieth century and also ran a stage line from Tucson to Gunsight.

On an April afternoon in 1934, on her way home from school in Tucson, six-year-old June Roblés, Bernabe's granddaughter, was abducted. A ransom note for $15,000 arrived at her home a couple of hours later. For several days, the family heard nothing. Crowds of anxious citizens waited outside the Roblés's home for some word of her fate. After nineteen days, Governor Ben Moeur received a letter postmarked from Chicago disclosing where June could be found. Combing the desert outside Tucson, searchers found a long sheet-iron box buried in the sand. June was inside, exhausted but alive. The story got sensational press; little June was even invited out to Hollywood. The kidnapper was never found.

Kitt Peak National Observatory

Fifteen miles west of Robles Junction is the turnoff to Kitt Peak (AZ 386). According to one story, surveyor George Roskruge named the peak in 1893 after an Indian named Kit who worked for surveying parties in the area. Another story says it was named for Roskruge's sister, whose married name was Kitt. In 1958, taking advantage of Arizona's crystal clear air, a national observatory was built here that boasted the largest concentration of facilities in the world for stellar and solar research. The observatory is on the Tohono O'Odham Indian Reservation. Visitors are welcome; the complex includes a visitor center, museum, and tours on which visitors may look through some of the telescopes.

SELLS AND THE TOHONO O'ODHAM INDIAN RESERVATION

Back in 1909 Sells was called Indian Oasis. The town began when Joe and Louis Menager dug a well and opened a store and post office. In 1919 the name was changed to honor Cato Sells, Commissioner of Indian Affairs.

Sells, about sixty miles west of Tucson on AZ 86, is the agency headquarters for the Tohono O'Odham Indians. The nearly 2.8-million-acre reservation, with a population of approximately 23,600, is exceeded in size only by the Navajo lands to the north and east. The southern boundary of the reservation abuts the U.S.-Mexico border. The reservation covers some of the tribe's original homelands.

The Tohono O'Odham, or "People of the Desert," are also known as the Papago. As with the name Pima, Papago was a name the Spanish gave the tribe; in Spanish it means "Bean Eaters." The two tribes, Tohono O'Odham and Pima, are closely related. Jesuit father Eusebio Kino first visited the Tohono O'Odham in 1694. Up until about 1950, what Kino wrote about them and their lifestyle would still have fit, more or less. Traditionally, the aridity of their lands made them less agrarian than the Pima. Instead, they were a seminomadic, or rancheria, people, moving between favorable climates within their homeland, Papagueria, as the seasons changed. Rainfall in this area varies from four to twelve inches; elevation runs from 1,400 to 3,000 feet.

Father Kino first introduced the Tohono O'Odham to cattle ranching in the 1600s, and cattle still graze the sparse grasslands of Papagueria today. Without a single permanent stream or lake on the reservation, these hardy people have survived droughts through hard work and resourcefulness. Most of the villages have only one well; residents haul water home in oil drums. During drought, cattle subsist on prickly pear and other desert plants. But the inhospitable environment has been a blessing in disguise for the desert dwellers. No one else has wanted to live here. In fact, the need to establish reservation boundaries didn't even arise until late in the twentieth century.

QUIJOTOA AND COVERED WELLS

Quijotoa and Covered Wells (Maish Vaya) are neighboring towns on the Tohono O'Odham Reservation, twenty-two and twenty-five miles northwest of Sells, respectively. Quijotoa was the Papago name for nearby Ben Nevis Mountain. It means "Carrying-Basket Mountain," and indeed, the top of Ben Nevis resembles a basket. Covered Wells was a water-supply place for the mining towns at Quijotoa during the 1880s. The name comes from the wooden covers used at the wells.

As early as 1774, Spanish *gambusinos* (miners) were working mines in this area and shipping the ore to Baja California. The region boomed in 1883 when Alexander McKay found outcroppings of silver and copper on Ben Nevis Mountain. Soon several mining companies were setting up operations. Four mining camps sprang into being within a year: Logan, New Virginia, Virginia City, and Brooklyn. Ultimately the four towns, with about 200 buildings among them, merged into the desert megalopolis Quijotoa.

Real estate was a sure path to prosperity. Reportedly, one man spent $500 to erect a building, then turned around and rented space for $75 a month. Drinking water sold for 75 cents a bucket; it was almost cheaper to wet a parched throat with whiskey. Lots of money was made here, but, as in mining camps across the West, more of it came from mining the miners than from mining the ore. Mine boosters had a field day promoting Quijotoa; they surrounded the place with a magical air of mystery and promise. But in 1885 the ore played out, and several thousand residents moved on to greener pastures. Four years later a fire nearly finished off Quijotoa.

WHY

At the junction of AZ 86 and AZ 85—a Y in the road—the town of Why was founded in the 1960s. At the junction, AZ 86 ends and AZ 85 leads north to Ajo and south to Lukeville, on the Mexican border. Supposedly, residents called the town "Y," but tourists thought they were saying "Why." Others say the name comes from so many tourists asking, "Why do you want to live out here?" Now the most common question is, "Why is your town called Why?" After years of trying to provide real answers to this question, locals have shortened their reply to "Why not?"

AZ 286
Mexican Border—Robles Junction
46 MILES

ALTAR VALLEY

From the border with Mexico, AZ 286 runs north through the Altar Valley to meet up with AZ 86 at Robles Junction. The southern part of the valley is dedicated to the Buenos Aires National Wildlife Refuge.

Father Kino first mentioned the Altar Valley in 1693; he called it simply El Altar. The Altar River, which has its headwaters in the area, flows close to the site of the ancient Tohono O'Odham village of Ali-Shonak, or "Place of the Small Springs," about twenty-five miles southwest of present-day Nogales.

In 1736, near Ali-Shonak, a Yaqui Indian miner named Antonio Siraumea made the fabulous "Planches de Plata" silver strike. The silver occurred in sheets, or "planks"—hence *planches.* One chunk was said to weigh a ton. Over two tons of silver, most of it in the form of large balls and slabs, were mined in a relatively small area. As word of the strike spread, Spanish miners poured into the area. It is said the silver there was so rich and pure, you could cut it with a knife. The name of this tiny, obscure place was soon on every New World Spaniard's lips—lips that pronounced it "Arissona." This story supports one theory of where the state's name came from.

I-8
I-10—Gila Bend
62 MILES

From I-10, I-8 strikes boldly west across desert country, heading almost straight for Gila Bend. Before the arrival of the freeway system beginning in the 1950s, this road was known as AZ 84. Travelers were advised to carry extra fan belts and radiator hoses, and to carry drinking water. Earlier, in the nineteenth century, weary travelers on the way to Yuma Crossing from Tucson first went north to the Pima villages on the Gila River to barter for supplies and rest stock before venturing across the desert to Gila Bend.

GILA BEND

Near Gila Bend, or Big Bend as local people called it, the southbound Gila River makes a ninety-degree turn to the west and flows toward Yuma. A stopping place in the desert between Casa Grande (or in older days, Maricopa Wells) about forty miles to the east and Yuma Crossing to the west, Gila Bend has been a welcome sight to generations of travelers.

In 1774 Father Francisco Garcés reported a Papago (Tohono O'Odham) rancheria at Gila Bend, which he named Santos Apostales San Simon y Judas. In the 1850s there was a Butterfield station called Gila Ranch about four miles south of present-day Gila Bend. When the Southern Pacific Railroad line arrived in the area around 1878, the town relocated to its present site to be close to the station.

Touring cars in the desert (no date)
—Southwest Studies, Scottsdale Community College

The stretch across the desert between Maricopa Wells and the mountains of California was the most torturous on the entire twenty-four-day, biweekly run of the Butterfield Overland Mail. Stations spaced fifteen to twenty miles apart bore a litany of picturesque place names like Murderer's Grave, Flapjack Ranch, and Filibuster Camp.

In the late 1800s Gila Bend proudly boasted one of the West's most appropriately named saloons, "Whiskey, the Road to Ruin." Today that sign hangs over the false-front saloon at the Pioneer Arizona Living History Museum, twenty-five miles north of Phoenix on I-17. When US 80—today, I-8—was built across Arizona in the 1920s, Gila Bend was one of the few places where weary travelers could get water and gas. The auto repair business was the most lucrative in town. Residents still refer jokingly to this desert community as the "fan belt capital of the world."

Breakdown in the desert; the early days (no date) —Southwest Studies, Scottsdale Community College

AZ 238
Casa Grande—Gila Bend
62 MILES

AK-CHIN INDIAN RESERVATION

The Ak-Chin Indian Community is in the Santa Cruz Valley immediately south of the Gila River Reservation. It was created in 1912, the same year Arizona became a state. Ak-Chin residents include Tohono O'Odham and Pima people. Today fewer than 1,000 people call Ak-Chin home.

Nearly 15,000 acres of the reservation are under irrigation, with cotton the leading crop. The tribe also has a 109-acre industrial park. The proximity of fast-growing Phoenix adds to the community's economic prospects. Today, much of the tribe's revenue comes from Harrah's Ak-Chin Casino Resort near Maricopa. After the Arizona Water Settlements Act, which gave control of 1.5 million acre-feet of water per year back to Arizona's tribes (see historical overview), the tiny Ak-Chin Indian community became the water supplier for the huge Del Webb Anthem development north of Phoenix.

MARICOPA AND MARICOPA WELLS

Maricopa is at the junction of AZ 238 and AZ 347, about thirty miles south of Phoenix, on the Ak-Chin Indian Reservation. Maricopa Wells, about ten miles northwest of Maricopa, was an important oasis on the banks of the Gila River. It no longer exists, though the wells or natural springs are still there. Because of the water and because of the place's location on the eastern edge of the formidable Forty-Mile Desert and along the Gila Trail, Maricopa Wells has had centuries of notable visitors. Whether they were traveling in an east-west line or north-south, they usually passed through the Wells.

Naturally, the Wells was a good location for a stage station. The short-lived San Antonio & San Diego Mail—also known as the "Jackass Mail"—first established a station there in 1857. Later, the Butterfield Trail passed through. In 1873 a military telegraph linked Maricopa Wells with the outside world.

On April 29, 1879, the Southern Pacific reached Maricopa Station, about eight miles south of the Maricopa Wells stage station. It became the terminus for travelers connecting by stage to Phoenix, the upstart Salt River community thirty miles north, and to Tucson, nearly 100 miles to the southeast. With the arrival of the railroad, the old Butterfield stage station at Maricopa Wells, and Maricopa Wells itself, sank into oblivion. In 1887 a new railroad line opened between Phoenix and a station called Maricopa Junction a few miles east of Maricopa Station. Also in 1887, Maricopa Junction became simply Maricopa, and Maricopa Station was changed to Heaton.

Farther west on AZ 238, near present-day Enid, was the old stage station at Desert Wells, the only stop on the Forty-Mile

Desert crossing. The old adobe station walls stood until as late as the 1950s, but are gone now. West of Desert Wells, treacherous Pima Pass was notorious for ambushes. On the west side of the pass, the Butterfield Company constructed a water tank, hauling water in from Gila Bend. Perhaps with the thirsty traveler in mind, the place was called Happy Camp.

AZ 85
Mexican Border—I-10
115 MILES

ORGAN PIPE CACTUS NATIONAL MONUMENT

Set aside in 1937, 500-square-mile Organ Pipe Cactus National Monument honors and preserves an extraordinary desert ecosystem. Here one can find lizards, kangaroo rats, and other desert animals that go their entire lives without taking a drink of water, instead taking in moisture by eating succulent desert plants. The organ pipe cactus itself is so named because its arms spread upward like the pipes of an organ. To protect its delicate flowers from the harsh sun, it blooms only at night. The Desert Botanical Garden in Phoenix maintains a telephone hotline for late-breaking news about which desert plants are flowering.

AJO

Ajo is a town of about 3,000, ten miles north of Why on AZ 85. *Ajo* means "garlic" in Spanish, but contrary to popular belief, the town wasn't named for that pungent plant, but another—a tasty plant full of vitamins that grows along the washes in the area, and that probably saved the lives of a few miners running short on food: the ajo lily, a wild onion. Another theory holds that the name comes from the Tohono O'Odham word for paint, *au'auho*. The Indians used a pigment from a red ore found here to paint their bodies.

Spanish miners found a rich deposit of silver ore in this area around 1750, though there is no record that they mined it. Later, in 1864, legendary Arizona pioneer Pete Brady reported finding rich silver ore deposits around Ajo. Investors organized the American Mining & Trading Company, making Ajo the site of one of the first American-operated mines in Arizona. However, the high-grade surface stringers—small veins near the surface—weren't as rich as those at Bisbee, Jerome, and Clifton, and technology had not yet advanced for operating stringers at a profit, so the mine owners abandoned the project. The deposits around Ajo lay dormant until the twentieth century.

About 1900 a smooth-talking promoter named A. J. Shotwell picked up a few ore specimens at Ajo and took them to St. Louis. He had little trouble raising capital from usually skeptical Missourians for a mine at Ajo—after all, it was Arizona, where every coyote hole was a potential gold mine. When these investors lost their money, another group was waiting to take their place. The second group, less credulous than the first, wanted a firsthand look at Ajo. Wisely, Shotwell chose the rainy season for their visit—water is necessary for mining. The investors were suitably impressed, and on the way back to St. Louis, they organized the Cornelia Copper Company. But when the water holes around Ajo evaporated, so did the money and the investors' enthusiasm.

Along with some business associates, John C. Greenway, a former Rough Rider and the manager of Bisbee's Calumet & Arizona Company, picked up the Cornelia Copper Company in 1911. The reorganized and refinanced company brought in new technology and geological expertise. They discovered a huge underground reservoir of water and began an open-pit operation. Soon Ajo became one of Arizona's richest copper camps, peaking in time for the copper boom of World War I. By 1916 the town of Cornelia, just north of Ajo, had a population of over 5,000. In 1914, in the belief that beautiful surroundings make happier workers, Greenway hired architects to revamp Ajo. Today Ajo's distinctive Spanish-style plaza, completed in 1917, is one of several legacies from that effort. But that same year, older Ajo burned. Supposedly, the only thing salvaged was a phonograph record, "There'll Be a Hot Time in the Old Town Tonight."

Phelps-Dodge, the eventual owner of the Ajo mine, shut it down in 1985. Plans are to resume mining in the giant open pit, but the market price for copper will determine when.

BUCKEYE

Long before the arrival of white settlers in the Buckeye Valley, Hohokam Indians channeled water from the nearby Gila River to their crops. In 1877 Thomas Newt Clanton led a small band of settlers from Creston, Iowa, into the valley. Ill health brought Clanton west, and the move seemed to work—he lived another forty-nine years, to age eighty-two.

The Buckeye Canal, completed in 1886, gave the area its first great boost. In 1888 Clanton, Malin M. Jackson, and William "Buckey" O'Neill, later a famous Rough Rider, laid out a town site on a portion of the Clanton homestead. They named the town Sidney in honor of Jackson's hometown in Ohio, but in 1910 the town was renamed for the Buckeye Canal, which Jackson and Clanton had built and Jackson named for his home

Buckeye, 1955 —Southwest Studies, Scottsdale Community College

state. The arrival of the Arizona Eastern Railroad in 1910 brought another economic boom to the area. The next year the first automobile arrived. By 1912 Buckeye was connected to Phoenix by rail, and by 1915 a state highway ran through town.

For over a century Buckeye was a sleepy little agricultural community, but creeping suburbia and the construction of I-10 north of town are bringing great changes. Housing developers are planning gated communities, golf courses, and luxury homes. In 2000 the town's population was 6,500, but more than 160,000 new homes are planned on more than 60,000 acres of former farmland near the interstate. The many examples of good and bad development in the area should be invaluable for the townspeople of Buckeye. By 2020 Buckeye is expected to be one of the three largest cities in the valley.

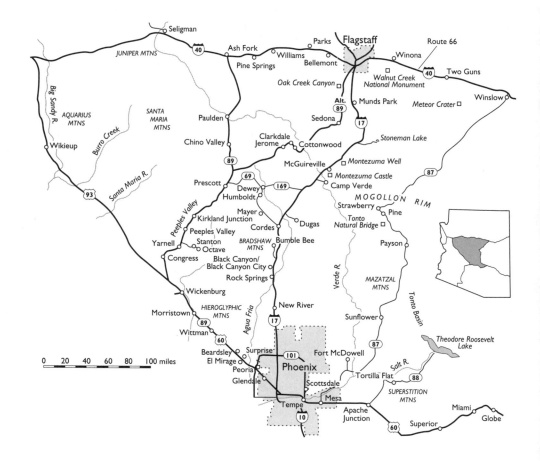

Seligman

JUNIPER MTNS

40

Ash Fork

Parks

Flagstaff

Route 66

Williams

Winona

Pine Springs

Bellemont

40

Two Guns

Walnut Creek
National Monument

Oak Creek Canyon

Big Sandy R.

*AQUARIUS
MTNS*

*SANTA
MARIA
MTNS*

Paulden

Alt.
89

Munds Park

Meteor Crater

Winslow

Burro Creek

Sedona

17

Stoneman Lake

Wikieup

Chino Valley

Clarkdale
Jerome

Cottonwood

89

Santa Maria R.

McGuireville

Montezuma Well

87

Prescott

69

Dewey

169

Montezuma Castle
Camp Verde

93

Peoples Valley

Humboldt

Mayer

Strawberry

MOGOLLON   RIM

Pine

Kirkland Junction

Cordes

Dugas

*Tonto
Natural Bridge*

Peeples Valley

Yarnell

Stanton
Octave

*BRADSHAW
MTNS*

Bumble Bee

Payson

Congress

Black Canyon/
Black Canyon City

Verde R.

*MAZATZAL
MTNS*

Rock Springs

Tonto Basin

Wickenburg

*HIEROGLYPHIC
MTNS*

New River

Sunflower

*Theodore Roosevelt
Lake*

Morristown

89

Agua Fria

17

Wittman

60

87

Beardsley
El Mirage

Surprise

101

Fort McDowell

Salt R.

88

Peoria

Phoenix

Tortilla Flat

Glendale

Scottsdale

Mesa

*SUPERSTITION
MTNS*

Tempe

10

Apache
Junction

Miami

60

Superior

Globe

0   20   40   60   80   100 miles

Part 2

Peaks and Valleys

US 60
Globe—Tempe
78 MILES

Long before US 60 came into existence in the 1920s, automobiles and wagons used this road. The future US 60 was first chiseled out of sheer rock walls in 1870 as a military road by soldiers from Camp Pinal, six miles west of present Miami.

Before the highway was built, motorists traveling to Phoenix from east-central Arizona had to drive down today's AZ 88 to Roosevelt, then down the dusty, winding Apache Trail past Fish Creek Hill and Tortilla Flat to Apache Junction, then on to Phoenix. On November 29, 1922, citizens gathered at Miami for the ground-breaking ceremony for US 60 between Globe and Phoenix via Miami and Superior. The highway was completed in 1926. US 60 south of Top of the World is among the most scenic stretches of road in the state.

MIAMI AND BLOODY TANKS WASH

Miami sits in a small valley at the foot of the Pinal Mountains. The business district is laid out on the valley floor, while most of the residences are perched on the slopes of the foothills. Bloody Tanks Wash runs through the middle of the valley, which is known as Miami Flat. The old Miami Copper Company and Inspiration Mines, along with company offices and dwellings, were on the north side of town near where today lies a massive man-made mesa of bleached-out dirt.

King Woolsey
—Southwest
Studies, Scottsdale
Community College

Bloody Tanks Wash was named for a battle that took place in 1864 between rancher King Woolsey's Indian fighters (see Dewey) and a party of Apache. The fight occurred during a "peaceful parley" between the two groups on January 24. The 250 warriors were "painted and feathered up" for battle, and Woolsey's 40 men were carrying concealed weapons. After Woolsey offered gifts of tobacco and pinole (ground corn mixed with sugar) to the natives, he touched his hat, a prearranged signal, and the militiamen pulled their guns and opened fire.

When the smoke cleared, at least nineteen Apaches were dead. It was said the water in the creek turned red from the blood, inspiring the grim name. Woolsey's casualties were understandably light—one killed and another, a man named Tonto Jack, receiving an arrow wound in the neck.

The late Gila County historian Clara Woody believed that the battle between Woolsey and the Apache occurred at Fish Creek, and that Bloody Tanks was named for an encounter between Lt. Howard Cushing's troops and a band of Pinal Apache on June 4, 1870. Cushing and his troops trailed the warriors into the Pinal Mountains. The Apaches, thinking they had evaded the soldiers, made camp and posted no guards. Cushing's men surrounded the camp and opened fire, killing about thirty Apaches.

In 1907 "Black Jack" Newman, a Polish immigrant, found a rich prospect in Big Johnny Gulch and named it the Mima for his girlfriend, Mima Tune. At about the same time, a group from Miami, Ohio, staked a claim near Bloody Tanks Wash. When the tent city went up, Black Jack wanted to name the fledgling community Mima, but the others insisted on calling it Miami. They reached a compromise when both sides agreed to spell it "Miami" but pronounce it "Mima." Some old-timers still pronounce it that way.

In 1908 a developer named Cleve Van Dyke bought the town site for $25,000, acquired a newspaper, the *Silver Belt,* and began promoting Miami to prospectors and merchants. By the end of World War I, the "Concentrator City," as Miami was sometimes called, had a larger population than Globe. Like most of the old copper towns, however, recently Miami has fallen on hard times. The market has been glutted with imported copper, and the local companies have deemed it unprofitable to update the mines with modern equipment. Meanwhile its rival town, Globe, has prospered.

TOP OF THE WORLD

Before US 60 was built, the old highway used to wind its way farther east, past the Top of the World "guest ranch," a famous bordello popular during the 1950s. The interior was paneled with white pine, and the lobby had a coke machine and a jukebox that lit up like a Las Vegas casino. But the main attraction was the girls, who were among the prettiest in Gila County and known far beyond the county borders.

When the Top of the World brazenly advertised in a 1960 Phoenix phone book, the Phoenix paper began a successful moral campaign to have it closed. It's gone but not forgotten; it remains in the fondest memories of the miners and college kids from ASU who frequented the place. The area around the summit between Miami and Superior is still called the Top of the World.

PINAL CITY AND THE SILVER KING MINE

Pinal City, a ghost town three miles southwest of Superior, was a mill town for the fabulous Silver King Mine (today on private land). In November 1870 Gen. George Stoneman established a military post near the headwaters of Mineral and Pinto Creeks in Mason Valley. In 1871 Stoneman moved his troops, about 400 of them, about ten miles west to a new fort, Camp Picket Post, near Picket Post Mountain.

In 1873 a soldier from the camp named Sullivan picked up a curious chunk of black rock and showed it to a friend, local farmer Charles Mason. Mason recognized it as nearly pure silver. When his enlistment was up, Sullivan disappeared, having mentioned only that he found the ore near the foot of Stoneman Grade.

Silver King Mine (no date) —Arizona Historical Society, Tucson

When Mason and three farmer friends went looking for the lode around the grade, an Apache war party jumped them. During the fight one of the burros wandered away. Afterward, the four found it standing directly atop a rich outcropping of the same black rock. It looked like the king of all silver mines, so they called it the Silver King.

Unsavvy prospectors, the four men tossed the high-grade ore onto a tailing dump and took the low-grade stuff to San Francisco. The freight bill alone was $12,000. However, Mason and his partners were saved from poverty when some mining men offered to work the Silver King for half the profits. The first shipment netted the four men $50,000. The Silver King was incorporated in 1877. When the boom ended eleven years later, the mine had produced more than $6 million in silver.

According to legend, during the Silver King's prosperous years, an old itinerant wandered into Pinal City and told the mine's owners he was Sullivan, the soldier who had made the original discovery. In California he'd heard of the fabulous Silver King and wanted to look at it before he died. The sympathetic owners believed his story and offered him a job with a pension for life.

The mill town of Pinal City, five miles from the mine, was established in 1878 as Picket Post, but the name was changed to Pinal a year later. The city boomed along with the mine, boasting such amenities as a brewery, two churches (Protestant and Catholic), several lodges, and the usual sundry businesses. Camp Picket Post was eventually abandoned by the army and absorbed into the bustling town. However, when the bottom fell out of the silver market in the early 1890s, the population of Pinal, which had reached 2,000, dwindled to 10.

SUPERSTITION MOUNTAINS

The Superstitions, the awesome, jagged range north of US 60 just east of the Phoenix metro area, are among America's most storied mountains. It was said that people who ventured into these mysterious mountains, with their twisting, steep-sided canyons, never returned. Here is the home of the Apache Thunder Gods, a white streak of limestone that is, according to legend, the high-water mark of a great flood that covered most of the earth.

The most enduring legend of these mountains is that of the Lost Dutchman Gold Mine. The Dutchman was Jacob Waltz, who supposedly found an old Spanish mine in the Superstitions and killed anyone foolish enough to try to learn his secret. After his death in the early 1890s, the legend of the lost mine created some local interest for a time. In 1893, a claim was filed on a rich outcropping of gold that became the Black Queen Mine. The Mammoth and Mormon Stope Mines were discovered not far from the Black Queen. The Mormon Stope alone produced $1 million in gold. One of these mines might have been the Lost Dutchman lode, but the legend endured.

In the 1930s, after the Lost Dutchman story had been mostly forgotten, a Dr. Adolph Ruth arrived at Apache Junction claiming to have a map of the mine. An elderly man in poor health, Ruth ventured into the mountains one hot summer day and was never again seen alive. Several months later his skull was found with what looked like a bullet hole in it. The newspapers around the country had a field day with the story as would-be millionaires came out of the woodwork to search for the fabulous lode. True believers continue the search to this day. Lost mines are much more interesting when they remain lost. The Lost Dutchman Museum in Goldfield has more on the story, as well as displays on local history and folklore.

The rugged Superstitions have some of the most spectacular vistas in America. In the early spring, nearly every canyon stream flows with sparkling clear water, and all summer the grass is emerald, with lupine and poppies everywhere. While the Lost Dutchman Mine remains a mystery, the real treasure in these mountains lies in simply being there.

APACHE JUNCTION

In 1944 Apache Junction, at the western end of the Apache Trail, consisted mainly of one combination gas station and hotel. Every Sunday a three-piece country music band played in the lobby. Out back was a crude zoo of boards and chicken wire, the most interesting part of which was the rattlesnake pen. The area around Apache Junction has always had a good supply of rattlesnakes.

In the 1960s a big diamondback crawled into the dugout at a major league spring-training game, sending the players scrambling. Today Apache Junction is a popular retirement community and recreation spot.

MESA

Mesa, west of Apache Junction and part of the Phoenix metropolitan area, started out as several separate Mormon settlements. In 1877 the first Mormon settlers to establish a community south of the Little Colorado River arrived in the Salt River Valley via the old road from Fort McDowell. They forded the river at the crossing known at various times as the McDowell, the Maryville, or the Whitlow Crossing. Maryville had been the first settlement near what is now Mesa. On the north side of the river, near the junction of AZ 87 (the Beeline Highway) and McDowell Road, Maryville boasted a store, hotel, and blacksmith shop, but it had already been abandoned when the Mormons arrived.

These early Mormon settlers were called the Lehi Pioneers. They built their colony near the site of Maryville, organizing work parties, digging irrigation ditches, and planting crops. They erected an adobe fort, named Fort Utah, near present-day North Mesa Drive and Lehi Road. (A replica of the fort currently stands in front of the Mesa Historical Museum.) The settlement was called Utahville, then Jonesville, and finally Lehi.

The following year, another group of Mormon settlers from Utah, known as the Mesa Pioneers, arrived at Lehi. They decided to build a new colony, on the tableland south of Lehi, and called it Mesa, or Mesa City. More Mormon settlers soon arrived and established Stringtown at the site of today's East Valley Institute of Technology. This settlement later became part of Mesa.

The phenomenal growth that has characterized the rest of the Salt River Valley has also occurred in Mesa. From a population of 7,000 in 1940, the town expanded to over 400,000 by 2000. The agrarian society that characterized early Mesa has been replaced by high-tech industry, as suburbia creeps over what was once lush farmland and sprawls across the desert.

Tempe, circa 1900 —Southwest Studies, Scottsdale Community College

TEMPE

They say that in 1879 British expatriate "Lord" Darrell Duppa (see also Phoenix, "A City Is Born") gazed out across the desolate desert south of Phoenix, with its dots of greasewood and clusters of grizzled mesquite, and said the place reminded him of the Vale of Tempe in Greece. We know Duppa was addicted to alcohol, so he may have been overcome with a moment of grandeur. In any case, Tempe it became and Tempe it is.

Tempe was first known as Hayden's Ferry, when merchant Charles Trumbull Hayden operated a ferry here across the Salt River. Hayden had come to Santa Fe in the late 1840s and moved to Tucson in 1858. A dozen years later he moved to the south bank of the Salt River, where he established a ferry landing, a flour mill, and a store. His former home, now the restaurant Monti's La Casa Vieja, was also the birthplace of famous Arizona senator Carl Hayden. Some referred to Hayden's Ferry as San Pablo or Butte City. By 1879 everyone had agreed on Tempe, and a post office was established under that name.

Tempe Bridge, 1913. On the bridge (second from right) is Governor George W. P. Hunt, who served seven terms as Arizona's chief executive. —Southwest Studies, Scottsdale Community College

In 1885 the population of Tempe was 800, and the main industries were Hayden's ferry business and grain mill. With the arrival of the Maricopa & Phoenix Railroad in 1887, Tempe developed as a cattle shipping point, railroad junction, and important agricultural area. After the completion of Roosevelt Dam in 1911, irrigation created a man-made oasis at Tempe, and the town flourished. The establishment and growth of the college that would become Arizona State University also contributed to the town's prosperity. Today the town's population is more than 160,000.

In recent times, one of Tempe's proudest accomplishments has been the restoration of its historic downtown. The classic story of its redevelopment has served as a model for other communities in the Salt River Valley. Faced with catastrophic decay, city government and commercial developers teamed up in 1973 to draw up a bold plan to revitalize the area. In just a few years, the downtown became a wonderland of trees, flowers, fountains, restored Victorian buidings, and bustling new stores

Tempe residents enjoy their restored downtown. —Tempe City Hall

and restaurants. The old Casa Loma Hotel was restored to become an office and restaurant complex, and Hayden Square is a prize-winning development of apartments, shops, and entertainment venues. The old Tempe Hardware building is now a community theater, and shacks at the foot of Hayden Butte were cleared away for the Sheraton Tempe Mission Palms Hotel, just a short walk from the 74,000-seat Sun Devil Stadium.

In addition, Tempe joined forces with Phoenix to spearhead the Rio Salado Project, a multimillion-dollar effort to restore the green banks and wildlife habitat of the Salt River. The project began in the late 1990s and even before its completion showed remarkable progress in attracting birds and nurturing plant life.

In Tempe, the 220-acre Tempe Town Lake is the centerpiece of a huge recreation area, complete with emerging waterfront resorts, shops, and services.

Much of the credit for the amazing rebirth of downtown Tempe and the visionary Rio Salado Project goes to longtime Tempe mayor Harry Mitchell. A Tempe native, Mitchell was a teacher at Tempe High School when he was elected mayor in 1978. Reelected seven times, he retired in 1994 after presiding over an era of unprecedented growth and progress. Tempe's ugly-duckling transformation was confirmed when a magazine in rival Tucson, no doubt grudgingly, pronounced Tempe the most beautiful city in Arizona.

Arizona State University

In 1885 the Territorial Assembly at Prescott created a normal school in Tempe, which led to the town's emergence as an educational center. The school opened in February 1886 with thirty-three students (thirteen men and twenty women) and a two-year operating budget of $3,500. One of the first graduates was James McClintock, who later gained fame as a historian, newspaperman, and captain in the Arizona contingent of Teddy Roosevelt's Rough Riders during the Spanish-American War.

The 1885 bill creating the school stipulated that land to build it had to be secured within sixty days. George and Martha Wilson, a generous, civic-minded couple, endowed fifteen acres of the original twenty-acre parcel and sold the rest for $500. The Wilsons (for whom Wilson Hall is named) impoverished themselves by making the donation in what is undoubtedly one of the most unselfish, public-spirited acts in Tempe history. Martha Wilson died soon after, but her husband remained a caretaker on the campus until his death in 1916.

In its first quarter century, the normal school only averaged twelve students a year. In 1929 it became a four-year teachers college. In 1945, the name was changed to Arizona State College and, with the return of GIs from World War II, grew from 1,200 to 2,200 students. The last name change, to Arizona State University, came in 1958.

Arizona State has a proud tradition in sports. Tempe's sports teams were known as the Bulldogs until 1946, when the name

ASU's first football team, 1896
—Southwest Studies, Scottsdale Community College

was changed to Sun Devils. The popular, devilish-looking mascot was designed by a cartoonist from Walt Disney Productions.

Emerson Harvey was the first African American to play football for Tempe, in 1937. After World War II, black athletes Morrison Warren and George Diggs returned from the service and joined the team. In those days, Texas colleges prohibited their teams from competing, at home, against schools with black players. In 1947, after a game in Texas in which Diggs and Warren were not allowed to play, the ASU student body spurred the athletic department to issue a declaration against playing schools with whites-only policies. Only one Texas school, Hardin-Simmons, agreed to ASU's terms. The other teams were dropped from the Arizona State schedule until policy change in 1951. Because of its stand, Tempe attracted such talented black athletes as Leon Burton and Bobby Mulgado.

Since the early 1970s, Arizona State has hosted one of the major New Year's Day games, the Fiesta Bowl. In 1988 the St.

Louis Cardinals moved to Arizona and settled in Tempe, playing at Sun Devil Stadium. On January 18, 1996, Tempe and Arizona State University hosted Super Bowl 30 between the Dallas Cowboys and the Pittsburgh Steelers.

Loop 101
Tempe—I-10
36 MILES

SCOTTSDALE

On a February day in 1888, Phoenix was a city of 3,000 and just one year away from becoming the permanent capital of Arizona when army chaplain Winfield Scott arrived to look at some real estate. Scott's reputation as a colonizer with integrity inspired local promoters to invite him to see the Salt River Valley. William J. Murphy had just completed construction of the Arizona Canal, opening vast new areas for irrigation. Scott crisscrossed the valley on horseback for about a week before finding his utopia in the east valley. Five months later he purchased a 160-acre homestead for $2.50 an acre under the Desert Land Act.

Since the Desert Land Act required that the land be irrigated within three years, Winfield Scott brought his brother George Washington Scott out to prepare the land, dig the irrigation ditches, and plant barley, citrus, and grapes. George erected a tent on the northeast corner of today's Scottsdale and Indian School Roads, the present site of a modern financial center. He is, therefore, considered Scottsdale's first citizen.

Winfield Scott, still in the army, continued to promote the area. In 1889 he was transferred to Fort Huachuca and spent much of his free time preaching at churches in Phoenix, Tempe, and Mesa. He retired from the army in 1893 and moved to his homestead, bringing along another retiree, an army mule named Old Maud. A painting of Old Maud by noted artist Marjorie Thomas hangs in the mayor's office at city hall.

In 1894 Albert J. Utley, a Rhode Island banker, bought a section of land south of Scott's and plotted forty acres into a town site. He hoped to create a resort community that would include a hotel, a tuberculosis sanitarium, and a streetcar line to Phoenix. Utley asked Scott to take charge of the project. Giving the town a name headed the list of priorities. Suggested names included Murphyville for the canal builder and Utleyville for the developer. Utley himself preferred Orangedale, and for a brief time the town used that name. But before lots were ready to be sold, the future community's name was changed to Scottsdale to honor the man primarily responsible for building it.

In the fall of 1896, the first Scottsdale school opened, with seventeen pupils and Mrs. Alza Blount as teacher. In 1911 Scottsdale had its first post office; that same year, the citizens voted for Prohibition. Scottsdale was founded by church-minded people, and the community leaders were determined to keep the "vices and moral decadence" of Phoenix out of their town. It wasn't easy—Johnny Rose ran a pool hall on Brown and Main Streets and made regular runs into Phoenix to buy tanglefoot whiskey to sell. The town also had several shooting frays. In 1900 "Popcorn John" Rubenstein, a mail carrier from Phoenix, shot and killed two men in an argument over their wagon blocking his path. During the 1930s, town constable Al Frederick shot and killed a winter visitor's chauffeur after the latter attacked him with a cue stick in a pool hall.

In spite of the occasional excitement, Scottsdale was mostly a quiet farm village. Scottsdale farmers grew everything from peanuts and olives to citrus and barley, but the big moneymaker was cotton. During World War I, when cotton was in great demand for uniforms and balloon tires, a farmer could pay off his mortgage in one year.

In the early 1900s, most of the houses were built of orange crates and canvas. Phoenix residents disdainfully referred to the town as "White City" because of all the white tent dwellings.

At that time too, Phoenix made it clear that people with lung disease weren't welcome, so many convalescents came to live in Scottsdale. Minnie Elliott, afflicted with tuberculosis, was given only six months to live when she came to Scottsdale in 1895. She became friendly with the local Pima Indians, and they took it upon themselves to cure her. Each day they gave Minnie a bitter tea brewed from the leaves of the creosote bush and buried her up to her neck in desert sand. In six months her lungs healed, and she lived to the age of eighty-six. Some believe the treatment cured Minnie; others believe she made herself well to escape the treatment. In addition to being a farm community and a haven for health seekers, Scottsdale has been a refuge for artists since the late 1940s, including Lew Davis, Jesse Benton Evans, Lon Megargee, Philip Curtis, John Hampton, and Fritz Scholder.

Great Escape

During World War II, a large prisoner-of-war camp was built near Papago Park. For reasons understood only by a bureaucratic army, the most incorrigible prisoners were assigned to Papago. Many were German naval personnel—the idea was to get them as far way from the sea as possible. But the prisoners schemed to tunnel out, float down the Salt River to the Gila, then to the Colorado and on to Mexico, where they could eventually arrange a safe return to Germany. Twenty-five tireless Germans, using spoons for shovels, dug a 178-foot tunnel through the claylike caliche, and on December 23, 1944, they escaped. They waded down the

Scottsdale, 1941 —Southwest Studies, Scottsdale Community College

Crosscut Canal carrying a prefabricated boat and headed for the Salt River. The river was dry, as it usually is, so the prisoners tossed the boat away and, after spending Christmas Eve huddled in the basement of Phoenix Union High School, they separated. Within about six weeks all had been rounded up and put back behind barbed wire, ending the largest World War II prisoner-of-war escape in the United States.

Scottsdale Landmarks

The first of Scottsdale's long history of zoning fights occurred in 1910, when city fathers forced George Cavalliere to build his "smelly, fly-attractin' blacksmith shop" at the edge of town—way out on Second Street and Brown Road. The shop still does business at that location and is one of Scottsdale's richest historical treasures. Another sits next door, the venerable Our Lady of Perpetual Help Catholic Church. The adobe building was erected in 1933 by Mexican citizens who came to Arizona as farm workers and wanted a church of their own.

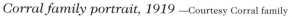

Corral family portrait, 1919 —Courtesy Corral family

Another Scottsdale landmark near Second Street and Brown Road is Los Olivos Restaurant, built by the Tomás Corral family, Mexican American farm workers who became prominent Scottsdale citizens. The Corral family migrated to Scottsdale in 1919, while the bloody revolution that had engulfed the Mexican Republic since 1910 still raged. Their sponsor, E. O. Brown, a prosperous merchant and rancher for whom Brown Road is named, gave them jobs. In the early 1930s, the family built an adobe pool hall, which was also used as a classroom for Our Lady of Perpetual Help.

During World War II, Tomás Corral's sons joined the military. They came home only to be denied some of the very civil liberties they had fought to preserve. After being refused service in a local restaurant, the Corrals converted their pool hall into a restaurant. Los Olivos continues to be one of Scottsdale's finest restaurants, its classic Mexican design a lasting tribute to the artistic talent of the Corral brothers.

Taliesin West

Northeast Scottsdale is also home to Taliesin (tal-ee-ESS-in) West, the winter home, studio, and architecture school of great American architect Frank Lloyd Wright. Born in 1867, Wright grew up in rural Wisconsin. A founder of the Prairie School of American architecture, he was one of the first truly American architects. After a lifetime of success, Wright began building Taliesin West in 1937, when he was seventy years old.

Wright first experienced the American Southwest on a job in Death Valley in 1923, and he came to Phoenix in 1927 to work on the spectacular Biltmore Hotel. Ten years later he bought 600 acres in the foothills of the McDowell Mountains and, with the help of his students, designed and in some cases hand built this remarkable complex of buildings, stone walls, and terraces that was inspired by and stands in harmony with its desert surroundings. Wright designed several other buildings in Arizona, all near Phoenix.

Taliesin means "Shining Brow" in Welsh. Both Taliesin West and Taliesin East, in Wisconsin, are National Historic Landmarks. Wright died at Taliesin East in 1959, at age ninety-two. Taliesin

West still houses a school of architecture and the Frank Lloyd Wright Foundation.

PARADISE VALLEY

The town of Paradise Valley, east of Phoenix, is tucked between Phoenix and Scottsdale. Like all cactus-strewn lands north of the Arizona Canal, it was unwatered and unused except for grazing land until World War II, when creeping suburbia jumped the canal and spread across the desert like molasses. The natural evolution of most of the land in the Salt River Valley has been from desert to agriculture to urban development. Paradise Valley skipped the middle part.

That might not have been the case if the Rio Verde Canal Company had had its way in the 1890s. Canal promoters planned to dig a canal west from the Verde River along the base of the McDowell Mountains, all the way to Union Hills. Then it would extend the canal over seventy miles west to the Hassayampa River and irrigate about 400,000 acres—an area one and a half times the acreage of the Salt River Valley Water Users Association. Paradise Valley certainly seemed like an appropriate name for the area. However, by 1892, after the company had drilled a 715-foot tunnel at Horseshoe Dam and dug eighteen miles of canal, financial woes halted the project, and the grand dream eventually evaporated.

PHOENIX

Beginnings

Phoenix's first residents were the ancient Hohokam Indians, who reached the Salt River Valley from Mexico around A.D. 700. During their 700 years in the valley, the Hohokam engineered the most extensive prehistoric canal system in the world and introduced both cotton and barley to this area.

After the Hohokam's mysterious disappearance around 1400 (see introduction), the Salt River Valley lay unclaimed for nearly 500 years. At the close of the Civil War in 1865, Fort McDowell was established near where Sycamore Creek joins the Verde River. Lt. John Y. T. Smith, mustered out of the army about that time, decided to stay on as a hay contractor and post sutler. He'd seen the fields of wild hay growing on the floodplains of the Salt River eighteen miles to the south and decided to set up a hay camp, which he built on the road to Fort McDowell (near today's Fortieth and Washington Streets in Phoenix). The place became known as Smith's Station.

Originally John Y. T. Smith was just plain John Smith, but when he ran for public office in 1879, a newspaper editor commented unfavorably on a man with a name like John Smith running for office. He went to the legislature and legally added the middle initials Y. T., which stood for "Yours Truly."

In September 1867 Smith's Station was visited by Jack Swilling, a thirty-seven-year-old, red-haired Confederate officer, ex-Indian fighter, adventurer, hellion, and most recently, gold prospector. Swilling was quick to note the opportunities for irrigating the rich, fertile soil by cleaning out the old Hohokam canals and

Jack Swilling —Arizona Historical Foundation

ditches. He went to Wickenburg, a thriving mining community fifty miles northwest, where he raised $400, recruited a party of strong-backed visionaries, and organized the Swilling Irrigation Canal Company.

Swilling, a generous and big-hearted man, was the product of the violent frontier. Originally from South Carolina, he had fought in both the Mexican-American and Civil Wars and had been involved in several scrapes with Apache and Comanche. One time a gun barrel fractured his skull, and he also carried a bullet in his left side from another incident. Because his old injuries caused a great deal of pain, he took morphine and whiskey and at times became a little crazy. Ultimately he died in a Yuma jail in 1878, accused of a crime he didn't commit.

Swilling and sixteen companions arrived at Smith's Station in December 1867 and began the laborious task of cleaning out the old canals. They began digging on the north bank of the Salt across from present-day Tempe, but when they hit caliche and rock they moved downriver near Smith's Station. By March 1868 the wheat and barley crops were in, and the population of Smith's Station had reached fifty.

Swilling's Ditch, as the watering system was called, ran northwest across the desert for half a mile, then curved back toward the river. Eventually it would be called the Town Ditch and would run along the north side of Van Buren to about Twenty-seventh Avenue. During its heyday the ditch was multipurpose: people dipped its waters for drinking, irrigation, bathing, and washing laundry. One newspaper complained that saloon keepers washed their spittoons in the ditch when nobody was looking. Nobody could have known at this time that from these humble beginnings the Salt River Valley would develop into one of the richest agricultural regions in the world.

The first permanent farm in the valley was started by Frenchy Sawyer in 1868. That site is marked by a small plaque on the southeast corner of Washington and Twenty-fourth Streets. The federal census of 1870 recorded a population of 164 men and 61 women. The ages of this hardy group ranged from twenty-one to thirty. Ninety-six people listed themselves as farmers. There wasn't a single doctor, lawyer, banker, or teacher in the whole community.

A City Is Born

On October 20, 1870, a committee of citizens gathered to select a town site. There were three proposed sites: one group wanted to build the town at today's northeast corner of Sixteenth and Van Buren; another preferred Thirty-second and Van Buren; and the third favored a mesquite-covered parcel between Seventh Street and Seventh Avenue.

Among the members of the selection committee was Bryan Philip Darrell Duppa, better known as "Lord" Duppa, reported to be a British lord who'd been something of an embarrassment to his family and had been exiled to the colonies. He received financial support as long as he remained out of England. The thirty-seven-year-old nobleman was addicted to ardent spirits, probably the reason for his exile. Though a well-traveled, educated man who spoke five languages, Duppa was hard to understand, his friends complained, because he was usually drunk and spoke all five languages at once.

Sometime between 1868 and 1872 Duppa built a two-room adobe house at 116 W. Sherman. Today that simple little casa, with its roof of cottonwood beams overlaid with salt-cedar poles and covered with arrowweed and mud, seems overwhelmed by the towering skyscrapers of downtown Phoenix. It is the oldest house still standing in the capital city and is the most obvious link with the city's past.

On the town site selection committee, Duppa had favored a site about four miles west of Smith's Station, near today's Central Avenue and Van Buren Street, but the committee finally chose the Seventh Street and Seventh Avenue site. Jack Swilling, who wanted the Thirty-second Street site, was so angry at the results he fired a round of bird shot, scoring a direct hit on one of those who had voted against him.

The first lot in the new city, on the southwest corner of First and Washington Streets, sold for $103. More than sixty lots, with prices ranging from $20 to $140, were sold by the end of the day. Not long afterward, a citizen came down from Wickenburg and planted the first tree, a cottonwood, on Washington Street.

The next task for the commitee was to choose a name for the town. Several were proposed, including Stonewall, Salinas, Pumpkinville, and Millville. Most historians credit the eccentric

Lord Duppa with suggesting the name Phoenix for the new town, after the mythical bird that rose from its own ashes. But others give credit to Jack Swilling, claiming he found the word in his Webster's dictionary and thought the name suited the place. In any case, on October 26, 1870, the little community of adobe houses, reborn from the ashes of the great Hohokam civilization, was christened Phoenix.

In 1871, when Maricopa County was organized, Phoenix became the county seat. The first election for sheriff of Maricopa County set an early precedent for political fireworks. Three candidates tossed their hats into the ring. The least conspicuous of the trio, Jim Barnum, wisely sat back and let the other two, "Whispering Jim" Favorite and J. M. Chenowth, fight it out. Each claimed the other was immoral, hated kids, and was rude to little old ladies. The feud drew so much attention that Barnum was almost forgotten and seemingly had no chance. The day before the election, Favorite and Chenowth grew tired of arguing politics and went for their six-shooters. When the smoke cleared,

Carnival Parade, downtown Phoenix, December 7, 1900
—Arizona Hall of Fame

Whispering Jim lay dead, and the city fathers asked Chenowth to leave town. Jim Barnum was elected by a landslide.

Bill Kirkland, another distinguished Arizona pioneer, moved to Phoenix in 1871. He and his family moved into a small adobe house on Washington Street between Central and First Avenues. His daughter May Ellen was the first Anglo child born in Phoenix, on August 15, 1871.

In 1879 Sam Lount opened the first ice-making plant. He sold his ice for seven cents a pound, and anyone who ever spent a summer in Phoenix before air conditioning will surely agree that there ought to be a monument dedicated to Lount. By 1880 Phoenix, zesty and full of optimism, boasted a population of 1,708.

Water to Grow

Since both transcontinental railroads bypassed Phoenix, it looked as though the isolated community on the banks of the Salt River was destined to remain small and unimportant. At the time, not even the most prophetic could foresee Phoenix's unlikely success as an agricultural center. But it would take men of vision and fortitude to bring it about. Historically, lands north of a canal were considered worthless. But bigger and better canals could change this.

Phoenix's future appeared in the person of William J. Murphy. In 1885 Murphy took on the difficult task of building the thirty-five-mile-long Arizona Canal, a project both massive and speculative, to open up irrigation north of the Grand Canal. Self-interest groups tried to block his efforts with political obstacles, but Murphy was undaunted. While Murphy traveled in the East raising funds for the project, his wife Laura supervised the construction. Despite falling heavily into debt, the Murphys finished the project on schedule and watched triumphantly as the first water flowed through the Arizona Canal in June 1887, right on schedule.

With the Arizona Canal a reality, agriculture on a much larger scale would now be possible. Yet delivery systems among Phoenix's four canals were poor and there was a lot of water loss. So Murphy organized the Arizona Improvement Company and built a cross-cut canal that connected all four canals, minimizing water loss and improving delivery. Now strong and prosperous,

Phoenix was able to challenge Prescott and Tucson in becoming the territorial capital.

Winning the Capital Battle

Tucson and Prescott had struggled bitterly in their campaigns to become Arizona's capital. Prescott had been named the first territorial capital in 1864. Three years later, the honor went to Tucson, where it remained until 1877, when the Prescott politicos garnered enough votes to get it back. In 1889 Phoenix exercised enough clout to move the capital to the banks of the Salt River, beating out Prescott by only one vote.

According to one tale, Prescott lost its bid because of a mishap with a glass eye. On the evening before the final vote, as the story goes, one of Prescott's delegates went to his city's red-light district to visit one of the ladies on the line. The man had a glass eye, about which he was self-conscious. That night, after blowing out the lamp, he removed the eye and placed it in a water glass next to the bed. Sometime during the night his companion became thirsty and, turning the water glass bottoms-up, swallowed the eye. The next morning the delegate found his eye

Phoenix courthouse, before 1900 —Arizona Historical Society Library

gone, and vanity prevented him from attending the legislative session. Thus Phoenix was named the capital by one vote.

Before Phoenix's capitol building was erected, the legislators met in the county courthouse. The beautiful new Capitol on West Washington Street was dedicated in 1901. On top of the huge domed structure was a weather vane designed in the shape of a beautiful woman, called "Winged Victory." Cowboys in town on a spree used to delight in taking potshots at the figure.

At certain times, prevailing winds caused "Winged Victory" to face west, thus turning her backside to those approaching the Capitol steps. Some of the legislators took exception to this indignity and had the lady welded in place to face the entrance. During the 1960s, when the building was remodeled, "Winged Victory" was freed again to reveal her derriere whenever the winds dictated.

Federal Projects Assure the Future

Even after the completion of the Arizona Canal, Phoenix faced serious water problems. Disastrous floods in 1890 and 1891 nearly wiped out the town. These were followed by long droughts in the 1890s, withering crops and killing livestock. Discouraged farmers began abandoning their land and leaving the valley.

Roosevelt Dam —Southwest Studies, Scottsdale Community College

Phoenix turned to Washington for help. In 1902 the federal government passed the National Reclamation Act (the Newlands Act) and chose the Salt River Valley as the site of the first major reclamation project in the West—the Theodore Roosevelt Dam. (See Roosevelt Dam under AZ 88.)

The dam, completed in 1911, marked the dawning of a new era; during the next few years, four more dams were built on the Salt and two on the Verde. With a reliable water supply, as well as a source of hydroelectric power, the future of Phoenix was assured.

Around 1926 the federal government funded a system of paved highways. Soon these roads crisscrossed Arizona, changing it forever. Phoenix remained in the center of this development: by the 1950s two interstates and a highway intersected there. In 1987 construction began on a new freeway system. Loop 101, finished in 2002, links I-10 with Glendale, Peoria, Scottsdale, and Tempe; AZ 51 has been extended to hook up with it in northern Phoenix. Loop 202, due to be completed in 2007, will run through Mesa and Chandler. A third loop, 303, began construction in 1990, and will link I-10 with I-17 through the western suburbs.

Valley of the Sun

Since World War II, with its water problems largely resolved, a number of major highways running through it, and several surges in popularity of the Sunbelt, Phoenix has grown spectacularly. Today greater Phoenix is the third-largest high-tech area in the country, and thousands of well-educated young people move here each year seeking employment in technology. Others come to live where the sun shines 85 percent of the time and recreation abounds.

Not long ago the Phoenix desert was perceived as uninhabitable except by cactus, coyotes, and rattlesnakes. Today desert living is infinitely attractive with its wide-open spaces and spectacular scenery. And Phoenix stands in the center of it all, a young city in an ancient land, its futuristic architecture reaching into the wide southwestern sky.

PEORIA

As is true with many communities in the Salt River Valley, huge tracts of farm land used to separate Glendale and Peoria. Today, however, only city-limit signs signal motorists traveling along Grand Avenue (US 60) that they are leaving one town and entering the next.

In 1888, when canal builder W. J. Murphy headed back east to interest people in settling along his canal, a group from Peoria, Illinois, bought over 5,000 acres in the district, thus the town's name. The farmlands were fertile, and from then on, people made a good living despite swarms of red ants, scorpions, and an occasional rattlesnake in the kitchen. One farmer reported killing eighty-five rattlers in one evening while he was irrigating his field.

Today Peoria is one of the nation's fastest growing cities and the state's ninth-largest city, with over 120,000 residents. It is the spring training home of the San Diego Padres and the Seattle Mariners. In 1994 the Peoria Sports Complex opened, with a 10,000-seat stadium and twelve practice fields.

GLENDALE

As with many other Arizona towns, water—specifically, William J. Murphy's Arizona Canal (see also Phoenix, "Water to Grow"), completed in 1887—made Glendale, in northwestern metropolitan Phoenix, possible.

While in the East raising funds for the canal project, Murphy encouraged folks to come to his new settlement, which he named Glendale. Some of the first settlers who came there belonged to the Church of the Brethren. In 1891 they established a temperance colony called Glendale Valley, and by 1892 seventy families had arrived, though a drought three years later drove some of them on to California. For a time, while the influence of the God-fearing Brethren dominated, the town had no hell-raising cowboys, miners, painted ladies, or gunfighters.

The railroad came to Glendale in 1895, thanks again in part to Murphy. Murphy also helped fund the construction of a five-story red brick beet-sugar factory in 1906. Between the successful agriculture in the area and the railroad, it became possible to ship hundreds of carloads of produce from Glendale, leading to

❀GLENDALE❀

ATTENTION IS CALLED TO THE

Temperance Colony of Glendale.

The location is made upon the choicest fruit lands of the valley.   No more beautiful site could be selected.
The town is well planned for convenience and beauty.

BROAD AVENUES, PUBLIC SQUARES, AND LARGE LOTS,

→ THE SALE OF INTOXICANTS ←

IS FOREVER FORBIDDEN

IN THE CONVEYANCE OF THE LAND.

———•———

School Houses and Churches,

But no saloons or gambling houses ! No drunken brawls !
No jails ! and no paupers !

The design is to furnish opportunities for BEAUTI-FUL, PEACEFUL HOMES, combining as fully as possible the advantages of the city with the security and quiet and charm of the country. This will be appreciated by a very large class of people. It is the **First Colony** located in the territory, planned on this basis.

Address:—**GLENDALE COLONY CO.,**
PHŒNIX, A. T.

The new town of Glendale put heavy emphasis on the high moral character of its prospective citizens.
—Arizona Historical Foundation

the founding of the Glendale Ice Company in 1910. Soon, the company was the town's biggest employer and Glendale was the largest produce shipper in Arizona.

In the early years of the twentieth century, until World War I, many people in the area were making a living through ostrich ranching. The fashions of the day prescribed ostrich feathers for hats, bustles, and more. However, when styles changed, the colorful era of "ostrich boys" (as opposed to cowboys) and their thundering herds came to an end. During the war, here as in other parts of the state, the demand for Pima long-staple cotton helped settlers improve their economic situation.

Glendale has had many Russian and Japanese settlers over the years. In 1911 a large party of Russians called Molokans, fleeing political oppression, purchased 400 acres in Glendale and began farming sugar beets. The Molokans were religious dissidents who had broken from both Catholicism and the Russian Orthodox Church. *Moloko* means "milk" in Russian; the Molokans earned their name by drinking milk on days when Church doctrine forbade it. By the end of World War I, 200 Russian immigrants were living in Glendale. People with names like Popoff, Treguboff, Tolmachoff, and Conovaloff still live in the Glendale area and are a part of its rich agricultural heritage.

The first Japanese immigrants came to Arizona early and individually, to mine, farm, or work as servants or cooks. In 1905 the Southwest Sugar Company brought 120 Japanese sugar-beet laborers to work at the beet-sugar factory, but by 1915, combined instances of bad luck, including heat and pests, had closed the factory, and the workers moved away. (The abandoned factory still stands in Glendale.) Glendale's more permanent community of Japanese came to farm. On small leased farms and plots of land bought in the name of American-born children, a community of ultimately about 120 hardworking and thrifty Japanese farm operators innovated the growing of lettuce, cantaloupe, strawberries, and flowers. By the 1950s the flower fields around Glendale had become a tourist attraction in themselves.

The Japanese in Glendale and in the rest of Arizona encountered support but also cruel prejudice. In 1902 an Arizona law forbade intermarriage between Anglos and Asians. Some Anglo neighborhoods forbade Asians to live nearby. In 1934, with the Great Depression, Japanese farmers became a target of many frustrations. In the Salt River Valley, Japanese homes were bombed, farmers were shot at, and crops were flooded out. Six hundred Anglo farmers gathered for an anti-Japanese demonstration and discussed how to rid the valley of their competitors. Business interests outside the state and the federal government—which provided money for Arizona dams—managed to persuade white farmers it was in their best interest not to discriminate against their neighbors. But by 1940, about half of the Japanese farmers around Glendale had left.

World War II brought further trials, with the relocation of some Japanese residents to detention camps. After the war they were allowed to reclaim their property, and they flourished again. Today, however, most of their former farmland has been developed into homes. World War II also brought thousands of servicemen to train at Thunderbird and Luke Air Fields. Luke Air Force Base, built in 1941 and named for Frank Luke Jr. of Phoenix, a World War I Medal of Honor recipient, was the biggest training base for the Army Air Corps during World War II. Today it's the largest jet training base in the world—and Glendale's biggest employer.

Glendale's most famous native was country music artist Marty Robbins. Born Martin David Robinson in Glendale in 1925, Robbins grew up poor and sometimes picking cotton in Glendale. He learned to play the guitar in the navy during World War II. After the war he made his start musically on local radio and television. Before long he found himself in Nashville with the Grand Ole Opry, where he became one of its most popular performers. Robbins went on to have an interesting and diverse life with many outlets for his talents. His song "El Paso" won a Grammy and is a western-music classic. Robbins died in 1982, just after being voted into the Country Music Hall of Fame.

For many years, Glendale had a beloved semiprofessional baseball team, the Greys, founded in 1916. In the days before television and air conditioning, families spent their summer evenings at the local ballpark, and many towns had teams. This writer played for the Glendale Greys when they were the Cinderella team in the 1956 state tournament. After a lackluster regular season, the Greys caught fire in the state tourney and made it to the semifinal against the Phoenix Blue Sox. That was a special evening for me since I got four hits, drove in the tying run, and scored the winning run in the tenth inning, putting Glendale in the state finals against Casa Grande.

Glendale had to win only one of two games against the powerful Casa Grande Cotton Kings. But it wasn't meant to be. A Casa Grande pitcher from the University of Arizona, Dave Baldwin, who went on to pitch for the Washington Senators, shut the Greys down on successive nights. I had a good tournament, though, hitting over .400. I never came close to playing that well again. Neither did the Greys. Hard times hit local semipro baseball as Little League, American Legion, and a myriad of other sports teams competed for crowds and revenue. The Greys disbanded in 1958.

Since they arrived from St. Louis in 1988, the National Football League's Arizona Cardinals have played their home games at Sun Devil Stadium in Tempe. In 2000, voters approved construction of a multipurpose stadium somewhere in the valley. However, plans for a stadium fell through in Tempe, Phoenix, Mesa, and the Gila River Indian Reservation. Finally, in 2002, Glendale was awarded the $350-million Arizona Cardinals Stadium. A year earlier, Glendale also landed the Phoenix Coyotes of the National Hockey League, who had also been looking for a new home.

Today Glendale is still a diverse city and hard to categorize. It isn't a blue-collar town or a college town (though there are three colleges in the area) or a military town or a bedroom community for Phoenix or a high-tech community; yet it is a combination of all those things and more. It has a strong sense of community and a dynamic vitality that has defined it for more than a century.

I-17 and AZ 69
Phoenix—Prescott
102 MILES

Long before there were interstates, central Arizona settlements were connected to one another by wagon roads, used by freighters, stage lines, and the military. The earliest roads between Tucson and Prescott bypassed the new farm community of Phoenix, following the transcontinental Gila Trail, but as Phoenix grew and gained influence the road eventually shifted east of the South Mountains, becoming the forerunner of today's I-10. The Vulture Road, aka the Wickenburg Stage Road, linking Phoenix to Prescott via Wickenburg, evolved into US 60 and AZ 89. Another route, the Black Canyon Road, dating back to the 1860s, headed almost due north to Prescott, skirting the west end of the Phoenix Mountains. Black Canyon Road follows part of today's I-17.

During the late nineteenth century the Arizona Stage Company made the 140-mile run from Prescott to Phoenix on the Black

Canyon Road every Monday, Wednesday, and Friday, leaving Prescott at 8:00 A.M. and arriving in Phoenix the following day at noon. In 1893 a ticket for the Black Canyon stagecoach from Phoenix to Prescott cost $12.50, cheaper than the Vulture Road stage to Prescott and ten hours shorter. But the ride was rough.

The steepest grade and the sharpest curves on Black Canyon Road were on Antelope Hill. Stagecoach drivers used to announce their arrival at a hairpin turn with a shrill blast of a tin horn. A driver coming from the other direction replied with two blasts. If the two rigs met in a place too narrow to pass, it was customary for the driver on the downside to unhitch his team and ease the wagon downhill to the first wide spot in the road. The rough country and steep grades made this route an ideal place for ambushes by both Indians and outlaws. Highwayman Dick Fellows is thought to have made the largest haul. Though his attempt to rob a $42,000 payroll was foiled by Wells Fargo detectives, the persistent outlaw tried again the next day and got away with $17,000.

Motoring near Prescott —Arizona Historical Foundation

By 1917 the stagecoaches had been replaced by their upstart nemesis, the horseless carriage, but because of the rugged terrain and small population, it's not surprising that as late as 1929 there were still less than 300 miles of paved highway in the state of Arizona. The Black Canyon Road was still a dirt road into the 1940s, having changed little from the days of stagecoach travel.

I-17, begun in Phoenix in 1955, follows the Black Canyon Road until Cordes Junction, where Black Canyon becomes AZ 69 to Prescott and I-17 heads north through the Verde Valley to Flagstaff. The interstate, completed as a freeway in 1978, at long last provided a direct link between Phoenix and Flagstaff. Today, driving north from Black Canyon City to Cordes Junction on I-17, travelers can look off to the west and see the old dirt road winding up Antelope Hill.

PIONEER ARIZONA LIVING HISTORY MUSEUM

Opened in 1969, the Pioneer Arizona Living History Museum, off I-17 at exit 225, twenty-five miles north of Phoenix, is a re-creation of a pioneer town on ninety acres of state land. Many of the buildings at the museum are original structures that were hauled in from elsewhere in the state, including Senator Henry F. Ashurst's log cabin and an old church from Globe. Costumed interpreters show visitors the blacksmith shop, bank, tin shop, opera house, bakery, and many other buildings that also grace the place. Park your car outside; motor vehicles are not allowed on the grounds.

BRADSHAW MOUNTAINS

The rugged, sprawling mountains west of I-17 between New River and Prescott are among the richest of all the mineral-laden ranges in Arizona. They were originally called the Silver Range because of rich silver lodes. For a time in the 1860s they were known as the Silver Bradshaws in honor of the prospector who discovered their wealth, Bill Bradshaw; by the 1870s, the name had been shortened to the Bradshaws. In the early 1860s, Bill and his brother Ike ran a freighting business from San Bernardino, California, to La Paz (near today's Ehrenberg). Near La Paz, they built a ferry across the Colorado River; Ike operated the ferry while Bill went prospecting. In 1863 Bill found rich silver ore in these mountains, and soon created the Bradshaw Mining District, encompassing dozens of mines with picturesque names like Tip Top, Tiger, Minnehaha, Oro Belle, Hum Bug, Crown King, and Gazelle.

While some of the mines ceased to be profitable by the 1880s, others continued to produce through the early twentieth century. At their height, the Bradshaw mines produced millions of dollars in gold and silver and left an indelible mark on Arizona history. Visitors can see the remains of many of these mines and ghost towns off I-17, AZ 69, and AZ 89.

In 1871 Bradshaw City sprang up a few miles west of today's town of Crown King. At its peak, the town boasted about 500 residents. The bubble burst quickly, however, and within a decade Bradshaw City was a ghost town. Today nothing remains but a sign on Crown King Road marking the site. Crown King remains an active town and center for the ghost towns in the area.

In 1899 the vast riches still flowing from the Bradshaws prompted railroad man Frank Murphy to take on what seemed to be a mission impossible, building a railroad from Mayer to the source of the minerals at Poland, on the north side of the mountains, and another line to Crown King, on the south side. Building railroads over rough terrain was nothing new to Murphy—he'd already completed a line from Ash Fork to Phoenix and another from Prescott to Mayer. This one would be called the Bradshaw Mountain Railroad.

Murphy advertised in eastern newspapers for strong-armed track layers willing to work for a dollar a day, twice the usual pay of that time. By October 1901, 350 men were ready to tackle what was called an impossible railroad project. The determined crew of track layers and gandy dancers sliced their way into the Bradshaws, across rough arroyos and along steep barrancas. When a dynamite blast exposed a rich body of ore, Murphy lost most of his workers to gold fever, but he had no difficulty replacing his crew at the wages he offered. On April 21, 1902, the first locomotive steamed into Poland.

The other part of Frank Murphy's "impossible" railroad headed southwest of Mayer to Crown King, clinging tenaciously to the sides of the lofty Bradshaws, with more kinks than a cheap lariat. Twelve switchbacks had turns so tight passengers in the caboose could look across and see the engine going the other way. The line was finally completed in 1904, after exceeding its projected cost by about 300 percent. It was worth every penny—by 1907 the mines at Tiger, Hum Bug, Turkey Creek, Pine Grove, and Crown King were producing over a million dollars annually in gold and silver.

The boom lasted until the end of World War I. By then old age was catching up with the Bradshaw Mountain Railroad; furthermore, the price of metals was down, freight costs were up, and the mines were starting to play out. By 1920 both the Poland and Crown King lines were abandoned.

ROCK SPRINGS

In the late 1920s, a spring emerging from some rocks provided the inspiration for the name of Rock Springs, just south of Black Canyon City. In 1922 settler Ben Warner put up a tent store at Rock Springs to serve miners, prospectors, and motorists. Later he built a permanent hotel, restaurant, and store. The business continues to thrive today. The Rock Springs Cafe sells arguably the best pies in the West.

BLACK CANYON AND BLACK CANYON CITY

Black Canyon City goes back at least to 1875, when a stage station called Black Canyon was located where the Agua Fria River crosses the road. When a post office opened here in 1894, the settlement was called Cañon. Charles Goddard was postmaster, so it was sometimes referred to as Goddard. Later a new post office opened under the name Black Canyon, from the canyon through which I-17 now passes.

The canyon itself is the setting of a few legends, including that of the fabled Lost Pick Mine. The story begins in the 1870s in the small community of Phoenix, when two itinerant prospectors known as Brown and Davies, hanging around a general store, noticed an Indian paying for supplies with gold nuggets. They learned from the proprietor that the Indian was a Yavapai who lived in a canyon about fifty miles north of town. They also learned he came into town once a year, always with enough gold to purchase whatever he needed.

The two prospectors decided to follow the Indian to discover his source. The Yavapai made no attempt to evade the pair as the trail led deeper into the *malpais* (badlands) north of town. They crossed three streams—Skunk Creek, the New River, and the Agua Fria—going deeper into the steep-sided recesses of Black Canyon. The Indian entered a side canyon and seemed to vanish into thin air. While trying to pick up the trail, Brown and Davies stumbled into a boulder-strewn arroyo, a tributary to the Agua Fria. Before their eyes was the unmistakable glitter of gold! Every chunk of rock seemed to be laced with the yellow metal.

The two men worked tirelessly for the next several days mining high-grade ore, amassing an estimated fortune of nearly $80,000. In their single-minded pursuit of gold, however, they had forgotten the ever-present danger of Indians. When a band of warriors attacked, Davies was killed in the first volley of gunfire. Brown hit the ground and rolled into the brush; to his relief, the warriors turned and rode away. He quickly cached the ore, marking the site with his pick, and headed west toward the Colorado River.

Brown didn't return to reclaim his treasure until many years later. He was sure he could find it, but a fading memory and the desert terrain played tricks with his mind. On his deathbed, the old man told the story of his fabulous gold strike somewhere in Black Canyon. Years later someone claimed to have seen a rusty prospector's pick buried in a rock outcropping, but he had ignored it. To this day the Lost Pick is believed to be one of Arizona's richest lost mines.

At milepost 249, tour guides like to point out the last saguaro you will see as you go north. Easy to spot with its upraised arms, it's just west of the interstate, near the top of the rim of the canyon. It signals the end of the lower Sonoran Desert and the beginning of the upper Sonoran, with its piñon pine, juniper, and chaparral.

BUMBLE BEE

Bumble Bee, perched on the west bank of Bumble Bee Creek, is one of the more easily accessible ghost towns along I-17. The road from exit 248 is paved. Calculations show that the place nearest the geographical center of the state is Bumble Bee.

Bumble Bee in the 1930s —Arizona Historical Foundation

There is a question about the former town's unusual name: some say hostile Indians in the area were "thick as bumblebees"; another version has it that soldiers overheard a band of Indians holding a conference that sounded like "a swarm of bumblebees." Most likely, early prospectors found—and perhaps were attacked by—a nest of bumblebees along the creek.

Bumble Bee evolved from a stage stop called Snyder's Station. Established as Bumble Bee in 1879, it was never a boomtown in the true sense of the word, although there was some placer mining there. It was better known as a way station and general store that sold groceries, hardware, and gasoline, at night turning into a dance hall and saloon. A one-room school sat east of the road.

In 1949 developers bought the town to become part of the 74,000-acre Bumble Bee Ranch resort, still in existence. During the 1960s Phoenix entrepreneur Ed Chilleen tried to turn the town into a tourist attraction, complete with frontier-style facades, but the venture failed to materialize. Today the false fronts decay along with the original remains, although the place is still maintained as a tourist site.

CORDES

Cordes, an old ranching community and road stop, is three miles off I-17 at exit 259, just before Cordes Junction. Situated on a plain above notoriously difficult-to-negotiate Antelope Hill, the town was originally called Antelope Station and was a regular stop for weary travelers on the old Black Canyon wagon road.

The town takes its name from John Henry Cordes, who came to the area with his family in the 1880s. Lured by the silver strikes in the Bradshaw Mountains, Cordes arrived in 1883 and built a store at the top of Antelope Hill. In 1915 he began selling gasoline from a one-gallon pump. Antelope Hill was so steep that the old Model Ts, with their gravity-fed fuel pumps, had to go up the hill in reverse.

Henry Cordes, a grandson, took over in 1937 and ran the business until it shut down for good in 1972. For years Henry waited tables, cooked, pumped gas, and fixed flats. In 1947, he was a genial host to this writer, then eight years old, and my family for several days when our car broke down trying to climb Antelope Hill.

When the new highway opened in the mid-1950s, Cordes was left off the beaten path. Today the stillness of the place is broken only by the occasional passing of an auto headed down dusty AZ 69 to Mayer. Descendants of the Cordes family still live in the area.

Also off exit 259 is Bloody Basin Road. Some say the place got its name from a battle between Indians and miners in 1864. Others maintain that a suspension bridge over a canyon gorge here collapsed and hundreds of sheep fell to their deaths in the basin below.

ARCOSANTI

Arcosanti, just west of Cordes Junction, is not an official town, but rather an experimental model city, brainchild of Italian-born architect Paolo Soleri. Soleri came to Arizona in 1947 to study with Frank Lloyd Wright at Taliesin West in Scottsdale. Nine years later he started the Cosanti Foundation to design energy- and space-efficient communities. In 1970, on the side of a canyon at Cordes Junction, the visionary architect began building such a community and called it Arcosanti. Since then, students have come from all over the world to work on Arcosanti, some staying to live and work there permanently. The project is supported in part by Cosanti Originals ceramic and bronze creations, specializing in bells.

Visually reminiscent of ancient cliff dwellings, Arcosanti is designed to meld architecture and ecology into what Soleri calls "arcology." He and his students attempt to address some of the world's problems through the theory and practice of arcology, seeking to make the best use of energy and land. Buildings expand vertically, with pedestrian walkways and elevators replacing busy streets and freeways. Buildings use solar energy.

When complete, the city will have 7,000 residents. Soleri envisions even greater vertical metropolises, three times the height of the Empire State Building and home to millions. Arcosanti is open for tours and overnight visits and has regularly scheduled events.

MAYER

Mayer is part ghost town but mostly a live town catering to visitors. Merchant Joseph Mayer, the town's namesake, arrived here in 1882 and opened a store, stage station, and saloon along the Black Canyon Road. Mayer was a tourist-minded entrepreneur. A newspaper article in 1902 mentioned his marketing "Indian toothpicks," which were spines from prickly pear cacti. The general store is now a souvenir shop.

The towering smokestack standing alone on the edge of town was the result of some best-laid plans that went awry. An optimistic developer planned a smelter on the site and contracted for a smokestack and a smelter. Before the project began, the mine played out, and the developer tried to break the contracts. The smelter builder accepted the bad news with grace, but the Weber Chimney Company was adamant that a deal was a deal and sent a crew to build the pointless smokestack.

POLAND JUNCTION

Four miles north of Mayer, Poland Junction is another former mining town along AZ 69. The rich Poland Mine, named for Davis

R. Poland of Tennessee, produced $750,000 in its lifetime—mostly in silver. Around 1900 Frank Murphy, part owner of the mine, began work on a railroad line. By 1902 Poland Junction was a bustling community with a post office, fourteen-room boardinghouse, and a general store. Its population peaked at about 800.

In 1913, the post office discontinued service; the mines and town were fading. Yet, even though it doesn't appear on many maps, Poland Junction is inhabited. Visitors can still see the entrance to the Poland-Walker Tunnel nearby, an 1,100-foot tunnel built in 1902 through the mountains from Poland to Walker, six miles west. Miners began the tunnel unintentionally when they followed a vein of gold through the mountain.

HUMBOLDT AND DEWEY

Humboldt, just off AZ 69 two miles south of Dewey, is the site of the Iron King Mine, a source of boom and bust for nearly 100 years. Around the turn of the twentieth century, Arizona was the center of many wild and woolly promotional schemes, and it was said that the Iron King Mine sold more stock than ore. The mine did produce a respectable amount of gold and silver, however, and the town prospered. Just as Humboldt and its mine were peaking, the Panic of 1907 brought operations to a standstill for three decades.

By the late 1920s Humboldt had begun to take on the appearance of a ghost town, but the demand for lead and zinc during World War II brought new life to the Iron King and Humboldt. In 1959 the mine generated 3 million tons of ore, making it the largest producer of lead and zinc in the state.

Today the Iron King is still open, producing iron and other nutrient minerals for fertilizer since 1978. Many of the old buildings in town are still in use.

Dewey sits at the intersection of AZ 69 and 169. In 1864 Arizona hero King Woolsey established a ranch along the Agua Fria River at Dewey. When Woolsey arrived in Arizona in 1860 he had nothing more than his horse, saddle, rifle, pistol, and the clothes on his back. He took a job in Yuma hauling supplies and invested his savings in mining ventures and, later, ranching. When

Woolsey Ranch today —Courtesy M. K. McKenna

gold was discovered in the Prescott area in 1863, Woolsey was among the first to arrive. Soon afterward he established a ranch at present-day Dewey, calling it the Agua Fria Ranch after the river that ran through it.

Woolsey quickly gained renown as a formidable Apache fighter. The fearless rancher became a hero for his expeditions against Indians. In 1867 Woolsey left his ranch and eventually wound up at the new settlement of Phoenix.

PRESCOTT VALLEY

A new community, Prescott Valley, may soon rival Prescott in population. Founded in 1966, it's on AZ 69 between Dewey and Prescott. Since 1990, the town's population has more than doubled. The area used to be known as Jackass Flats, something the town's boosters don't necessarily advertise.

PRESCOTT

First Territorial Capital

One of famous frontiersman Joe Walker's last great adventures was his gold-hunting expedition in early 1863, the year Arizona became a territory, in the area that would become Prescott. Captain Walker and his party of prospectors found rich gold placers there, a discovery that would soon lead to the founding of Prescott as a wilderness capital.

Walker was one of the most indestructible frontiersmen in American history. He stood well over six feet tall and weighed 200 pounds. During the 1830s he was one of the nation's foremost scouts and mountain men. In 1833 he became the first Anglo American to lead a winter expedition over the Sierra Nevada, and the first to see what would become Yosemite National Park. He explored much of Arizona, including, in 1851, along the thirty-fifth parallel. Mountain man Daniel Conner said of Walker, "He don't follow trails, he makes them."

In the 1860s, despite old age and failing eyesight, and acting on a tip from Union general James Carleton, military commander of New Mexico, Walker struck gold in the Bradshaw Mountains. After President Abraham Lincoln proclaimed Arizona a territory on February 24, 1863, it was naturally assumed the capital would be Tucson, the hub of culture at the time, but Walker's gold strike convinced newly appointed governor John W. Goodwin and his party to head for Prescott instead. Tucson, General Carleton reminded them, was a hotbed of secessionist activity. It would also help Union interests to have the seat of government near a money source, and Fort Whipple, already established to safeguard prospectors, would offer protection.

The governor's party arrived at Fort Whipple on a chilly January day in 1864. The resourceful Secretary of the Territory, Richard C. McCormick, had brought along a small printing press, and by March a newspaper, the *Arizona Miner,* northern Arizona's first paper, was in business. The following month Governor Goodwin selected a capital site on Goose Flats above Granite Creek, in a settlement of a dozen or so shacks the miners had been calling Granite City.

Although miner Van Smith had established squatter's rights to most of the land at the site, with a grand display of public spirit characteristic of Prescottonians down through the years, he agreed to give it up. Robert Groom surveyed the site, using an old prospector's skillet for a transit. Soon afterward, Fort Whipple was moved a short distance northeast of the new capital site, where it stands today, on the grounds of the Sharlot Hall Museum.

On May 30 the governor held a meeting in a humble log-cabin mercantile store known as Fort Misery, to choose a name for the new capital. Among the suggestions were Goodwin, Audubon, Gimletville, and Azatlan (for the area's prehistoric ruins, mistakenly thought to be Aztec). But Secretary McCormick, who had a copy of William Hickling Prescott's classic work on the history of Mexico, suggested the community be named in honor of that great historian, which suited everyone.

Prescott remained the territorial capital until 1867, when, with Civil War concerns past, Tucson displaced the young mining town for the position. Prescott became capital again ten years later, but in 1889 Phoenix won the honor permanently.

Prescott's Early Days

By the summer of 1864 Prescott was Arizona's biggest new boomtown. Prospectors, freighters, cowboys, tinhorn gamblers, merchants, shady ladies, and other denizens of frontier society were walking the capital's wide streets. Freight wagons hauled supplies over the treacherous roads between Prescott and the Colorado River landings at Ehrenberg and Hardyville. The population of Prescott was overwhelmingly Anglo American, a rarity in the Southwest.

Fort Misery was Prescott's first building. A man named Manual Ysario had built it as a store, but the supplies ran out and he left. Then Caroline Ramos, better known as "Virgin Mary" (apparently for her tender care of sick and injured miners), turned it into a boardinghouse. A sign tacked outside stated "Room and board, $25 in gold, cash in advance." The menu didn't offer much variety, but the hungry miners didn't complain. Breakfast consisted of venison with chiles, coffee, bread, and goat's milk. Lunch was roast venison, chile bread, coffee, and goat's milk. Supper was venison, chile sauce on a tortilla, coffee, and goat's milk. Fort

Prescott street scene (no date) —Arizona Historical Society Library, Tucson

Misery was also used as a church on Sundays, and during the week, Judge John "Blinkey" Howard dispensed justice, or "misery" as the miners called it, in the building.

Prescott's first saloon, the Quartz Rock, was a rustic collection of timber with a plank for a bar, where tangleleg whiskey was dispensed. This establishment was perched on the banks of Granite Creek but was later moved to Montezuma Street. Several reasons have been passed down as to why it was moved. One version says that sober citizens grew tired of pulling drunks out of the creek. Another has it that imbibers became sick at the sight of the stream's pure water.

Railroad Follies

In 1886 a fast-talking promoter named Tom Bullock convinced Prescottonians to raise $300,000 to construct a seventy-five-mile rail line connecting their town with the main line at Seligman, which was known in those days as Prescott Junction. The spur had to reach Prescott no later than midnight on December 31, or Bullock would face a stiff $1,000-a-mile penalty.

No sooner had construction begun than entrepreneurs began setting up tent saloons along the route, undermining worker productivity. Furthermore, local cattlemen, angry over the railroad right-of-way across their grazing lands, had their cowboys stampede cattle through the construction sites. In Prescott the betting was heavy as to whether or not Bullock would meet his deadline. Some residents tried to hedge their bets by vandalizing the line: one group tried to blow up a caboose; another set fire to a trestle, but a rainstorm doused the flames; others tried to derail a work train by removing a section of track, but the plot failed when the engine ran aground before reaching the damaged area.

At one point, odds against the Bullock line reaching Prescott on time were as high as twenty to one. Some who had taken those odds tried to ensure their bets by joining the construction crew as volunteers. Working feverishly against the clock, track layers reached Granite Dells with a day to go, and by the evening of the final day, they were only two miles from Prescott. In the end, the Bullock line reached Prescott with five minutes to spare. Throngs cheered as the territorial governor, Conrad Zulick, drove a gilded spike into a tie painted red, white, and blue. Prescott, at last, was linked by rail to the outside world.

In operation, the Prescott & Arizona Central Railroad was the epitome of inefficiency. During its first months, the entire railroad consisted of only two small steam engines—the *F. A. Tritle* and the *Hassayampa*—four boxcars, and one passenger car, all secondhand. The fare was ten cents a mile, but customers could usually get a better deal buying a ticket from one of the crew. Trains made unscheduled stops along the way, for "beer calls" at Del Rio Springs and hunting trips in Chino Valley.

Since the turntable at Prescott was not ready, the trains had to make the trip to Prescott Junction in reverse. After a heavy rain, the rails would sag, tossing the little locomotives into mud holes. The poor old *Hassayampa* once lay on its side for three weeks before someone got around to hauling it out. By 1891 local people were beginning to call Bullock's line the "Mudball Express."

In 1893 the Prescott & Arizona Central Railroad went out of business. Bullock promptly tore up the track and moved his railroad to California. Arizona taxpayers and investors had lost several million dollars thanks to this smooth-talking huckster.

World's Oldest Rodeo

The first rodeos took place during the days of the open range, when cowboys from neighboring ranches began competing during roundup. Each ranch took pride in the riding and roping ability of its cowpunchers, along with their ability to sit on the hurricane of an unbroken horse. From these early beginnings grew the sport of rodeo. On July 4, 1888, Prescott held the first paid-admittance rodeo in the world, called simply a "cowboy tournament," sponsored by local merchants. The turnout for that event was about 2,000. For more than a century, what is now called the Frontier Days Rodeo has been the highlight of the weeklong Independence Day festivities around Prescott, attracting the nation's finest professional rodeo cowboys.

Whiskey Row

By the turn of the twentieth century, there were forty saloons on the west side of Montezuma Street—an area known as Whiskey Row. Before drinking and gambling were outlawed, Whiskey Row ran under a full head of steam twenty-four hours a day. The macho custom of thirsty cowboys in off the range was to start their binge, or "whizzer" as they called it, at the Kentucky Bar, at the corner of Goodwin and Montezuma, and take a drink in every bar all the way to the Depot House, thirty-nine saloons away. If one were really feeling his oats, he drank all the way back again. Noted cowboy poet Gail Gardner, a Prescott native, immortalized Whiskey Row in his poem "Sierry Petes, or Tyin' Knots in the Devil's Tail," written in 1917.

Fire of 1900

July 14, 1900, was like any other summer day in Prescott until some careless miner jammed his pick candle into the wall of the Scopel Hotel, on the corner of Goodwin and Montezuma, and forgot about it. The hotel caught fire and the flames spread quickly through the business district. Volunteer fire companies with names like the Toughs, Dudes, O.K.'s, and Hook & Ladder arrived, but the town's water supply was low and all anybody could do was save a few furnishings. Customers in the Palace Bar grabbed the storied backbar with its contents, carrying it across the street to the plaza. Another group carried a piano to safety, and while someone played "Hot Time in the Old Town Tonight," roulette wheels and faro tables were moved into the plaza. Business resumed at the gaming tables and bar while flames licked the sky over Prescott. Sheriff George Ruffner led a group of powdermen

Prescott's Whiskey Row after the fire, July 1900
—Southwest Studies, Scottsdale Community College

into the area ahead of the holocaust and began dynamiting structures. By about three A.M. the fire had burned itself out.

The next morning Prescottonians took inventory: twenty-five saloons and five of the town's largest hotels were gone, as was the entire red-light district. The area was still smoldering as shopkeepers sifted through the ruins hoping to find something worth salvaging. By mid-morning they had set up counters on the sidewalks in front of their burned-out buildings to conduct business as usual.

Prominent Prescottonians

Pauline Weaver is often called "Prescott's first citizen"—more honorary than strictly chronological. Weaver was born in Tennessee around 1800, the son of a white father and a Cherokee mother. He arrived in Arizona in the late 1820s, and soon had the reputation of knowing Arizona's mountains, deserts, and rivers better than any other white man.

*Pauline Weaver
(artist unknown)*
—Southwest Studies,
Scottsdale Community
College

After scouting for the Mormon Battalion, Weaver trapped beaver along Arizona's streams and grew to be friendly with most of the Indian tribes. In 1862 natives along the Colorado River in western Arizona showed him some rich gold placers. The strike he found produced $12 million in gold and led to the establishment of La Paz. Weaver moved north the next year and was already camped on Granite Creek, the future site of Prescott, when the Walker party arrived.

Later that year he guided the Abraham H. Peeples party up the Hassayampa River in search of the yellow metal. A few miles north of Wickenburg they stumbled on a treasure trove of gold nuggets on top of a rocky knoll that became known as Rich Hill, the richest single placer strike in Arizona history. Weaver worked tirelessly to keep peace between the native tribes and newcomers, but as more whites poured in, it became well-nigh impossible.

In the mid-1860s a Yavapai war party jumped Weaver and seriously wounded him. The old scout, thinking he was about to die, went into his "death song," a custom he had adopted from the Plains Indians. The warriors, not familiar with the ritual, believed he had gone crazy and quickly left. When Weaver saw he was not going to die, he arose and walked home. When he did die on June 21, 1867, he was buried at Camp Verde with full military honors. Later the post was abandoned, and his remains were taken to California. In 1929 poet-historian Sharlot Hall organized a campaign to have Weaver's remains returned to Prescott. With funds raised by the Boy Scouts and Prescott schoolchildren, he was reburied on the grounds of the old territorial capital.

Another prominent Prescottian was Morris Goldwater, son of pioneer merchant Mike Goldwater (see Ehrenburg). He arrived in Prescott with his father in 1876 to work in the family mercantile business. He rented a room from a young widow, Sarah Fisher. After six months, the city council passed a proclamation suggesting that he should marry the lady, and he obeyed.

Goldwater was elected mayor of Prescott in 1888 and served four terms. He also helped bring the Prescott & Arizona Central Railroad to Prescott and, in his store, established the first bank in the city. He served in the territorial legislature from 1883 to 1885 and in 1910 was elected vice president of the constitutional convention. Morris Goldwater is considered the "Father of the Democratic Party" in Arizona, though the next generation of Goldwaters became famously Republican—Morris's nephew was Senator Barry Goldwater. In 1964 Prescott, celebrating its 100th anniversary, chose him as their "Man of the Century."

One of Prescott's most famous landmarks is Solon Borglum's majestic bronze statue of the Rough Rider in front of the old county courthouse, thought by most to represent William "Buckey" O'Neill, who was, next to Teddy Roosevelt, the most famous Rough Rider of them all. It is actually a tribute to all Arizonans who served in the First Volunteer Cavalry, better known as the Rough Riders, in the Spanish-American War.

Arriving in Prescott in 1882, O'Neill, who earned his nickname Buckey from betting against the house in faro—called "bucking the tiger"—was a popular political figure and newspaperman

*Prescott's Rough
Rider statue (by
Solon Borglum)*
—Southwest Studies,
Scottsdale Community
College

before he enlisted in the army. He served as the Yavapai County sheriff from 1890 to 1894. He was elected mayor in 1897.

O'Neill was killed in 1898 by a Spanish sniper shortly before the Battle of San Juan Hill. His death was deeply felt not only in Prescott but throughout Arizona, as his colorful personality, daring exploits, and strong stand for statehood had made him a bona fide folk hero.

Buckey's widow, Pauline Schindler O'Neill, was, during her long lifetime, a suffragette, teacher, businesswoman, writer, and politician. After Buckey's death she moved to Phoenix, and in 1901 she married Buckey's brother Eugene. From 1917 to 1921 Pauline O'Neill served as an Arizona legislator. She lived to be ninety-six.

William O. "Buckey" O'Neill
—Southwest Studies, Scottsdale Community College

Prescott's most famous sheriff, George Ruffner, served from 1894 to 1898 and again from 1922 until his death in 1933. Before his death at age seventy-one, he was the oldest Arizona sheriff. In 1958 the National Cowboy Hall of Fame in Oklahoma City chose him as the first Arizonan to be inducted into that select association of authentic Western heroes.

One of the more unusual episodes in Ruffner's career involved an obscure outlaw named Fleming Parker in 1898. Parker's career as a badman was not spectacular; in fact, as an old friend of Sheriff Ruffner, he might have escaped hanging if he'd kept his temper in check.

One day, two of Parker's string of horses wandered onto the railroad tracks and were killed by a passenger train. When the Atlantic & Pacific Railroad offered a measly recompense, the indignant cowboy retaliated by robbing the train at Peach Springs. Sheriff

George Ruffner
—Southwest Studies,
Scottsdale Community
College

Ruffner quickly picked up the trail, and a few days later Parker was behind bars in Prescott.

Residents were sympathetic to Parker's dispute with the railroad, and it looked as though he would get a light sentence until he broke out of jail and killed Lee Norris, the deputy district attorney. Then he headed for Ruffner's livery stable, stole the sheriff's prize white gelding, Sureshot, and fled north.

The outlaw knew his old companion would be following, so he reversed Sureshot's shoes to throw the sheriff off track. When the animal went lame, Parker turned him loose and continued on foot. Ruffner finally caught up with the renegade north of Flagstaff, and he returned with his prisoner to Prescott.

On the evening before the scheduled execution, Ruffner visited Parker and asked if he had any last request. Parker asked if Flossie, one of the girls on Whiskey Row, could pay him a visit. The obliging sheriff found Flossie and brought her over to the jail, where she bid the prisoner adios for an hour or so. Parker's other request was that Ruffner carry out the sentence; the outlaw wanted the man who cashed him in to be someone he respected.

Another prominent Prescottian arrived in Arizona from Kansas with her family in February 1882. Age twelve at the time, Sharlot Hall rode the entire distance on horseback. During the journey, she was thrown from her horse and suffered a painful spine injury that would linger through her lifetime.

As an adult she helped manage the family horse ranch, Orchard Ranch, east of Prescott. She was also a gifted poet, writing mostly about Arizona. In 1909 Governor Richard Sloan appointed her territorial historian, making her the first woman in Arizona to hold a political office.

In 1924 Hall was chosen to represent Arizona in the electoral college, but she turned down the offer because she couldn't afford the proper clothes. Officials at the United Verde Mine in Jerome stepped in and bought her a blue silk dress with a fine copper-mesh coat and accessories. Her "copper dress" was a hit back

Sharlot Hall at the territorial governor's mansion —Sharlot Hall Museum

East, and Arizona's copper industry benefited from the publicity. During the trip, she visited numerous museums and vowed to create a historical museum in Arizona. After she returned she began the project for which she is best remembered—the restoration of the territorial governor's mansion.

The old governor's "mansion" was a log structure built in 1864, the oldest territorial building still at its original location. In 1927 the city of Prescott granted Hall a lifetime lease on the mansion and grounds on West Gurley, and she got to work. The clapboard sidings were stripped away, exposing the original logs, and various elements were reconstructed. The restored structure opened as a museum in 1928. The following year Hall moved into the mansion and lived there until her death in 1943. Today the Sharlot Hall Museum complex is one of the finest historical-preservation institutions in the state. In 1981 Sharlot Hall was among the first inductees to the Arizona Women's Hall of Fame.

I-17
Cordes Junction—Flagstaff
78 MILES

CAMP VERDE AND CAMP VERDE
INDIAN RESERVATION

Camp Verde, off I-17 about fifty miles south of Flagstaff, is one of the eight main population centers of Yavapai County. Camp Verde is also the name of Arizona's second-smallest Indian reservation, on 636 acres west of the town. The town, on the banks of the picturesque Verde River, is the oldest white settlement in the Verde Valley. The reliable Verde River, along with four other streams that flow all year long—Clear Creek, Beaver Creek, Oak Creek, and Sycamore Creek—made the Verde Valley one of the richest agricultural areas in Arizona.

In June 1865 James Swetnam led a party of nine from Prescott into the valley to explore farming possibilities. Before long,

Hauling freight down the steep inclines into the Verde Valley required a skilled driver with an inexhaustible vocabulary (no date).
—Southwest Studies, Scottssdale Community College

farmers were digging irrigation ditches and planting crops. At first the only market for cash crops was at the military post of Camp Verde, but the mining booms beginning in the 1870s opened vast new markets for Verde Valley farmers well into the twentieth century. Today Camp Verde still thrives as an agricultural area, as well as a recreational and tourism center.

Verde Tribes

In prehistoric times, the Sinagua, Hohokam, and other Indian tribes prospered for hundreds of years in the Verde Valley before abandoning their villages about A.D. 1400. After they left, the area became the home of the Yavapai and Tonto Apache peoples. The Yavapai were of Quechan stock, while the Tonto were an

Athabascan-speaking group. Despite the Yavapais' differences, writers often called them Apache, since ecological and environmental conditions made the two groups' ways of life similar.

When whites began to encroach on their lands, these tribes fiercely resisted, but in 1873, after a long winter spent dodging Gen. George Crook's persistent soldiers and Indian scouts, Cha-Lipun (Charley-Pan), leader of some 2,300 Apache, rode into Camp Verde and surrendered. Crook was convinced that the nomadic Indians could become productive farmers, and for a while, on a new reservation established near the fort, his plan seemed to be working. Then, in spring 1875, after General Crook was transferred out of Arizona, the Indians were removed from the Camp Verde Reservation to the San Carlos Reservation, known as "Hell's Forty Acres." Finally, in 1909, the Camp Verde Reservation was reestablished and the Yavapai and Tonto Apache were allowed to return to their homeland.

Fort Verde State Historic Park

In 1866, construction of Camp Verde, a small fortress at the junction of the Verde River and Clear Creek, was completed. Moved a mile south in 1871, the fort became the supply base for patrols and punitive expeditions into the Tonto Basin, including Gen. George Crook's famous winter campaign of 1872–73.

According to Crook's mandate, all bands who refused to move to reservations by November 21, 1871, would be pursued relentlessly until they surrendered. A year later he sent his troops into the field. The campaign ranged from the cactus-strewn deserts around the Superstition Mountains to waist-deep snows above the Mogollon Rim. "A dirtier, greasier, more uncouth looking set of officers and men it would be hard to encounter anywhere," one officer recalled. However, the campaign worked; Chief Cha-Lipun, or Charley-Pan, surrendered in spring 1873. Troops at Camp Verde continued to round up resistant Indian bands over the next decade. In 1879 Camp Verde became Fort Verde.

After Geronimo surrendered in 1886, it was only a matter of time before the post shut down. In 1891, it was officially abandoned. In 1970 it became a state historic park and a year later was placed on the National Register of Historic Places.

Fort Verde, early 1890s —Arizona State Library

Crook Military Road

When General Crook first arrived at Camp Verde in 1871, after exploring nearly 700 miles on muleback, he decided to construct a military road along the Mogollon Rim from his post to Camp Apache. Part of his 200-mile road followed a trail used hundreds of years ago by Hopi Indians and during Spanish times by explorers Espejo, Farfán, and Oñate. Following the precipitous escarpment, the road provided a critical supply and communication link during the 1872–73 campaign.

Today the wagon ruts of Crook's old mule trail are still visible. Milepost blazers on tree trunks and strands of telegraph wire can still be seen, and there are a few sandstone grave markers along the trail. Although the Crook trail continued to be used well into the twentieth century, it was replaced as a main route when the railroad reached Holbrook in 1881.

MONTEZUMA CASTLE NATIONAL MONUMENT

Off I-17, between the Middle Verde and McGuireville exits, Montezuma Castle—a misnomer (the Aztec leader never came

Montezuma Castle cliff dwellings —Arizona Historical Society Library, Tucson

near the place)—was the prehistoric rendition of a frontier town. Archaeological evidence indicates the existence of several cultures in this region, and items found around Montezuma Castle suggest the area was a major trade center for prehistoric peoples of the Southwest.

The first inhabitants were the Hohokam, the master farmers of the Southwest, probable descendants of earlier desert cultures. Arriving in this area around A.D. 700, they lived in clusters of pit houses—one-room structures made of poles, mud, and brush. Spring-fed Beaver Creek provided a reliable source of water, allowing the natives to irrigate their crops of maize, beans, squash, and cotton. During the latter part of the eleventh century, some Hohokam moved to the San Francisco Mountains. The eruption of Sunset Crater in 1064 had left a layer of rich ash mulch, making the region around Wupatki ideal for farming, and many peoples gathered to take advantage.

The Sinagua (Spanish for "without water"), who arrived in the Verde Valley about 1100 from the Flagstaff area, were dry farmers. As pueblo dwellers, they lived communally. Apparently the Hohokam and Sinagua lived harmoniously, sharing customs, practices, and arts. There is also evidence of people from Ancestral Pueblo, Cohonina, and Mogollon cultures in the area.

Around 1250 the Sinagua began work on the grandiose stone dwelling known today as Montezuma Castle. The twenty-room pueblo, nestled beneath a limestone overhang above Beaver Creek, was occupied between 1100 and 1400, serving as home for about twelve families, or fifty people. Like other cliff dwellings in the Southwest, Montezuma Castle, with its exposure to the winter sun, took advantage of solar heating, while the overhang protected it from rain and snow and shaded it from the blistering summer sun. Another pueblo about 100 yards west was even larger, with more than forty-five rooms. The total population of this pueblo might have been about 200.

Overcrowding was one possible reason for the abandonment of these pueblos. A long drought between the years 1276 and 1299 was also a contributor, probably causing friction between the two cultures as they competed for water. Perhaps there was increased pressure from nomadic, warlike tribes. By 1450 the entire area was deserted.

The first white man to visit Montezuma Castle was the great scout Antoine Leroux, in 1854. By the end of the 1890s the site had been badly vandalized and was in a state of near collapse. In 1906 President Theodore Roosevelt proclaimed Montezuma Castle and Montezuma Well national monuments, assuring their preservation.

MONTEZUMA WELL

From the McGuireville exit on I-17, Montezuma Well, a huge, natural sinkhole, is about four miles northeast on Beaver Creek Road. The sink is what remains of an ancient cavern created by an underground spring percolating through limestone. The spring's seventy-five-degree water flows out at nearly 1.5 million gallons a day. The sink is slightly under 500 feet in diameter, and the well is about 55 feet deep. During prehistoric times, limestone-lined irrigation ditches carried the springwater to the crops of

"Montezuma's Well," circa 1880s (photo by Leo Goldschmidt) —Arizona Historical Society Library, Tucson

the Sinagua and Hohokam farmers. Many Native American tribes today consider the well a sacred place.

About 800 years ago, at least two limestone pueblos existed at Montezuma Well. The smaller one had twenty rooms, while the larger, a two- or three-story structure, had more than fifty. About 1864 a tiny white settlement called Montezuma City developed here around a small adobe fort. Rocks from the prehistoric pueblos were used in the construction of the community.

STONEMAN LAKE

Fourteen miles east of I-17 on Stoneman Lake Road (exit 306), Stoneman Lake is in the crater of an ancient volcano. Some writers claim it is the only natural lake in Arizona. Originally it was called Chavez Lake after Lt. Col. Francisco Chavez of the New Mexico Volunteers. Chavez, the son of an illustrious New Mexico family, provided military escort for Governor John Goodwin and his party in 1863–64 on their way to establish the first territorial government. The lake was renamed for Gen.

George Stoneman, who came to Arizona with the Mormon Battalion in 1846. Apparently a cantankerous man, Stoneman achieved fame in the Civil War and some degree of immortality in the 1960s, when he was mentioned in the song "The Night They Drove Old Dixie Down."

FLAGSTAFF

In 1911, movie producers Jesse Lasky and Cecil B. DeMille packed up their New York motion-picture company and headed west. Traveling on the Santa Fe Railroad, they were intrigued when the train halted at Flagstaff, a small community at the foot of the spectacular San Francisco Mountains. It looked like an ideal place to shoot outdoor movies, and they unloaded the equipment. Suddenly, a bone-chilling wind swept down from the towering peaks, followed by an icy drizzle and soon, a heavy blanket of snow. Lasky and DeMille packed up their gear and boarded the next westbound train, not stopping until they reached sunny Southern California. Thus did Flagstaff almost become the movie capital of the world.

Buildings along Santa Fe Avenue, the whole of Flagstaff in 1882 —Southwest Studies, Scottsdale Community College

Early Exploration

Flagstaff, in one of the most picturesque settings in America, seemed destined to become an important city. Its two springs, Leroux and San Francisco, and its location at the foot of the loftiest mountains in Arizona made it a natural campsite for natives and later travelers. Its position at the thirty-fifth parallel put it in the path of road builders.

During the 1850s, Secretary of War Jefferson Davis commissioned the Army Corps of Topographical Engineers to survey a possible transcontinental railroad route along the thirty-fifth parallel. The first survey was led by Lt. Amiel W. Whipple in 1853. Whipple's party spent a snowy Christmas Day camped where Flagstaff is now. They turned south in the vicinity of the west fork of the Verde River, then went west to the headwaters of the Big Sandy River, following it to the Bill Williams River, then down that stream to the Colorado. They continued on to the California coast along the thirty-fifth parallel.

During these same years, Lt. Edward F. "Ned" Beale made his legendary survey using camels as beasts of burden, part of the army's experiment to use a pack animal more naturally suited than mules to crossing deserts. The experiment was beset with problems. Mule skinners, known for being able to swear in paragraphs, found their oaths falling on deaf ears. The independent camels simply refused to learn English and looked upon their American handlers with contempt. The Americans, for their part, couldn't speak Arabic. It was said the breath of a camel could wilt the Yellow Rose of Texas (though nobody bothered to ask the camels what they thought of the mule skinners' breath). The stalemate was broken when the army imported camel drivers from the Middle East, and the survey proceeded on schedule.

All these military surveys along the thirty-fifth parallel during the 1850s would prove invaluable later on, when the Atlantic & Pacific Railroad built the first transcontinental line. The construction was delayed for several years, however, by the Civil War. Arizona would not have a line along the thirty-fifth parallel until 1883.

First Settlers

Although the area was well traveled by adventurers during the 1850s, the next recorded activity of note near the future site of Flagstaff came in the spring of 1876, with the arrival of the first colonists from Boston. The party of fifty, all men, were inspired to settle northern Arizona by Samuel Cozzens, who had come to southern Arizona during the 1860s. During his travels, Cozzens visited the Zuni pueblos and viewed the vast, sprawling rangeland to the north, where he visualized rich, fertile farmland with cool mountain streams—a land crying out for settlers. When the well-meaning but uninformed Cozzens returned to New England, he wrote an enthusiastic book about Arizona called *The Marvellous Country* and went on the lecture circuit to promote colonization of this rich breadbasket. It mattered little that Cozzens had never actually set eyes on northern Arizona.

This first Boston group expected to settle along the Little Colorado River, but a colony of Mormons from Utah had already arrived there, so they headed west to the San Francisco Mountains, which, some were convinced, were laced with veins of gold. The men laid out a town near Leroux Springs, in Fort Valley (a few miles northwest of downtown Flagstaff). The colonists quickly became discouraged, and within a short time most left.

Around July 4, 1876, a second party of Boston colonists arrived at the foot of the San Francisco Mountains. According to legend, they cut the branches off a tall pine tree and raised the American flag. The second group didn't stay any longer than the first, but the old flagpole remained a landmark for many years afterward and inspired the name Flagstaff. On July 4, 1985, a ceremony was held at this site and a tall pine flagpole and monument were dedicated.

Flagstaff's first permanent settler was Thomas F. McMillan, a native of Tennessee. In the spring of 1876 he built a cabin and corral at Antelope Spring, at the foot of Mars Hill. As the town grew up west of Antelope Spring, McMillan's original ranch became known as Old Town, and the spring was called Old Town Spring, or Flagpole Spring (the site is just west of today's Milton Road underpass). Today the Museum of Northern Arizona still makes use of McMillan's cabin.

The Coming of the Railroad

The area south of Flagstaff boasted the largest stand of ponderosa pine in the world, and by 1880 timber and cattle were the stalwarts of northern Arizona's economy. A railroad was needed to transport these commodities to outside markets. Since the 1860s, the government had been making large land grants to railroad companies to encourage them to build lines in western territories. In northern Arizona, the Atlantic & Pacific was awarded twenty-mile sections along each side of the track. When the line was completed, the value of the land soared, and the railroad recouped its expenses by selling it to ranchers and settlers. Thus the railroad arrived in Flagstaff in 1881. A boxcar served as the town's first depot. A more substantial station was built west of Antelope Spring, and the settlement grew up around it. By 1886 Flagstaff was the largest city on the main line of the Atlantic & Pacific between Albuquerque and the Pacific coast.

Cattle Boom

The arrival of the iron-bellied locomotives marked the real beginning of the cattle business in northern Arizona. John W. Young, a son of Brigham Young and a pioneer settler in the area,

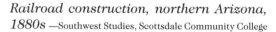

Railroad construction, northern Arizona,
1880s —Southwest Studies, Scottsdale Community College

founded the Mormon Cattle Company and stocked the ranges around Flagstaff on a large scale for the first time, but had to make a hasty exit in 1885 when a warrant was issued for his arrest for polygamy. His partners renamed the operation the Arizona Cattle Company. By the late 1880s, the A-1, as it was known, was running about 16,000 head of cattle from south of Flagstaff near Lake Mary, north to the Grand Canyon, and from Ash Fork east to the Little Colorado River. The A-1 was one of the biggest ranches in Arizona when the famed Babbitt brothers bought it in 1889.

Not everyone in Flagstaff was happy about the cattle boom. Newspaper accounts of the time tell of citizens' outrage when cowboys periodically drove several hundred range cows down the town's main street, or when law-abiding folks were sent scurrying for safety as drunken cowpunchers rode hell-for-leather through town, waving their revolvers in the air and "shootin' holes in the sky." As the *Chronicle* expressed it on September 20, 1883:

> They are bragging, whiskey-drinking bummers who delight in sixshooters, fine horses, saddles, and fast women. Their aim in life seems to be to have a good time. They delight in disconcerting the eastern tenderfoot. Nearly all die with their boots on and no one mourns their death.

Babbitt Dynasty

Flagstaff was still rough around the edges on a chilly March morning of 1886 when two aspiring cattlemen named Dave and Billy Babbitt arrived. A fire had recently destroyed the small business district, and the sounds of sawing and hammering heralded the emergence of a new town atop the smoldering ashes of the old. "Unchurched, unmarried, and unwashed" was a good description of most of the residents.

The Babbitts had run a grocery store in Cincinnati with their brothers C. J. and George, who would arrive later. Seeking new opportunity in Arizona, the brothers, including Edward, the youngest, who never moved to Arizona, pooled their cash and came up with $20,000. To some, Flagstaff wouldn't have seemed like a likely place to invest life savings, but the Babbitts were visionaries who dreamed of becoming cattlemen. In developed

The Babbitt brothers, 1908; from left: George, Charles "C. J.," Edward,
William, and David —Southwest Studies, Scottsdale Community College

areas, their money would have bought very little, but the railroad was selling Arizona cattle country for pennies an acre, so the Babbitts were off.

A few weeks after they arrived, they bought a small outfit between Flagstaff and Winslow. As a tribute to their hometown of Cincinnati, they stamped a "C O" with a bar underneath on the hides of their "hairy banknotes." A few months later, they shipped their first herd—seventeen carloads—to California, and the storied Babbitt dynasty had begun.

At the urging of Gerald Vercamp, father-in-law to three of the brothers, the Babbitts diversified their business. Dave opened a mercantile store and George got involved in real estate while C. J. and Billy ran the cattle operation. In 1889 they formed the Babbitt Brothers Trading Company. Drought and bad markets would have bankrupted the cattle operation several times had it not been for the other interests.

In 1889 the C O Bar doubled in size when the Babbitts bought the Arizona Cattle Company's A-1 Ranch. During its golden age,

Bar building in Fort Valley, north of Flagstaff, former headquarters of the Arizona Cattle Company (no date) —Southwest Studies, Scottsdale Community College

1909 to 1919, the C O Bar Ranch ran thousands of sheep and cattle on ranges that extended from Ash Fork on the west to the New Mexico line on the east and from the Grand Canyon on the north to the Mogollon Rim on the south. The Babbitts also owned large ranches in Kansas and California.

Through the years, the Babbitts diversified their holdings far beyond what Gerald Vercamp could have imagined. They operated a vast network of trading posts on the Hopi and Navajo reservations; opened Flagstaff's first automotive garage; and owned a bank, an ice plant, a livery stable, a slaughterhouse, an opera house, and a mortuary. It's been said the Babbitts "fed, clothed, equipped, transported, entertained, and buried Arizonans, doing it more efficiently and more profitably than anyone else."

During these years, Flagstaff became the cultural and mercantile center of northern Arizona, and the industrious brothers from Ohio no doubt had a powerful influence on politics and business in the region, but they did not wield a heavy hand.

*Earle Forrest, a C O
Bar Ranch cowboy
who carried a
camera and recorded
some of Arizona's
ranching history*
—Earle Forrest Collection,
Museum of Northern Arizona

Rather than construct opulent mansions as testament to their wealth, they lived in unpretentious homes, setting an example for benevolent power rare in the annals of dynasties.

Today the C O Bar Ranch is still one of the state's largest cow outfits, and it's still a family business. During the 1990s, the Babbitts scaled back their operations and liquidated all their trading posts, but they still own two ranches in addition to the C O Bar, as well as three stores in Flagstaff. The Babbitt Ford dealership is one of the oldest in the western states. One of C. J.'s grandsons, Bruce Babbitt, served two terms as governor of the state (1978–86) and was Secretary of the Interior under President Clinton.

The Riordan brothers' Arizona Lumber Company (no date) —Northern Arizona University

Timber Barons

The Babbitts weren't the only brothers to find business success in Flagstaff. Timothy and Michael Riordan came to the area in 1886 and had soon acquired some of the leading companies in northern Arizona's other major industry, timber. In 1903 Tim built a dam at the end of a long cienega south of town and named it Lake Mary in honor of his oldest daughter. The lake later became Flagstaff's main source of water. The innovative brothers also built the town's first electric plant.

In 1904 the two Riordans built an impressive log mansion and named it Kinlichi, Navajo for "red house." The house had separate living quarters at each end for the two families and a common area in the center. It became the social hub in the area. In 1927 tragedy darkened the house when young adult children in both families contracted polio. An iron lung ordered by rail failed to arrive in time, and they died on the same day. The Riordan

Kinlichi, home of the Riordan brothers and their families (no date) —Southwest Studies, Scottsdale Community College

mansion, a unique and interesting vestige of Flagstaff's lumber dynasty, is open to the public.

Continuing Growth

As in most communities of the "real West," Flagstaff citizens worked hard to build schools, fraternal organizations, and churches. In 1883 a preacher passed the hat in local saloons to raise money to build the town's first Protestant church. A Jesuit priest came to the administer the needs of Roman Catholics, and a chapter of the Women's Christian Temperance Union was organized.

The town bragged about its healthful climate and opportunities for a "fresh deal," as Bret Harte said, for those who would give up Eastern security to settle in a new community nestled at the foot of the grandiose San Francisco Mountains. In what could pass for a Department of Tourism commercial, newspaperman George Tinker wrote in 1887:

> The air is dry, the soil porous, the water pure, scenery cheerful and sunlight brilliant. . . . The value of the climate as a remedial

agent is demonstrated daily. . . . Around Flagstaff the sun shines nearly every day, and but few are cloudy. Even during the rainy season which begins in July and lasts about six weeks, the daily showers are followed by the brightest sunshine.

By 1891 the population of Flagstaff had grown to about 1,500. With its lumber, ranching, and railroad, Flagstaff, in a short decade, had become Arizona's most important city north of Prescott.

In the twentieth century, tourism became Flagstaff's new major industry as large numbers of visitors came to the Grand Canyon. The building of Route 66 in the 1920s made the tourist industry one of Flagstaff's most important sources of income.

Northern Arizona University

Northern Arizona University (NAU), the newest and smallest of the state universities, has come a long way since 1901, when four young ladies stepped forward to receive their teaching degrees—the normal school's first graduating class. The school had opened its doors September 11, 1899, with a faculty of two and a handful of students.

After years of haggling about the college's funding, its purpose, and even its name, the 1925 legislature approved the creation of Northern Arizona State Teachers College. When the school began offering a master's degree in education, Flagstaff became known as an ideal place for teachers to go for summer school.

On November 28, 1964, the regents changed the school's name one last time to Northern Arizona University, and on May 1, 1966, its university status became official. Today, in addition to the downtown Flagstaff campus (with about 14,000 students), the university offers degree programs at NAU-Yuma (about 700 students), and courses in several other Arizona communities (nearly 4,000 students). The school boasts impressive research programs including the Colorado Plateau Research Station and the Social Research Laboratory and awards degrees up through the doctoral level.

Lowell Observatory

The Lowell Observatory sits on top of Mars Hill, at the west end of Flagstaff. In 1893 Dr. Percival Lowell selected the observatory site in Flagstaff because the clear mountain air gave it the best visibility in the United States. Lowell expected to chart the path of Mars, which was to come closer to Earth than ever before observed. He believed intelligent life had constructed irrigation canals on the Red Planet. Before his death in 1916, Lowell predicted the discovery of an unknown planet. In 1930 the observatory's Clyde W. Tombaugh discovered Pluto in the exact position indicated by Dr. Lowell.

AZ 88 (Apache Trail)
Apache Junction—Roosevelt Dam
46 MILES

The Apache Trail begins at Apache Junction and travels some forty-five miles to the Roosevelt Dam. This stretch of country is blessed with some of the most spectacular desert scenery in Arizona. In prehistoric times, Salado Indians inhabited this area. Later, nomadic Tonto Apache and Yavapai bands used these twisting canyons as sanctuaries from warring Pima Indians living along the Gila River. During the Apache Wars, U.S. troops scoured these uncharted regions in search of their cunning and elusive adversaries.

As the Salt River Valley became settled, residents needed a consistent source of water for farming. Eventually the federal government stepped in to fund the Tonto Dam, later renamed the Theodore Roosevelt Dam. Surveying for a new road to the dam that would trace the old Tonto or Yavapai Trail—later known as the Apache Trail—took place from September 1902 to April 1904. Funds were approved in 1903 and construction on the road began.

By the following year, over 400 road workers were on the job. Building the sixty-two miles of road through rough terrain cost just over half a million dollars. The Apache Trail was completed early in 1905, and soon after, the first Concord stage rumbled

Fish Creek Hill on the Apache Trail (no date) —Salt River Project

along the rough road to the dam site. On August 23 of that year, the first automobile chuffed its way up the canyon.

However, some sections of that road now lie under the waters of Canyon Lake. In 1925, Mormon Flat Dam was completed and Canyon Lake formed behind it. The new post-1925 Apache Trail now passes along the dam. On February 25, 1987, the Apache Trail was officially dedicated as one of the first Arizona Historic Roads. Visitors can stop and take a spectacular trip up the lake on the steamboat *Dolly*.

TORTILLA FLAT

Boundary commissioner William Emory, here in 1853 to survey the United States' newly acquired land after its war with Mexico, supposedly named the flat-top mountains in this area the Tortillas after the cornmeal cakes so ubiquitous in the region. However, another story traces the name of this town back to famous Tonto Basin cowman John Cline. Cline said the town site had served, perhaps as early as the 1860s, as a cowboy campsite during cattle drives. One time flood waters stranded some cowboys here with nothing to eat but tortillas, so they named it Tortilla Flat.

Originally the town, with as many as 100 residents, was on the opposite side of the road. However, residents moved it to higher ground after a flash flood. In the 1920s, the community even had a small zoo with wolves, coyotes, mountain lions, snakes, wild pigs, and a bear to entertain tourists. The post office was established in 1927.

Today Tortilla Flat calls itself the friendliest town in Arizona. It may certainly be the smallest, with six full-time residents. In addition to an old stage station, a restaurant, and the 100-year-old Superstition Saloon—papered with enough dollar bills to open a small bank—the town has a country store that serves a specialty: prickly pear ice cream.

In 1987 a devastating fire destroyed several buildings in Tortilla Flat, including the restaurant. It caused over $200,000 in damages, none of them covered by insurance. When loyal patrons—local, national, and international—heard about the demise of this favorite hangout, they donated money, supplies, equipment, and even labor. The town was reborn and dedicated on July 1, 1988. Looking at it today, one would never know the difference.

ROOSEVELT DAM

The completion of the Roosevelt Dam in 1911 is still, without a doubt, the most significant historical event in the history of central Arizona. Without this dam and the others that followed, the Phoenix metro area would still be a small desert community relying on the fickle Salt River for its water.

Though the Arizona Canal had begun carrying water to the area in 1887, Salt River Valley residents were still at the mercy of the river's floods and droughts. The community realized that if the river were harnessed, the valley could become one of the nation's richest agricultural regions.

The citizens made their appeal to the federal government, but Arizona was not the only western territory seeking funding for water projects in 1900, and there was a lot of politicking going on in Washington. The Newlands Act of 1902 (also called the National Reclamation Act) called for the sale of public lands to finance reclamation projects in the West. With some hard lobbying by Arizonans and a little luck, the Congress decided that the best place to start was with a massive dam in Arizona Territory, at the confluence of Tonto Creek and the Salt River.

Before construction began, the government wanted a guaranteed repayment plan (the original estimate for the project was $3 million; the final cost was $10 million). To raise enough collateral, Arizonans had to unite—thus was born the Salt River Valley Water Users Association (today's Salt River Project). Led by men of vision like Ben Fowler, William J. Murphy, Dwight Heard, Joe Kibbey, and John Orme, the association took on the difficult task of overcoming the prevailing attitude of "every man

Construction on Roosevelt Dam, February 1908 —Salt River Project

for himself" and convincing landowners to offer their lands as collateral for the common good.

Construction on the dam began in 1905. A road was built from Mesa, as each piece of machinery and all supplies had to be hauled in from the nearest railroad, sixty miles away. Before the year was out, more than 1.5 million pounds of freight had been hauled up the road to the dam site. Italian stonemasons were brought in to quarry huge granite blocks that eventually ridged a canyon 680 feet wide at the top. The dam, rising 284 feet from bedrock, formed a reservoir with a capacity of 1.3 million acre-feet of water (one acre-foot is about 326,000 gallons).

On March 18, 1911, former president Theodore Roosevelt led an automobile entourage up the Apache Trail for the dedication ceremony. Up to this time, the dam had been called the Tonto Dam, but henceforth it would carry the name of the old Rough Rider.

President Theodore Roosevelt on his way to dedicate Roosevelt Dam in 1911 —Southwest Studies, Scottsdale Community College

AZ 87 (Beeline Highway)
Mesa—Winslow
168 MILES

AZ 87 follows an 1880s wagon road that crosses the 1868 Crook Military Road above the rim. A few miles farther north, the road joins part of the Chavez Trail and Sunset Pass, continuing into Winslow. This is also the Palatkwapi Trail.

Palatkwapi Trail

An ancient trail led through northern and central Arizona, heading west from the Zuni pueblo of Santa Fe to the Little Colorado River, then on to the springs at the foot of the San Francisco Mountains. From there the trail drifted southwest of the Bill Williams Mountains and into Chino Valley, ending at present-day Prescott. Some parts of that old road are still visible from AZ 87.

The Hopi Indians call it the Palatkwapi Trail, and their legends tell of several clans that lived among the beautiful red rocks in the Verde Valley. Their name for the place was Palatkwapi, "Warm Valley among the Rocks." According to the Hopi, life was so easy the people became degenerate, and the gods grew angry and drove them out. Eventually they wound up at Walpi, on the Hopi mesas about sixty miles north of Winslow.

Spanish explorers Antonio de Espejo, Marcos Farfán, and Juan de Oñate followed this route in the late 1500s and early 1600s while searching for rich Indian mines and the fabled Northwest Passage. It was also the trail followed by Lt. Col. Francisco Chavez in 1863–64, when he escorted the first territorial officers to Arizona.

Beeline Highway

During the 1950s it took about five hours to make the trip from Mesa to Payson. Today it takes about an hour and a half. Earlier one had to go up the old Bush Highway, a washboard dirt road, to Blue Point, then take a long, dusty road north of Saguaro Lake. One had the choice of driving dangerously fast to get ahead of the other cars or going slow and eating their dust. The journey

The bad old days —Southwest Studies, Scottsdale Community College

required crossing several creeks, the largest being Sycamore, which sometimes flooded. The plunge down Slate Creek was an adventure and usually was good for at least one flat tire.

In the early 1940s the State Highway Commission agreed to build the road, but it was the late 1950s before AZ 87, the Beeline Highway, was paved all the way to Payson. The road made a beeline from Mesa to Payson, hence the name.

In the years following the Beeline's completion, weekend, holiday, and summer traffic became a nightmare. In 1969 the Arizona Department of Transportation began building a four-lane highway from the Salt River Valley to Payson. The divided four-lane highway was finished in 2001, completing the long-awaited project on one of the state's busiest highways.

FOUNTAIN HILLS

This new and fast-growing community is just off AZ 87 at Shea Boulevard, northwest of Phoenix. The site where the town of

Fountain Hills is today was for most of the twentieth century a working cattle ranch, the P-Bar Ranch, owned by the Page Land & Cattle Company.

In 1968 the Page Land & Cattle Company sold 4,500 acres to the McCulloch Oil Corporation. McCulloch Properties, a subsidiary, was developing Lake Havasu City and was interested in building a planned community in the Phoenix metropolitan area. Robert McCulloch Sr. teamed up with C. V. Woods, the man who had developed Disneyland in California. The new community was originally called Chaparral City. McCulloch and Woods believed that Chaparral City needed something unique to bring it cohesiveness and identity. A Phoenix reporter proposed a fountain—not just any fountain, but the biggest one in the world.

A Swiss firm that had designed the Delacorte Fountain in New York City was commissioned to design Chaparral City's fountain. McCulloch invested $1.5 million in the project. The resulting fountain could send a jet of water 560 feet into the air, 10 feet more than the height of the Empire State Building.

On December 15, 1970, the "World's Tallest Fountain" was turned on for the first time. At the time, the fountain ran for fifty-five minutes on the hour from 9 A.M. to 10 P.M. Today it runs every hour on the hour for about ten minutes, depending on weather conditions.

Work began on Fountain Hills's first homes in the fall of 1971, and the first residents moved in February the following year. Many of the new residents arrived by way of McCulloch's "fly to see" sales program, where prospective buyers from eastern and midwestern states were flown to Arizona in the company's fleet of airplanes.

Between 1985 and 1990 the town's population doubled from 5,000 to 10,000. A decade later it had doubled again. In 1993 the community was listed in the book *50 Fabulous Places to Raise Your Family*. A 1999 poll taken by a local television station showed that Fountain Hills was considered one of the most desirable places to live in the Phoenix metro area. A big part of the attraction is the high Sonoran desert and the mountains that surround the community.

FORT MCDOWELL INDIAN RESERVATION

East of AZ 87, Red Mountain looks down on the Fort McDowell Indian community. Viewers can sometimes see the profile of a man in the mountain's side. From the highway, around milepost 191 is the best place to see it—optimally, in early morning. To the Yavapai Indians, this "Man in the Mountain" is sacred; he looks out for the people of the community.

On May 12, 1992, the deity was up to the task. That day several large moving vans loaded with the Fort McDowell Indian community's slot machines sat in the gaming center's parking lot waiting to haul them out. Armed federal agents were positioned on the gaming center's roof, and other agents in riot gear stood nearby. At the exit, the reservation's residents had gathered to blockade the road. Yavapai men and women, young and old, made their stand, unarmed. Here in the Arizona desert, one of this nation's smallest and poorest Indian tribes stood in defiance of the government for three weeks. Finally the feds backed off, soon to negotiate gaming contracts with all the tribes in the state. The stand taken by the Fort McDowell Yavapai Nation was a moral and political victory for all Native Americans.

Originally the Yavapai, whose name translates as "People of the Sun," inhabited the rugged region from the Salt River Canyon to the Bradshaw Mountains. Living in the same area as the Tonto Apache, the two tribes shared certain ways of life, such as traveling in small family groups or bands, and they also intermarried. Like the Apache, the Yavapai are recognized for their fine basketry. Today about 1,000 Yavapai live on the Fort McDowell Reservation.

Fort McDowell

On September 7, 1865, five companies of California Volunteers established Fort McDowell at the confluence of Sycamore Creek and the Verde River. The site was a strategic location for scouting and punitive expeditions against the Yavapai and Tonto Apache bands, who had been raiding Pima Indians and whites alike. Named for Gen. Irvin McDowell, military commander in the area, the original adobe fort washed away in a thunderstorm. Undaunted, the troopers built another. By 1870, the new

Remains of Fort McDowell, 1990 —Author photo

department commandant, Gen. George Stoneman, was calling Fort McDowell one of the finest forts in the territory.

During Gen. George Crook's famous winter campaign of 1872–73, the Yavapai and Apache bands were defeated and moved to reservations at Date Creek and Camp Verde. In 1875 the Yavapai were rounded up and herded like cattle in the humiliating March of Tears to the San Carlos Apache Reservation. On April 10, 1890, they were allowed to return to Fort McDowell, where 24,400 acres had been set aside as a reservation. Most residents of the Fort McDowell reservation today are descended from the survivors of the March of Tears.

TONTO BASIN

South of Payson, AZ 87 passes through the Tonto Basin, which runs south from the Mogollon Rim to the Salt River and is bordered on the east by the Sierra Anchas and the west by the Mazatzal Range. In the old days it was rough country—remote, mountainous, with few roads—and it bred a tough, formidable people. They used to say that if you could hold a job cowboying in the Tonto Basin, you could work anywhere.

The families who ranched this rugged land were a close-knit community, and their social lives centered around the old Packard Store on Tonto Creek, now known as Punkin Center (on AZ 188). Here ranch families picked up their mail, bought supplies, and even held dances. Residents used to have an annual pumpkin-growing contest, and the Packard Store was the official weighing station. The post office at Punkin Center was closed in 1929, but descendants of pioneer families with names such as Haught, Conway, Armer, and Cline still congregate at the store to catch up on the latest happenings in the basin.

The area takes its name from the Tonto Apache, who used to live here. *Tonto,* a Spanish word meaning "fool," is said to have been bestowed on those Indians by their relatives, the White Mountain Apache, for refusing to renounce the warpath for reservation life.

In 1867 Camp Reno was established a mile west of what became Punkin Center on Tonto Creek. (The site can be reached from AZ 188 via a dirt frontage road.) Until it was abandoned in 1870, Camp Reno, at the entrance to strategic Reno Pass, would play a major role in subduing the Apache bands that roamed the region.

The army drove in the basin's first cattle herds to feed the soldiers at Camp Reno. It wasn't until a few years after the post had closed and the Apache had been relocated that the private ranchers arrived. The first was David Harer of California, in 1872.

PAYSON

The Mogollon Rim (pronounced muggy-OWN), called the "backbone of Arizona," is most prominent above Payson, where it serves as a panoramic backdrop for the town. The huge escarpment was named for Juan Ignacio Flores Mogollon, governor of New Mexico from 1712 to 1715.

Payson began its existence in 1876 when Bill Burch built a cabin on the site of what is today the fifth green of the local golf course. In 1882, when father and son John and Frank Hise opened a store, the community was born. For years, Payson was one of the most remote communities in Arizona. The two best roads—to Flagstaff and Globe—were both five tough days of travel by wagon.

Payson in 1900 —Arizona State Library

Payson's social gathering place in the early days was the Pioneer Saloon. The town also had another saloon, two stores, two cafes, and "one street." During spells of western-style trouble, typically on Saturday nights, the town marshal chained errant cowboys to a tree until they sobered up enough to ride home. The "jail tree," a tall oak in front of the library, later became known as the "tree of knowledge."

Cowboy Games

In 1884, when Payson was not yet Payson but was called Union Park, citizens began celebrating "August Doin's." After a huge town picnic, local cowboys would compete in a contest of skills that included riding and roping in the town's main street. Today, the Payson Rodeo bills itself as the "World's Longest Continuous Rodeo."

"Arizona Charlie" Meadows earned the title "Father of the Payson Rodeo" by competing in and helping organize the first one. In 1882 he was working as a packer for the army in the Verde Valley when Apaches killed members of his family near Payson. Called home to take care of the family ranch, he entered that first Payson rodeo and, on a horse named Snowstorm, won nearly every event. From that time on Charlie had show business in his blood and refused to spend the rest of his life taking care of cows. On August 16, 1890, he got out of the cow business by announcing at the double wedding of his sister and one of her friends that the two couples were welcome to all the cattle they could rope and brand by sundown on his ranch.

Soon after, Meadows left the Payson area to perform all over the world, riding with Buffalo Bill's Wild West Show. Late in life he settled in Yuma. He often said, "It'll be a snowy day in Yuma when they bury this old Hassayamper." (Back before Arizonans called themselves "Zonies," they were called "Hassayampers" after the Hassayampa River.) Arizona Charlie Meadows died on December 12, 1932. On that day, it snowed one and a half inches in Yuma.

Although gambling had been outlawed by the territorial legislature in 1907, it was wide open in the Payson saloons in the early days. The county sheriff looked the other way because the vice paid for the annual rodeo. During the event, the action took place under a tent set up in the middle of town. One time, when some "city slickers" were winning most of the money at the expense of locals, an enterprising cowboy slipped out back and cut the tent ropes, causing the tent to collapse. This was also done periodically to stop free-for-all fighting among revelers.

Cowboys could be quite creative when it came to games of chance. Bronc rider George Felton placed a half-dollar in each of his stirrups and bet $100 they'd still be there when he finished his ride. Another favorite was to toss dollar coins to a line to see who finished closest. Eventually Payson held horse races, which always caused excitement. Most early races were between cow ponies. Later on, when the stakes became higher, professionals began bringing in bred racehorses.

Lion Wrangling

One of Arizona's more bizarre episodes occurred on September 16, 1927, when a plane carrying Leo the Lion, the famous MGM mascot, crashed in the mountains east of Payson. Fortunately, the pilot and his feline cargo survived. The pilot walked for three days for help. Five Payson-area cowboys responded: "Green Valley Sam" Haught, Columbus "Boy" Haught, Lou Pyle, Henry Steele, and Ernie Sweat. All were seasoned cowhands who had doctored wild range bulls at least as dangerous as an African lion.

At the crash, they found Leo battered but alive. They cut two oak limbs for a drag sled, pulled the lion, in his cage, from the wreckage, and had to convince some fearful mules to be hitched to the sled. Later, when the mules balked at a steep grade, all Sam had to do was lift the tarp covering the lion's cage and give the mules a peek.

When they reached Bear Flat, the cowboys pondered how to treat Leo's wounds. They opened the cage gate, and when the lion charged out, they roped his hind then his front legs, stretching him on the ground, and wedged a chunk of oak in his mouth. Two bad wounds were crawling with screwworm maggots. As they had on many cows, the cowboys applied a salve for the maggots and cleaned the wounds, then covered them in pine tar to keep the flies away. Now they had to get Leo back in his cage. They tied one end of a rope to the beast and threaded the other through the back of the cage, securing it around Sam's saddle horn. Then Sam dragged the lion like a dead cow back into the cage.

By then, Leo was one mad lion, and the cowhands let him cool off before hauling him out. In no time the big cat was back in Hollywood filming the opening credits for MGM's first talkie, *White Shadows in the South Seas*. Undoubtedly the recollection of his ordeal in Arizona inspired the magnificent, angry roar that symbolizes MGM.

Modern Payson

In 1959, AZ 87 was finally paved, and Payson, at last linked up with the "outside world," has never been the same. Following the completion of the Beeline Highway, the tiny community at the foot of the Mogollon Rim saw a surge of population that continues to this day. After AZ 260 was paved from Payson to Show Low in the 1970s, it became the popular road to the White Mountain area. By 2000 Payson had a population of 13,600.

Tourism has become Payson's number one income-producing industry. Each September some 5,000 fiddle fans gather in the cool pines under the Tonto Rim to enjoy the Old-Time Fiddlers Contest, with entrants from around the country. At the annual

Tonto Natural Bridge, circa 1885 (photo by Willis P. Haynes) —Arizona Historical Society Library, Tucson

"Loggers Jamboree," lumberjacks compete in some twenty-six events, including a log toss and pulp and ax throws.

TONTO NATURAL BRIDGE STATE PARK

A frontage road from AZ 89, about ten miles north of Payson, will take you to Tonto Natural Bridge, on Pine Creek. The first white men to see this great natural arch, which is 183 feet high and 400 feet long, were army troops from Gen. George Crook's command during the 1870s. They were watering their horses in the creek when one of them noticed the huge limestone formation 100 yards away.

In 1877 a Scotsman named Davy Gowan was trekking through the mountains of central Arizona when a band of Apache picked up his trail. Gowan fled deeper into the mountains but the Indians followed. In a beautiful green valley watered by a stream, Gowan was about to be cornered when he saw a big stone arch looming in his path and, nearby, a cave opening. He entered the cave and hid for three days. When he was sure the warriors were gone, Gowan emerged and staked a claim to the magnificent green valley. In 1890 he invited his nephew, David Goodfellow of Durham, Scotland, to settle there. Goodfellow recognized the wonder of the bridge and developed it as a tourist attraction.

Goodfellow later built a lodge, completed in 1927, allowing as many as sixty tourists at a time to visit the site. The lodge still stands, as well as the fruit trees Gowan planted in the 1880s. Tonto Natural Bridge is now a state park with several hiking trails.

PINE AND STRAWBERRY

Today Pine and its sister town Strawberry are quiet havens for hikers and retirees. Many historic buildings remain in downtown Pine, and there's a historical museum in the old Mormon chapel. Strawberry got its name from its profusion of wild strawberries. For several years before the first white settlers arrived in 1877, cowboys drove cattle in and out of this area seasonally to graze on the good forage.

The Old Strawberry School House *(by Bill Ahrendt)* —Courtesy artist

Strawberry's residents built a school from hand-hewn logs in 1887. The arrival of the Peach family's eleven children in 1882 increased the enrollment dramatically. Alfred and Frances Peach made a rhyme of their offspring's names to keep them straight: "Kate, Ede, Ide, and El; Alf, Hank, Gus, Bob, and Will; Tuff and Tom, the baby—he's the last, well maybe." The school building still stands, the oldest in Arizona.

WINSLOW

In 1973 the Eagles released a song, "Take It Easy," cowritten by Jackson Browne and Glenn Frye. The lyric "Standin' on a corner in Winslow, Arizona" made the town a household name all over the country. In the 1990s, Winslow built a park "on the corner" at Kinsley and Second Streets that includes a mural by artist John Pugh and a six-foot-tall statue of a young man leaning against a lightpole, by Ron Adamson. The mural and statue were dedicated in 1999.

Mural and statue in Winslow inspired by "Take It Easy" —Author photo

Winslow was probably named for Gen. Edward Winslow, a railroad executive, although a prospector near Mayer named Tom Winslow later claimed the honor. Winslow remains the Arizona headquarters for the Santa Fe Railroad.

During its heyday in the 1920s and 1930s, bustling Winslow was the largest city in northern Arizona. Charles Lindbergh designed an airport that became a major stop between Los Angeles and Chicago. During those years it was the busiest airport in the state.

The economy of Winslow today relies on tourism, transportation, and a state prison south of town. The Old Trails Museum traces life in the Winslow area from prehistoric to modern times. Some of the exhibits include artifacts from the nearby Homolovi ruins, railroad memorabilia, Route 66 history, and the famous Harvey House restaurants. Resident Janice Griffith was the driving force behind the development and success of the museum, the "Standin' on a Corner" Park, and the La Posada restoration.

La Posada Hotel

The La Posada Hotel, with its classic Spanish architecture, was Winslow's Harvey House, one of the legendary eating establishments built along the Santa Fe line by Fred Harvey. Before the days of railroad dining cars, passengers had to eat in whatever hash houses there were at the train stops. The food was usually terrible, and the service even worse. It took a gentleman from England named Fred Harvey to bring top-quality cuisine to the American Southwest.

After experiencing the deplorable eating conditions along the rail lines, in the early 1870s Harvey put forth to the Santa Fe Railroad a visionary plan that would provide passengers with attractive surroundings, superior service, and above all, good food. The railroad company accepted the proposal enthusiastically and agreed to supply buildings, restaurant furnishings, and even personnel free of charge. Harvey would receive all the profits.

The first Harvey House opened for business in Topeka, Kansas, in the spring of 1876 to immediate success. Over the next twenty years, Harvey's restaurant-hotels opened throughout the

Southwest. Eventually, Arizona had five Harvey Houses: at Ash Fork, Kingman, Needles, Williams, and Winslow, where La Posada was the crown jewel.

Before reaching a station, the brakeman would take orders and wire the information ahead. When the train was a mile away, it would blow its whistle, which signaled the waitresses to set up the first course. By the time the train arrived and the hungry passengers were ushered in, the meal was ready to serve. The chefs were French, hired away from prominent Eastern restaurants, and the food was fresh and local.

It wasn't just the excellent food that attracted Southwesterners to Harvey's establishments. In a land where women were scarce, Harvey brought in as wholesome a group of young women as had yet been seen in that region. "Harvey Girls" were recruited in the East through newspaper advertisements that read, "Young women 18 to 30 years of age, of good character, attractive and intelligent, as waitresses in Harvey Eating Houses in the West.

Harvey Girls, Winslow, circa 1910
—Southwest Studies, Scottsdale Community College

Good wages with room and meals furnished." For many, the job was a dream come true, and the girls didn't always stay single for long. Humorist Will Rogers once said, "Fred Harvey kept the West in food and wives."

During the 1920s the Fred Harvey Company chose Winslow as the site for its major hotel in northern Arizona. Southwest architect Mary Jane Elizabeth Colter designed La Posada, "The Resting Place," as a Spanish hacienda. Colter, one of America's greatest architects, believed buildings should be sympathetic to their environment, not copies of European styles. In 1910, at a time when women architects were few, she became chief designer and architect for the Fred Harvey Company. Among her designs in Arizona were the El Tovar, Desert View, Bright Angel Lodge, Hermit's Rest, Lookout Studio, and Hopi House at the Grand Canyon. She felt La Posada was her masterpiece.

The hotel cost more than $2 million, a huge sum in 1929. The original hotel had seventy guest rooms, three dining rooms, restful arcades, and fancy lounges. It was surrounded by eight acres of grounds with a garden, greenhouse, stables, and two tennis courts. The grand opening, in 1930, was a typically boisterous western affair. Local lore says some cowboys rode their horses into the spacious lobby, hoisted the laughing Miss Colter up on one of the horses, and fired shots into the ceiling. Celebrities who stopped at La Posada over the years include Charles Lindbergh, Errol Flynn, Mae West, Howard Hughes, Albert Einstein, James Stewart, Dorothy Lamour, John Wayne, Bob Hope, Will Rogers, Gary Cooper, Clark Gable, and Carole Lombard, who spent her last night at La Posada before her fatal plane crash in Nevada. Today each room is named for a celebrity guest.

As times began to change, La Posada's star faded, and the hotel closed in 1957. Fortunately, in the 1990s local citizens recognized La Posada as a "lost treasure" and, with grants from the Arizona Department of Transportation, the Historic Preservation Heritage Fund, and private donors, the legendary hotel and restaurant opened again for business.

AZ 89
US 93—Prescott
50 MILES

CONGRESS

Congress is three miles west of Congress Junction, which is ten miles north of US 93 on AZ 89. In 1883 Dennis May found the fabulously rich Congress Mine in the rugged foothills of the Date Creek Mountains, nine miles west of Pauline Weaver's Rich Hill discovery. "Diamond" Jim Reynolds, a Mississippi riverboat gambler with a flamboyant lifestyle, owned the mine in the late 1880s. He built a twenty-stamp mill, and by the time of his death in 1891, more than $600,000 in gold had been taken out. By 1897 the rough-and-tumble city of Congress was at its peak, with

President William McKinley (second from left on train) in Congress, 1900 —Arizona State Library

425 men employed at the mine. President William McKinley paid a visit to Congress in 1900 to see the bonanza firsthand.

Congress was really two towns—Mill Town and Lower Town. At Mill Town were the mill, a hospital, homes for the employers and employees, bunkhouses, and company offices. Lower Town was strung out along a canyon and included saloons like the Red Front and the Silver Dollar, boardinghouses, restaurants, churches, mercantile stores, and a variety of other boomtown enterprises. The only source of water in town was a small spigot in front of the company store at Mill Town. Residents rolled an empty fifty-gallon barrel up the hill each day, filled it up, and let gravity carry it down the hill to Lower Town.

Fires in 1898 and 1900 and the scarcity of water to fight them destroyed portions of Lower Town. Though there was some rebuilding, by the 1930s the boom times were long gone and nothing much was left of Congress but the fallen walls of miners' cabins and rusted mining equipment.

STANTON, OCTAVE, AND WEAVER

Two miles north of Congress Junction, a dirt road leads off to the east toward the old ghost towns of Stanton, Weaver, and Octave. Eight miles down, at the base of Rich Hill on Antelope Creek, is Stanton, named for Charles P. Stanton, one of the most ruthless, conniving scoundrels in Arizona history. At its peak in the 1890s, the town of Stanton had about 200 residents, a five-stamp mill, a boardinghouse, and various other businesses, as well as Charles Stanton's own store.

Nearby, at Antelope Station, Yaqui Wilson operated a stage stop, and about half a mile away an Englishman named William Partridge was also running a stage station. Apparently the two were not-so-friendly competitors, so Stanton figured that if he could start an open feud, he could get a corner on all the business. The scheme worked, and in a gunfight, Partridge killed Wilson. The Englishman was tried for murder and sent to the territorial prison at Yuma.

Before Stanton could take over the Englishman's station, however, a silent partner named Timmerman appeared and brought in a new partner, Barney Martin. Undaunted, Stanton hired a cutthroat named Francisco Vega and his band of rogues to kill Timmerman and Martin. After murdering Timmerman, the outlaws set out to get Martin. They got not only him, but his whole family as they traveled in a wagon. A few weeks later their charred remains were found in the desert near Morristown. Since there were no witnesses willing to testify in the case, no charges were pressed.

Later that year, Charles Stanton learned the lesson of living by the sword. On November 13, 1886, after Stanton had insulted the sister of one of Vega's henchmen, Cristo Lucero, Lucero entered Stanton's store and filled him full of lead. No one lamented his passing.

The next town, Weaver, about two miles east of Stanton, was named for famed scout Pauline Weaver. In 1863 the rugged explorer was hired to guide the Abraham Peeples party into the nearby mountains. At the top of what became known as Rich Hill, they found a fabulous pocket of gold nuggets. Other rich placers were found along Weaver and Antelope Creeks, and eventually a community sprang up.

Eventually Weaver was absorbed by the adjacent underground-mining community of Octave. A relative latecomer to this trio of ghost towns, Octave came into existence in the late 1890s. The mine was developed by eight entrepreneurs, hence the name Octave. At its height the community boasted 3,000 residents, a school, a post office, a grocery store, a stage station, and a general store. At one time the mine was said to be netting $50,000 a month, but in 1942 the Octave Gold Mining Company shut down operations and demolished the buildings.

KIRKLAND AND KIRKLAND JUNCTION

Kirkland Junction, on AZ 89, and Kirkland, four miles northwest, were named for William Kirkland, the area's first settler and one of Arizona's most illustrious pioneers. Kirkland moved his family to this valley in 1863 and established a stage station. The excellent meals at Kirkland's Station made it a favorite stopping place for travelers. Kirkland farmed and mined in the area until 1868, when he moved his family to Phoenix.

Kirkland, a big strapping Virginian, first came to Arizona in 1856, and the following year ranched at Canoa. With cattle from Mexico, he was the first Anglo American to ranch in Arizona.

William Hudson Kirkland, 1909
—Courtesy Ben and Fern Allen

Kirkland was one of the few who came to Arizona in the turbulent 1850s and lived into the twentieth century. He died in 1909.

Kirkland had several encounters with hostile Indians while living in the Kirkland area. On one occasion, Kirkland was stopped by a band of Indians, and a warrior demanded his shirt. When the Indian tried to remove the garment, Kirkland shoved him away. Another warrior rode up behind him and ran a lance into his back. Although the wound was painful, Kirkland refused to flinch. Eventually, they tired of the game and rode away. Years later at Fort McDowell, Kirkland recognized one of his attackers, a one-eyed Indian. The warrior gave the Kirkland a hard but respectful look and called him *valiente capitan,* "brave captain" in Spanish. Kirkland proved his bravery on many occasions, but he knew when it was time to steer clear of trouble. "I've helped bury a lot of men," he used to say, "who insisted they had as much right to a place as the Indians did."

AZ 89
Prescott—I-40
51 MILES

FORT WHIPPLE

The site of old Fort Whipple is one mile northeast of Prescott on AZ 89. In May 1864, the fort known as Camp Clark was moved, along with Prescott, the territorial capital, eighteen miles south to a site closer to the gold diggings at Granite Creek. The post was renamed Fort Whipple for Gen. Amiel Whipple (see I-40, Lupton–Flagstaff, Part 3), who had recently fallen in the Battle of Chancellorsville, though it was sometimes called Prescott Barracks.

During the 1860s Fort Whipple was a primitive post with a scattering of rough-hewn log cabins. Hostile bands of Yavapai and Apache kept the soldiers on constant alert. Post records indicate that numerous punitive expeditions went out from the fort during these years. The thriving community of Prescott offered those stationed there amenities not found elsewhere in Arizona.

Following the end of the Apache Wars in 1886, Fort Whipple quieted down, and it was abandoned in 1898. The army reopened the fort four years later, but in 1913 it was permanently closed as an army post. In 1922 the facility was turned over to the Public Health Service and Fort Whipple became a veteran's hospital, which it still is today.

GRANITE DELLS

The spectacular outcropping of salmon-colored granite boulders four miles north of Prescott was a favorite rendezvous for Indians bent on mischief to miners and freighters going to and from Prescott. The misleading name "Dells" developed from *dalles,* French Canadian vernacular for a rocky enclosure, the name given the place by an early trapper. Another descriptive name for the picturesque area, Point of Rocks, appears in early stories.

Granite Dells was a favorite spot for shooting Hollywood westerns in the 1930s through 1950s. Nestled in a giant stone

Point of Rocks, or Granite Dells (no date) —Arizona State Library

amphitheater is a tree-shrouded recreational area complete with a natural swimming pool among the boulders. Today, much of Granite Dells has become private property and is being developed, but parts are still accessible. The area also draws rock climbers.

CHINO VALLEY

During his historic 1853–54 survey, Lt. Amiel W. Whipple named Chino Valley for its carpeting of curly range grass, which the Mexicans in the party called *chino*. This vast, windswept region begins northeast of the Juniper Mountains near Seligman and stretches south all the way to Prescott Valley. The Verde River has its headwaters on the north side of the Chino Valley, along AZ 89 near Paulden.

During the 1820s mountain men like Ewing Young and Kit Carson had great success trapping beaver in this area. The old narrow-gauge railroad built in 1892 ran into the Chino Valley from Jerome. Special trains had to be built to negotiate the twisting curves and switchbacks through the valley. One thirteen-mile stretch had 168 curves, or as one old cowpuncher said, "more kinks 'an a cheap lariat." Local people quickly dubbed it the "world's crookedest railroad." Passengers claimed they could look out the window and see the engine passing them going the other way.

HELL CANYON

During the 1950s the new AZ 89 took the thrill out of the drive through Hell Canyon, between Paulden and Ash Fork, with its treacherous twists and turns. Today motorists glide by hardly noticing the deep chasm.

In 1885 a raging snowstorm at Hell Canyon delayed the stage that the Tucson delegation to the Thirteenth Territorial Assembly was taking to Prescott. High waters on the Salt River had already caused a major detour, and now time was of the essence as the delegation, hoping to bring Arizona's "capital on wheels" back to Tucson, tried to get to the assembly in time to make their bid. When the stage became snowbound, desperate delegate Bob Leatherwood rode a mule the rest of the way to Prescott, carrying a satchel full of money to throw some vote-winning galas. But Leatherwood arrived too late; Prescott's political warrior Buckey O'Neill had already "partied" his way into victory, and Prescott retained its capital status.

Alternate AZ 89
Prescott—Flagstaff
89 MILES

JEROME

Spanish explorers were the first to record the mineral wealth at the site of what would one day become the "billion-dollar copper camp" called Jerome, in the Black Hills, thirty miles northeast of Prescott on Alt. AZ 89. The silver specimens Antonio de Espejo brought back from his 1583 expedition into the Verde Valley rekindled Spanish interest in resuming the explorations that had ended with Coronado's unsuccessful quest for gold forty years earlier. In 1598 Governor Juan de Oñate, the great colonizer of New Mexico, sent Marcos Farfán to search for the lost mines, and Farfán returned with rich silver ore from the vicinity of Prescott. But the area's remoteness and rough terrain made transporting ore too difficult, so the Black Hills kept their treasure for nearly 300 years, until a narrow-gauge railroad made it economically worthwhile to mine there.

During the 1870s, one of Arizona's most illustrious frontiersmen, army scout Al Sieber, worked claims on what became known as Cleopatra Hill, but he gave them up before realizing their value. The reddish, cone-shaped Cleopatra Hill, on which Jerome is precariously perched, was a veritable treasure trove of gold, silver, and copper. Jerome's reputation as the "billion-dollar copper camp" matches the fame of Cripple Creek and Leadville, Colorado, and the Comstock Lode of Nevada. Unfortunately, records of Jerome's history are hard to come by because fires wiped out the town three times around the turn of the century.

In 1882, when Cleopatra Hill's new owners ran short of money, they brought in New York financier Eugene Jerome as a backer. After putting up $200,000, he insisted that the community that had sprung up near the mine be named after him. Jerome never visited his namesake town.

World War I brought Jerome to its highest pinnacle of success. Between 1914 and 1920, the population reached 15,000, making it Arizona's third-largest city. Housing became a critical problem. Residents attached lean-to rooms to their houses and became landlords. Three miners might share the same sleeping quarters, taking turns using the room.

Huge stockpiles of copper at the end of the war sent the market plunging. By 1920 the price had dropped from thirty cents to twelve cents a pound. During tough economic times, shop owners, fearing the miners were not spending enough money in their stores, tried to close down the saloons and cathouses. However, as soon as times improved, the drinking establishments and the ladies of easy virtue were back in full swing.

Jerome, 1923 —Arizona Historical Society Library/Tucson

During Prohibition bootlegging became Jerome's biggest industry, next to copper. On July 4, 1920, the town jail, which was reputed to have spikes in the floor to prevent prisoners from getting any sleep, was overflowing, so the town marshal chained twelve drunks to a huge mill wheel. The prisoners picked up the wheel in unison and hauled it to the door of the nearest speakeasy, then demanded an ax to widen the doorway.

Colorful characters in Jerome included "Doctor" Lee Hawkins, a self-trained dentist who was not really a doctor but liked the title, and since his remedies were harmless, residents let him practice. Doc Hawkins was also an inventor of gadgets that usually did not work. Jerome's magistrate, Lewis St. James, was totally deaf and could not hear testimony, but he had the uncanny ability to know how much cash a defendant was carrying and set his fine accordingly.

In the mid-1920s, miners discovered a rich body of ore directly beneath the town. Hundreds of thousands of tons of dynamite were used to wrest the ore from the mountain's clutches. Above-ground, years of choking smelter smoke had destroyed the flora on the mountain. With nothing to hold the soil, the entire town began to slide downhill. But Jerome's citizens never lost their sense of humor—Mayor Harry Mader proclaimed Jerome "a city on the move."

Mining Wars

Copper king William Andrews Clark was secretive to a fault and trusted no one, not even his accountant. It was said that the diminutive mogul's bookkeeper in New York kept only the left side of Clark's ledger while Clark kept the right side in Jerome. Clark fired any employee who discussed the company's wealth with an outsider and any underground miner who talked to an aboveground worker about the richness of the United Verde's ore.

Around 1912 another mining investor, Jimmy Douglas, came to Jerome to speculate on the mines around Cleopatra Hill. Son of Dr. James Douglas (see Bisbee), "Rawhide" Jimmy, as he was known, was a flamboyant wheeler-dealer. After buying the Little Daisy Mine at the foot of Cleopatra Hill, he spent half a million dollars in the first year to mine it without success. But two years later, he hit a vein of pure copper five feet thick, the richest ever found in American mining. In 1916, Rawhide Jimmy's United Verde Extension mined $10 million in gold, silver, and copper.

Soon Rawhide Jimmy was smelting more ore in one furnace than Clark was in three. Competition between the two copper kings was fierce, and the local citizens loved it. If a worker was unhappy at one mine, he could quit and go to work at the other without having to move to another town.

Clark died in 1925, while his mine was still producing. It would finally shut down in 1953. Douglas's United Verde Extension played out in 1938, but not before making $50 million in dividends. Rawhide Jimmy Douglas died in 1949 a multimillion-aire. The Douglas Mansion is now a state park and historical museum.

A Ghost Town Resurrected

Jerome was nearly abandoned after the last mines shut down in the early 1950s, but soon afterward the few citizens who remained banded together to make Jerome a tourist destination. Many of the original buildings are still standing, so it is a popular stop for history buffs. During the 1970s, Jerome also became known as a haven for artists. Today the town's galleries, shops, B and Bs, historic museum, and other attractions keep Jerome's economy—and history—alive and well.

CLARKDALE

In 1914, United Verde Mine owner William Andrews Clark spent $2 million to establish the smelter town of Clarkdale four miles east of Jerome. He also lent $3.5 million to the Santa Fe Railroad to build a line into the new town. Residents lived in company housing and shopped in company stores. When the smelter closed in the early 1950s, the Phoenix Cement Company came in, keeping the town's economy alive.

The building and interior of First Interstate Bank in downtown Clarkdale have not changed much since Arizona's biggest bank robbery up to that time took place there in June 1928. Earl Nelson and Willard Forester, Oklahoma outlaws, held the bank up for $40,000 then jumped into their getaway car just as seventy-year-old Jim Roberts, the town constable, was making his rounds. One of the robbers shot at the old man as his partner hit the accelerator.

The two outlaws did not know that the old man was one of Arizona's legendary gunfighters. Jim Roberts had tamed more towns than most people in those days had even seen. Before he became a peace officer in the 1890s, Roberts had been a participant in the famous Pleasant Valley War (see Pleasant Valley). All agreed he was the deadliest gunman on either side of the law.

Roberts calmly drew his Colt revolver and shot the driver, Forrester, through the head. In moments, Nelson meekly surrendered. After the incident, Roberts went home for lunch. He was late, and when his wife asked what had delayed him, his only reply was, "There was a little trouble downtown." She only found out later what had happened.

Today, Clarkdale has a major tourist attraction in the Verde Canyon Railroad, which winds its way up the canyon from Clarkdale to Perkinsville and back, passing through Sycamore Canyon on the way. The railroad made its maiden voyage in 1990

Jim Roberts
—Courtesy Bill Roberts

and was an instant success, especially since Verde Canyon is accessible only by rail and makes up some of the most scenic country in Arizona.

SEDONA

Dorsey Elsworth Schnebly was one of the original settlers among the beautiful red rocks on Oak Creek, about twenty-five miles south of Flagstaff. In October 1901 he came from Gorin, Missouri, to Jerome, not to mine but to farm. After he found a place some thirty miles north of Jerome, he sent for his brother, T. Carleton Schnebly, to join him. Two weeks later, T. C.'s wife Sedona and the couple's two children arrived at the farm.

Soon the family had a thriving truck farm, hauling produce over to Jerome. They soon realized there was an even better market in Flagstaff, but the road to that town was beyond a high

Red Rock Crossing, Sedona —Author photo

mountain rim. Using picks and shovels, the brothers built a road up the steep cliff now known as Schnebly Hill. Today that road, which runs from Sedona to I-17, is one of the state's most scenic routes.

The Schnebly home beside Oak Creek soon became a favorite way station for travelers. The family called for a post office, proposing the name Oak Creek Canyon Station, but postal authorities thought it was too long. Upon hearing this, Dorsey turned to his sister-in-law and said, "What do you think we should call it, Sedona?" Before she could respond, he had his answer.

After T. C. and Sedona's youngest daughter was dragged to death by a horse, the grief-stricken family returned to Missouri for several years. They came back in 1930, and Sedona Schnebly died in the town that honors her name on November 13, 1950.

Until the 1950s, the beauty of Sedona was one of Arizona's best-kept secrets. But after several Hollywood westerns were shot there, including *Johnny Guitar* and *Broken Arrow,* the whole

Movie set, Sedona, late 1940s; today, houses dot this area.
—Southwest Studies, Scottsdale Community College

world knew about Sedona. Soon the town was inundated with tourists and, before long, new residents.

The Sedona Heritage Museum, nestled in the spectacular red rocks, takes visitors back to both pioneering days in Sedona and the area's moviemaking history. In addition, in Red Rock State Park, visitors can picnic near Red Rock Crossing, one of the most photographed places in the state. The crossing has featured in many western films. The park also offers rewarding bird-watching and hiking.

Four local men founded the Cowboy Artists of America organization at the Oak Creek Tavern in downtown Sedona in 1965. The four set some lofty ideals in their charter: "To perpetuate the memory and culture of the Old West [and] to insure authentic representation of the life of the West as it was and is." Today these artists are earning what Charlie Russell used to call "dead man's wages" for their works. A recent cowboy art show in Phoenix drew 2,000 viewers and grossed over $1.75 million.

First meeting of the Cowboy Artists of America, June 23, 1965, at Oak Creek Tavern, Sedona; from left: Joe Beeler, Charlie Dye, John W. Hampton, George Phippen, and (back to camera) Robert MacLeod —Elizabeth Rigby photo

OAK CREEK CANYON

Just north of Sedona, drivers on Alt. AZ 89 wind through stunning Oak Creek Canyon, sometimes called "the Grand Canyon with a road." Around 8000 B.C., nomadic Paleo-Indians roamed this area. The water of Oak Creek and the abundant animal life were an obvious draw for these hunters. About A.D. 700, Hohokam farmers moved in, also drawn by the water. They were followed by Sinagua Indians, who mostly dry-farmed. By the late 1300s, for mysterious reasons, the prehistoric peoples had left the area.

The original settlers in the canyon were the Thompson and Purtymun families. Jim Thompson moved to the area called Indian Gardens in the 1870s and started ranching. In 1901 the entire student body at the Oak Creek school was named Thompson or Purtymun. Later, two Thompson girls married Purtymun boys. Descendants of the Purtymun and Thompson families are still scattered throughout the Verde Valley.

Canyon settlers sold most of their crops in Flagstaff, though they sometimes hauled them south to Jerome and Fort Verde. Before a road was built through the canyon, to get to Flagstaff settlers had to climb trails called "ladders" to the top, where they kept wagons and mules to take them to town. The trail into Flagstaff roughly follows today's I-17.

In the early 1920s, western author Zane Grey came to Oak Creek Canyon and wrote *Call of the Canyon*. In 1923 Grey convinced Hollywood producer Jesse Lasky to film a movie based on his popular novel at the same site. This was the first of many movies, television commercials, and music videos to use beautiful Oak Creek Canyon and Sedona as a backdrop.

Slide Rock State Park, about seven miles up the canyon from downtown Sedona, is open year-round, but becomes especially busy in summer when hot city dwellers seek out its refreshing natural chutes and frigid swimming pools.

Oak Creek Canyon, 1931 —Southwest Studies, Scottsdale Community College

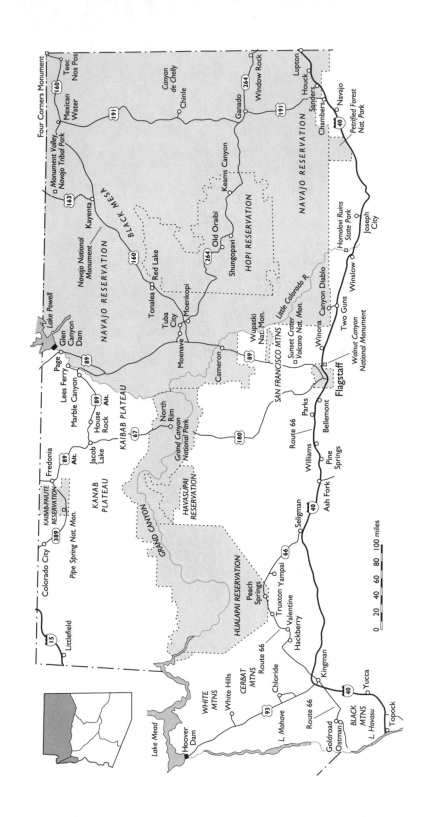

Part 3

The Colorado Plateau

I-40
Lupton—Flagstaff
163 MILES

Most of the towns and cities along I-40, which roughly parallels old Route 66 through Arizona, trace their ancestry to the Santa Fe Railroad or its forerunner, the Atlantic & Pacific Railroad. Many of these settlements were named for railroad officials or those closely associated with the company. For the railroads to come through, however, the route had to be blazed and surveyed.

First Survey

In 1853 the U.S. government commissioned four railroad surveys from the Mississippi River to the Pacific coast. The task was assigned to the Army Corps of Topographical Engineers, and, as testimony to a job well done, all four routes eventually became transcontinental railroads. Two of these routes were to cross Arizona—one along the thirty-second parallel near the Gila Trail, and the other along the thirty-fifth parallel. The latter route eventually became today's I-40. Experienced engineer Lt. Amiel W. Whipple led the survey of the thirty-fifth parallel route.

By the time the party reached the San Francisco Mountains, on Christmas Eve, slogging through heavy snows had left the pack animals exhausted. Whipple called a halt to allow the stock to recuperate and let the men celebrate the holiday. While opening up the packs, Heinrich Baldwin Möllhausen, the expedition artist, wrote that the men uncovered "some well preserved bottles of what makes glad the heart of the traveling

271

Gen. Amiel W. Whipple —Southwest
Studies, Scottsdale Community College

man." The wine and food were turned over to the cooks "for the glorification of our Christmas dinner in the Wilderness."

One pack included eggs that by some miracle had survived the journey. While the cooks were preparing venison, wild turkey, and other tasty delights, Lieutenant John, a resourceful young officer in the party, took the eggs and liquor and conjured up a punch that would grow hair on a Gila monster. Möllhausen describes the celebration:

> All gentlemen are requested to assemble after supper before Lieutenant John's tent, and to bring with them their tin drinking mugs.
>
> No one had a previous engagement, nor was it at all tempting to decline, and as soon as the night set in and the stars began to flitter in the deep blue firmament, and to look down upon us

between the snowy branches, the company began to assemble at the appointed spot. . . .

Lieutenant John was busy with his brewage and that fragrant steaming pail, with the inviting froth at the top, was a most agreeable sight to men who had been so long limited to water. Lieutenant John made a speech, as nearly as I can remember to this effect:

"Let us now forget for a few hours our hardships and privations, the object of our journey, and the labours still before us; and here, under a roof of boughs, and on the spotless white carpet that God Almighty has spread for us, for as we are far from our homes, let us think of our friends, who, very likely, are thinking of us as they sit around their firesides; and drowning our cares in a social glass of toddy, drink to their health, and to our own happy return."

We sat in a circle, smoked, drank, toasted and told jokes— —hearts became lighter, blood ran more swirly in veins, and all joined in a hearty songfest that echoed through ravines and mountains and must have sadly interfered with the night's rest of the sleeping turkeys.

The Mexicans threw firebrands into the cedar thickets, making them blaze and spark over the glittering snow. Later, they sang traditional Mexican Christmas songs while the Americans offered Negro spirituals. Two men, former prisoners of the Navajo, topped off the multicultural event with native dances they had learned in captivity.

Christmas Day was spent in quiet observance and with a sense of nostalgia: "We looked up at the sublime summits of the San Francisco Mountains and needed no temple made with hands within to worship our Creator." This marked the first recorded Christmas observance in Arizona north of the Gila River.

The expedition eventually reached the Mojave villages near the mouth of the Bill Williams Fork. The meeting with the villagers was cordial, although the six months' growth of whiskers on the explorers evoked laughter among the Mojave women. After this pleasant interlude, Whipple's party continued on to California and the completion of their historic survey.

Camel Corps

The next major survey of the thirty-fifth parallel was the famous Beale Camel Experiment in 1857. Jefferson Davis, U.S. Secretary

*Mojave women
(no date)* —Arizona
Historical Society

of War from 1853 to 1857, was the Washington official primarily responsible for the camel project. The use of camels in America was not a new idea—someone had suggested the idea as early as 1701—but it wasn't until the opening of the arid lands west of the ninety-eighth meridian in the 1840s that the idea of using camels as pack animals was taken seriously. In 1855 Congress appropriated $30,000 for "the purchase and importation of camels and dromedaries to be used for military purposes."

Davis placed Maj. Henry Wayne in charge of the experiment, assisted by navy officer David Porter and former navy officer Edward F. "Ned" Beale. Wayne and Porter traveled extensively in the Middle East during the next few months on the ship *Supply* to make their selection of animals. Wayne turned the ship into a camel stud farm, certainly a first for the United States Navy. He hired several Arabs, Greeks, and Turks to tend the animals. The ship, carrying thirty-four camels, arrived on the Texas coast in May 1856. Less than a year later, another shipload increased the herd size by forty-one.

The camels passed all tests of durability and adaptability with flying colors, including winning a race against mule-drawn wagons, in spite of carrying a heavier load. During rainy weather they plodded right through the slick Texas gumbo that mules couldn't manage.

In 1857 Major Wayne was called to Washington, and the task of implementing the camel experiment fell on the shoulders of young Ned Beale. Beale's life story reads like an adventure novel. He was with Gen. Stephen Watts Kearny at the siege of San Pasqual, sneaking through the Mexican lines and reaching San Diego in time to bring back a rescue party. When gold was

Lt. Edward F. "Ned" Beale (artist unknown)
—Southwest Studies, Scottsdale Community College

discovered in California, Beale was chosen to carry the news to President Millard Fillmore, making an epic dash across the continent in 1848 disguised as a Mexican. During the trip, Beale shot his way out of several attempted holdups, outriding his pursuers. His accomplishment ultimately helped trigger the California gold rush.

Beale's assignment was to survey a wagon road from Fort Defiance (near today's Window Rock, Arizona) to the Colorado River along the thirty-fifth parallel using the camels as pack animals. By the middle of August, the camel brigade was on its way. Accompanied by the Middle Eastern "camel conductors" in their traditional garb, the caravan made a colorful spectacle as it passed through villages along the way. Beale looked and played the part of circus ringmaster, riding on a wagon painted bright red. The camels were hauling 700 pounds each, about twice what a mule could carry. Beale generally rode a mule, but once, for a social call at a military outpost, he climbed up on a white dromedary named Seid. No doubt the appearance of this dashing young officer sitting high on a white camel had the desired effect.

Beale couldn't have been more pleased with his camels. The camels endured the arid lands between Flagstaff and the Colorado River especially well. During a stretch of thirty-six hours without water, the horses and mules suffered, but the camels did not falter. "One of the most painful sights I ever witnessed," Beale wrote, "was a group of [horses and mules] standing over a small barrel of water and trying to drink from the bung hole, and seemingly frantic with distress and eagerness to get at it. The camels appeared to view this proceeding with great contempt, and kept quietly browsing on the grass and bushes."

After the expedition, Beale took his camels to his ranch at Fort Tejon, California. He made another trip along the thirty-fifth parallel the following year, but the camel corps, although highly successful, was doomed. The outbreak of the Civil War ended all plans for a southern railroad to the Pacific in the near future. When the railroad did come across northern Arizona in the 1880s, it closely followed the trail blazed by Ned Beale and his camels nearly a quarter of a century earlier.

Route 66

Much has been written of the railroad era, which marked the closing of the American frontier, the "great and glowing West." About the time the trail dust had settled for good and the history of the frontier was fading into the realm of romantic nostalgia, Americans began their enduring love affair with the horseless carriage. Henry Ford had figured out a way to mass-produce his product, and soon nearly everybody could afford a car. America had become, in one generation, a mobile society. A national clamor arose for decent highways, and by the 1920s the nation had embarked on an unparalleled road-building program.

Of all America's great highways built during the big road boom, none epitomized American culture better than the National Trails Highway, better known as Route 66. Stretching from Chicago to California, it rambled hundreds of miles through the Midwest and across Oklahoma, Texas, New Mexico, and Arizona. Route 66 was the twentieth-century rendition of the golden road to the promised land—the Gila Trail, the Beale Camel Road, and the Oregon Trail all rolled into one.

Route 66 near Ash Fork, 1920s —Southwest Studies, Scottsdale Community College

On November 11, 1926, federal highway officials put the finishing touches on the new 2,400-mile interstate route linking Chicago with Los Angeles. In Arizona, Route 66 began its 376-mile journey across the state at Lupton, on the New Mexico line, and angled southwest to the former frontier town of Holbrook. From there the narrow, two-lane dirt road headed west across the windswept high desert, past Winslow and Flagstaff, snaking its way through tall pine forests and grassy meadows to Williams before beginning its long descent down treacherous Ash Fork Hill.

Beyond Ash Fork, a high, windswept plateau with countless islands of cedar-studded mesas and rolling hills spread for miles in all directions. At 5,000 feet, the plateau was carpeted with native grasses and spotted with piñon and juniper, and herds of antelope raced across the plain at the speed of an automobile. A few miles past Kingman, the highway approached Oatman Hill, the last great obstacle before reaching the California line. Twisting and winding its way through the rugged Black Mountains, the Oatman Hill section of the highway was the standard by which drivers measured other treacherous hills.

Route 66 was many things to many people. To refugees of the Oklahoma dust bowl, it was the yellow brick road to the promised land of California. During the post–World War II years, others came "to get something or someplace or to get away from something or someplace," or, as Bret Harte said a century earlier, they were "looking for a fresh deal all around." They found their theme song in Bobby Troup's "Get Your Kicks on Route 66." From 1960 to 1964, the television generation learned about Route 66 from watching two idealistic young hipsters behind the wheel of a shiny Corvette in an innovative show named after the famous road.

Construction of the new I-40 began in the early 1950s. On December 13, 1983, at Williams, the final stretch of the interstate was opened, and old Route 66 began fading into legend. The old route separates from I-40 at exit 139, just west of Ash Fork, and becomes AZ 66 at Seligman. It arcs north through the Hualapi Reservation, then angles south to Kingman. West of Kingman, the post-1950s route again merges with I-40, but the original Route 66 cut through the Black Mountains.

LUPTON

Lupton, near the New Mexico border, was named for G. W. Lupton, train master at Winslow in the early 1900s. Today Lupton is on the Navajo Indian Reservation. Now more a roadside attraction than a town, it has several trading posts and curio shops to entice tourists traveling I-40.

HOUCK

In 1874 Houck's namesake, James D. Houck, was employed as a mail carrier between Prescott and Fort Wingate, New Mexico. Three years later he established a trading post on the lonely road between Fort Wingate and Horsehead Crossing. At first the local Navajo resented the intrusion of this white man, but Houck was stubborn and tough enough to make a stand. Eventually the Indians began to come into the trading post to swap sheep and wool for the white man's merchandise, and Houck accumulated a large flock in the exchanges. After the railroad arrived in 1881, a small station was built at the post along with a water tank for the steam-driven locomotives, and a community grew up around it.

Houck was always careful to avoid direct confrontation with the Navajo. On one occasion, when his horses were missing, the trader locked the doors to the store and waited. A few days later some Navajo leaders appeared and wanted to know what was wrong. Houck told them the store would be reopened when his horses were returned. They went away silently, and the next day Houck's horses were back in the corral.

Houck was involved in the Pleasant Valley War (1887–92) on the Tewksbury side. He moved to the Paradise Valley when large sheep outfits around Flagstaff had begun wintering their flocks there. He settled at Cave Creek, opened a shearing station and saloon, and soon became known as the "Sheep King of Cave Creek." But a long drought in the early 1900s brought hard times to the area. In April 1921 Houck, despondent over financial losses and old age, calmly swallowed poison, lay down, and died.

CHAMBERS

The railroad named a station Chambers in honor of Charles Chambers, who had opened a trading post several years earlier at the site. A post office opened in 1907. Near Chambers is the Kin Tiel ruin, a Hopi-affiliated pueblo that dates back to the thirteenth century. The site, one of the largest in the Southwest, is characterized by high-quality masonry and includes kivas, a walled spring, a plaza, and burial grounds. Kin Tiel means "Wide Rock" or "Pueblo House" in Navajo.

NAVAJO SPRINGS

Navajo Springs, three miles southeast of the town of Navajo, was a favorite watering place for Indians traveling between the Zuni pueblo and Horsehead Crossing (Holbrook). The "springs" at Navajo Springs were more like seeps, but the water was pure and lay in the middle of an open meadow that provided good grazing for animals. Lt. Amiel Whipple, camping here in 1853, named the springs, noting that the Navajo frequented the area. Today, a locked gate keeps visitors from the springs.

On December 29, 1863, the territory's first gubernatorial party, on its way to establish the new capital, camped at Navajo Springs in a raging snowstorm. Despite the weather, they planned to swear in the new territorial governor that day. First they had to ascertain they were on Arizona soil, since there was confusion about the exact location of the new boundary between Arizona and New Mexico. Lt. Col. Francisco Chavez, who provided military escort for the group, assured them that Navajo Springs was in Arizona. After a feast of antelope and champagne, Governor John C. Goodwin took the oath of office, and the territory of Arizona was formally established.

A railroad station was established at Navajo Springs in 1881. The name was shortened to Navajo in 1883. Between Navajo and Leroux Wash are the exits for the Petrified National Forest and Holbrook.

LEROUX WASH

At milepost 285, I-40 crosses Leroux Wash. The wash was named for Antoine Leroux, a western hero little known in Arizona, yet as deserving of recognition as Jim Bridger or Jed Smith. Unlike many who were recruited to become fur trappers from the grog shops of St. Louis, Leroux was a member of an affluent French merchant family and educated in the finest St. Louis academies. But there was a sense of adventure in his blood, and in 1822 he joined the storied Ashley-Henry Expedition, which left St. Louis in 1822 to explore to the headwaters of the Missouri River. The roster of that expedition reads like a who's who in the mountain man hall of fame, including Jim Bridger, David Jackson, Jed Smith, Tom Fitzpatrick, Hugh Glass, Jim Kirker, "Frenchy" Sublette, and Jim Clyman. Most of these adventurers were in their early twenties at the time.

Two years later Leroux was trapping in the Gila watershed of Arizona and New Mexico—between 1830 and 1848, often assisted by Kit Carson. By the time the Americans took over the region after the Mexican-American War ended in 1848, Leroux was considered the most experienced, competent, and celebrated scout in New Mexico.

Antoine Leroux's achievements in the opening of the Southwest are impressive. In 1846 he was a guide for the Mormon Battalion on their historic road-building trek from Santa Fe to California.

Mormon Battalion (by George Ottinger)
—Scottsdale Community College, Southwest Studies

In 1851 he led the first of several expeditions by the Army Corps of Topographical Engineers charged with locating proposed railroad routes. Of the four proposed routes, Leroux guided three: the thirty-second, thirty-fifth, and thirty-eighth parallels. During the 1851 expedition, under the leadership of Capt. Lorenzo Sitgreaves, Leroux walked into an ambush near the Big Sandy River and received three arrow wounds from Hualapai warriors. It was said the humiliation of getting ambushed hurt the tough frontier veteran more than the arrows themselves.

After guiding the Sitgreaves reconnaissance party to San Diego, Leroux was hired to lead U.S. Boundary Commissioner John R. Bartlett and Lt. Amiel Whipple east across the desert to Yuma, then along the Gila River and across New Mexico to El Paso. In early 1853 Leroux was with Capt. John W. Gunnison on his ill-fated surveying expedition across central Colorado, but he had to leave Gunnison in Utah to keep his commitment to lead the Whipple party through Arizona. Later Gunnison and his men were murdered by Ute Indians; most historians believe that the experienced Leroux could have avoided the massacre had he been present.

JOSEPH CITY

In this area, the Little Colorado River was known by the Navajo as Tol-Chaco, meaning "red" or "bloody." Coronado named it Rio de Lino—the Flax River—because of the wild flax that grew along it. In 1604, explorer Don Juan Oñate called it the Rio Colorado, or "Red River." This muddy brown river of many moods has its headwaters near 11,470-foot Mount Baldy. It empties into the Grand Canyon after cutting a 250-mile gorge across the Colorado Plateau. Although the Little Colorado isn't as famous as some other rivers in Arizona, it is still a force to be reckoned with.

In 1876 a Mormon mission was established at the ancient Hopi community at Moenkopi. Over the next two years, fiery red-headed frontiersman Lot Smith and other church leaders such as William C. Allen, George Lake, and Jesse O. Ballinger led parties of colonists to the lower Little Colorado River Valley near today's Joseph City, Sunset Crossing (Winslow), and Holbrook. Town sites were marked, irrigation ditches dug, dams erected, and crops planted. The Mormons took permanent root in Arizona.

Four colonizing parties, each numbering about fifty, established camps and named them for their respective captains. Lake's Camp later became Obed; Smith's Camp was changed to Sunset, for the river crossing nearby; Ballinger's Camp became Brigham City; and Allen's Camp became St. Joseph, then Joseph City.

St. Joseph, the only one of the four communities that survived, is considered the oldest Mormon colony in Arizona. Despite numerous crop failures and dams destroyed by the rampaging Little Colorado, the gritty colonists stood firm. At last in 1939 a durable dam tamed the river, but not before Obed, Sunset, and Brigham City had all succumbed not only to the capricious river and its floods, but also to probable dissension and lack of cooperation among the colonists.

HOMOLOVI RUINS STATE PARK

Homolovi Ruins State Park is located on the Little Colorado River, a few miles northeast of Winslow, just off I-40 on AZ 87. Arizona's first archaeological state park, Homolovi is made up of several pueblo ruins and various other remains of the ancient Indian villages that once stood here, as well as trails and camping areas for visitors.

Homolovi means "Place of the Low Hills." The pueblo sites are numbered, one through four. Prehistoric Ancestral Pueblo (Anasazi) Indians lived here from about A.D. 600 to 1450. Early inhabitants dwelled in clusters of pit houses. Later, the structures grew into two- and three-story pueblos. There were at least half a dozen villages in the vicinity of present-day Winslow, with a total population of several thousand. Homolovi Two had 700 to 1,200 rooms in structures centered around a plaza, and it may have had as many as 3,000 residents. The people subsisted on crops of corn, beans, and squash, and also grew cotton.

When, either from prolonged drought or the arrival of the Navajo and Apache, the villages went into decline, the Homolovi Ancestral Pueblo moved to the present-day Hopi Mesas. The Hopi believe their ancestors came from many different places and peoples, Ancestral Pueblo from Homolovi among them. The Hopi people consider this site sacred and leave prayer feathers or *pahos* for the spirits.

Meteor Crater —Southwest Studies, Scottsdale Community College

"Anasazi" is a Navajo word of hostility that now neither the Hopi nor the Navajo prefer. "Ancestral Pueblo" is the name in English for these ancient ancestors. The Hopi call them Hisatsonom, or "People of the Remote Past of Ancient Time." *Sinom* in Hopi means "people."

METEOR CRATER

Meteor Crater, off I-40 at exit 233, is said to be the best preserved crater in the world. It was formed about 49,000 years ago when a giant nickel-iron ball weighing several million tons and traveling at a speed of 43,000 miles per hour slammed into the earth. It exploded with a force scientists believe was equal to 20 million tons of dynamite, destroying all life within a 100-mile radius and projecting fragments of itself as far as 3,000 feet beneath the surface of the earth. One scientist estimated the meteorite to be only 81 feet in diameter. The crater is nearly 600 feet deep, has a lip of about 150 feet, and is nearly a mile in diameter. Apparently some prehistoric peoples found the crater a suitable place to settle, as ruins have been found inside the rim. Prior to their moon landings in the late 1960s, the Apollo astronauts trained at Meteor Crater.

White men first noted the crater in 1871, but it was not thought to have been caused by a meteorite until 1886, when sheepherders found pieces of meteorite near Canyon Diablo. In the early twentieth century, mining engineer Daniel Barringer led the search, underground, for the meteor that had caused the crater. His search was largely futile, and modern technology reveals why: about 80 percent of the meteorite vaporized on impact; only about 10 percent still lies beneath the crater's south rim.

TWO GUNS

Two Guns sounds like a Wild West name conjured up for the benefit of the tourist trade, but Two Guns, thirty-five miles east of Flagstaff, had a brief, violent history that befits its name. The original inhabitant of the site was an ornery individual who called himself "Two Gun" Miller and claimed to be an Apache. The eccentric Miller lived in a cave in the walls of Canyon Diablo and was reported to be hostile to visitors. He once killed a neighbor in a fight, but the jury ruled it self-defense and Miller was acquitted. Some of the victim's friends inscribed on the grave marker, "Killed by Indian Miller." This angered Miller, so he painted out the uncomplimentary epitaph and was jailed temporarily for defacing a grave.

Just west of modern-day Two Guns is an interesting collection of "Indian pueblos" erected during the heyday of Route 66. Some of the old tourist-attracting signs are still hanging from the crumbling rock walls.

CANYON DIABLO

Because this 250-foot-deep gorge, spanning miles north and south of Two Guns, presented the greatest natural obstacle to Lt. Amiel Whipple on his historic thirty-fifth parallel survey in 1853 (see I-

The Atlantic & Pacific crossing Canyon Diablo,
1880s —Southwest Studies, Scottsdale Community College

40, Lupton–Flagstaff, Part 3), he called it Canyon Diablo (Devil's
Canyon). After Whipple's party reached the edge of the canyon,
Whipple wrote, "[W]e were all surprised to find at our feet, in
magnesian limestone, a chasm probably one hundred feet in
depth, the sides precipitous, and about 300 feet across at top.
[Whipple seriously underestimated the depth.] A thread-like rill
of water could be seen below, but descent was impossible."

The canyon itself runs for several miles on either side of I-40.
The canyon walls are literally covered with remnants of old rock
dwellings, all within sight of the highway. However, these
"ancient" pueblo ruins really date back to the 1930s; they were
built by entrepreneurs attempting to captivate tourists. A short
hike from Two Guns along a rock ridge leads to a closer view.

During construction of the railroad bridge over the gorge, a
settlement sprang up east of the bridge, called Canyon Diablo
after the gorge. For a time it was reputed to be one of the roughest
towns in the territory. During its peak, more men died in

gunfights, robberies, and murders than in Dodge City, Abilene, and Tombstone combined. At least thirty-five graves have been found in Canyon Diablo's boot hill; all but one were those of men who died with their boots on. The exception was a prostitute who had her throat cut.

Today Canyon Diablo, off I-40 on a rough dirt road, three miles north of Two Guns, is silent. The name is still partly visible on a white stucco adobe building on the north side of the tracks. Nearby are the melted mounds of adobe ruins, all that remains of the old town. The stillness is broken only by the occasional passing of a Santa Fe train.

WINONA

"Flagstaff, Arizona, don't forget Winona . . ." There's no doubt that Bobby Troup's lyrics in the hit song "Get Your Kicks on Route 66" gave tiny Winona more fame than one would expect. A mile east of Walnut Creek, Winona was originally a railroad stop called Walnut. In 1886 its name was changed to Winona. In the 1920s, Billy Adams, a local rancher, opened a gas station and campground along the National Trails Highway (Route 66); Winona locals boast it was the nation's first tourist campground. In the mid-1920s a new highway was built farther south, and the original community relocated there.

WALNUT CANYON NATIONAL MONUMENT

Walnut Canyon National Monument is several miles south of I-40 at exit 207 or 204. Sinagua Indians made their homes under the natural overhangs of steep-sided Walnut Canyon over 850 years ago. Their rock and clay dwellings are among the most unusual in the Southwest, built on the cliff's ledges. To get down to the home sites on the canyon's ledges, visitors must descend nearly 200 steep feet along a narrow trail.

To build their homes, the natives walled up the front between two ledges (one overhead and one underfoot) and made partitions with rocks mortared with clay. They smoothed the floors with plaster. Although the average height of the Sinagua was five foot six, the doorways were much smaller, probably to minimize the loss of warm air. Animal skins covered the doorway, and a small opening above the door allowed campfire smoke to escape.

A permanent stream flowing at the bottom of the 400-foot-deep chasm allowed native farmers to grow abundant crops of corn, beans, and squash. At one time the Sinagua occupied about 120 sites with about 400 rooms. Then, around A.D. 1250, they left the area, perhaps because of drought.

I-40
Flagstaff—Seligman
77 MILES

WILLIAMS

The picturesque town of Williams, about forty miles west of Flagstaff, takes its name from Bill Williams Mountain, which towers above the town, and the mountain is named for old Bill Williams, the "greatest fur trapper of 'em all."

Bill was as colorful a man as any who ever forked a horse or mule and headed toward the setting sun. To those who knew the tireless mountain man, he'd always seemed old and eccentric. His drunken sprees around Taos set a standard others tried to match but never could. He rode alone into forbidding hostile Indian country where no other white man before dared venture and always returned, his pack mules laden with beaver pelts.

Williams was a tall, skinny redhead with a high-pitched voice. His body was battle-scarred and weathered. Even in his later years, he had amazing endurance. He was known to run all day with six traps on his back and never break into a sweat. His walk resembled a stagger; it was never in a straight line. On horseback he wore his stirrups so short his knees bobbed just beneath his chin, and he leaned forward in the saddle, so he looked like a hunchback.

Williams fired his long-barreled "Kicking Betsy" with unerring accuracy, using a technique people called the "double wobble"— since he couldn't hold his gun steady for long, he just let it wobble back and forth until his sights crossed the target, then squeezed

Bill Williams Street, Williams, 1917
—Southwest Studies, Scottsdale Community College

the trigger. He bet on himself in shooting matches, at $100 a shot, and never lost.

People called Williams "Old Solitaire" for his lonesome ways, though he always seemed to have an Indian woman waiting somewhere. He spoke several Indian dialects and was more at home among the friendly tribes than he was with his own people. It was said he came west as a missionary to the Osage Indians, but they converted him. He married an Osage wife, who died after bearing two daughters, so he headed for the mountains and became a trapper.

Old Bill had more lives than a cat, surviving one hair-raising adventure after another. His luck finally ran out after thirty years in the wilds, when on March 14, 1849, a war party of Utes killed him near the headwaters of the Rio Grande in southern Colorado.

The first settlers arrived in Williams in 1876, about the same time that Flagstaff was settled. Like most communities in this area, nothing much happened until the railroad arrived on September 1, 1882. After that, the most important industries in the mountain settlement were cattle and lumber. That same month the *Prescott Miner* reported that Williams had 100 houses and over 500 residents, about the same number as Flagstaff.

Good help was hard to find in those new towns. In 1881 the *Miner* reported: "Geo. Rich, Deputy Sheriff of Williams, has resigned his position. He is supposed to have had a hand in the robbery lately committed upon the wholesale liquor firm of W. E. Talbott & Co., of Williams."

The Santa Fe laid track from Williams to the Grand Canyon in 1901 and began hauling tourists to the South Rim, giving Williams a legitimate claim to being the "Gateway to the Grand Canyon." The opening of Route 66 in the mid-1920s turned Williams into a first-class tourist town, as millions of cars passed through annually. In 1956 the federal government approved the construction of multiple-lane interstate freeways. Doomsayers claimed that the completion of these freeways would sound the death knell of towns like Williams, the last town on Route 66 to be bypassed by I-40; however, Williams continues to prosper with the reopening of passenger rail service to the Grand Canyon, and still bills itself as the Gateway to the Grand Canyon.

ASH FORK

The town of Ash Fork lies slumbering on gentle, juniper-studded slopes fifteen miles west of Bill Williams Mountain. In the late 1500s Spanish conquistadores found rich deposits of silver, gold, and copper in the mountains a few miles to the south. When this area was part of the Republic of Mexico, traders and fur trappers like Ewing Young, Antoine Leroux, Bill Williams, and Kit Carson went through today's Ash Fork on their way from Santa Fe to Los Angeles.

Cooper Thomas Lewis came to Ash Fork in 1882 and opened a grocery store next to the railroad tracks. Five generations later, some of Lewis's descendants still call Ash Fork home. On April 21, 1883, a post office was established in the town, and two years later Wells Fargo opened a station. The original town site, on the north side of the tracks, burned in 1893, and the present town was rebuilt on the south side.

Water, the arid Southwest's most precious commodity, was always scarce in Ash Fork. The porous lava that lies just beneath the surface in that region does not hold water. Water had to be hauled by train from Del Rio Springs in Chino Valley, thirty miles south. During the 1960s drillers finally hit water and a small well was able to provide an adequate supply.

A rail line running south to Prescott was finished in 1893. Because of its many curves and switchbacks, it was quickly dubbed the "Peavine." Two years later the line reached Phoenix, circumventing the mountains to do so. "It may take all day to get to Phoenix," it was said, "but you can see the country two or three times on one trip." This linking of Phoenix to Ash Fork in 1895 is regarded by many historians as marking the closing of the frontier period of Arizona's history.

In 1907 Fred Harvey opened one of his famous Harvey Houses, the Escalante, in Ash Fork (see Winslow). Citizens of Prescott thought nothing of driving fifty miles over a rough dirt road to dine at the Escalante. Cowboys rode forty miles just to sample the hot biscuits and catch a friendly smile from a "Harvey Girl." Few of Harvey's waitresses remained single for long.

When the Santa Fe moved its main line ten miles north of town in the 1950s, Ash Fork's prosperity faded. A tragic fire swept

The Escalante Harvey House —Southwest Studies, Scottsdale Community College

through the old business district in the mid-1970s, wiping out historic buildings. The famous old Escalante was torn down, the victim of an Arizona law that requires property owners to pay taxes on structures whether they are occupied or not. This law has contributed to the destruction of many important historical sites in the state. What many consider the fatal blow to downtown Ash Fork came in 1979, when the new I-40 bypassed the town.

Towns like Ash Fork don't die easily, however. Today, the town's few businessmen believe the worst is over and that the outlook is bright. Travelers on I-40 still stop for gas, food, and lodging. Mexican immigrants and other locals make a living as flagstone splitters. The freeway bypass may have been a blessing in disguise—eighteen-wheel trucks and out-of-state cars no longer come speeding through town at full throttle. Ash Fork is a quiet

This all-star baseball team with players from Williams, Ash Fork, and Seligman competed in Arizona's first Little League tournament in 1951, losing the title game to Prescott, 2-0. Author, middle row, left end. —Courtesy author

community again, reminiscent of bygone days when people weren't in such a hurry. The mountain setting is a refreshing change from the crowded streets of Phoenix.

SELIGMAN

Seligman, twenty-four miles west of Ash Fork, was established a few years later than the other communities stretched out along the Santa Fe line. Originally called Prescott Junction, Seligman takes its name from a pair of New York bankers. The Seligman brothers had helped bankroll and were part owners of the spectacular Aztec Land & Cattle Company (the Hashknife outfit). They were also large stockholders in the Atlantic & Pacific Railroad.

First the railroad, then the tourist traffic along Route 66 were Seligman's main sources of economic security for the first three-quarters of the twentieth century. In the late 1970s the new I-40 bypassed the town, and in February 1985 an even more serious blow to the local economy came when the Santa Fe closed its operations. Seligman had been a terminal point on the line between Winslow and Needles, and dozens of railroaders had rented rooms, eaten in local cafes, and patronized other businesses in town during their layover. Today, express trains flash through Seligman without stopping, declaring the end of the town's illustrious railroad history.

I-40
Seligman—Topock
123 MILES

Between Seligman and Kingman, the interstate, more direct here than Route 66, runs close to the old Hardyville-Prescott Road. In 1864, when most freight reached Arizona by steamboat, William Hardy established a port on the Colorado River. Now Hardyville lies buried beneath the waters of Lake Mohave. The stretch of road between Kingman and Topock, opened in the 1950s to bypass treacherous Oatman Pass in the Black Mountains, hugs the old 1883 railroad line.

FORT ROCK

Now just a name on the map south of I-40 near milepost 95, Fort Rock was once a stage station called Mount Hope on the Hardyville-Prescott Road. The place received its new name in an unusual way. Between 1866 and 1868, the Walapai War took place between the Hualapai people and the U.S. Army. At the beginning of the war, in 1866, stationmaster J. J. Buckman's young son Thad was building a stone playhouse when a large party of Hualapai attacked the station. Caught outside when the shooting started, Buckman and a soldier jumped behind the playhouse for protection. From both inside the station and behind the playhouse's low rock wall, the defenders held off more than fifty warriors for an entire day before finally driving them off. In 1879, after a post office had been established, the station was dubbed Fort Rock in honor of the occasion thirteen years earlier.

Also in 1866, near Fort Rock, a battle took place between Troop E of the 1st U.S. Cavalry and Hualapai warriors after the soldiers happened upon a Hualapai camp. Twenty warriors were killed; sixteen women and children were captured; and seven troopers and Lt. Patrick Hasson were wounded.

KINGMAN

Kingman, at the junction of I-40, AZ 66, and US 93, was established as a railroad stop in 1883 on the last leg along the thirty-fifth parallel line. Because of the railroad, Mohave County's most important city was selected as county seat in 1887.

In addition to its importance as a rail stop, Kingman was a regular stop for early mail and passenger airlines. On July 8, 1928, more than 1,500 Arizonans greeted Charles A. Lindbergh, the first pilot to fly solo across the Atlantic, when he arrived in Kingman to inaugurate a new forty-eight-hour airmail service between Los Angeles and New York.

An interesting piece of Hollywood trivia is that Clark Gable and Carole Lombard were married in the little Methodist church

Kingman, looking north on Fourth Street, 1919
—Mohave County Historical Society

in Kingman. Actor Andy Devine, though born in Flagstaff, was raised in Kingman and always referred to it as his hometown. The town's main street is named for Devine, considered one of Hollywood's greatest character actors.

The construction of dams along the Colorado River during the first half of the twentieth century and gold mining in the mountains of Mohave County brought further prosperity to Kingman. During World War II, the military built an air force base in Kingman, at the site of today's Mohave County Airport, increasing the town's growth even more. After the war, the base served as a storage area for surplus war planes.

Since World War II, Kingman has continued its spectacular growth, illustrating the importance of its location at the juction of two major highways: to the north on US 93 are Hoover Dam and Las Vegas; US 93 southbound goes to Phoenix; westbound I-40 leads to Los Angeles; and eastbound I-40 connects with every major highway system in the eastern United States.

YUCCA

Yucca, twenty-six miles south of Kingman, has been here since 1905, when a post office was established. The town took its name from the prolific growth of yucca in the area. The best-known yucca in these parts is the Joshua tree, which has dense clusters of spiky leaves atop a tall trunk. At the height of gold mining in the mountains nearby, the trees' thick trunks were used for fuel. Yucca was important to prehistoric people and Native Americans. People have long used its tough leaf fibers for rope, mats, sandals, and basketry, eaten its fruits and seeds, and used the roots for soap and shampoo.

TOPOCK

Nobody seems to know the origin of the name Topock; it's probably a corruption of a Mojave word for either "wave" or "bridge." Topock was originally called Needles, after the pointed mountains on the California side of the Colorado River. It has also been called Powell, after the Grand Canyon explorer, Red Rock, and Mellon, after the legendary Colorado River steamboat skipper Capt. Jack Mellon. In 1916, a bridge with a graceful arch spanned the Colorado River. Route 66 crossed the river on the bridge. The bridge is still there, though today its only function is to support a pipeline—cars no longer use it.

AZ 66, Oatman Road, and Old Highway 66
Seligman—Topock
160 MILES

Northwest of Seligman, old Route 66 becomes AZ 66 and follows Ned Beale's 1857 survey across the Aubry Valley to Kingman ("Aubry" is usually misspelled on maps as "Aubrey"). The valley was named for the great "Skimmer of the Plains," François Aubry. Until 1952, the original highway then went in a southwesterly direction, cutting and twisting its way through the Black Mountains and the picturesque towns of Goldroad and Oatman. This section is now called Oatman Road. South of Oatman, the road is marked as Old Highway 66. It has a few potholes here and there, but the trip is worth the extra time and wear.

YAMPAI

Yampai is about twenty miles north of Seligman on AZ 66. The town was named for the Yampai Indians, a nomadic people. They were probably the ancestors of the Hualapai tribes of today, but not much is known of them. They are mentioned in the reports of Sitgreaves, Whipple, and Beale, and their remarks are not complimentary. Some historians believe "Yampai" was a misspelling of "Yavapai," the name of another group of Arizona Indians.

PEACH SPRINGS

Recorded history of Peach Springs goes all the way back to the days of that tireless Franciscan explorer, Father Francisco Tomás Garcés. On June 15, 1775, Garcés named this spring Pozos de San Basilio (St. Basil's Wells). Lt. Ned Beale, who visited with his camel entourage on September 17, 1858, called it Indian Spring. The peach trees in this area apparently grew from pits the Mormons planted, since no mention of peach trees was made before their arrival.

The springs in Peach Springs Canyon provided water for steam locomotives in early railroad days. The railroad built a water tank and station at this site, and a community grew up around the station. In 1883 a traveler wrote in his diary that the town had ten saloons; he did not mention the number of churches or schools.

Peach Springs is the tribal headquarters of the Hualapai Indians. The Hualapai Reservation, established in 1883, and the adjacent Havasupai Reservation both border Grand Canyon National Park. Both tribes are related linguistically to the Yuma, or Quechan, people. Hualapai means "Pine Tree People" and Havasupai, "People of the Blue-Green Water."

Traditionally the Hualapai were hunters and gatherers in a vast area bounded by the San Francisco Peaks to the east, the Bradshaw Mountains to the south, the Grand Canyon to the north, and the Colorado River to the west. The Havasupai, their close relatives, learned to grow corn, beans, and squash from the Hopi Indians when they took up residence in fertile Cataract Canyon. Early accounts refer to the Havasupai as Cosninos, a name given them by the Hopi. "Cosninos" had several spelling variations, one of which was "Coconino"—a name chosen, later, for Coconino County.

Originally the primary villages of the Hualapai were scattered along the Colorado River above the Mojave villages; across the Aquarius Mountains; and in the Hualapai, Sacramento, and Yavapai Valleys. The discovery of rich minerals in the Cerbat Mountains, part of the Hualapai range, brought in prospectors, freighters, and inevitably, conflict. In the 1860s the Hualapai, under their chiefs Wauba-Yuba, Scherum, and Walapais Charley, fought the U.S. army. After Wauba-Yuba was murdered at Beale Springs by a party of whites, all-out war between the Hualapai and the army followed. However, no match for the soldiers, the Hualapai were quickly defeated and moved to a reservation in the malaria-infested tules along the Colorado River. After a few years they were allowed to return to the beloved home surroundings that had inspired their name.

Today some 2,200 Hualapai live on nearly a million acres along the Colorado River and south of the Grand Canyon. Among other enterprises, they operate the only Indian-owned-and-operated river rafting company on the Colorado.

HACKBERRY

The spring near Hackberry is probably the same site Lieutenant Beale called Gardiner. In the 1870s prospectors found a rich vein of gold a mile and a half west of the spring. A large hackberry tree nearby inspired the name for the mine and the settlement that followed, as a newspaper of the time explained: "[After] this tree which in summer bears an abundance of fruit . . . they have named the beautiful mine with the hope that it may prove as prolific of bullion as the tree of edible berries."

For a time, Hackberry prospered with a population of over 100. The hackberry tree continued to bear fruit, but the mine eventually played out. Today, the main attraction is the Old Route 66 Visitor Center, built in 1934 as the Hackberry General Store. The revival of interest in Route 66 means many "roadies" are visiting these towns bypassed by I-40 and pumping new life into them.

From Hackberry, AZ 66 continues west and south twenty-four miles to Kingman, where it again merges with I-40. Ten miles farther south, at the town of McConnico, Oatman Road follows the route of the original Route 66 southwest to Goldroad.

GOLDROAD

Though a party of prospectors led by John Moss first discovered gold deposits here in the 1860s, Goldroad only really came to life when prospector Joe (José) Jerez's pick struck pay dirt in 1902. Jerez and the man who grubstaked him, Henry Lovin, sold their claim for $25,000, and Lovin opened a store in the town. For a time Goldroad was known as Acme. A post office opened in 1903. By 1907 the high-grade ore was starting to play out, and the mine soon closed—at least for a time. For the next few decades, the town hung on, with the post office closing and opening periodically. Finally in 1949, remaining buildings were torn down for tax purposes. Today only the crumbling rock walls of a few miners' homes still stand.

The Goldroad Mine remains, however, and has gone back into production on and off over the years. Between 1995 and 1997, under the ownership of Addwest Minerals, it produced 92,500 ounces of gold. But in 1998, when the price of gold dropped, the company suspended operations. While the company waits for prices to rise, portions of the mine are open for tours.

OATMAN

Oatman, a few miles west of Goldroad, had its rise to prominence about the same time as Goldroad. In 1902 Ben Taddock was riding along a trail when he saw the unmistakable glitter of yellow. A year later Taddock sold out to several speculators, who in turn sold the property to the Vivian Mining Company. The next three years were boom times, the mine producing more than $3 million in gold. It was during this period that Oatman came into existence. At first it was called Vivian, but in 1909 the name was changed to Oatman.

There has been some speculation that the town was named for Olive Oatman, the girl kidnapped by a war party in 1851 near Gila Bend and later traded to Mojave Indians (see Oatman

Oatman in the early 1900s —Southwest Studies, Scottsdale Community College

Flat). In 1857 Henry Grinnell was able to secure Olive's release. According to local legend, Olive was found near the site of present-day Oatman. Another account says the town was named for a half-blood Mojave Indian named John Oatman, who claimed to be Olive's son. The town might have been named for him, but he was not Olive Oatman's son, as she did not have any children during her captivity.

In 1910, just as the Vivian Mine was beginning to play out, another rich discovery, the Tom Reed Mine, brought new life to Oatman's economy. In 1916 the Tom Reed Mine and the Goldroad Mine were combined into the Oatman District. Mining historians consider the Oatman District to be the richest gold-mining area in Arizona. Oatman remained a prosperous mining community into the 1930s before hard times came once again. Hollywood discovered the town in the late 1930s, when, to escape reporters, Clark Gable and Carole Lombard honeymooned in the old hotel in downtown Oatman.

When old Route 66 closed in 1952, Oatman's population dwindled to sixty. During the early 1960s, a major segment of the epic movie *How the West Was Won* was filmed in Oatman. Some of the false-front buildings from the movie set are still standing. Today, Oatman has come back and thrives as a tourist town. Descendants of the mining town's ubiquitous "desert canaries"—the burros who hauled the ore—still stalk the streets of Oatman, adding to its colorful character.

A mile or so south of Oatman, drivers can pick up Old Highway 66, a stretch of the original Route 66, to Topock.

US 191
Chambers–US 160
137 MILES

CANYON DE CHELLY NATIONAL MONUMENT AND CHINLE

The 140-mile stretch of open highway between Chambers, on I-40, and Teec Nos Pos, on US 160 near the Utah border, runs through the Navajo Indian Reservation. At Canyon de Chelly National Monument, two canyons, Canyon de Chelly (pronounced duh-SHAY) and Canyon del Muerto, come together like a giant turkey footprint. It is thought that "de Chelly," probably derived from Spanish, Navajo, and English, means "Among the Cliffs" or "Rock Canyon." In places, sheer, salmon-hued sandstone walls rise 1,000 feet from the canyon floor. The monument encompasses about 2,000 prehistoric sites and twelve major ruins. About 2,000 years ago, nomadic tribes roamed these canyons. The Ancestral Pueblo (Anasazi) arrived around the time of Christ. Around A.D. 1100 they built dwellings in the canyon walls, housing an estimated population of 1,000. For mysterious reasons, however, the culture went into decline after 1300, and the villages were abandoned.

Canyon de Chelly —Southwest Studies, Scottsdale Community College

Navajo moved into the canyon and began farming there around 1700. The canyon was their hideout and retreat during raids on Indian and Spanish neighbors. Canyon del Muerto (Canyon of the Dead) takes its name from a retaliatory massacre of Navajo by Spanish troops in 1805. Pursued by the Spanish, the Navajo scaled the 1,000-foot cliff to shelter in a shallow cave. When Lt. Antonio Narbona's soldiers arrived on the canyon rim, however, they were able to fire their muskets down into the cave and kill 115 people. Today, the site honors a Navajo woman who lunged at one of the soldiers and pulled him off the cliff with her. In Navajo, the place is called Adah Aho doo nili, or "Two Went Off."

Chinle, located at the junction of the two canyons, is best known as the gateway to Canyon de Chelly. Near Chinle in 1864, Col. Kit Carson held a parley with the Navajo that ended a long war between the Navajo and the Americans. Carson had been ordered to exterminate the Navajo; instead, he drove them into these canyons and starved them into submission. Following his relentless campaign, more than 8,000 Navajo surrendered and were taken on the famous "Long Walk"—300 to 400 miles—to the Pecos River Reservation, also known as Fort Sumner, at Bosque Redondo, New Mexico.

It had been prophesied that if tribal members ever crossed three rivers, terrible things would happen. Indeed, the "Long Walk" took them across the Rio Puerco, the Rio Grande, and finally the Pecos. What followed were four years of disease, hunger, terrible living conditions, conflict with Apache camp mates (their age-old enemies), and white efforts to change their ways. Many died on the way to Bosque Redondo; more died after they reached it. Finally in 1868 the government entered into a peace treaty with the Navajo and allowed them to return to their northern Arizona home. The column of people, animals, and wagons that headed west in June stretched ten miles long. In 1968 portions of Fort Sumner and Bosque Redondo Reservation were declared a New Mexico State Monument.

At Canyon de Chelly, visitors can drive around the top of the various canyons. Hikes must be in the company of a guide; unaccompanied hikes are acceptable along the White House Trail. At the end of the nineteen-mile South Rim Drive, the 800-foot monolith rising from the canyon floor is the legendary home of Spider Woman, a Navajo deity. Navajo parents warn their children when they misbehave that Spider Woman takes bad little kids, carries them to the top of the monolith, and devours them. The white limestone cap atop the rock is supposed to be their bleached bones.

AZ 264
Window Rock—Tuba City
156 MILES

AZ 264 winds north of I-40 through canyon country, crossing the Navajo and Hopi Indian Reservations. The 25,000-square-mile Navajo Reservation, which extends into Utah and New Mexico and is the largest in North America, surrounds the Hopi Reservation.

WINDOW ROCK AND THE
NAVAJO INDIAN RESERVATION

Window Rock, near the New Mexico border, is the tribal capital of the Navajo Nation, the largest Native American tribe in the United States. An eighty-five-acre tribal park surrounds the town, named for the Window Rock formation, a circular, fifty-foot opening in a huge sandstone ridge. This unique natural formation is a sacred place to the Navajo.

Origins of the Navajo

Along with the Apache—their relatives, long ago—the Navajo are Arizona's only Athabascan-speaking Indians. They arrived in the Southwest from Asia via Canada perhaps as early as A.D. 1100. While their name for themselves is *Diné* (the People), the Zuni name for them, *Apache de Navahu* (Enemies of the Arroyo with the Cultivated Fields), shortened to Navajo, lasted. Navajo lands are known as *Dinetah* (Among the People).

Eventually, the Apache and the Navajo broke into separate groups. The Navajo moved into the Four Corners area, where the Arizona, Utah, Colorado, and New Mexico borders meet. More sedentary than their Apache cousins, the Navajo farmed some of the old areas previously occupied by the prehistoric Ancestral Pueblo (Anasazi). They began to adopt the customs and culture of the area's Pueblo Indians, including certain origin myths and ceremonies; matrilineal and clan systems of organizing society; and crafts such as sandpainting and weaving. Despite these adaptations, they preferred living in their own style of circular, domelike hogans.

A Warring Nation

From the 1600s onward, the Navajo in the Four Corners area and Spanish settlers living along the Rio Grande continually raided each other. The Spanish used captured Navajo as slaves on their ranches. The Navajo took Spanish women, children, and livestock, often raising the children as their own. Not all the Navajo were guilty of these transgressions. Navajo society divided into two groups: the *Ricos* or wealthy Navajo (with much livestock), who had no need to raid the Spanish; and the *Ladrones* or outlaws, who stole as a way of life.

Navajo hogans —Author photo

When American troops arrived in New Mexico in 1846, they agreed to protect Spanish settlers from Navajo raiders if the settlers would support the new American government. American soldiers began riding into Navajoland on punitive expeditions. Unfortunately they paid no attention to the distinction between Rico and Ladrone. Seeing only "Navajo," they took the peaceful Ricos' sheep and "returned" them to the Spanish. Soon the Ricos were becoming poor and the Ladrones were running free.

In the 1850s the army launched several military campaigns against the Navajo, but the Indians evaded the soldiers by hiding out in Canyon de Chelly and other remote canyons. The army established Fort Defiance in 1851 as a base for continued action against the Navajo. After Navajo nearly captured the fort, the army called in Kit Carson, whose 1864 "scorched earth" campaign finally forced the Navajo to abandon their homeland—at least temporarily (see Chinle and Canyon de Chelly). After their return to their ancestral lands in 1868 and the creation of their reservation, the Navajo gave up their warlike ways.

Navajo scouts (no date) —Southwest Studies, Scottsdale Community College

A Family of Leaders

Henry Chee Dodge was the last chief of the Navajo tribe and first chairman of the Navajo Tribal Council. He was born at Fort Defiance on February 22, 1860, the son of a Navajo-Jemez mother and a Mexican father, Juan Cocinas. Orphaned and lost at age four, he was found by a young Navajo girl and her grandfather. The three later surrendered to American soldiers. By age twenty, Chee had become the official interpreter for the Navajo people, and four years later, he was made head chief of the Navajo tribe. After accumulating several thousand dollars, Chee invested in a trading post and farmlands, and his herds increased rapidly.

*Henry Chee
Dodge as army
interpreter*
—Southwest Studies,
Scottsdale Community
College

Throughout his career, Chee encouraged both education and the continuance of traditional Navajo customs. Investing in sheep and cattle, he became even wealthier. When the Navajo Tribal Council formed in 1923, Chee served as its first chairman until 1928, then again from 1942 to 1946. He died at Ganado on January 7, 1947, one of the most honored and respected leaders of his time.

Annie Dodge, Henry Chee Dodge's daughter, was born in 1910. Annie tended her father's sheep until she was old enough for the boarding school at Fort Defiance. When she was eight, the great flu epidemic of 1918–19 hit the Navajo Reservation, and the young girl aided nurses during the outbreak. Four years later a trachoma epidemic struck Navajoland. These devastating events would influence the course of Annie's life.

At school in Albuquerque, Annie Dodge met George Wauneka and married him in 1929 in a traditional Navajo ceremony. It was an unusual marriage for a Navajo girl in that she, not her parents, chose George. The pair went on to have six children. Her father also lived with the family in their home at Klagetoh. In addition to her duties as mother, wife, and daughter, Annie Wauneka traveled with her father as his aide, attending meetings in chapter houses across the vast Navajo Reservation. Her travels made her acutely aware of the poverty, disease, and malnutrition plaguing her people.

In 1951, four years after Chee Dodge's death, the people of Klagetoh voted Annie onto the tribal council. The first woman elected to that governing body, she served until 1978. During her run for a second term in 1954, one of the men she defeated for the council seat was her own husband, George.

Annie's prime mission was to bring medicine men and white doctors together to fight tuberculosis, the greatest killer on the reservation. She also wrote a dictionary defining Navajo medical terms in English, and the white man's medical terms in Navajo. She reached out across the reservation through a regular radio program on topics of health and sanitary living conditions.

During her life Annie Wauneka was honored with many awards, including the Presidential Medal of Freedom, presented by President Lyndon B. Johnson. She died on November 10, 1997. In 2000 she became the fourth Native American woman inducted into the National Women's Hall of Fame.

Navajo Code Talkers of World War II

During World War II, Navajo "code talker" marines saved countless American lives at Guadalcanal, Saipan, Iwo Jima, Okinawa, and other Pacific battles and campaigns by fooling the Japanese with their ingenious code. Originally there were 29 Navajo volunteers but ultimately they numbered as many as 1,500.

The first news of war brought a surge of volunteers from remote Navajoland. The young men's warrior heritage and traditional Navajo pride called for them to join the roughest, toughest fighting outfit in the service, the Marines.

Navajo marine "code talkers" —United States Marine Corps

Japanese intelligence officers, often schooled in America, spoke fluent English and were well-versed in American pop culture, from Betty Grable's measurements to Babe Ruth's home-run record. They succeeded in intercepting messages and creating chaos on American military radios—until the Navajo arrived. Recruited on the reservation and trained at Camp Pendleton, California, the code talkers used their native language to create a code that confused and confounded the Japanese. The code was never broken and was so hush-hush that the Navajo were sworn to secrecy even after the war.

After the project was declassified in 1968, the code talkers still received no official recognition. It was more than fifty years after the end of the war before they were finally awarded a special Congressional Gold Medal. By that time only five of the original twenty-nine code talkers were still alive.

Navajoland Today

Worldwide, the Navajo are perhaps best known for their arts and crafts, highly valued by collectors and tourists. The Navajo learned silversmithing from the Spanish and weaving from the Hopi. From there they took both skills to higher levels, eventually making themselves and their art famous.

Navajo life today is changing rapidly. The desire for consumer goods causes more people to seek wages outside the reservation. Although farming and sheepraising are still symbolically important, fewer people are living in the traditional way. With a wealth of coal, uranium, and gas on the reservation, one of the greatest challenges facing the Navajo today is how to develop these resources while preserving time-honored values. Another challenge is a long-standing land dispute with the Hopi (see Keams Canyon and the Hopi Indian Reservation).

GANADO AND HUBBELL TRADING POST NATIONAL HISTORIC SITE

Trader John Lorenzo Hubbell named the town he founded for his friend Ganado Mucho (Many Cattle), a local Navajo chief. The community grew up around the trading post, built in 1883. In its early days, Hubbell Trading Post was one of the foremost posts in the Southwest, taking in $250,000 in wool and hides alone. Amazingly, the trading post is still in business. The oldest continuously operating Navajo trading post, it is now a national historic site run by the National Park Service.

John Lorenzo Hubbell was born of a Spanish mother and Anglo father in Pajarito, New Mexico, in 1853. He came to Ganado at age twenty-three and remained here until his death in 1930. Hubbell homesteaded this piece of land before it became part of the Navajo Reservation, but he almost lost it when the reservation was enlarged in 1880. With help from his friend Teddy Roosevelt, he was allowed to keep his property. One of Roosevelt's first acts as president was to sign a bill confirming Hubbell's title to his land.

Don Lorenzo, as he was called, was a remarkable man, fluent in four languages—English, Spanish, Navajo, and Hopi. He was always trying to improve the economic lot of the Indians through

Hubbell Trading Post —Author photo

various ventures. One time he brought a silversmith from Mexico to teach silverworking to the natives. Hubbell was also a politician. He was elected sheriff of Apache County in 1882. Later he was a member of the territorial legislature, and from 1912 to 1915 he was a state senator. He ran unsuccessfully for the U.S. Senate in 1914.

Though a friend of presidents, Hubbell was happiest at his remote trading post dealing with the people he had come to know and respect. For the most part, the natives reciprocated these feelings. Dubbed "Lorenzo the Magnificent" by author Hamlin Garland, John Lorenzo Hubbell represented the highest ideal of the Indian trader.

Today, walking into the Hubbell Trading Post is like taking a long step back in time. The long, flat-roofed building is constructed of large, salmon-hued sandstone rocks. The inside walls are of thick plaster reminiscent of an old Spanish hacienda, and the floor is of well-worn hardwood. Huge beams of ponderosa pine stretch across the ceiling, acting as hangers for such former

Early tourists at Hubbell Trading Post, 1920s —Arizona State Library

essentials as saddles and horse collars. Stark, bare lightbulbs dangling at the ends of electrical cords illuminate the room. Except for these 1920-vintage electric lights, the venerable trading post has not changed much since 1883. While most of the post's business today is with tourists, Navajo still come in to trade wool blankets or silver jewelry, bartering with a white trader in their native tongue.

KEAMS CANYON AND THE HOPI INDIAN RESERVATION

Keams Canyon, in the Hopi Reservation, is the seat of tribal government for the Hopi. It was named for Thomas V. Keams, an Englishman who established a trading post here in 1872. The government built an Indian school at Keams Canyon in 1886 and a Hopi agency three years later.

Hopi women (no date) —Southwest Studies, Scottsdale Community College

The correct name for Arizona's only Pueblo Indians is Hopitu, meaning "the Peaceful People." Descended in part from the prehistoric Ancestral Pueblo Culture, the Hopi are a melting pot of different peoples. It is said that each new arrival had to demonstrate some contribution before being accepted into the tribe.

The Hopi have inhabited these lands since the twelfth century. Most of the villages on the reservation are perched on top of three barren limestone mesas that extend out on the south end of Black Mesa. These mesas are called First, Second, and Third, moving east to west, though the Hopi number them west to east. There are also numerous springs and washes throughout the area.

The first whites to visit Hopi lands were soldiers from Coronado's expedition in 1540, during his quest for the mythical Seven Cities of Gold. Other Spanish explorers, including Espejo,

Walpi Pueblo on First Mesa (no date) —Arizona Historical Foundation

Farfán, and Oñate, all visited the mesas in the late 1500s. Franciscans established the first mission on Hopi land in 1629. Although the Hopi are generally peaceful, they fiercely resisted the missionaries' attempts to Christianize them. Finally, during the Great Pueblo Revolt of 1680, the Hopi destroyed the church, killed four priests, and drove the rest of the missionaries out. They used beams from the church to construct a new kiva at the pueblo of Oraibi, still in use today. Since the revolt, Catholics have not been allowed to build churches on the mesas. Other church groups have also met resistance. In 1901, Mennonites built a church on the mesa near Oraibi without village consent. Lightning struck the church not once, but twice.

The Hopi villages have a complicated, interwoven social structure. Like the city-states of ancient Greece, each village is a separate power. Each individual has a particular responsibility, and each clan is designated for particular duties. The clan system is much stronger among the Hopi than among other Pueblo peoples. Although a man marries and lives with his wife near her clan, he still has responsibility to his own clan—his "real home." Women own the pueblo, gardens, and furnishings, while men take care of herding, farming, and activities away from the village.

Religion is a seven-day-a-week affair with the Hopi. All villages have kivas, or underground ceremonial chambers, characterized by long ladder-poles extending through a hole in the roof. Hopi ceremonial life is complex. Agriculture figures prominently in Hopi ritual, with corn an important symbol. All ritual really has to do with being Hopi—achieving "Hopiness." Ceremonies begin in January and last until the crops are harvested in the late summer. Today these celebrations are usually held on weekends to accommodate tribal members who live off the reservation.

Spiritual kachinas visiting a village (artist unknown)
—Southwest Studies, Scottsdale Community College

Hopi kachina doll maker —Southwest Studies, Scottsdale Community College

In Hopi culture, "kachina" refers to three things: spirit beings, the male dancers who impersonate these beings in ceremonies, and masked figurines or dolls of the dancers. According to Hopi beliefs, the spirit kachinas reside high in the San Francisco Mountains and visit the villages periodically, bringing gifts. Not all kachinas are benevolent, however. Some are ogres who handle discipline. The purpose of figurine kachinas is to teach Hopi youngsters about their religion.

Hopi-Navajo Land Dispute

Sometime during the late 1700s, the Navajo began encroaching on the vast stretches of Hopi land surrounding the mesas. In 1864 Col. Kit Carson and his troops rounded up about 8,000 Navajo and confined them to a reservation in New Mexico. Four years later, however, they were allowed to return to the Four Corners area, where a reservation was established. In 1882 the Hopi Reservation was vastly reduced to about 2.5 million acres, while the Navajo continued to grow. Soon the Navajo were moving onto Hopi lands again.

In 1962 a federal panel declared 1.8 million acres formerly occupied by Navajo to be a joint-use area owned equally by the two tribes. In further legislation in 1974, this land was partitioned, requiring 100 Hopi and 10,000 Navajo to move. Today, the Hopi and Navajo are still working out the difficulties of coexistence.

SHUNGOPAVI

Shungopavi (pronounced shum-oh-PAH-vee) is known as the home of Louis Tewanima, the "happy Hopi from Shungopavi." Perhaps the world's best-known Hopi, Tewanima was one of America's greatest distance runners. He received his early training chasing jackrabbits, and just for sport he used to run sixty-seven

Hopi runner Louis Tewanima (front, third from right) and Jim Thorpe (front, fourth from left) at Carlisle Indian School; Glen "Pop" Warner, who later gained fame as a football coach, in suit —Courtesy Charlotte Thorpe

miles along what is today AZ 87 from Shungopavi, on Second Mesa, to Winslow to watch the trains; then he'd run back home again—the same day.

Tewanima attended school at the famous Carlisle Indian School in Pennsylvania with Jim Thorpe, another great athlete and a Sac Fox from Oklahoma. In the 1908 Olympics in London, Tewanima finished ninth in the marathon. In 1912 he won the silver medal in the 10,000-meter run at Stockholm, a record not matched by an American until another Indian, Billy Mills, won the gold in 1964.

Tewanima died in 1969, at age ninety-two. Going home from a ceremony on a dark night, he took a wrong turn at Second Mesa and fell seventy feet to his death. When the Arizona Sports Hall of Fame was created in 1949, the first athlete selected was Louis Tewanima.

OLD ORAIBI

Old Oraibi, sitting on top of Third Mesa, has been occupied since about A.D. 1100 and is considered by many scholars to be the oldest continuously inhabited village in America. It was the largest of the pueblos until 1906, when a rift occurred within the tribe, and the so-called "hostiles" and "friendlies" had a falling out. The two factions' leaders had a traditional shoving match, after which the loser and his followers moved out, settling at Hotevilla. It was a hard year for the defeated, and a few decided to return to Oraibi. The returnees were refused permission to reenter, so in 1907 they established the community of Bacabi.

MOENKOPI

In 1870 Chief Tuba, or Tuvi, village leader at Oraibi, established a farming settlement along Moenkopi Wash—a place for the people on Third Mesa to irrigate their crops. Moenkopi, which means "Place of the Running Water" in Hopi, is the only Hopi pueblo with a reliable source of surface water for farming. The Hopi, long known for their ability as distance runners, used to jog from Oraibi to Moenkopi, a distance of sixty-two miles, to tend crops. There is evidence that Hopi lived at Moenkopi before Chief Tuba's settlement, as well.

Hopi men emerging from underground kiva at
Old Oraibi, Third Mesa (no date) —Southwest Studies,
Scottsdale Community College

In 1879 the Hopi allowed John W. Young to establish a Mormon colony at Moenkopi and run a woolen mill using native labor. Believing the Native Americans to be descendants of the "lost tribes of Israel," the Mormons attempted to assist and to maintain friendly relations with all Indian tribes. However, the Moenkopi enterprise had a short life; the Hopi didn't like working with machinery.

Today, the community has two sections. The upper village participates in the Hopi Tribal Council, while the more conservative lower village does not. In recent years, the growth and encroachment of Tuba City, a Navajo community barely two miles away, has created tension among the people of Moenkopi.

TUBA CITY

In the 1870s a supply station was established at Musha Springs, the site of present-day Tuba City, two miles north of Moenkopi, for Mormons traveling into Arizona from Utah. Jacob Hamblin was in the area during the 1850s and 1860s. Hamblin was a trailblazer and an excellent goodwill ambassador to the Indians, especially the Hopi. In 1878, the Mormon apostle Erastus Snow mapped out a town at the site and named it Tuba or Toova City in honor of the Hopi leader at Oraibi, Tuvi. When the Navajo reservation was enlarged in 1880, Mormon settlers in the area found themselves on land set aside for the Indians. The federal government bought them out in 1903.

Dating from 1870, the Tuba City Trading Post is the oldest trading post on the western portion of the Navajo Reservation. Around 1900 the Babbitt Brothers Trading Company bought the store and operated it for nearly a century. The two-story octagon was added in 1920. The trading post remains a popular tourist attraction. The old lodge was the launching point for President Theodore Roosevelt's expeditions into the uncharted region in the early 1900s. Zane Grey penned three of his books at the lodge, and legendary Hollywood director John Ford used it as a darkroom to process the film shot in his Monument Valley movies of the 1950s.

US 160
Tuba City—Four Corners Monument
150 MILES

US 160 from Tuba City to Four Corners spans most of the Arizona section of the Navajo Reservation from west to east, passing through several tiny reservation towns. About halfway across is the turnoff for Monument Valley.

NAVAJO NATIONAL MONUMENT

In the settlements they built in canyons throughout the Four Corners area, the Ancestral Pueblo people had an advanced culture. Some of the most interesting and best-preserved Ancestral Pueblo sites in Arizona are at Navajo National Monument, on AZ 564 off US 160. The pueblos' occupants abandoned the sites around A.D. 1300 after occupying them for only about fifty years.

Betatakin, situated under an impervious dome at the bottom of an 800-foot-deep canyon, exemplifies the ingenious Ancestral Puebloan awareness of solar energy. Settlements in these cliffs were always situated to receive maximum sunlight in the cold winter months and shade during summer. Great kivas— underground ceremonial centers—indicate a rich and advanced culture. This people's mastery of agriculture allowed them to store large amounts of surplus food in large baskets or pottery containers. They also had the ability to construct multistoried masonry buildings without mortar. From the visitor center, one can see Betatakin in the distance, but to explore it or another site, visitors must hike five or more miles and join a tour with a ranger.

TEEC NOS POS

Teec Nos Pos (pronounced tees-NAHS-pas), population approximately 300, is in the farthest northeast corner of Arizona on the Navajo Reservation. In Navajo, Teec Nos Pos refers to a circle of cottonwood trees. One particular style of Navajo weaving—characterized by bold, intricate designs and subtle color—bears the name of this town and the surrounding area. The trading post at Teec Nos Pos, run by the Foutz family, has been the community gathering place since 1905.

FOUR CORNERS MONUMENT

About five miles north of Teec Nos Pos on US 160 is Four Corners Monument. Four Corners aptly fits the old description of going "from no place through nothing to nowhere." Its real significance lies in the fact that it is the only place in the United States where four states—Arizona, Colorado, Utah, and New Mexico—come together. There are no towns close by. Despite the roughly 2,000 travelers who pass through each summer, the average stay ranges from a five-minute photo op to a slightly longer ramble past the tents and tables of vendors selling curios.

An unprepossessing slab marks where the four states meet. In 1949, a tablecloth was laid over the slab so the governors of the four neighboring states could have lunch together, each seated in his own state. Among the items on the agenda was resolution of a boundary dispute dating from an 1868 survey that erroneously placed the state line 100 yards south of where it should have been, along the thirty-seventh parallel. Despite proof of the error, the Supreme Court decided in 1925 to let the boundary stand—to the frustration of the Ute and Navajo peoples. The Navajo treaty with the United States sets the Navajo Reservation border at the thirty-seventh parallel. The Ute Reservation ends at the Colorado–New Mexico line. The governors' luncheon did nothing to resolve the issue.

US 163
US 160—Utah Border
22 MILES

MONUMENT VALLEY NAVAJO TRIBAL PARK

North of Kayenta on US 163, visitors can glimpse some of Monument Valley Navajo Tribal Park's massive buttes, mesas, and canyons—which cover nearly 30,000 acres in Arizona and Utah on the Navajo Reservation—from the road. To enter the park, however, one must go to the visitors center, on the Utah side about twenty-five miles north of Kayenta. Visitors can view the park from an overlook there or take the seventeen-mile, rough dirt road off US 163 into the park; this is the only park access permitted without a guide.

The date the Navajo arrived in Monument Valley is uncertain. It is known that during Kit Carson's Navajo campaign in the early

Monument Valley —Southwest Studies, Scottsdale Community College

1860s, many Navajo escaped the "Long Walk" to the Bosque Redondo Reservation in New Mexico and found refuge among these majestic sandstone skyscrapers.

In 1923 Harry and "Mike" (his wife) Goulding opened a trading post on the Arizona-Utah border, where they took an active interest in helping the Navajo make the sometimes painful adjustment to the twentieth century. They not only purchased wool blankets and crafts created by Navajo artists but also settled disputes among the people and acted as a liaison between the Indians and the federal government.

During the Great Depression, in an effort to boost the local economy, Harry Goulding came up with a plan to entice the movie industry to come to Monument Valley to film westerns—normally filmed in the hills around Hollywood—in hopes that the producers would hire the Navajo as extras at good pay. Goulding knew that the spectacular red sandstone monoliths would make a dramatic backdrop and believed that if he could convince director John Ford to take a firsthand look, Monument Valley would sell itself. He headed for Hollywood with pictures of the area.

It proved difficult for Goulding to get an appointment with the famed director, so the persistent trader hauled his bedroll into the receptionist's office and spread it out on the floor, saying firmly that he would camp there until Mr. Ford was available. The tactic was successful: Ford looked at the photos, made a trip to Monument Valley, and the rest is movie history. The setting, Ford thought, was perfect for *Stagecoach,* the epic western he was planning. A young actor named Marion Morrison, stage name John Wayne, would play the Ringo Kid, his first starring role in a major motion picture. *Stagecoach* became an American classic, thanks in part to its stunning location, and put Monument Valley on the map.

During the production, hundreds of Navajo were cast as Apache, Cheyenne, Comanche, and other Indians. In the film there were moments of dialogue between natives and hard-riding heroes in which the native actors spoke Navajo as a generic "Indian language." Some of the lines would never have made it past a Navajo-speaking censor. When the film played in theaters in Flagstaff and Winslow, whites were bewildered by the snickers of the Navajo in the audience during what was supposed to be serious dialogue.

Since the filming of *Stagecoach,* dozens of other movies have been shot in Monument Valley, both westerns and nonwesterns. The valley was a setting not only in several more John Ford features, but also in scenes from *2001: A Space Odyssey, Thelma and Louise, Forrest Gump, Planet of the Apes,* and *The Ten Commandments.*

Harry Goulding died in 1981, but area residents will never forget him and Mike and all they did for the Navajo of Monument Valley. The old Goulding Trading Post is now a museum.

US 89
Flagstaff—Lake Powell
135 MILES

SUNSET CRATER VOLCANO
NATIONAL MONUMENT

Sunset Crater Volcano National Monument is about fifteen miles north of Flagstaff on US 89, and a few miles east of the highway. Sunset Crater was the last volcano to erupt in Arizona. In the fall of A.D. 1064 the mountain blew its top, sending billowing smoke and ashes into the atmosphere and a molasses-like lava flow toward the Little Colorado River to the north. A heavy layer of ash remained on the land around the volcano, a condition that created an ideal situation for dry-farming. Soon the Sinagua Indians were raising crops; however, about 1300, a long drought coupled with dry winds that blew the ash mulch and topsoil away caused the Sinagua to abandon their farms.

The volcano was named by famous Arizona explorer John Wesley Powell, who led an expedition through the Grand Canyon in 1869. Supposedly the red and yellow hues of the rim inspired the name. The cinder cone rises 1,000 feet above the plain; the crater is 400 feet deep. Ice caves near the cone provide bone-chilling air and ice year-round. During the 1880, saloon keepers in Flagstaff hauled blocks of ice into town for their customers' drinks in the summer. The site was made a national monument in 1930.

WUPATKI NATIONAL MONUMENT

Wupatki National Monument was designated in 1924. The exit is about eighteen miles north of Sunset Crater on US 89. The original Indian settlement was hardly isolated—the ruins of some 800 other villages have been located in the area—but Wupatki was the largest. Wupatki, a Hopi word, means "Tall House." Here on the windswept plains, with the towering San Francisco Peaks as a backdrop, the prehistoric Sinagua people farmed for about a century.

During its cultural peak in the twelfth century, about 300 people at Wupatki occupied more than 100 rooms. A large "amphitheater," unique in the Southwest, is a circular depression that may have been an adaptation of the kiva, a ceremonial chamber used by the cliff-dwelling Ancestral Pueblo in the Four Corners area. Wupatki also has an oval prehistoric ball court. Such ball courts are common in Mexico, where the Spanish wrote of them and the games played in them, which involved a ball and a small hoop. However, such courts are rare this far north. Some others have been found in Hohokam pueblos, including Snaketown on the Gila River.

CAMERON

The first bridge across the Little Colorado River was erected in 1911, and at the same time a Navajo named Scott Preston opened a trading post on the west side of the bridge. A small community soon grew up around the store, on the Navajo Reservation. Hubert Richardson, an early trader, named the community for Senator Ralph Cameron. A post office was established in 1917. For years now, the trading post, like others of its kind in the state, has played a vital role in its community. In the early days, Indian people came from miles around to trade there. The trader bought and sold goods, but perhaps more importantly he was also an interpreter and go-between, in culture as well as in language.

MOENAVE

Moenave is several miles east of US 89 on Reservation Road 23, five miles due west of Tuba City. The ubiquitous Father Francisco Tomás Garcés visited the natives in this area in 1776. A century later, in 1871, Mormon Jacob Hamblin, the "Buckskin Apostle," established a colony here in the spring-fed area at the foot of the Moenave Cliffs. Remains of the buildings the Mormon colonists erected are still in evidence.

Moenave lay along a trail Hamblin blazed in the 1870s from Utah to the Little Colorado River Valley, opening the Mormon colonial period in Arizona. Since there were no temples in Arizona until 1926, young Mormon couples desiring to solemnize their wedding vows had to travel on Hamblin's trail to St. George, Utah.

Jacob Hamblin, Mormon missionary and explorer —Arizona Historical Society Library/Tucson

The exhausting journey took weeks and covered several hundred miles. Mormons affectionately referred to this road as the Honeymoon Trail.

Just as travelers on the Oregon Trail scribbled their names on Independence Rock in Wyoming, and Spanish conquistadores from the 1500s scratched their names on the sedimentary stone cliff at El Morro, near Zuni, New Mexico, Arizona pioneers had their inscription rock in Moenave Wash. Dozens of names and dates going back to the 1870s are carved in the reddish sandstone there.

PAGE

Page, off US 89 at Lake Powell, near the Utah border, was a planned community developed in the 1960s by the Bureau of

Reclamation to provide headquarters and to house workers for the building of the Glen Canyon Dam. The town, destined for success as a gateway to Lake Powell and the Glen Canyon National Recreation Area, was named for John C. Page, who spent many years planning and developing the proposed dam site while serving as commissioner of reclamation. Page died in 1955 before construction of the dam began. It was completed in 1964.

A short distance east of Page was the Vados de los Padres, or Crossing of the Fathers. The historic crossing, now buried beneath Lake Powell, was made by Fathers Escalante and Domínguez in 1776 as they tried to find a route from Santa Fe to San Gabriel (Los Angeles). Their journey took them across the Four Corners area and northwest nearly to Salt Lake before, discouraged and disappointed, they decided to head back to Santa Fe. They crossed the Colorado River at this site. The route to Los Angeles, the Old Spanish Trail, would not be set for a half century after the brave padres made their futile attempt.

GLEN CANYON DAM AND LAKE POWELL

Glen Canyon Dam, just northeast of Page, is on the Arizona side of the Glen Canyon National Recreation Area, which lies mostly in Utah. Lake Powell, a 186-mile-long reservoir, was created from the Colorado River when the Glen Canyon Dam was built, beginning in the mid-1950s, to provide water and power to surrounding desert communities. The lake, which did not reach its full water capacity until 1980, is one of the Southwest's most popular recreation spots.

Lake Powell was named for explorer John Wesley Powell, who named Glen Canyon in 1869. Awestruck by the beautiful red-rock chasm, Powell noted the "carved walls, royal arches, glens, alcove gulches, mounts and monuments; from which of these features shall we select a name? We decide to call it Glen Canyon."

The reddish chasms and arches of Glen Canyon, once among the most remote and spectacular hiking areas in this nation, are now buried beneath the waters of Lake Powell. For better or worse, depending on one's point of view, a former pristine wilderness was transformed into a boating enthusiast's wonderland. In recent years some environmentalist groups have been lobbying to decommission the dam and drain the lake in an attempt to restore the Colorado River and Glen Canyon.

US 180
Flagstaff—South Rim, Grand Canyon National Park
83 MILES

GRAND CANYON NATIONAL PARK

Wherever we look there is but a wilderness of rocks—deep gorges where the rivers are lost below cliffs and towers and pinnacles, and 10,000 strangely carved forms in every direction and beyond them, mountains blending with clouds.

John Wesley Powell, 1869

The Grand Canyon, the world's most glorious natural architectural masterpiece, has stirred the human imagination since we first gazed into its magnificent abyss. Words cannot express the canyon's sublime beauty and tapestry of color, nor can the camera capture the majestic splendor of its infinite vistas. At 277 miles in length, 4 to 18 miles in width, and about a mile in depth, "grand" hardly begins to describe this canyon's immensity. From Flagstaff, US 180 takes you directly to the South Rim, one of several entrances to the park. Ninety percent of the canyon's visitors come to the South Rim.

The first missionary to come upon the great canyon noted that such a wonder could only have been created by the Almighty. Author-naturalist Joseph Wood Krutch called it "the most revealing single page of Earth's history open on the face of the globe." On his visit in 1903, President Theodore Roosevelt expressed his feelings about the canyon in a plea for its preservation: "Do nothing to mar its grandeur . . . keep it for your children, your children's children, and all who come after

you, as the one great sight which every American should see."
And naturalist John Muir, in his assessment of this labyrinth,
wrote: "There's nothing quite like the Grand Canyon. No matter
how many famous gorges and valleys you have seen, the Grand
Canyon will seem novel to you, as unearthly in the color and
grandeur of its architecture as if you had found it after death, on
some other star."

Others have been less poetic in their commentary. "Today, I
spit a mile," wrote a youngster in the park's guest registry. "What
a marvelous place to throw your mother-in-law," mused a famous
French politician. A cynical voyager remarked that it was nothing
but a bad case of soil erosion. "Golly, what a gully!" former
president William Howard Taft allegedly quipped.

In the Grand Canyon, one can view 20 million centuries of
geologic history. The timeless chasm provides a layer-by-layer
record of the planet's history. The exposed rocks at the edge of
the Colorado River are some of the oldest on earth. The ancient
metamorphic Vishnu Schist on the canyon floor dates back 2
billion years.

The dark, craggy walls of the Inner Gorge—the vertical cliffs
that make up the bottom third of the canyon—are the core of an
ancient mountain range that was once five to six miles high. The
upper part of the canyon lies in horizontal sedimentary layers.
Into these layers are carved the colorful buttes, temples, mesas,
and spires that make the Grand Canyon one of the seven natural
wonders of the world.

The Colorado River began cutting through the land that became
the Grand Canyon about 6 million years ago. Scientists don't
agree on exactly how this came about. One theory, the ancestral
river theory, holds that about 65 million years ago, the Kaibab
Plateau began uplifting and the ancestral Colorado River started
carving through the soft upper surface, eventually creating the
giant chasm.

A second theory, the stream piracy theory, maintains that
about 35 million years ago the Kaibab Plateau separated the
ancestral Colorado and Hualapai Rivers, the latter flowing west
of the plateau and the former flowing east toward the Gulf of
Mexico. About 12 million years ago the Colorado formed a huge
lake, which scientists call Lake Bidahochi, in today's Little

Colorado Valley (the Winslow-Holbrook area). At the same time, the Hualapai River was cutting its way eastward through the plateau, toward the Colorado. Eventually the Hualapai cut through and connected with the Colorado, "pirating," or diverting, its flow westward into the Sea of Cortez (Gulf of California). Increased rainfall during the ice ages followed by melting glaciers in the Rocky Mountains sent water cascading down the new Colorado, chiseling out the Kaibab Plateau and sculpting the Grand Canyon.

Today, the Colorado River is still slicing through the canyon as it flows between Marble Gorge and Lake Mead. At a rate of one foot every 2,000 years, the Grand Canyon will continue to widen. It's estimated that in another 5 million years the canyon will have lost much of its beauty and grandeur. So don't wait to visit!

Early Inhabitants

Nomadic Paleo-Indians were the first to arrive in the Grand Canyon area, about 11,000 years ago. The Archaic (Desert) Culture followed, ending about 3,000 years ago. These prehistoric Southwesterners left behind very little to tell us about their settlement and subsistence patterns. Archaeologists have discovered stone spear points and tiny, split-twig figurines of deer and bighorn sheep that date back 4,000 years in the canyon's caves of Redwall Limestone. The figures were believed to provide sympathetic magic for a successful hunt. After the Archaic Culture people left, the area may have been uninhabited for 1,000 years or so.

From about A.D. 1 to 1250, the prehistoric Ancestral Pueblo and Cohonina peoples resided within the canyon's steep walls. Around 1400, the Cerbat Indians arrived at the west end of the canyon. The Cerbat were hunters, gatherers, and farmers who dwelled in caves and brush shelters. They are believed to be the ancestors of today's Hualapai and Havasupai Indians, as well as some segments of the Hopi peoples.

The Hopi still maintain shrines in the Grand Canyon. One sacred place, a formation near the Little Colorado River called the Sipapu, is what the Hopi believe was the "birthing hole" where their ancestors first emerged into this world. More recent arrivals to the Grand Canyon were the Paiute on the north and the Navajo on the east.

White Exploration

The first white men to view the canyon were in Coronado's expedition in 1540. Upon hearing from the Hopi Indians of a great river, which Coronado believed could be the fabled Northwest Passage, Coronado sent García López de Cárdenas with a small party to investigate. Upon reaching the canyon's edge, they attempted, in vain, to climb down. Certain it was not the passage to India, the men returned to the main group at Zuni.

Others came to the canyon over the next three centuries. In 1776 Father Garcés descended into the canyon (though not all the way down) and visited the Havasupai Indians. Trapper James Ohio Pattie saw it in 1826, but he was not favorably impressed, describing the ". . . horrible mountains, which cage it up, as to deprive all human beings of the ability to descend its banks and make use of its waters."

Coronado's men at the Grand Canyon, 1540 *(by Bill Ahrendt)* —Southwest Studies, Scottsdale Community College

In 1857 Lt. Joseph C. Ives, after his journey up the Colorado, headed overland for New Mexico and on the way viewed the canyon from the South Rim. Like Pattie, he appraised it as altogether valueless: "It can be approached only from the south and after entering it there is nothing to do but leave. Ours has been the first and will doubtless be the last party of whites to visit this profitless locality."

The first to actually explore the Grand Canyon was the courageous John Wesley Powell. In 1869 Powell, a one-armed Civil War veteran, led an adventuresome band of ten men in four small wooden boats on a daring expedition down the uncharted Colorado River into the Grand Canyon. The company covered 1,000 miles, through rugged canyons and treacherous rapids, in just ninety-eight days, as Powell made extensive notes on the flora, fauna, geology, and native inhabitants of the region.

The brave explorers faced danger at every bend as the river tried again and again to devour their tiny boats. Fearing the last stretch of rapids through the canyon's deep and fearsome gorges, three of Powell's men left the expedition and were never seen again. Powell led another expedition through the canyon in 1871–72, during which he coined the name Grand Canyon. During the years immediately following the expeditions, the canyon became home to prospectors, bootleggers, horse thieves, and hermits.

Captain Hance

The Grand Canyon's first promoter was Capt. John Hance, a lean, weather-beaten man with a long, angular face, wiry whiskers, and mirthful, deep blue eyes that wore a permanent squint from years of gazing into the far distance. He was the first to provide accommodations for tourists, in 1886. From his lodge and camp on the South Rim, Hance also built the first trail down into the canyon and led the first tourist excursions. Until 1902, Grand Canyon Village was known as Hance's Tank.

Captain Hance was a master of dry humor. One day he was pointing out the sights to a group of tourists at the canyon's edge. "Mr. Hance," a lady from the East interrupted, "how did you lose your finger?" Hance stopped talking for a moment and looked down at his hand, pretending to notice the missing finger for the first time. "Why, ma'am," he replied, straight-faced, "I musta wore

Captain John Hance
—Northern Arizona Pioneers
Historical Society

that thing plumb off pointin' at all the beautiful scenery around here."

The crowd loved it, and a legend was born. From that time on, until his death in 1919, John Hance provided lodging and lying, pulling the legs of thousands of tenderfeet. Since his audience came from all parts of the globe, Hance's fame spread far and wide—a person had not really experienced the canyon unless he had heard a Captain Hance whopper.

Sometimes Hance's windies backfired. One day a stranger asked him how the deer hunting was around the South Rim. "Why, it's jest fine," Hance replied. "I went out and killed three all by myself jest this morning."

"That's wonderful!" the stranger exclaimed. "Do you know who I am?"

"No, I don't," Hance admitted.

"Why, I'm the game warden, and it looks like you've been breaking a few game laws."

"Do you know who I am?" snorted the old bull peddler.

"No, I don't," the game warden replied.

"Well, I'm the biggest damned liar in these parts!"

Captain Hance spent the last forty years of his life sharing tall tales with visitors to the canyon. In 1906 he sold his homestead and moved to Grand Canyon Village, where the Fred Harvey Company gave him room and board for life. All they asked in return was that he regale tourists with his tales—obviously, an easy task for the captain. It would have been difficult if they had asked him *not* to talk to them.

Nobody knew for sure just how old Hance was. Voting records showed him to be sixty-four in 1906 and only sixty in 1908, a net loss of four years in two years' time. A newspaper listed his age as eighty-four when he died in 1919.

Growing Tourist Industry

Despite its grandeur, the canyon was a well-kept secret until the turn of the twentieth century. Up to then, a few entrepreneurs around Flagstaff hauled tourists by stagecoach over a rough road to the Bright Angel Trail, but only the most durable of visitors dared make the eleven-hour trek. In 1901 the Santa Fe Railroad began running excursion trains from the main line at Williams to the Bright Angel Trail on the South Rim. It also constructed Bright Angel Camp on twenty acres at the head of Bright Angel Creek. The camp, the forerunner of today's lodge, started out with a log hotel and several cabins. The sixty-four-mile Bright Angel Santa Fe line ran until 1968. In 1989 the Grand Canyon Railroad reopened it, and today visitors can take a nostalgic ride in vintage passenger cars pulled by a 1910 steam locomotive.

In 1902 Ellsworth and Emory Kolb, brothers from Pennsylvania, set up a photography studio at Bright Angel Camp. It's estimated that over the years they took pictures of 1.5 million canyon visitors. Footage from films they began making in 1911, the first ever of the canyon, still plays in park visitor centers. Today the old Kolb Studio houses the Grand Canyon Association bookstore.

One of the first big hotels built at the Grand Canyon was the El Tovar, named for Pedro de Tovar, one of Coronado's officers. Perched precariously on the South Rim, it is truly Arizona's

El Tovar at the turn of the century —Grand Canyon National Park

grandest hotel. Opening in 1905, with Fred Harvey as concessionaire for the National Park Service, the El Tovar was originally a playground for the rich during the days when only the affluent could afford the expense and leisure of travel. The architectural design was a blend of a Swiss chalet and a Scandinavian hunting lodge, built partly by local Hopi labor with massive Kaibab limestone blocks and durable split logs from Oregon. A stone's throw from the El Tovar, the Hopi House gift shop features Indian arts and crafts and the performance of traditional dances and ceremonies.

The Grand Canyon became a National Monument in 1908, and in 1919 it was upgraded to a National Park. In 1979 it became a World Heritage Site—a place recognized by UNESCO, the United Nations Educational, Scientific and Cultural Organization, as having "outstanding universal value." In 1975 the government doubled the park's area, extending the boundaries northeast to Lees Ferry, and west to Grand Wash; it now covers 1,904 square miles. The number of visitors has also grown. In 1919, less than 45,000 people visited the canyon in the entire year; today, more than twice that visit each day, around 5 million each year.

Mystery of the Lost Honeymooners

One of the Grand Canyon's most enduring and intriguing mysteries is that of Glen and Bessie Hyde, newlyweds who vanished without a trace while running a homemade boat down the Colorado River to celebrate their honeymoon. Glen was from Ketchum, Idaho, where he had run the Salmon River. Bessie Haley met Glen in California, where she attended art school. They were married in 1928.

The 1920s was a time of record setting by adventurous people like Babe Ruth and Charles Lindbergh. Glen Hyde wanted to run the mighty Colorado River faster than anyone had before. He persuaded Bessie to join him and become the first woman to run that section of the Colorado. On October 28, 1928, the couple launched in a homemade wooden scow, without fanfare or lifejackets and with scant supplies. On November 16, the Hydes stopped at Phantom Ranch and hiked up the trail to South Rim,

Glen and Bessie Hyde, 1928
—Emory Kolb photo

where the famous Kolb brothers took their picture. They also took on a hitchhiker, Adolph Sutro, the grandson of the famous San Francisco mayor, who rode with them to Hermit's Camp. He was the last to see them alive.

Glen's father was supposed to meet them at Needles. When they didn't show, he organized a massive search. On Christmas Day, searcher Emory Kolb spotted their boat, snagged in rocks but upright and loaded. The Hydes had come 600 miles and were just 46 miles from the mouth of the canyon when they vanished. They were presumed drowned, but soon rumors and speculation grew. Had Glen killed Bessie, or Bessie killed Glen, to live to old age under another name? Over the years the legend has resurfaced now and then, with people claiming to be Bessie or Glen or their children, or to know what happened, but no claims have been substantiated. Around campfires along the Colorado, river runners still tell the story of Glen and Bessie Hyde's disappearance in the chilly depths of the Grand Canyon.

US Alternate 89
US 89—Fredonia
85 MILES

MARBLE CANYON AND VERMILION CLIFFS

This is a marvelous drive through some of the Arizona Strip, the 3 million acres of undeveloped land between the Arizona-Utah line and the Grand Canyon. It's hard to get to the strip from most of Arizona, since you have to drive around the Grand Canyon. The result is a relatively lonesome, pristine land.

Alt. US 89 starts in the small town of Bitter Springs, located on the Navajo Reservation. One crosses out of Navajoland at the Colorado and into the town of Marble Canyon, on the west side of the river. The canyon itself, through which the river runs, is south of town, inside the northern boundaries of Grand Canyon

National Park. The 500-foot-deep canyon is some sixty miles long and made of multicolored limestone that resembles marble.

Grand Canyon explorer John Wesley Powell is responsible for naming many places in this region. As his tiny boats passed through the deep chasm here, Powell looked up at the titanic cliffs and, believing them to be marble, dubbed the place Marble Canyon. Powell also named the Vermilion Cliffs, west of the canyon, describing them thus: "I look back and see the morning sun shining in splendor on their painted faces; the salient angles are on fire and the retreating angles are buried in shade, and I gaze on them until my vision dreams and the cliffs appear on a long bank of purple cliffs plowed from the horizon high into the heavens."

The stretch of the Colorado River through Marble Canyon is fraught with swift currents and crashing rapids, giving river runners then and now a thrill a minute. In 1925 the U.S. Geological Survey officially named this canyon Marble Gorge. The name was changed to Marble Canyon in 1961, and eight years later it was made a national monument.

LEES FERRY

At Marble Canyon, a side road off Alt. US 89 takes you about five miles north to Lees Ferry, the noted river crossing on Jacob Hamblin's trail to Utah. In 1864 Jacob Hamblin crossed the Colorado River here, at its confluence with the Paria.

In 1871 John Doyle Lee, a fugitive from justice, arrived here and figured this was about as good a place as any to hide. He had been an instigator in the notorious 1857 Mountain Meadows Massacre, where some Mormon settlers and Paiute allies attacked a wagon train of anti-Mormon emigrants from Missouri. After four days, the Mormons murdered them all except seventeen children.

When John Wesley Powell passed through Lee's hideout later that year on his second Grand Canyon expedition, he gave a boat he didn't need to Lee, who converted it into a ferryboat. Lee's ferry business soon began to thrive, and people began calling the place Lees Ferry.

United States marshals finally caught up with Lee here in 1874. At his trial Lee insisted that he was a scapegoat, a defense many

Lees Ferry (no date) —Southwest Studies, Scottsdale Community College

historians believe. He was found guilty and sentenced to die by firing squad at Mountain Meadows, the site of the massacre, in southern Utah. He was also excommunicated.

On March 2, 1877, Lee stood inside his own coffin and faced his executioners. "I am ready to die," he said, "I trust in God. I have no fear. Death has no terror." Five shots rang out, seemingly ending a dark chapter in Mormon history. For seventy-three years the Mormon Church denied any involvement in the massacre, but after years of pressure from Lee's descendents and others, the church reinstated Lee to full membership in 1961.

After Lee's death his seventeenth wife, Emma, remained with her children five more years at Lees Ferry, which she called Lonely Dell. Most of the time the young woman ran the ferry alone, 100 miles from the nearest community. One night she discovered a party of Navajo warriors camped in her yard. Not wanting to show fear, she gathered her brood and spread their blankets around the Navajo's campfire, where they all went to sleep. The next morning the Indians' leader pronounced her the bravest woman he'd ever met and declared that she would never have to fear harm by the Navajo.

Lee's old ferry operation continued until 1928, when a bridge was built across the Colorado River at Marble Canyon. The National Park System acquired the property in 1973, and five years later it was added to the National Register of Historic Places.

HOUSE ROCK

The site of House Rock is down an unpaved road just off Alt. US 89 near the border of the Kaibab National Forest. The House Rock area is best known for the House Rock Buffalo Ranch, twenty miles south of the highway, reached via partially paved roads. In the 1880s, Charles J. "Buffalo" Jones brought bison (aka buffalo) into the area. He tried to breed them with cattle for a meat called "beefalo," but the experiment didn't work. Jones sold the animals

House Rock —Author photo

to his friend "Uncle Jim" Owens, celebrated hunter and guide and longtime warden of the Kaibab National Forest. The herd multiplied rapidly on the grassy plateau, where they still thrive today. The government bought the herd in 1931.

The House Rock Ranch is also home to Arizona's native elk (wapiti). In the early 1900s the species nearly became extinct. During Teddy Roosevelt's administration, the government imported a small herd from Yellowstone National Park. Like the bison, the elk continue to thrive on the vast, remote ranges of the Kaibab Plateau.

JACOB LAKE

Jacob Lake, a small lake and campground area on Alt. US 89 at AZ 67 in the Kaibab National Forest, is named for the legendary Mormon explorer Jacob Hamblin. Hamblin, known as the "Buckskin Apostle," explored much of northern Arizona from the 1850s to the 1870s, searching for sites for prospective Mormon colonies. He was the first American missionary to go among the Hopi and Navajo. In 1869 Hamblin helped guide John Wesley Powell's expedition north of the Grand Canyon. He also helped Powell negotiate several treaties with natives. Hamblin died in 1886 and was buried at Alpine. A restored cabin dating from 1910 overlooks Jacob Lake, which can be dry.

FREDONIA

Fredonia, four miles south of the Utah border and just east of the Kaibab-Paiute Indian Reservation, is another of those towns created by Mormon polygamists evading federal prosecution in Utah. Settlement began in 1885, and originally the town was called Hardscrabble. The noted Mormon apostle Erastus Snow suggested Fredonia instead—a clever combination of "free" and *doña* (the Spanish feminine title for "Mrs."), indicating that Arizona was a relatively safe haven for plural wives.

As part of an agreement with the federal government to allow Utah admittance into the union, the Mormon Church outlawed polygamy in the early 1890s. Many patriarchs did not want to give up the practice, however, so they established towns in Arizona near the Utah border. In some houses, it was said, the living rooms were in Utah, but the bedrooms were in Arizona. People also joked that the houses were built on skids and could be dragged back and forth between Utah and Arizona, depending on the political climate.

AZ 67
Jacob Lake—North Rim, Grand Canyon National Park
43 MILES

AZ 67 runs through the Kaibab National Forest from Jacob Lake south to the Grand Canyon's North Rim. John Wesley Powell believed the Paiute Indians called this area Kai-vav-wi (pronounced KYE-babb), or "Mountains Lying Down." The idea of mountains lying down makes sense considering that the Kaibab is a huge plateau rising more than 3,000 feet above the valleys to the east and west. To the south, the plateau drops off abruptly into the Grand Canyon. To the north are lofty mountains in Utah. Old maps refer to the plateau as either Kaibab, Bucksin, or Buckskin. *Bucksin* is a Paiute word that referred both to the plateau and to themselves as people who lived there. However, whites misheard and thought they were saying "Buckskin."

NORTH RIM

The first tourist facility at the town of North Rim was called Wylie Way Camp. In 1926 a post office opened there and took the name Kaibab. In 1947 the National Park Service changed the name to North Rim, a term that also refers to all Grand Canyon country north of the Colorado River. The North Rim is 1,000 to 1,500 feet higher than areas to the south, and gets 60 percent more precipitation. Roads into the North Rim are closed in the winter, when snow piles up six to ten feet deep. At 8,803 feet, Point Imperial offers one of the North Rim's most spectacular vistas.

AZ 389
Fredonia—Colorado City
33 MILES

AZ 389 passes through the Kaibab-Paiute Indian Reservation and the northern end of the Arizona Strip, that part of Arizona north of the Grand Canyon between the Nevada line on the west and the Colorado River on the east. The Strip is considered some of the most remote "inhabitable" land in America. The natural barrier of the Grand Canyon and a lack of major highways through the Strip cut it off from the rest of Arizona and link it more closely to Utah. In fact, several times during the 1800s, Utah tried to persuade the government to redraw the boundary lines to include the Arizona Strip within its borders.

PIPE SPRING NATIONAL MONUMENT

Fifteen miles southwest of Fredonia, just off AZ 389 on the Kaibab-Paiute Reservation, is Pipe Spring National Monument. Pipe Spring was a welcome sight to Jacob Hamblin and his fellow Mormons when they came here in 1852, as it was the only water for sixty miles. While resting at the spring, William "Gunlock Bill" Hamblin, brother of Jacob, showed off his marksmanship by shooting the bottom out of a pipe placed on its side on a rock. In honor of this accomplishment, the place received its name.

The first Mormon settlers to attempt to establish a colony at Pipe Spring in 1863 were killed by Navajo. A decade later, Mormon ranchers combined their efforts and formed the Winsor Castle Livestock Growers Association. They built a castlelike fort of huge stone blocks to protect themselves against Indian attacks. Over the years Winsor Castle, the fort, became a sanctuary for

Pipe Spring National Monument
—Southwest Studies, Scottsdale Community College

polygamists escaping indictment in Utah. In 1923 Pipe Spring National Monument was created as a memorial to the pioneers. The forty-acre tract encompasses Winsor Castle and other pioneer buildings. Today Winsor Castle is a museum with living history demonstrations.

The Kaibab-Paiute Indians, residents of the area around Pipe Springs National Monument, belong to the Ute-Aztecan language group. Back in the 1860s when Mormon ranchers and farmers began settling in their homeland, the Paiute were a small, semi-nomadic group of hunters and gatherers, and they could not resist the white encroachment. Since religious practice among the Paiute was not strong, many converted to the Mormon faith. Today about 250 people live on the Kaibab Reservation near Pipe Springs. They make their livelihoods from livestock, tourism, fruit orchards, and other trades.

COLORADO CITY

Colorado City was founded in 1909 as Millennial City by "unreconstructed" polygamists out to establish a colony. Later, the town's name was changed to Short Creek. During the early and mid-twentieth century, outsiders claimed that young girls were being taken into polygamous marriage against their will. At the same time, Mohave County officials complained of an increasing number of women requesting welfare, noting that many of them listed the same man as their husband. Short Creek's leaders denied these accusations and, in effect, demanded that outsiders mind their own business.

In the summer of 1953 a large force of the Arizona Highway Patrol made a surprise raid on Short Creek, rounded up the polygamists, and jailed them in Kingman. The women and children, considered victims, were bused to the Phoenix area. The children were placed in foster homes and enrolled in urban schools, where their old-fashioned customs and clothes made them conspicuous. Several months later the state's case against the citizens of Short Creek fizzled, and all were allowed to go home.

With the shower of national notoriety the incident brought, in 1958 Short Creek residents changed the town's name yet again to Colorado City. Polygamy is practiced to this day in the thriving community. Citizens view the 1953 raid as their "holocaust," a badge of honor in their fight for the right to choose.

I-15
Utah Border—Nevada Border
30 MILES

As I-15 passes through the western United States from Montana to southern California, it cuts across the far northwest corner of Arizona, following the path of the Virgin River along this stretch. During his search for a road to California in 1776, Franciscan padre Silvestre Escalante called the river the Rio Virgin, presumably for the Virgin Mary. Another theory holds that the river is a misspelling of Thomas Virgen's name. Virgen passed through this valley with famed explorer Jedediah Smith, searching like Escalante for a route to California. The Paiute, who lived here for centuries and knew the river better than anyone, called it Pah-Roose, meaning "Very Muddy Stream."

LITTLEFIELD

Littlefield is about twenty miles southwest of the Utah border on I-15. Daniel Bonelli, a native of Switzerland who accompanied Brigham Young on the first ox-train trip to Utah, settled Littlefield in 1863, giving this community bragging rights as the first in Arizona of Anglo American origin. That same year, floods along the Virgin River washed out Bonelli's place, forcing him to move. He went on to build a ferry crossing on the Colorado River near the mouth of the Virgin River and establish a prosperous freighting business, salt mine, and farm. Floods along the Virgin continued to flood settlers out, though in the mid-1870s a group of Mormons established small farms with "little fields," hence the town's name.

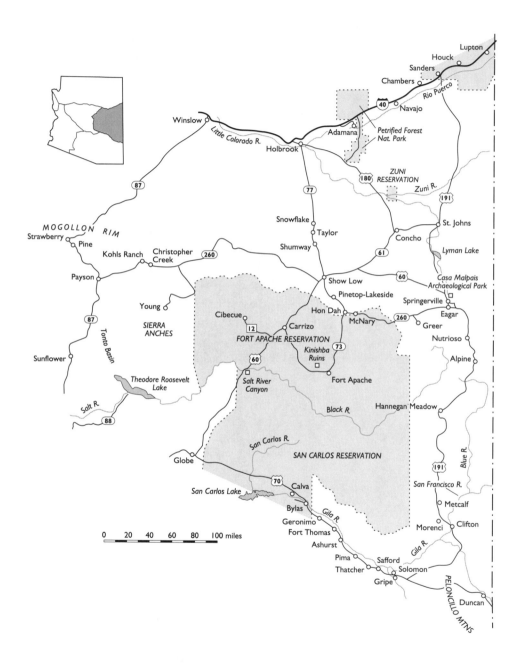

Winslow
Little Colorado R.
Holbrook
Adamana
Petrified Forest Nat. Park

Lupton
Houck
Sanders
Chambers
Rio Puerco
Navajo

ZUNI RESERVATION
Zuni R.

MOGOLLON RIM
Strawberry
Pine
Kohls Ranch
Christopher Creek
Payson

Snowflake
Taylor
Shumway
Show Low
Pinetop-Lakeside
Hon Dah
McNary

St. Johns
Concho
Lyman Lake
Casa Malpais Archaeological Park
Springerville
Eagar
Greer
Nutrioso

SIERRA ANCHES
Young
Cibecue
Carrizo
FORT APACHE RESERVATION
Kinishba Ruins
Fort Apache

Sunflower
Tonto Basin
Theodore Roosevelt Lake
Salt R.
Salt River Canyon

Black R.
Hannegan Meadow

Alpine

San Carlos R.
SAN CARLOS RESERVATION

Globe

Blue R.

San Carlos Lake
Calva
Bylas
Geronimo
Fort Thomas
Ashurst
Pima
Thatcher
Gila R.
Safford
Solomon
Gripe

San Francisco R.
Metcalf
Morenci
Clifton

Gila R.

PELONCILLO MTNS
Duncan

0 20 40 60 80 100 miles

Part 4

The High Country

US 70
New Mexico Border—Globe
124 MILES

DUNCAN

Seven miles northwest of US 70's entry point into Arizona from New Mexico, in the shadow of the Peloncillo Mountains to the west, is Duncan. When the Arizona & New Mexico Railroad connected Clifton with the main line in 1883, they built a rail stop on the property of Duncan Smith, hence the name. "Black Jack" Ketchum, notorious stagecoach robber, and his gang were among many desperadoes who passed through Duncan.

In 1880 Henry Clay Day arrived in this part of Arizona from Connecticut by way of Kansas. He came to homestead a ranch a few miles south of Duncan. Day called his outfit the Lazy B, and the ranch, despite an occasional drought, became one of the most successful in Arizona. In 1922, when he grew too old to run it any longer, he turned the 260-square-mile property over to his son Harry. Unfortunately, the ranch was in financial trouble by that time.

In 1927 Harry married Ada Mae Wilkey, the college-educated daughter of a prosperous cattle dealer from El Paso. Harry and Ada Mae raised two daughters, Sandra and Ann, and a son, Alan. Both girls were pretty—the story is still told around Duncan that the young cowboys used to come from all over Graham and Greenlee Counties to social functions on Saturday night just to look at Harry Day's daughters.

*Sandra Day
O'Connor on Chico
at the Lazy B*
—Courtesy Sandra Day
O'Connor

Sandra wanted to stay on the Lazy B and be a cowgirl, but her brother was so much better at working cows she decided to go to college instead. She attended Stanford and received a law degree. After graduation she married classmate John O'Connor and settled down to raise a family. When she began her own career as a lawyer, Sandra found many openings as a secretary but few firms wanted to hire a woman attorney. She persevered, however, starting her own firm in Phoenix. In the late 1960s she was elected to the Arizona Senate, and eventually she became the senate majority leader, the first woman in American history to hold that post in a state legislature. It was not a surprise to those who knew her when in 1981 Sandra Day O'Connor was appointed the first woman justice on the U.S. Supreme Court.

The Day family ended up selling the Lazy B, but a memoir of growing up there written by Justice O'Connor and her brother Alan was published in 2002.

SOLOMON

Isador E. Solomon came to America from Germany when he was sixteen and settled in Arizona in 1876, at a settlement then called Munsonville, near the confluence of the San Simon and Gila Rivers. Munsonville was named for Bill Munson, who in 1873 had built an adobe house and a store there. Solomon bought Munson's store and enlarged it, and he soon became the town's most prominent citizen. When the mines around Clifton began operation, Solomon built charcoal ovens to supply them. Pioneer rancher William Kirkland, working as a mail carrier here in 1878, suggested the town be renamed Solomonville (shortened in 1950 to Solomon). Geronimo's renegade Apache bands fleeing the San Carlos Reservation were a threat to settlers here, including the Solomon family. Once, Apache raided Solomon's ranch and killed 12 men, a woman, and a child, and slaughtered 500 sheep.

Augustine Chacon, a notorious Mexican outlaw who boasted of having killed nearly thirty gringos (not bothering to count the number of his own countrymen), finally got his just deserts in Solomon. In 1896 Chacon robbed a store in Morenci and in a rage hacked the owner to pieces with an ax. Later, when a posse

*The hanging of
Augustine Chacon
at Solomon*
—Southwest Studies,
Scottsdale Community
College

had him surrounded, a deputy named Pablo Salcido, an old friend of Chacon, tied a white handkerchief to his rifle barrel and called for a parley. Chacon asked Salcido to step out into the open and spoke to him from a concealed place. Then he shot his friend in cold blood.

The outraged posse eventually caught their man, and he was taken to Solomon and sentenced to hang. But a lady friend of Chacon's hid a hacksaw blade in the binding of a Bible and delivered it to his cell. The next night she sweet-talked the jailer into taking her into his office for some lovemaking. Meanwhile, the inmates sang *corridos* with a guitar and concertina while Chacon sawed away on the bars. Less than twenty-four hours before Chacon was to hang, the jailer released himself from a fond embrace to check on his prisoner, only to find the cell empty. Chacon had made his escape and headed for the Mexican border. Chacon remained free until 1902, when Arizona Ranger captain Burt Mossman slipped into Mexico and made a daring capture. Chacon was returned to Solomon, and this time the hanging came off on schedule.

GRIPE

Just southeast of Solomon was a produce and plant inspection station known as Gripe, whose name has an interesting origin. In the 1930s, to prevent the spread of plant disease and insects, the Arizona Agricultural Board established the station. While the state's intentions were laudable, weary motorists still tended to resent the inconvenience of being stopped. When employees were thinking of a suitable name for the place, some clever wag suggested Gripe. The inspection station was closed in the 1970s, and there is no longer a town at Gripe.

ASHURST

Ashurst, a few miles up the road from Pima on US 70, was originally called Redlands because of its reddish soil. In 1918 the new post office arrived and the town became Ashurst, after U.S. senator Henry Fountain Ashurst. Henry Ashurst came to Arizona from Nevada in 1877, at the age of three. In his youth he worked as a cowboy around Flagstaff, and he later practiced law in Flagstaff and became well-known for his knowledge of Shakespeare and his ability as an orator. In the late 1890s Ashurst was elected to the territorial legislature, and when Arizona became a state in 1912, he went to Washington as a U.S. senator. He served five terms and became known in the Senate as the "silver-tongued orator of the Colorado."

FORT THOMAS

The fort, named for Civil War hero Gen. George Thomas, was established along the Gila River in 1876 to replace Fort Goodwin, which had been abandoned due to malaria. The new post offered no relief from health problems, however—doctors reported severe cases of malaria, typhoid fever, and chronic depression, the latter of which was blamed on the climate and location. The fort's twenty-seven adobe, shingle-roof buildings had piped-in water but no sewer system. Considered by many to be the worst post in the whole U.S. Army, it was closed on December 3, 1892.

In 1965, a monument honoring Melvin Jones, a founder of the humanitarian service organization Lions International, was erected here. Jones was born at the fort in 1879 and lived there with his family until he was eight. He later wrote that his boyhood memories consisted of "horses, blue-clad troopers, bugles and war cries, wagon trains, gaunt settlers and dust."

On May 11, 1889, a crime with one of Arizona's most vexing outcomes occurred on the road between Fort Thomas and Fort

Fort Thomas in the 1880s —Southwest Studies, Scottsdale Community College

Grant, about thirty miles due south. Maj. Joseph Wham, army paymaster, and his 24th Cavalry escort were ambushed and robbed of $26,000 in gold and silver by a gang of between eight and twenty men. The outlaws fired down on the troops from a high, rocky ledge, forcing them to abandon the money wagon and run for cover. Seven of the eleven soldiers were wounded.

Later, one by one, some of the outlaws were rounded up. They turned out to be members of prominent families in the area. The families hired a battery of high-powered attorneys, including Tombstone lawyer Marcus Smith. At that time, resentment of the federal government in Arizona was fierce (a feeling that survives in some rural parts of the state), making citizens disinclined to take the military's side. Despite overwhelming evidence presented by the prosecution, the jury found the robbers innocent. Some consider the case one of the worst miscarriages of justice in Arizona history. Oddly, in the 1920s, the Wham robbery was reenacted during a local Pioneer Days celebration, with descendants of the outlaws playing the robbers.

GERONIMO

Little remains of this community five miles northwest of Fort Thomas, just outside the border of the San Carlos Indian Reservation. It was named in honor of the notorious Chiricahua leader. When the railroad was laying track up the Gila Valley in 1895, the Apache refused to allow it to cross their reservation. The company negotiated a settlement in which the Indians were allowed to ride for free.

In its heyday, the town was a sanctuary for outlaws during warm weather. Its buildings were mostly adobe with flat roofs, and by climbing up on the roofs and pulling the ladder up behind them, those on the lam could get a good night's rest without worrying about someone sneaking up on them.

Geronimo, like the rest of lawless Arizona Territory, had its share of frontier con men, ranging from tinhorn gamblers to stock swindlers. Today's disreputable land promoters selling lakeshore lots on the edges of mirages have nothing on the wheeler-dealers of yesteryear. One of Geronimo's was "Doctor" Richard Flower. Before coming to Arizona, Flower made a living selling bottles of cure-all medicine. He claimed his recipe would cure everything

*Freight wagons at the tent city of Geronimo in
the 1880s* —Southwest Studies, Scottsdale Community College

from baldness to toothache. Although the nostrum had no
medicinal value, it contained enough alcohol to mellow "Doc"
Flower's patients enough so they didn't feel cheated.

Eventually Flower, growing weary of small-time scheming,
decided to play for higher stakes. Fortunes were being made in
the Arizona mines, but he did not have a bona fide mine to call
his own—so he created one. Although he had never been to
Arizona and would not have known a gold nugget from rolled
oats, he rushed ahead with his scheme. He erected a fake, movie-
set mine complete with headframe near Geronimo, bought a few
samples of ore, and headed east to promote his "strike."

Flower called his mine the Spendazuma: "mazuma" was slang
for money, so in effect he was promoting the "spend your money"
mine. The scam worked at first. Would-be millionaires were
waiting in line to buy stock in Doc's mine. But the balloon burst
when the *Arizona Republican* (today's *Republic*) reporter George
Smalley rode out to have look at the mine that was creating such
a stir back east.

When Smalley's exposé hit the papers, Flower's lawyer indignantly threatened to sue for $100,000 and demanded a retraction. Smalley could hardly keep from laughing, so they offered him $5,000 to rewrite the story to say he had made a mistake. When the spunky reporter assumed a pugilist's stance, the lawyer retreated, and Doc Flower's blossoming Spendazuma scheme withered away.

SAN CARLOS INDIAN RESERVATION

Just past Geronimo, the highway passes into the San Carlos Reservation, home to 10,000 Apache and others. The San Carlos Reservation encompasses nearly 2 million acres just south of the slightly smaller Fort Apache Reservation and includes San Carlos Lake, a reservoir created by Coolidge Dam in the 1930s. The town of San Carlos sits on the San Carlos River about a mile from its junction with the Gila.

Along with the Navajo, the Apache are Arizona's only Athabascan-speaking Indians. Some anthropologists believe the Apache and Navajo came to North America about 6,000 years ago in the second of three great migrations from Asia. They arrived in the Southwest perhaps as early as A.D. 1100 after a long journey from Canada. While the Apache still call themselves Diné or Inde (the People), in those early times, others had less kind names for the nomads. The Zuni called them *Apache,* or "Enemies," and the name stuck.

Around 1400 the Apache and their relatives broke into various groups and went in different directions. The Navajo and Jicarilla Apache settled in the San Juan River basin in the Four Corners region. The Mescalero Apache migrated into southern New Mexico. The Chiricahua Apache occupied southern Arizona, northern Mexico, and southwest New Mexico. The Lipan Apache spread into west Texas, where they adopted customs and warfare techniques of Plains Indians, as did the Kiowa Apache. With many subgroups including the Gila, Pinal, Aravaipa, Coyotero, and Tonto, the Western Apache roamed the rugged central mountains of Arizona.

Essentially hunters and gatherers, the Apache adjusted to their harsh environment by living in small bands. Later, the fact that the Apache did not see themselves as one political entity would prove confusing to whites. To the Apache, military defeats or peace treaties with one band weren't considered binding by other bands. From the seventeenth century until they went to reservations, the Apache increased their numbers by taking captives from other peoples. For as long as they could, they clung to their nomadic lifestyle, offering fierce resistance to European encroachment on their lands and way of life.

Soon after it was created in 1873, the San Carlos Reservation came to be known as Hell's Forty Acres. Gen. Oliver Howard established San Carlos, along with the White Mountain and Fort Apache reserves, during his peace mission of 1872, simultaneously abolishing reservations at Fort McDowell, Date Creek, and Beale Springs. Over the next three years Indians from the closed

Coyotero Apache man on left, San Carlos Apache man on right, San Carlos Reservation, circa 1883 —
Southwest Studies, Scottsdale Community College

reservations were taken to San Carlos. Gen. George Crook opposed the plan, feeling that the gathering together of so many Indian bands hostile to each other was bound to cause trouble. In fact, the animosities among the Indians provided unreconstructed rebels like Geronimo the opportunity to recruit malcontents for renegade forays off the reservation.

By 1876, 4,000 Apache, Mojave, and Yavapai were crowded into San Carlos, and tensions grew, not only among the Indians, but between the Indians and the soldiers. That year, Geronimo broke from the reservation and cut a wide swath of terror and death across southern Arizona and Mexico. The following year Indian agent John Clum and his Apache police made a daring capture of both Geronimo and the notorious Victorio, successor to Apache chief Mangas Coloradas.

The soldiers left Camp San Carlos in 1900. At first, the Bureau of Indian Affairs did much of the governing for the reservation. Now, tribes govern themselves, with a tribal council and chairman.

SAN CARLOS LAKE AND COOLIDGE DAM

In 1924 President Calvin Coolidge signed the bill authorizing the building of Coolidge Dam on the upper Gila River to provide water to reservation and area farmers. Construction began in 1927. After the 249-foot-high, 920-foot-wide dam's completion in 1930, it took San Carlos Lake over fifty years to fill up behind the dam. Gazing out on the weed-filled area behind the dam after its dedication in 1930, American humorist Will Rogers remarked, "If that was my lake, I'd mow it."

US 191
US 70—Sanders
245 MILES

CORONADO TRAIL

Between Clifton and Springerville, US 191 roughly follows the northern part of what is believed to be Francisco Vasquez de Coronado's route through Arizona. In February 1540, the Coronado expedition, numbering over 1,000 people, left Compostela, Mexico, in search of fabled lands of gold to the north (see also Coronado National Memorial). They entered present-day Arizona near Bisbee and continued north through the San Pedro Valley, heading for the Zuni pueblo called Hawikuh and hoping it was what they sought.

On July 7, 1540, they reached the pueblo's first village, Cibola—today, a ruin on the Zuni reservation. It was small and poor, and the explorers' disappointment was bitter. Their arrival did not go unnoticed; soon a crowd of Zuni and ally warriors had gathered. Attempts at communication ended with cornmeal scattered on the ground in a symbolic line the newcomers should not, but did, cross; battle resulted, with the Spanish the winners. The battle of Hawikuh was the first clash of many between white men and native people in what would become the continental United States.

The Zuni told Coronado of seven villages about twenty-five leagues west. There, on high mesas, lived a "warlike people" who paradoxically called themselves the Hopitu (the Peaceful People). Coronado sent Pedro de Tovar with a party to explore. They found the mesas in the evening, crept to the edges, and waited. At dawn the villagers saw them and prepared for battle. As at Hawikuh, Tovar's attempted communications drew only catcalls, cornmeal, and a skirmish, which lasted just a few minutes and caused no deaths. Tovar was preparing for a real attack on the village when chiefs appeared bearing gifts. They told him of a great river to the west (the Colorado) that might be what he sought. However, exploratory parties brought back only bad news. Coronado returned to Mexico City in disgrace and died a few years later, never dreaming he would one day be numbered among Spain's greatest explorers.

CLIFTON AND MORENCI

Clifton and Morenci are two of a cluster of mining and cattle towns around the San Francisco River near its confluence with the Gila. Clifton, twenty-four miles north of US 70 via AZ 75 and US 191, may have been named for Henry Clifton, one of the first settlers to arrive in the Prescott area following the discovery of gold in 1863. Others claim the town was named for the cliffs along the San Francisco River, which flows through town.

In 1872, a mining camp sprang up near Clifton. It was called Joy's Camp, after mineral surveyor Capt. Miles Joy. Around 1874, investor William Church arrived at Joy's Camp, bought four claims, and organized the Detroit Copper Company, incorporated in 1875. Joy's Camp was renamed Morenci after a town in Michigan.

Chase Creek, one of Clifton's main streets, 1890s —Arizona Historical Foundation

In the early 1870s several men, including army captain John Bourke and brothers Jim and Bob Metcalf, reported rich copper ore in the area. Copper, not gold, would bring the Clifton-Morenci Mining District its wealth. The Montezuma, Copper Mountain, and Yankie claims, staked in 1872, would prove to be among the richest mines in the Southwest. But in the 1870s, mining in the area was difficult. It was more than 700 miles to the nearest railroad, at La Junta, Colorado, and more than one prospector lost his scalp to an Apache.

Apache and Comanche attacked many ox trains as they hauled smelted copper some 1,200 miles over the Santa Fe Trail to Kansas City. Killing the drivers and taking the oxen for meat, the warriors left the copper ingots—of no value to them—for the next ore train to retrieve. The cost of operating these ox trains was high in money, time, and lives. In 1879 a steam locomotive replaced the ox trains.

Morenci, circa 1910 —Arizona Historical Society Library/Tucson

In 1921 the Arizona Copper Company and the area's other main operation, the Detroit Copper Company, both became part of the Phelps-Dodge Corporation. Over the next half century the Clifton-Morenci area became one of Arizona's greatest copper-mining districts. In 1939 Phelps-Dodge began a massive open-pit operation that, by the late 1960s, had swallowed up the picturesque city of Morenci. A new community was built on a nearby hill. By the 1950s, the Morenci Mine was the second-largest mine in America and the fourth-largest in the world.

At the same time the mines were starting up, cattlemen were moving in. Today, they still run cows on the Blue River at the historic Triple X Ranch, established in 1885.

When Clifton was still a raw town, residents demanded the construction of a suitable place to lock up intractables. The result was a most unusual, escape-proof jail. Built in 1881, it was blasted out of a solid rock cliff on the floodplain above the river (which meant that whenever the river flooded, prisoners had to be quickly evacuated). The town hired a hard-rock miner to gouge out the jail, and after being paid, he went on a binge at the nearest whiskey mill, Hovey's Dance Hall. Later that evening he proposed

The Clifton Cliff jail —Arizona Historical Foundation

a toast to the world's greatest jail builder, and when no one would lift a glass in his honor, he proceeded to shoot holes in the ceiling. Escorted to the new jail, he became not only its creator, but its first inmate.

In 1904, Clifton-Morenci was the site of a big hoopla about forty poor orphans. Nuns from New York had brought the children west to new homes with good Catholic families. However, the children were white, and the mining families that had agreed to take them were Mexican. Led by the town's indignant white matrons, a vigilante squad kidnapped the children to ensure their protection from what, in the whites' eyes, was practically child abuse. The squad also nearly lynched the nuns and the town's priest. Later, when the Catholic Church sued to get the children back, every court up the line to the Supreme Court in Washington supported the vigilantes.

ALPINE

At the junction of US 191 and US 180, Alpine, nestled in some of Arizona's most spectacular high country, was originally called Bush Valley for Anderson Bush, its first settler, who arrived in 1876. Three years later, a party of Mormons renamed it Frisco for the nearby San Francisco River. Finally, because of the tall mountains, the town was named Alpine.

Jacob Hamblin, the greatest of all Mormon trailblazers of the Southwest, is buried here. Hamblin explored much of northern Arizona from the 1850s to the 1870s, searching for sites for prospective Mormon colonies. He was the first American missionary among the Hopi and Navajo. In 1869 he helped guide John Wesley Powell's expedition north of the Grand Canyon. He also helped Powell negotiate treaties with natives. Hamblin died in 1886.

SPRINGERVILLE AND EAGAR

Springerville, at the junction of US 191 and US 60, is an important center of tourism, trade, ranching, and lumber. About 2,000 people live here. The first settlers, Mexicans, arrived in this area from New Mexico sometime prior to 1871 and named the place Valle Redondo, or "Round Valley." Horse thieves used Round Valley as a refuge where they could alter the brands of livestock stolen in northern Arizona to sell them later down south. On the way back, they rustled herds from southern ranches to sell up north.

Springerville's namesake, merchant Henry Springer, unwittingly extended credit to most of the unsavory characters in Round Valley and eventually went broke. Neighboring Eagar, at the foot of the majestic White Mountains, is an interesting contrast to Springerville—the latter settled primarily by Catholic Hispanics, the former by Anglo Mormons. Eagar was named for its first homesteaders, brothers John, Joe, and William Eagar, who arrived in 1878.

The stability of the settlements around Springerville was shaken when Texas cattlemen drove large herds of cattle into the area in the 1880s. With them came cattle rustlers and other unsavory characters, including the two Clanton brothers who survived the infamous Earp-Clanton feud in Tombstone (see Tombstone, "The Gunfight and Its Aftermath").

The Westbrook and Snider gangs worked out of the Springerville area as well. Infighting in the Snider gang climaxed in a shoot-out one day on the hill behind the Eagar cemetery. When the smoke cleared, nine lay dead. On Christmas Day, 1887, members of the Westbrook gang shot and killed Springerville citizen James Hale as he walked down the street. They gave as their reason the desire "to see if a bullet would go through a Mormon."

In 1928 the National Old Trails Association and the Daughters of the American Revolution dedicated twelve "Madonna of the Trail" statues depicting the hardy but largely unsung pioneer women who "wested" in the nineteenth century. One of the eighteen-foot granite statues stands in the center of Springerville. The town also has a small but fine collection of European art at the Cushman Art Museum.

Casa Malpais Archaeological Park

On the northern outskirts of Springerville are the ruins of the prehistoric Mogollon village of Casa Malpais, Spanish for "Badlands House." Occupied between A.D. 1265 and 1380, the pueblo sits on a large lava flow, which inspired the name. Underneath the pueblo, a series of caves form a system of

The Madonna of the Trail statue in Springerville, (by August Leimbach) 1981 —Author photo

catacombs—something quite rare in the Southwest. The masonry pueblo itself rose two to three stories and had more than 120 rooms. It is believed to have been a major ceremonial and trade center.

The city of Springerville owns the site of Casa Malpais and provides tours and interpretive programs. The sacred underground catacombs, however, are not open to visitors. The Raven and White Mountain archaeological sites are also nearby.

ST. JOHNS

St. Johns, about twice the size of Springerville, sits at the junction of US 191 and AZ 61 on the Little Colorado River. People have lived along the Little Colorado River since at least 8,000 years ago when bands of Paleo-Indians stalked game across the grasslands and camped along the river's banks. Ancestral Pueblo people (Anasazi) and, later, Pueblo Indians including the Zuni and Hopi followed. Later, nomadic Athabascan-speakers who would become the Apache and Navajo ranged throughout this area.

The first American settler was a Prussian immigrant named Solomon Barth. It was said Barth had fought with guerilla Confederate forces in Arizona in 1862. A few years later, he began hauling ore from the mines at Wickenburg to the railhead at Dodge City, Kansas, then driving back with supplies for the military posts and mining camps along the way. With oxen, the round trip took six weeks.

Barth saw agricultural potential in the Little Colorado Valley. When Fort Apache was built in the area in 1871, a ready market for meat and crops opened, and Barth seized his chance. He recruited settlers from Cubero and Cebolleta, New Mexico, to raise sheep and crops. In 1872, Barth moved the families to a place Mexican sheepherders called El Vadito (Little Crossing), where water was plentiful. The settlers' houses fanned out along the river, and the road to Fort Apache ran across Barth's front yard. Barth named the new town San Juan after its first female resident, Señora María San Juan de Padilla. However, the postmaster general decided San Juan was too "foreign-sounding" and anglicized it.

In the spring of 1876, Mormon immigrants from Utah discovered the Little Colorado and spread quickly along its banks. Soon they were running out of land, and they approached Barth

St. Johns, Arizona, circa 1895 —Arizona Historical Society Library/Tucson

about purchasing property in St. Johns. Thinking of the land as his own, Barth sold squatters' rights to the Mormons for 750 cows and $2,000 in goods.

Forced off what they had believed was their land, many original St. Johns settlers left. For the ones who stayed, a line divided them from the Mormons. Well into the twentieth century, no Mormon lived east of the road, and no non-Mormon lived west of it. Tensions between the two groups often broke into violence.

Perhaps it was justice that, before too long, Barth and the Mormons became political enemies. During the 1880s Barth was a primary figure in a corrupt, strongly anti-Mormon group of politicos known as the "St. Johns Ring." But over the next several years the Mormons gained political sophistication. During the election of 1888, the Mormons joined forces with Democrats in the area and elected several of their number to county offices.

Barth was later convicted of forgery and did time in prison, though payments to officials cut that time short. When he returned home, he resumed the mercantile and hotel business he had previously established and continued his life as a prominent figure in St. Johns.

Udall Family

Among the more famous people born and raised in St. Johns were Stewart and Morris Udall. Their father, Levi S. Udall, was one of Arizona's leading citizens and was for years a justice on the state supreme court. Their grandfather, David K. Udall, was leader of the first Mormon colonizers at St. Johns. Both Morris and Stewart were basketball stars at the University of Arizona. After World War II, the brothers returned to the university to attend law school.

In 1954 Stewart Udall was elected to Congress. Six years later, President John F. Kennedy appointed him Secretary of the Interior. He was the first Arizonan to hold a cabinet post. Morris replaced his brother in Congress in 1961. "Mo," as he was called, had a folksy, homespun personality that made him one of Washington's most popular politicians. In 1976 he ran a strong campaign for president in the Democratic primaries before losing out to Jimmy Carter. He retired from the House of Representatives in 1991, and died in 1998.

Stewart (left) and Morris Udall —Arizona Historical Foundation

ZUNI RIVER

A few miles north of St. Johns is the Zuni River, which is often dry except after a hard rain. For hundreds of years Indians of the Zuni pueblo of New Mexico have held this area sacred. In fact, though few if any Zuni live in Arizona, a tiny seventeen-mile-square Zuni reservation, known as Zuni Heaven, exists near here especially for the tribe's religious ceremonies. The Zuni believe the spirits of their ancestors reside in this area. Once every four years, during summer, the Zuni travel forty-five miles from their pueblo to the reservation for the ceremonies. Anthropologists believe the Zuni have been holding these ceremonies in this place since A.D. 900. In 1985, recognizing the area's religious significance for the Zuni, the state of Arizona gave the land to the tribe through a land swap, and the reservation was established.

AZ 260
Eagar—Payson
138 MILES

GREER

A few miles south of AZ 260 on AZ 373 is Greer, in the beautiful, lush Greer Valley near the headwaters of the Little Colorado River. Today Greer is a popular, upscale vacation town, near several lakes and streams as well as the Sunrise Park Resort ski area. A few miles northwest of Greer, travelers on AZ 260 can spot a small, round-top mountain cluttered with a few remnants of the ski area known as Big Cienega. Before Sunrise was built, Big Cienega's gentle slopes offered the only skiing in the White Mountains.

Located in Greer is the Butterfly Lodge Museum. Housed in a cabin built in 1913, the museum traces the lives of a famous father and son. James Willard Schultz (1859–1947), originally from a wealthy New York family, came west in the 1870s and fell in love with the country. He worked all over the West as a hunting guide, trapper, and Indian-rights advocate. He also wrote thirty-seven books of adventure, three set in Arizona. During his time in Arizona he lived with the Pima Indians and worked closely with the Hopi, Navajo, and Apache.

With his Blackfoot wife, Schultz had one son, Hart Merriam Schultz (1882–1970). The son, also called Lone Wolf, came under the influence of Thomas Moran and became a well-known artist. Although both father and son were outsiders in Greer, a close-knit Mormon community, they spent much time here writing and painting. Exhibits in the museum show glimpses of the lives and work of these two men.

A few miles west of the Greer exit, AZ 260 enters the Fort Apache Indian Reservation, which lies directly north of and adjacent to the San Carlos Reservation. The Black River serves as the border between the two reservations. Both encompass fine ranch land and recreation areas. From here, AZ 260 more or less follows the scenic 200-mile-long Mogollon Rim all the way to Clarkdale in the Verde Valley.

MCNARY

Today McNary is a small community on the Fort Apache Reservation, but it was once a booming milltown. Before that, back in 1879, Oscar and Alfred Cluff harvested wild hay here and sold it to the government at Fort Apache. The place was then known as Cluff's Cienega (*cienega* is Spanish for "marsh").

During World War I, Tomas Pollock, a Flagstaff entrepreneur, and Amasa McGaffey, a lumberman from Albuquerque, leased some land on the Fort Apache Reservation and built a sawmill at Cluff's Cienega. In 1919 they founded a town there and later built a railroad. But in 1924, hard times fell on the two, and they sold out to James G. McNary and William H. Cady of McNary, Louisana.

Contrary to popular belief, Cady did not rename the town directly for his partner James McNary but for their hometown of McNary, Louisiana, which was itself named for James McNary's family. The McNary Lumber Company, which later became known as Southwest Forest & Lumber Mills and eventually Southwest Forest Industries, prospered for several decades.

Soon after Cady and McNary took over, Cady transported 800 workers from his operation in Louisiana. Most of these employees were black, and segregation between the races was strictly enforced. For many years in McNary, the blacks lived in the "Quarters" near the sawmill, and the whites on the "Hill."

The town had a peak population of nearly 2,000 in 1950. But when a fire destroyed the sawmill in 1979, the company did not rebuild, and the town decayed quickly. By 1980 the population had dwindled to fewer than 500. Vandals destroyed some of the old wooden dwellings, but many of the abandoned homes are now occupied by Apache families. The tribal resort-casino in nearby Hon Dah, built in 1998, has led to new growth and jobs in McNary.

HON DAH

Hon Dah, at the junction of AZ 260 and AZ 73, on the edge of the Fort Apache Reservation, is a gateway to the White Mountains. By most accounts, the name comes from the Apache word for "welcome." Some, however, claim it is an abbreviation of a longer phrase that means "I will not kill you, at least not today." The

Hon-Dah Casino & Resort, with its luxury hotel, restaurants, and gambling palace, opened in 1998.

PINETOP-LAKESIDE

Pinetop-Lakeside, once two adjacent ranching towns, is now an incorporated resort community just north of the Fort Apache Reservation. The origins of the name of Pinetop lie in a saloon operated in the 1880s by Johnny Phipps; it was a favorite watering hole of black cavalry troopers stationed at Fort Apache. When Phipps died in 1890, Bill Penrod took over, and for a time the saloon and town were called Penrod. However, the soldiers insisted on calling the place Pinetop. The name was inspired not by the lofty trees that abound in the area, but by tall, lanky, bushy-headed Walt Rigney, a bartender who worked at the saloon and was known affectionately by that name. In 1895 the post office officially renamed the town Pinetop.

SHOW LOW

Corydon E. Cooley was a noted scout for Gen. George Crook during the Apache Wars. Cooley lived in the Show Low area with his two Apache wives, Molly and Cora. Both were daughters of Pedro, a well-known chief of the Carrizo Creek area. Cooley and his neighbor Marion Clark decided they were living too close together and that one had to move, so they decided to settle the issue with a game of cards. On the last hand, Cooley needed a low card to claim victory. "If you can show low, you win," Clark said. Cooley drew the deuce of clubs and replied, "Show low it is." So the town was named. The main street through Show Low, the "gateway to the White Mountains," is called Deuce of Clubs in honor of Cooley's lucky draw.

Cooley's ranch was a favorite resting place for soldiers traveling along the Crook Military Road from Fort Apache to Fort Verde. Army bride Martha Summerhayes stayed at the ranch briefly in 1874. Her host's domestic arrangement unsettled her.

> Towards night we made camp at Cooley's ranch, and slept inside, on the floor. . . . There seemed to be two Indian girls at his ranch; they were both tidy and good-looking, and they prepared us a most appetizing supper.

Martha Summerhayes
—Southwest Studies, Scottsdale
Community College

The ranch had spaces for windows, covered with thin unbleached muslin (or manta, as it is always called out there), glass windows being then too great a luxury in that remote place. There were some partitions inside the ranch, but no doors; and, of course, no floors except adobe. . . . As we prepared for rest . . . I lay gazing into the fire which was smouldering in the corner, and finally I said, in a whisper, "Jack, which do you think is Cooley's wife?"

"I don't know," answered this cross and tired man; and then added, "both of 'em, I guess."

Now this was too awful, but I knew he did not intend for me to ask any more questions. I had a difficult time, in those days, reconciling what I saw with what I had been taught was right, and I had to sort over my ideas and deep-rooted prejudices a good many times.

Between Show Low and the turnoff for Young, AZ 260 passes through a number of small, quiet lumber and ranching towns including Linden, Clay Springs, Pinedale, Overgaard, and Heber. The highway between Show Low and Overgaard was not even

Show Low, mid-1940s —Southwest Studies, Scottsdale Community College

paved until the mid-1970s. In 2002, the Rodeo-Chedeski fire raged in this area, destroying 500,000 acres—the worst forest fire in Arizona history.

PLEASANT VALLEY AND YOUNG

Young, named for a local rancher, is a quiet stop in cattle country, about twenty miles south of AZ 260 on unpaved AZ 288, in the heart of Pleasant Valley. In spite of its name, Pleasant Valley was an area of much violence. The most notable conflict took place between 1887 and 1892 in the bloody family feud known as the Pleasant Valley War.

In 1879 a widower named John Tewksbury and his sons Ed, Frank, Jim, and John Jr. came to Pleasant Valley from California amd started a cattle ranch. Three years later the Graham family— Tom, John, and Billy—arrived in the valley from Ohio. In the meantime, another rancher, Jim Stinson, had come to the area with a sizable herd. Foolishly, Stinson branded his cattle with a simple "T"—an easy brand to alter, which is just what some of his neighbors started doing, with enthusiasm.

In 1883, Stinson began complaining that his cattle were being rustled. His foreman, John Gilliland, who didn't like the Tewksburys, rode to the family's ranch with some companions and

Edwin Tewksbury
—Southwest Studies,
Scottsdale Community
College

accused them of stealing cattle. Tom and John Graham were visiting at the ranch that day. Without warning, Gilliland pulled his gun and fired at Ed Tewksbury but missed. Tewksbury grabbed a rifle and fired back, slightly wounding two of Gilliland's party. For this, Tewksbury was charged with murder. Since there was no murder, the charges were ultimately dismissed as frivolous, but the Tewksbury brothers still had to ride all the way to the county seat at Prescott to deal with the legalities. On the chilly ride home, Frank Tewksbury contracted pneumonia and died soon after.

Many historians believe that Stinson and Gilliland made a deal with the Grahams to help Stinson prosecute the Tewksburys, and that it was actually the Grahams who'd been rustling Stinson's cattle.

Eventually the community divided into two factions, one siding with the Tewksbury family, the other with the Grahams. On the Graham side were Texan Mart Blevins and his many sons, one of whom was the notorious Andy Blevins, wanted in Texas, also

Tom Graham
—Southwest Studies,
Scottsdale Community
College

known by the alias Andy Cooper. Over the next several years, nearly thirty men would die in Pleasant Valley.

In February 1887 the Daggs brothers, a sheep outfit from Flagstaff, hired Bill Jacobs, a Tewksbury partisan, to drive a herd of sheep into Pleasant Valley. On the way, one of the herders was killed and beheaded. Hollywood and pulp writers have presented this feud as a sheepmen-cattlemen war, but in reality the issue of sheep versus cattle played a minor role in the drama.

In July 1887, Old Man Blevins rode off into the hills and was never seen again. It was presumed someone from the Tewksbury clan had plugged him. Two weeks later a group of Graham supporters, including Hamp Blevins, picked a fight with the Tewksbury brothers and ally Jim Roberts. When the smoke cleared, Blevins and one of his pals lay dead. A few days later trader Jim Houck, a Tewksbury sympathizer, killed eighteen-year-old Billy Graham. Clearly, up to this point the Grahams were getting the worst of it.

On September 2, 1887, the Grahams and Andy Cooper (Blevins) got revenge. The gang surrounded Tewksbury's ranch house before sunrise and waited. When Bill Jacobs and John Tewksbury stepped outside, their bodies were riddled with bullets. Further bloodshed was averted when a posse from Prescott arrived and drove off the Graham-Blevins gang.

Two weeks later the Grahams tried another early-morning attack. This time Jim Roberts, waking early, saw the men setting up the ambush. Roberts and the Tewksburys, all expert marksmen, opened fire, killing one and wounding several others. Meanwhile, John Graham and Charlie Blevins were killed when they tried to outrun a posse that was sent out to bring them in.

Later, prominent members of both groups were arrested and brought to Prescott, but charges were dropped when witnesses failed to appear. Athough the Graham-Tewksbury war was technically over, the killing didn't stop. Vigilantes determined to rid the area of rustlers and opportunists hoping to claim the ranches of the feuding families went on a campaign of terror. Any outsider was suspect, and at least three innocent men were hanged. Historians consider this the most dangerous period of the whole feud.

Tom Graham, the last man standing on his side, moved to Tempe, got married, and settled down. But feuds die hard—in 1892 Ed Tewksbury shot and killed Graham near Double Buttes, just east of today's I-10 and Broadway. Tewksbury, with the help of some clever attorneys, was released on a legal technicality. He then moved to Globe, where he spent his last days as a peace officer.

KOHLS RANCH

As AZ 260 winds and climbs over the top of the precipitous Mogollon Rim toward Payson, it passes small towns like Kohls Ranch, Tonto Village, and Star Valley. Kohls Ranch, a relative newcomer, established a post office in 1939 for residents and summer refugees escaping the heat of the Phoenix area. Just north of Kohls Ranch is Woods Canyon, in which western writer Zane Grey had a cabin where he produced some of his best works, including *To the Last Man,* a fictionalized account of the Pleasant

Zane Grey cabin, 1987 —Gary Johnson photo

Valley War, and *Under the Tonto Rim*. For a time after his death, the cabin was part of a museum, but the museum and cabin burned down in the 1990 Dude fire that ravaged the rim country.

AZ 73
Hon Dah—US 60
45 MILES

FORT APACHE

Fort Apache still exists as a town on AZ 73, about eighteen miles south of Hon Dah. Fort Apache Historic Park covers nearly 300 acres, including the Apache Museum and Cultural Center. Some of the old buildings—including the commanding officers' quarters, the adjutant's office, and Officers Row—are still standing. Fort

Fort Apache, 1870s —Southwest Studies, Scottsdale Community College

Apache saw its last action during the Pershing Expedition into Mexico, 1916–17.

Theodore Roosevelt Indian Boarding School was established at the fort in 1923, though the rest of the fort was abandoned the following year. Children age three to eight, mostly Navajo, received vocational training. Founded like most Indian boarding schools at the time to "take the Indian out of the Indian," the school still exists, but it focuses now on the value and cultivation of traditional Indian beliefs and customs.

Thanks in part to the silver screen, Fort Apache is one of the best-known military posts in the West. Although it was in one of the most remote parts of Arizona, it was strategically placed between the Apache tribes to the south and the Navajo Nation to the north. During the waning days of the Apache Wars in 1886, Chiricahua bands were gathered here, taken to Holbrook, and put on trains for Florida.

The military installation at this site, originally called Camp Ord, was established in the spring of 1870 by Maj. John Green. The name changed twice more that year—to Camp Mogollon, then Camp Thomas. The most likely explanation for the next change, to Camp Apache, is simply that the installation was in the middle of Apache territory. The post officially became Fort Apache in 1879.

Despite the beautiful scenery surrounding it, Camp Apache was a lonely, primitive duty station. Army wife Martha Summerhayes and her husband Lt. Jack Summerhayes arrived at Camp Apache in October 1874.

In January Martha gave birth to a son, the first Anglo child born in these parts. Area sheep ranchers and cattlemen joined the soldiers at the fort to celebrate the baby and congratulate the parents. The infant was of great interest to the Indians as well, including several Apache women on the nearby reservation:

> The seventh day after the birth of the baby, a delegation of several squaws, wives of chiefs, came to pay me a formal visit. They brought me some finely woven baskets, and a beautiful pappoose-basket or cradle, such as they carry their own babies in. This was made of the lightest wood, and covered with the finest skin of fawn, tanned with birch bark by their own hands, and embroidered in blue beads; it was their best work. I admired it, and tried to express to them my thanks. These squaws took my baby (he was lying beside me on the bed), then, cooing and chuckling, they . . . found a small pillow, which they laid into the basket-cradle, then put my baby in, drew the flaps together, and laced him into it; then stood it up, and laid it down, and laughed again in their gentle manner, and finally soothed him to sleep. I was quite touched by the friendliness of it all.

KINISHBA RUINS

The three-story-high Kinishba Ruins, off AZ 73 a few miles west of Fort Apache, on Reservation Route 41, are among the best examples of the prehistoric Mogollon Culture found in Arizona. In the 1930s Dr. Byron Cummings of the University of Arizona and his team of archaeologists restored a part of Kinishba, excavated other ruins, and left a mound for future scientists to explore. It is estimated that as many as 2,000 people lived in this 210-room sandstone building between A.D. 1100 and 1300.

The Mogollon people lived mainly in the central mountains of Arizona. They're believed to have descended from the Cochise Culture, so named simply because many of their sites were found in modern Cochise County. The Cochise Culture (circa 6000 to 300 B.C.) is the link between the ancient Paleo-Indian elephant hunters and the Ancestral Pueblo (Anasazi), Hohokam, Mogollon, and other tribes. The Mogollon natives abruptly left this area in the early 1300s for mysterious reasons. Evidence indicates they moved to Casas Grandes, Chihuahua, in northern Mexico.

AZ 61 and US 60
St. Johns—Globe
132 MILES

CONCHO

A few miles west of St. Johns on AZ 61 is Concho. The shallow basin around the community inspired the name, which means "Shell" in Spanish. Among the earliest settlers here was sheepman Juan Candaleria. Navajo raiders stole Candaleria from his home in Cubero, New Mexico, when he was nine. Soon after, the Navajo family to whom he belonged lost him to some White Mountain Apache in a gambling match. An Apache mother raised him, and he became a warrior. But at age nineteen, Candaleria went back to Cubero and married Regina Baca. He came to Concho in 1886 and, with the help and protection of his Apache relatives, he prospered and became a wealthy sheepman, raising fine merinos known for their wool rather than their meat. By the time his sons were grown, the family was running 100,000 sheep around Concho. His sons inherited the ranch, livestock, and town.

CIBECUE

Cibecue is a small Indian community about twelve miles west of US 60 on the partially paved Reservation Route 12. The exit is twenty-eight miles south of Show Low.

Most people are familiar with the Ghost Dance furor that culminated in the Battle of Wounded Knee in South Dakota in 1890, but few realize that a similar situation occurred among the Arizona Apache nearly a decade before that. An Indian mystic named Nock-ay-del-Klinne, mixing Apache and Christian religion, claimed the return of two dead chiefs who would lead a revolt against the whites. His teachings were loose and could be

Concho, 1936 —Arizona Historical Foundation

interpreted to suit individual believers. Soon not only Apache on the reservation but also army scouts were coming under his spell.

The government became uneasy about the Indians' behavior and decided to put a stop to Nock-ay-del-Klinne's troublemaking. On August 30, 1881, Col. Eugene A. Carr was sent from Fort Apache to Nock-ay-del-Klinne's home in Cibecue with 117 men, including 23 Apache scouts, to arrest him.

Geronimo, the eternal opportunist, was there and incited a riot over the arrest. As the troops were leaving Cibecue with their prisoner, several Apache opened fire. When the shooting ended, Nock-ay-del-Klinne was dead, as were eight soldiers, including Capt. Edmund Hentig. Most of the Apache scouts, torn between alliances, had sided with their own people during the melee. This was the only time in the history of Apache warfare that Apache scouts were disloyal to the army. Later, three of the scouts were hanged and two more sent to prison at Alcatraz.

After the incident at Cibecue, Apache warriors rallied around a chief named Na-ti-o-tish and rode into the Tonto Basin to raise hell. Militia were raised in Globe to pursue the Indians. The so-called Globe Rangers group, well fortified with whiskey, stopped to take a siesta at the Middleton Ranch. They had posted no guards, and while they were sleeping, several Apache crept in and stole their horses. It was a long walk back to town for the humiliated heroes of Globe.

The rebellious Apache were finally defeated on July 17, 1882, at Big Dry Wash, north of Payson. The Indians had tried to set up

Apache camp, circa 1880 —Smithsonian Institution

an ambush, but crafty scout Al Sieber smelled a rat and set an ambush of his own. When the smoke lifted, about twenty Apache, including Na-ti-o-tish, were dead. The incident marked the end of an era, for it was the last Indian battle fought on Arizona soil.

SALT RIVER CANYON

Back in the days before freeways and fast lanes, truckers hauling freight to and from eastern markets traveled US 60. The highway through Salt River Canyon, about halfway between Show Low and Globe, was the most treacherous part of the trip. It's still a steep hill, but today's vehicles are more powerful.

The Salt River flows across Arizona's central mountains for 200 miles before emptying into the Gila a few miles west of Phoenix. The Salt River's twisting, steep-sided canyons were in the heart of Apache-Yavapai country, and the canyons were one of the last Indian refuges from the U.S. Army. Until at least the mid-1880s the area remained a sanctuary for renegade Apache who had escaped the reservations. Apache old-timers claimed they used to sit in caves high above the canyon floor and watch the cavalry troops plodding along below in fruitless pursuit.

Skeleton Cave

In December 1872 a young Yavapai scout led soldiers to a hostile Yavapai camp in Salt River Canyon near today's Horse Mesa Dam. The natives, caught by surprise, retreated into a large opening in the canyon wall. The soldiers quickly blocked the entrance and ordered all men, women, and children to surrender, a request met by defiant war cries. When the troops told the Yavapai men to send out the women and children, the trapped band refused.

The battle that followed was one-sided. The soldiers fired into the walls, causing bullets to ricochet down on the helpless Yavapai. A small party of soldiers climbed above the rock fortress and started a rock slide. When the dust and smoke cleared, the Yavapai band was nearly annihilated. Seventy-six Indians were dead. The few survivors were taken as prisoners to Fort McDowell.

For the next thirty-four years, the massacre site remained undisturbed. Then Jeff Adams, an area rancher and later sheriff of Maricopa County, came across the site. Inside the cave, skeletons from the almost forgotten battle were scattered around, inspiring the name Skeleton Cave.

MCMILLENVILLE

The mining town of McMillenville, now a ghost town off US 60, twenty-eight miles north of Globe, was named for prospector Charlie McMillen. The story is told that in 1876, McMillen and his partner, Dore Harris, went prospecting a few miles north of Globe after a night on the town. They had not traveled far before the hungover McMillen said he needed a siesta. While he was snoozing, Harris started breaking off chunks of rock with his pick, uncovering a rich outcropping of almost pure silver. By now McMillen was wide awake, and the boys staked their claims.

The partners named their mine the Stonewall Jackson, and the town that soon sprang up around it was called McMillenville. The fabulous ledge of Stonewall Jackson silver ran ten miles. Yet McMillen and Harris did not fare all that well, prematurely selling the claim in 1877. The new owner reaped $2 million. McMillen drank himself to death a few months later, and Harris lost his earnings in the stock market.

For a time, McMillenville outgrew Globe. By 1880 about 1,500 miners were living there, and a twenty-stamp mill had replaced the original five-stamp mill. In 1882, after the Apache uprising at Cibecue, an Apache band attacked the town. Women and children hurried into the Stonewall Jackson Mine tunnel while the men gathered in an adobe building to ward off the warriors. Sharpshooters succeeded at keeping the Apache at bay until soldiers from Fort Apache arrived. Within a few years, though, the population had shrunk to one man—old "Uncle Charlie" Newton, who sat on his porch chomping on a pipe and telling anyone who would listen that McMillenville would boom again.

AZ 77
Show Low—Holbrook
52 MILES

SNOWFLAKE

In 1878 Jim Stinson sold his ranch here, three miles north of the town of Taylor, to Mormon pioneer William J. Flake and moved to Pleasant Valley. Later that same year, Mormon apostle Erastus Snow arrived with a bedraggled party of colonists from the Little Colorado River area—the river had gone on a rampage and wiped out their tiny community. Flake's ranch became a town site, and the town's name honored its two founders. In its early years, Snowflake was large enough to be the county seat for Apache County from 1879 to 1881. In 1895 the western half of the county seceded and created Navajo County.

HOLBROOK

The history-rich town of Holbrook, at the junction of AZ 77 and I-40, grew from Horsehead Crossing, a small community at the confluence of the Rio Puerco and the Little Colorado River. Juan Padilla was the first settler in the area, arriving in 1878 with an ox team. He hired a man named Berado to run a saloon. Berado's

William J. Flake, age ninety-three—still able to fork a horse (no date) —Arizona State Library

enterprising wife opened a store and restaurant in one part of the tavern.

The saloon became a favorite watering hole for travelers along the thirty-fifth parallel, and apparently Berado's spirited wife became a favorite of a lonesome fellow from Show Low named Henry Hurning. The story goes that Hurning arranged to get Berado drunk on his own whiskey, then have the lady kidnapped and delivered to his house in Show Low. There were no documents recording how this caveman-style courtship culminated, but Berado eventually returned to Albuquerque without the missus.

In 1881 the Atlantic & Pacific Railroad contracted John W. Young, a son of Brigham Young, to provide ties for the new line. A year after the line's completion, Young founded a new town a few miles west of Horsehead Crossing and named it Holbrook, for H. R. Holbrook, first engineer on the A & P. The town became the county seat for Navajo County in 1895, and until 1914 it was the only county seat in the United States without a church.

Holbrook, 1902 —Southwest Studies, Scottsdale Community College

In 1881 the Santa Fe linked northern Arizona with the rest of the civilized world, bringing new life to Holbrook and the other sleepy little settlements along the old Beale Camel Road.

After the railroad came through, Holbrook, with about 250 residents, became an important shipping center, moving cattle, wool, hides, and merchandise to the army, Indians, cattlemen, and settlers. This activity attracted a full complement of social misfits who could usually be found bellied up to the bar in the saloons along both sides of the tracks.

Hashknife Ranch

In spring 1884 when Edward Kinsley, a stockholder of the Atlantic & Pacific Railroad, went west to inspect the main line across northern Arizona, unusually heavy winter rains had made the rangelands lush in the Little Colorado River Valley. Kinsley was sure he had found one of America's great feeding grounds, where one could turn a $4 yearling into a $40 steer. He returned to New York and persuaded a group of investors to put $1.3 million in a cattle ranch. Thus was born the fabled Aztec Land & Cattle Company, later known as the Hashknife.

The following year the railroad offered 20 million acres of grazing land at prices ranging from 40 cents to $1.50 an acre. The Aztec bought a million acres for 50 cents an acre and brought in a large herd of Texas cattle. They also imported many Texas cowboys, with all their vices and virtues. It was said that many of these punchers left Texas because they were not wanted there, and many others left because they were wanted there.

The Aztec Land & Cattle Company ran as many as 60,000 cows and 2,000 horses on 2 million acres of private and government land between Holbrook and Flagstaff. The outfit became known as the Hashknife because its brand resembled a cooking tool used on chuckwagons. Until the company sold out in 1902 to the Babbitts of Flagstaff, the Hashknife was the second-largest cattle ranch in the United States; only the legendary XIT in Texas was bigger.

Hashknife cowboys in Holbrook (no date)
—Southwest Studies, Scottsdale Community College

Burt Mossman
—Southwest Studies,
Scottsdale Community
College

Rustlers bent on "stealing a start" in the cattle business hung around the fringes of the big outfits like wolves. Public sympathy was usually against eastern-owned ranches like the Hashknife, and a small rancher caught rustling cows usually got off. The Hashknife went fourteen years without a single conviction.

Then, in desperation, the company hired Burt Mossman. Mossman's life story reads like a Louis L'Amour western. Born in the Midwest, Mossman was working as a cowboy in New Mexico by age fifteen. A hot-tempered youth who fought at the drop of a hat, Mossman was also dependable and honest. At age twenty-one, he was foreman of a ranch with 8,000 head of cattle. At thirty, he became superintendent of the Hashknife, where he would gain his greatest fame.

After he took over, Mossman didn't waste any time. His first day on the job, he captured three cattle thieves and tweaked the nose of Winslow's town bully. Next he fired fifty-two of eighty-four Hashknife cowboys and installed trusted cowmen as wagon bosses. Soon the Hashknife was turning a profit. In the end, however, drought followed by a great blizzard finished off the Hashknife in 1901. The owners sold out.

Despite the ranch's failure, Mossman had earned a place in Arizona history as the "man who tamed the Hashknife." When the Arizona Rangers organized in 1901 to resist rustlers, Mossman was their first captain. He is recognized in the National Cowboy Hall of Fame.

Shoot-Out at the Blevins House

Holbrook was the setting of one of the West's most spectacular gunfights. In September 1887 the Pleasant Valley War, or Graham-Tewksbury feud, was just getting started (see Pleasant Valley and Young).

At the same time, the new sheriff of Apache County, Commodore Perry Owens, arrived in town. When Owens first rode into Holbrook, he immediately found himself the subject of restrained amusement among the local citizenry. A handsome man with hair reaching past his shoulders, Owens wore his pistol with the butt forward, and Holbrook's residents considered him a dandy.

On September 2, Andy Cooper, whose real name was Andy Blevins, and members of the Graham faction murdered two men. Owens was probably unaware of the shootings when he arrived in Holbrook, but he was carrying a warrant for Andy Cooper's arrest—for horse stealing, not murder. Cooper was at the Blevins house on Center Street when Sheriff Owens stepped onto the front porch and attempted to serve him the warrant. Cooper cracked open the door and raised his revolver, but before he could fire, Owens, armed with a Winchester, put a round through the door, mortally wounding Cooper.

From the opposite side of the room, John Blevins pushed open a door and fired at Owens, who cranked another shell into his rifle, turned, and fired from the hip, wounding Blevins. A relative, Mose Roberts, leaped out a side window at the same time the sheriff moved back into the street. Before Roberts could get a shot off, the Winchester cracked once more, killing him. Meanwhile, fourteen-year-old Sam Houston Blevins ran out the

Commodore Perry Owens —Southwest
Studies, Scottsdale Community College

front door to join the fight. Before the youth could even take aim, Owens shot him through the heart.

Controversy over the gunfight continues to this day; whole books have been written about it. To most, Commodore Owens was a legendary hero. A few claim that he was no more than a hired assassin, brought in by county officials to rid the area of desperadoes—he gunned down the Blevins boys and Mose Roberts without giving them a fighting chance. Whichever side one chooses to believe, no one can doubt the courage of Owens that day, and few outside the family were sad to see Andy Cooper die.

An Ungracious Invitation

Another Holbrook sheriff attained notoriety in 1899. Sheriff Frank Wattron received a reprimand from President William McKinley for sending out an ornate invitation to a hanging. The guest of honor was George Smiley, and the card read as follows:

George Smiley, Murderer

His soul will be swung into eternity on Dec. 8, 1899, at 2 o'clock P.M., sharp.

The latest improved methods of scientific strangulation will be employed and everything possible will be done to make the surroundings cheerful and the execution a success.

Petrified Forest Road
I-40—US 180
26 MILES

PETRIFIED FOREST NATIONAL PARK

The 93,533-acre Petrified Forest National Park is off I-40 thirty-seven miles east of Holbrook. The so-called forest was formed about 170 million years ago when the area was part of a large valley that also included Utah, New Mexico, and west Texas. Eventually the valley flooded, uprooting the large *Schilderia, Woodworthia,* and *Araucaria* trees, which floated into the lowlands and were buried beneath 3,000 feet of sediment and volcanic ash. Mineral-laden water seeped into the logs before they decayed and replaced the wood cells with silica, iron, manganese, copper, and other minerals. Over eons, wind and water erosion exposed the "forest" of petrified logs.

According to Navajo legend, the petrified forest was created when a trail-weary goddess, hungry and exhausted, came upon the felled logs. After killing a rabbit she tried to make a fire with the logs, but they were wet and wouldn't burn. In anger she cursed them and turned them to stone.

Lt. Amiel Whipple passed through the petrified forest on December 2, 1853, and wrote: "Quite a forest of petrified trees was discovered today, prostrate and partly buried in deposits of red marl. They are converted into beautiful specimens of variegated jasper. One trunk was measured 10 feet in diameter, and more than 100 feet in length."

After whites discovered it, this ancient collection of petrified wood was soon depleted by pilferers. Before it was made a national monument in 1906, people gathered pieces of the wood and shipped them out by the carload to be polished and sold to tourists. In the 1890s a mill was erected to crush the wood into industrial grinding powder.

In 1962 the petrified forest was designated a national park. Giant logs are still being exposed by erosion—some have been found in deep arroyos 250 feet beneath the earth's surface. In 1985 the fossil remains of one of the earliest known dinosaurs was found in the petrified forest.

There are a number of Indian ruins and petroglyph sites in the park as well. Flattop Site, a seasonally occupied agricultural village near Adamana, was a point of contact between Ancestral Pueblo, Hohokam, and Mogollon Cultures around A.D. 600. The petroglyphs there, some of which were used to mark the solstice and equinox, are among the best preserved in Arizona. Another nearby prehistoric site, dating back to the thirteenth century, is Puerco Ruin. This one-story, rectangular compound had more than 100 rooms, including three kivas, or ceremonial chambers. The Twin Buttes Archaeological District contains a cluster of Ancestral Pueblo subterranean homesteads occupied from A.D. 500 to 900.

The Painted Desert, north of the preserved wood sites, became part of Petrified Forest National Park in 1932. The Painted Desert is an eerily beautiful landscape of utterly barren, brightly colored hills. It was Spanish explorers with Coronado who first referred to the area as El Desierto Pintado.

The stretch of brilliantly multihued land within the park, north of I-40, is the most spectacular of the 300 square miles of the Painted Desert. Its vividly banded purple, scarlet, and pink tints vary with changing temperature, sunlight, and air purity. Despite its beauty, cowboys refer to the place as *malpais,* or badlands, as it'd be a hell of a place to try to graze cattle.

The historic Painted Desert Inn, with its classic pueblo-style architecture and decor that includes murals by noted Hopi artist Fred Kabotie, is at Kachina Point. Built in 1924 as a hotel, the building is now a museum on the National Register of Historic Places.

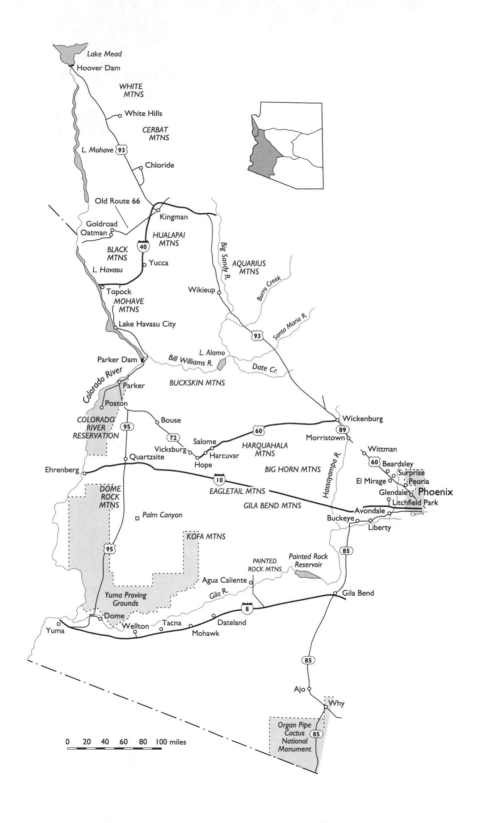

Lake Mead

Hoover Dam

WHITE MTNS

White Hills

CERBAT MTNS

L. Mohave (93)

Chloride

Old Route 66

Kingman

Goldroad
Oatman

HUALAPAI MTNS

(40)

BLACK MTNS

Yucca

L. Havasu

Big Sandy R.

AQUARIUS MTNS

Wikieup

Burro Creek

Topock

MOHAVE MTNS

Lake Havasu City

(93)

Santa Maria R.

Parker Dam

L. Alamo

Bill Williams R.

Date Cr.

Colorado River

Parker

BUCKSKIN MTNS

Poston

COLORADO RIVER RESERVATION

Bouse

Wickenburg

(95)

(60)

Morristown

(89)

Wittman

(72)

Salome

HARQUAHALA MTNS

Hassayampa R.

(60) Beardsley

Vicksburg Harcuvar

Surprise

Quartzsite Hope

BIG HORN MTNS

El Mirage Peoria

Ehrenberg

(10)

Glendale

Phoenix

EAGLETAIL MTNS

Litchfield Park

DOME ROCK MTNS

GILA BEND MTNS

Avondale

Palm Canyon

Buckeye

Liberty

KOFA MTNS

(95)

(85)

PAINTED ROCK MTNS

Painted Rock Reservoir

Agua Caliente

Yuma Proving Grounds

Gila R.

Gila Bend

Dome

(8)

Wellton Tacna

Dateland

Yuma

Mohawk

(85)

Ajo

(85)

Why

Organ Pipe Cactus National Monument

(85)

0 20 40 60 80 100 miles

Part 5

River Culture

COLORADO RIVER

In the far north-central part of the state, Lake Powell sits on the Arizona-Utah line, with the majority of the lake in Utah. From the southwestern end of the lake, the Colorado River begins its journey across the northwest corner of Arizona. After meandering through the Grand Canyon to Lake Mead, the Colorado turns due south and becomes Arizona's western boundary with first Nevada, then California. Then it passes into Mexico, ending at the Sea of Cortez.

Some 1,450 miles in length, the Colorado is one of the longest rivers in North America. It drains an area encompassing nearly 12 percent of the United States. The river averages about 300 feet wide and 35 feet deep—with depths of 100 feet in places. It flows at an average of four miles per hour, but at certain spots reaches speeds of twenty-five miles per hour. During its 277-mile rush through the Grand Canyon, the Colorado drops 2,200 feet—about 7.8 feet per mile. It has over 300 rapids, 70 of them considered major. Crystal and Lava are two of the most dramatic rapids.

Especially before it was dammed, the river was nicknamed "Big Red" because it flowed muddy red. Colorado means "reddish" in Spanish. The mighty Colorado was the last of the great rivers of the American West to be explored. John Wesley Powell first explored it along with the Grand Canyon in 1869 (see Grand Canyon, "White Exploration").

Steamboats on the Colorado

From 1852 to 1877, at the peak of the steamboat era, paddle wheelers churned their way up and down the muddy Colorado, unloading freight at landings along the banks and taking on firewood for their boilers. The steamers went as far north as Callville and Rioville. Landings between Yuma and Ehrenberg, about eighty miles north, once included Laguna, Castle Dome Landing, Eureka, Norton's Landing, Clip, Rhodes Ranch (also known as Cibola), and Mineral City. If these towns didn't die along with the steamboat business, the waters of Lake Mead and other dammed lakes would later cover most of them.

The high cost of freighting supplies overland to Fort Yuma drove the government to begin exploring navigation on the Colorado River. The army tried a steamboat in 1852, and one of Arizona's greatest nineteenth-century enterprises was born. During their heyday, before railroads and massive dams drove them out of business, such steamboats as the *Esmeralda, Mohave, Cocopah,* and *Gila* hauled freight and passengers to Yuma, Ehrenberg, and Hardyville. George Johnson, Jack Mellon, Isaac Polhamus, and other legendary captains skillfully piloted these craft around sandbars and underwater snags. The riverboats played an important part in opening up remote regions of the state.

The steamer that proved steamboats could navigate the Colorado was a sixty-five-foot side-wheeler named the *Uncle Sam*. A prefab affair, it arrived from San Francisco by schooner. In November 1852 the crew assembled it at the mouth of the Colorado; it reached Fort Yuma two weeks later. The return trip took only fifteen hours in the swift downriver current. The following year, the *Uncle Sam*'s career came to an abrupt end when a deckhand removed a bilge plug to soak and swell the wood, and the ship went down.

In fall 1853, Capt. George Johnson brought in a side-wheeler dubbed the *General Jesup*. It could haul fifty tons of freight. The *General Jesup* was an immediate financial success: at $75 a ton, Johnson's Colorado Steam Navigation Company was soon grossing $20,000 a month.

Compared with the floating mansions of Mark Twain's Mississippi, the steamboats of the Colorado were prosaic: they took mining equipment and supplies upriver into Arizona, and hauled ore back down to freighters at Port Isabel, Mexico, near the river's mouth. Larger boats had three decks and up to twenty staterooms for passengers. Traveling by steamboat cost less than by stagecoach.

Capt. George Johnson
—Southwest Studies, Scottsdale
Community College

The steamers traveled about thirty miles a day, tying up to shore at night. As business flourished, dozens of landings sprang up along the river. Small-time entrepreneurs made $5,000 a year supplying firewood for the paddle wheelers. At first, local Indians believed the noisy contraptions were the devil, spewing fire and smoke from his nose, and kicking the water with his feet. However, they soon became accustomed to the boats and began earning money cutting firewood.

During the 1857 Mormon War, the army hoped to transport soldiers and equipment to Utah by steamboat up the Colorado. To find out how much of the river was navigable, it ordered an iron-hulled stern-wheeler from Philadelphia, which Lt. Joseph C. Ives of the Army Corps of Topographical Engineers assembled and sailed with a crew to Fort Yuma in ten days. Christened the *Explorer,* the diminutive fifty-four-foot steamer was not the most graceful vessel on the Colorado; the expedition's artist, Baldwin Möllhausen, called it a "water-borne wheelbarrow."

Steamboat, docked at Yuma, circa 1880
—Southwest Studies, Scottsdale Community College

In the meantime, wanting to open commerce with Utah, Captain Johnson also decided to explore the river in the *General Jesup*. Johnson's curious crew included famed mountain man Pauline Weaver; the old Quechan chief Pascual; and an army officer and fifteen enlisted men. The *General Jesup* got as far as Pyramid Canyon—now buried under the waters of Lake Mohave, above Bullhead City—a distance of over 300 miles above Fort Yuma. Johnson determined that during high water the river would be navigable all the way to the Virgin River and into Utah.

The day after his start downriver, near today's Needles, California, the *General Jesup* met Lieutenant Beale and his camels on the east side of the river. The meeting was most fortunate for Beale: his beasts of burden, while great on the desert, stubbornly refused to swim the river. The *General Jesup* ferried the camels to the California side.

Near present-day Parker, the southbound *General Jesup* had a friendly meeting with Lieutenant Ives and his *Explorer*. The little *Explorer* traveled as far north as Black Canyon, the site of today's Hoover Dam, before it struck a rock. While the crew made repairs, Lieutenant Ives rowed a skiff another thirty miles to the mouth of the Virgin River, ascertaining for the army what Johnson had already discovered about the river's navigability. Ives took a land route home. Concluding that steamers on the Colorado were too expensive a proposition, he sold the *Explorer* to Johnson's Colorado Steam Navigation Company for $1,000.

From then on, the freakish-looking little *Explorer* was relegated to menial tasks, and ultimately, to hauling firewood on the Gila River. In 1864, after some workmen tied it to the trunk of a tree, it broke away and headed toward the Colorado, towing the tree behind. Somewhere downriver, it drifted into a slough and settled on the bottom. Eventually, the fickle Colorado changed its course, and the *Explorer* disappeared into the shifting desert sands. Nearly a quarter of a century later, a party of surveyors stumbled across a piece of iron hull sticking out of the sand.

The steamboat business declined with the arrival of the railroad at Yuma in 1877. The building of Laguna Dam above Yuma in 1907 capped the steamboat era for good.

I-8
Gila Bend—Yuma
116 MILES

Between Gila Bend and Yuma, I-8 runs roughly parallel to a portion of the Butterfield Overland Mail line and the old Gila Trail. The Butterfield line ran along the south bank of the Gila River. A few sites of the former stations are accessible by car. However, more and more, this area is coming under cultivation, and sites are becoming agricultural fields.

The Butterfield Overland Mail Company was a government-subsidized operation that ran from Tipton, Missouri, to San Francisco, California, from 1858 to 1861. The 2,800-mile route, dubbed the "oxbow," dipped down through El Paso to Tucson, then across to Los Angeles and up to San Francisco. Stations were spaced fifteen to twenty miles apart. It took the leather-slung coaches twenty-six days to make the trip, one way. The stage line ran with clockwork efficiency; Butterfield was a genius at keeping the stages running on schedule. Coaches, usually containing nine passengers, traveled day and night at an average speed of 5 miles an hour, making about 120 miles per twenty-four hours. On steep grades, able men were required to get out and push. In Arizona's hot desert, the company used lighter, open-air Celerity wagons instead of the more familiar Concord coaches. Canvas curtains could be lowered to provide shade but did little to keep out the dust.

Many passengers complained about the food served at the Butterfield stations, but traveler William Tallack was more understanding. "The fare, though rough, is better than could be expected so far from civilized districts and consists of bread, tea, and fried steaks of bacon, venison, antelope, or mule flesh—the latter tough enough." In Arizona, milk, butter, and fresh vegetables were as scarce as horseflies in December. Usually passengers were served jerked beef, slumgullion (meat stew), cornbread, beans, and black coffee. Jars of chile peppers and mustard added spice to the meal.

Little time was wasted at the stations. About two miles out, the driver blew a bugle to warn the hostler to prepare a fresh team of horses. When the coach stopped, mail sacks were exchanged and passengers headed for the outhouses. In ten short minutes, the stage was ready to roll again.

Newspapers advised passengers on proper conduct. Advice included: If a team runs away, don't jump out, just sit tight (some of the mules were so green they had to be blindfolded to be hitched); don't discuss politics or religion with your fellow passengers; don't drink hard liquor in freezing weather; and don't groom your hair with grease (too much dust). Many passengers literally drank their way across Arizona, tossing their empties out along the road. Later, airplane pilots claimed they could follow the route of the old Butterfield line by the glint of broken glass in the sun. Butterfield used this route until the Civil War.

PAINTED ROCK MOUNTAINS AND PAINTED ROCKS PETROGLYPH SITE

The Painted Rock Mountains were the natural boundary between the Maricopa Indians and their relatives and archrivals, the Quechan, or Yuma. Painted Rocks Petroglyph Site is just north of the mountains. To get there take exit 102 about fifteen miles north of the highway. The hundreds of petroglyphs in this area— etchings in rock of everything from insects and animals to people—likely inspired Father Eusebio Kino's naming of the mountains in 1699 as the Sierra Pinta. Father Jacob Sedelmayr also wrote of the place in 1754, as did explorer John C. Frémont in 1849. The site also includes historical inscriptions from such travelers passing through.

OATMAN FLAT

North of I-8 and southwest of Painted Rock Dam, on the south bank of the Gila, Oatman Flat was the scene of a grisly and infamous massacre. Here, on February 18, 1851, a war party of either Yavapai or Tonto Apache attacked a family of emigrants, the Oatmans, traveling alone on the Gila Trail. The lone survivors among the two parents and seven children were Olive, age fourteen; Mary Ann, seven; and Lorenzo, sixteen, who was clubbed and left for dead. After plundering the wagon, the Indians carried off the two girls.

Their captors eventually traded the girls to some Mojave Indians living along the Colorado. Mary Ann did not survive the ordeal—she died during a famine the following year—but Olive remained with the tribe, ultimately receiving the tattoo on the chin that was customary for Mojave women. Lorenzo recovered from his wounds, moved to California, and never gave up hope of finding his sisters. The bodies of the rest of the Oatman party were buried where they fell. For many years, travelers made solemn note of the graves in their diaries as they passed them on the Gila Trail. The site can still be seen; ask directions locally.

In 1856, Henry Grinnell, an employee at Fort Yuma on the Colorado River, learned of a white captive living with the Mojave and decided to investigate. When asked, the Indians denied that they knew such a person. Grinnell let it be known that a large military force was planning to sweep through the valley in search of white captives. This news persuaded the chief to exchange Olive for some gifts, and soon she was reunited with her brother.

Olive Oatman's ordeal became one of the most publicized events associated with the Gila Trail. In 1857 a preacher named Royal Stratton published a sensationalized account of the event.

Olive Oatman
—Southwest Studies,
Scottsdale Community
College

In it, poor Olive was supposed to have gone crazy and died in an insane asylum soon after obtaining her freedom. In reality, Olive lived a long, full life, married, raised a family, and lived to age sixty-four.

Seven years after the Oatman incident, in 1858, the Butterfield Overland Mail established a station at Oatman Flat. Supposedly the route ran right over the Oatman gravesite.

AGUA CALIENTE

Taking exit 87 at the town of Sentinel and going nine miles north leads to the ghost town of Agua Caliente. In the 1730s Jesuit Father Jacob Sedelmayr gave the place—formerly a native rancheria—the name Santa Maria del Agua Caliente, and recommended it as a site for a mission. In Spanish, Agua Caliente means "Hot Water," and the priest noted that natives used the warm mineral springs and mud in the spot therapeutically. Indeed, from prehistoric times, people soothed their bodies and spirits in the hot springs here.

One of Arizona's most illustrious early pioneers, King Woolsey, settled at Agua Caliente in 1865. Two years earlier, Woolsey had accompanied the Joe Walker expedition, which found gold in the Bradshaw Mountains. He also gained fame as an Indian fighter (see Dewey).

During the twentieth century, Agua Caliente was a popular health resort. A twenty-two-room hotel dating from 1897 still stands. However, a few decades ago, to accommodate more people at the springs, workers blasted out a larger bath area. In the process, the springs disappeared into a deep underground cavern, never to be seen again.

Opposite Agua Caliente is an old stage stop, Burke's Station, which was the site of a murder in the 1870s. After the station's stableman killed agent G. R. Whistler, King Woolsey pursued and captured him. Woolsey hanged the offender on the spot, leaving him swinging from a limb as a warning to other potential murderers—a common custom on the frontier before the arrival of organized law enforcement.

STANWIX

Nine miles northwest of Stanwix (west of Sentinel), off I-8, is the site of Stanwix Station, established in 1858. The station was also once known as Flapjack Ranch, and passengers looked forward to the stop because the station had a bathtub.

Some historians consider Stanwix Station the site of the westernmost skirmish of the Civil War. After Capt. Sherod Hunter's occupation of Tucson (see Tucson "Life in the Old Pueblo"), Hunter hoped to link up with Confederates in southern California to create an ocean-to-ocean Southern power. The plan failed when Union loyalists gained control of all of California in 1861. Hunter knew it was only a matter of time before his small force would have to evacuate. But in the time that remained, Hunter resolved to create as much havoc as possible.

On March 3, 1862, Hunter led his troops to the Gila River to destroy as many Union supply posts as they could. When Union captain William Calloway took his troops to the Gila River area to stop Hunter, one of his patrols ran into a small party of Confederates burning haystacks at the old Butterfield station at Stanwix. After the two sides exchanged shots, the Confederates gave their Yankee pursuers the slip and headed toward Tucson.

DATELAND

Dateland is sixty miles east of Yuma, about midway between Yuma and Gila Bend. It's home to about 400 people. During World War II, three army air corps auxiliary training fields were built in Dateland. Each facility had a 5,000- to 6,000-foot-long runway, which together formed a huge triangle. When the fields were abandoned, private investors bought them with visions of developing a "fly-in community."

Grinnell's Butterfield station was seven miles northwest of Dateland. Named for Henry Grinnell, the man who arranged Olive Oatman's release in 1856 (see Oatman Flat), the station was built in 1858, the first year of the mail line's operation. On later maps of the area, Grinnell's Station also appears as Teamster Camp and Texas Hill Station.

TACNA AND NOAH

With the arrival of the Southern Pacific in 1879, Tacna, originally established at Antelope Hill, moved closer to the rails, to a site along present-day I-8. The town had become little more than a railroad siding by the turn of the twentieth century.

In the early 1920s, Max Noah arrived from Texas with a barrel of gasoline and a hand pump and opened a gas station. Soon Noah, a teller of tall tales, had conjured a story of a seventeenth-century Greek padre named Tachnapolis who found his way into Arizona from California and spent his last days with the natives, who shortened his name to Tacna. Sometimes, Noah referred to his metropolis as "Tacna by the Sea," surrounded as it was by sand. He called the roadside restaurant he started Noah's Ark.

During the winter Noah always kept a small fire burning in his shack and a light on at night. In the language of the local Tohono O'Odham Indians, *tacna* came to mean "bright spot" or "bright light." In 1941, Noah sold the entire town at public auction. Afterward, the post office and railroad siding moved four miles down the road to its present location. The former site of Tacna became present-day Noah.

About two miles north of present-day Noah, the Butterfield station at Antelope Hill replaced Filibuster Camp, about five miles to the west, in 1859. The Southern Pacific Railroad went through the site of the old station and wiped out the remains.

WELLTON

Wellton, population 5,000, is twenty-nine miles east of Yuma. It was a water stop for the Butterfield line and later for the railroad—thus the name, "Well Town." Today, Wellton's livelihood depends more on agriculture than on transportation.

Approximately one mile north of Wellton, a stage stop called Filibuster Camp was established in 1858 on the campsite of the ill-fated Crabb Expedition of 1857. Henry A. Crabb was a filibuster—an adventurer or land pirate who joined up with other such men in their own private army. During the mid-nineteenth century, bands of American *filibusteros* invaded parts of Mexico and Central America to establish private empires or republics.

In 1857 Sonoran leader Ignacio Pesqueira asked Crabb to bring 1,000 "colonists" to Sonora, though in fact Pesqueira hoped Crabb and his men would help him overthrow Governor Manuel Gándara's regime and "liberate" the people of Sonora. With an army of fewer than 100 men recruited in California, Crabb set out in March 1857 for Sonora. They camped here before turning south toward Mexico.

When they arrived, Pesqueira had already overthrown Gándara's government, so he no longer needed Crabb's help. Seizing the opportunity to rally Sonorans to his side, the new governor declared war on the "hated gringo bandits." Outnumbered ten to one, Crabb and fifty-nine of his men held out for six days at Caborca before surrendering. Promised safe passage back to the border, they were lined up and shot instead on April 7. Crabb was saved for last; afterward, his head was cut off and placed in a jar of mescal. Pesqueria, the deceitful governor, came off as a patriotic savior. To this day, the brutal and cowardly slaughter of the Crabb Expedition is celebrated in Caborca as a glorious victory.

DOME

Dome is about fifteen miles northeast of Yuma. From I-8 it's reachable either by local roads or by AZ 95. In 1879 the Southern Pacific built a siding near the mining town of Gila City. They called the stop Dome for the Castle Dome Mountains and Mining District.

In 1858 Gila City was the site of the first important gold strike in Arizona. At its peak, the denizens of the boomtown numbered about 1,200, and by 1861 prospectors were panning out $20 to $125 in gold dust a day. However, the placers were quickly exhausted, and when the gold ran out, so did the miners. On a rampage in 1862, the Gila River washed out what was left of Gila City. By 1864, J. Ross Browne reported, only "three chimneys and a coyote" remained of the boomtown.

YUMA

Yuma, also called Yuma Crossing, sits near the confluence of the Gila and Colorado Rivers in the southwest corner of the state. Here, the Colorado narrows and calms, making for a naturally safer, easier crossing. The crossing made Yuma an important point on the route to California, and many key figures in Arizona history have passed through the town. The Colorado has been both friend and foe to Yuma. Major floods devastated the town in 1852, 1890, 1905, 1916, and 1920, but with their strong "sense of Yuma," the residents always recover. Today Yuma is Arizona's tenth-largest city, with a population of 80,000.

Yuma, 1880s —Southwest Studies, Scottsdale Community College

Quechan woman (no date)
—Southwest Studies, Scottsdale
Community College

It is believed that Quechan, Cocopah, Mojave, and other native peoples began farming this rich land more than 1,000 years ago. The Quechan (tribal members prefer Euqchan), also called the Yuma, may have been Arizona's first winter visitors, farming the floodplains around Yuma. When the hot, mosquito-infested summer came, they crossed the desert to the cool range of coastal mountains east of San Diego. However, in the 1600s, seeing how Spanish colonists coveted their farmlands, the Quechan began staying year-round to protect their interests.

In 1540, Spanish soldier Hernando de Alarcón sailed three supply ships for the Coronado Expedition to the mouth of the Colorado. At that river's junction with the Gila, he introduced himself to the Indians as the "Son of the Sun," in the belief that they were sun worshippers. Finding no sign of the Coronado Expedition, Alarcón moved on.

Quechan Uprising

Several more Spaniards passed through Yuma Crossing during the seventeenth and eighteenth centuries, including Father

Eusebio Kino. In 1774 another beloved priest, Francisco Tomás Garcés, trekked across Kino's old Camino del Diablo to Yuma Crossing. He was accompanying Juan Bautista de Anza, the commandant of the presidio at Tubac. New missions in California had been struggling, in desperate need of an overland supply route from Mexico; currents off the California coast were too treacherous for ships. At Yuma, Anza proved himself an able statesman when he successfully negotiated with the Quechan chief Palma for rights to cross the river.

Father Garcés stayed in the Yuma area and established two missions there in 1780: La Puerta de la Purisima Concepcion, on a bluff overlooking the confluence of the Gila and Colorado Rivers, and San Pedro y San Pablo de Bicuñer, twelve miles upstream.

Meanwhile, however, relations between the Spanish and the Quechan deteriorated. A belt-tightening program within the Spanish government drastically reduced funding for the missions at Yuma Crossing. Lavish gifts promised the Quechan never materialized, causing Chief Palma to lose prestige among his people. Spanish abuses and lack of respect added to a deepening resentment among the Quechan.

On the morning of July 17, 1781, the Quechan revolted, destroying the Spanish missions and dwellings. The slaughter went on for two days. When it was over, fifty Spaniards, including Father Garcés, lay dead. Later, forty-eight Spanish women and children were ransomed back to their government. For more than forty years after the incident, the overland road to California remained closed, and Indians near the crossing had little contact with whites.

Americans in Yuma

In the 1820s, Anglo American fur trappers penetrated the wilderness regions of Arizona. One of them, Kentuckian James Ohio Pattie, was the first American to write about Arizona. Though Pattie's adventures are highly exaggerated, the work provides an important piece of the history of the fur trade in Arizona.

Pattie came to Arizona as a trapper in 1825. The following year he and fellow mountain man Ewing Young trapped up and

Indian attack, original illustration from The Narrative
of James O. Pattie —Southwest Studies, Scottsdale Community College

down the Salt and Verde Rivers, then followed the Gila to Yuma
Crossing, becoming the first Americans to make this trip. Near
Yuma, the first encounter between the trappers and the Quechan
Indians seems to have been peaceful. Pattie wrote admiringly of
the Quechan:

> [One morning], a great many of these Indians crossed the river
> to our camp, and brought us dried beans, for which we paid
> them with red cloth, with which they were delighted beyond
> measure, tearing it into ribbons and tying it round their arms
> and legs; for if the truth must be told, they were as naked as
> Adam and Eve in their birthday suit. They were the stoutest
> men, with the finest forms I ever saw, well proportioned and
> straight as an arrow. They contrive, however, to inflict upon
> their children an artificial deformity. They flatten their heads,
> by pressing a board upon their tender scalps which they bind
> fast by a ligature.

In the fall of 1827 Pattie returned to the area with a trapping
expedition. This time the Quechans proved inhospitable, stealing
the Americans' horses.

When the war with Mexico ended on February 2, 1848, Article
V of the Treaty of Guadalupe Hidalgo stipulated that part of the

boundary line separating the United States and Mexico would be the Gila River. A joint commission from the United States and Mexico was to survey this line. Lt. Amiel W. Whipple of the Army Corps of Topographical Engineers took command of the American contingent. In late September 1849, Whipple set up headquarters on the banks of the Colorado—near the future site of Fort Yuma.

In 1854, after the Gadsden Purchase redefined the border, President Franklin Pierce sent the able and experienced Maj. William Emory of the Topographical Engineers to survey the new borders. Emory split his group, sending Lt. Nathaniel Michler to Yuma while he worked west from El Paso. The two men's detailed expedition record provided the first accurate information about the area.

Opportunity—and Violence—at the Crossing

After gold was discovered in California in 1848, thousands of argonauts took the Gila Trail to the goldfields. Whipple's survey team had arrived at Yuma Crossing during the height of the rush. Seizing the day, Whipple's military escort, led by Lt. Cave Johnson Couts, built a ferry to transport the would-be millionaires across the Colorado.

Within a year, several ferries had opened for business. Soon a notorious mercenary named John Joel Glanton and a gang of greedy ruffians decided to take over. After taking one successful operation by force and killing another's ferry operator, Glanton's men began abusing Indians and robbing emigrants. On April 23, 1850, the Quechan solved the problem by slaughtering Glanton and his gang. It is believed that Glanton's collected spoils, probably $15,000 in gold, was buried under a tree near the crossing. It has never been found, though the Indians did find another cache.

The few men who survived the Glanton Massacre staggered into Los Angeles with lurid tales of a slaughter of innocent whites at Yuma Crossing, inspiring Gen. Joe Moorhead to raise a band of 142 militiamen to punish the Quechan. The so-called Gila Expedition rode to the crossing in September 1850 under the guise of protecting travelers. They demanded that the Quechan hand over Glanton's treasure or receive a severe beating. Choosing to fight, the Indians gave Moorhead's marauders a sound thrashing. Next the militia turned its attention to fleecing Mexicans of gold they were taking home from the mines. Finally California authorities ordered the men home—but not before Moorhead had charged over $113,000 in expenses to the state treasury.

In the meantime, warrior tribes around Yuma Crossing had been attacking small parties of poorly armed emigrants along the Gila Trail. In November 1850, Capt. Sam Heintzelman established Fort Yuma on the western (California) side of the Colorado to protect the emigrants. The fort also served as a major supply depot for the army in the Southwest. Heintzelman ordered a series of punitive expeditions against the Indians, and by the end of 1852 most of the tribes ceased their aggressions against the whites. In 1884 the army deeded the fort to the Quechan, who today run it as a museum.

Founding of the City of Yuma

According to local legend and Charles Poston's memoir, when Poston (see Tubac) and a German engineer named Herman Ehrenberg reached the ferry at Yuma Crossing in 1854, they did not have the money for passage west. The ingenious Poston conceived a plan to survey a town site there on the Arizona side of the river called Colorado City. He and Ehrenberg mapped out city lots and convinced the ferry owner, Louis Jaeger, that he could get in on the ground floor of a real estate boom. For the sum of $25—the exact price of passage—Jaeger could have a choice city lot. The deal was consummated, passage was booked, and the future city of Yuma was born. While it is true that Poston and Ehrenberg drew up the plans for the city and registered them in California, the more colorful parts of the story are likely to be fiction.

Whatever its origins, the small community of Colorado City grew prosperous, with the military, steamboats, immigrants, and area gold strikes all playing a part in its growth and success. In 1858 citizens changed the name to Arizona City. During the Civil War the name was changed to Yuma, then back to Arizona City. Finally in 1873 it received the permanent name of Yuma.

Yuma continued to be an important center of commerce after the arrival of the railroad. Steamers loaded with cargo and

Fort Yuma and Jaeger's Ferry, around 1852 (from a sketch by J. R. Bartlett) —Southwest Studies, Scottsdale Community College

passengers went on plying the Colorado River until the building of the great dams in the 1900s. The ferry continued to haul wagons, horses, and, later, automobiles until 1915, when a bridge was constructed.

"The Great Western": Sarah Bowman

One of the most colorful women who ever graced the Old West was Sarah Bowman of Yuma. At a height of six feet, two inches, she was also known as "The Great Western," after the biggest sailing ship of her day. She could literally sweep men right off their feet—and did on more than one occasion. Bowman was born in Clay County, Missouri, in 1812, and seems to have led an uneventful life until the war with Mexico broke out in 1846. When her husband volunteered for service, she came along as a cook and laundress.

During the seven-day siege and bombardment of Fort Texas, Bowman won the undying admiration of the men, who compared her to Joan of Arc when they called her "the American Maid of Orleans." She and nine other women, along with fifty men, held out against a superior Mexican force until the arrival of Gen. Zachary Taylor's army. Bowman was supposed to be sewing sandbags but opted for more hazardous duty, defiantly dodging shells to bring hot soup and other encouragement to the troops. Once she joined a battle charge, declaring that if someone would lend her a pair of trousers, she would whip the whole Mexican army all by herself. Bowman traveled on with Taylor's army into northern Mexico. Her husband died in the fighting around Monterrey, Mexico, but the redoubtable "Great Western" continued to be the belle of Taylor's army.

When the war ended, Bowman loaded her wagons and rode along with Maj. Lawrence Graham's dragoons to California. When told that army regulations stated that a woman could not travel with the troops unless she was married to a member of the squadron, she gave a snappy salute and announced, "All right, I'll marry the whole squadron." She then climbed on her Mexican donkey and rode down the line shouting, "Who wants a wife with $15,000 and the biggest legs in Mexico! Come, my beauties, don't all speak at once—who is the lucky man?"

A soldier named Davis stepped forward. "I have no objections to making you my wife, if there's a clergyman here to tie the knot."

"Bring your blanket to my tent tonight," Bowman laughed, "and I will learn you a knot that will satisfy you, I reckon!"

Bowman's "marriage" to Davis did not last long; in fact, she switched husbands several times along the way. In Franklin, Texas, now El Paso, Bowman got sidetracked and spent a few months running an eating establishment and bordello. Back on the trail to California, Bowman stopped at Yuma—then called Arizona City—and set up business in a dirt-roofed adobe house. In 1861 author Raphael Pumpelly wrote that Bowman was the only resident of the eight-year-old town, which had been abandoned at the outbreak of war. Author-adventurer Capt. James Hobbs said she was "liked universally for her kind, motherly ways." Another observer, Jeff Ake, said she always packed two pistols, and "she shore could use 'em." Ake's father called her "the greatest whore in the West."

When Fort Yuma was evacuated briefly during the Confederate occupation and the soldiers prepared to march away to San Diego,

Bowman sent her working girls home to Sonora and "followed the guidon" once more. She came back to Yuma a few months later with the California Column, and she died there on December 22, 1866. Years later, when the fort was abandoned, her remains along with those of soldiers who had died at the post were reburied at the presidio in San Francisco. The community of Yuma pays Sarah Bowman the great compliment of calling her their "first citizen."

Territorial Prison, 1876–1909

On a rampage in 1852, the Colorado wiped out the town of Yuma. A new town was built on higher ground, and by 1870 the population numbered over 1,100. In 1876 the infamous territorial prison was built on a cliff on the west bank of the river. Some of the cells were carved out of solid rock. In its time, the prison at Yuma would house some of the West's most notorious men and women. In spite of the vast stretches of desert to the east and west, 26 of 3,069 prisoners between 1876 and 1909 managed to escape, and none were recaptured.

One of Yuma's most illustrious prisoners was Pearl Hart, the "girl bandit." In 1899 Hart and her boyfriend Joe Boot robbed a stagecoach north of Florence. A posse soon captured them, and

Territorial prison at Yuma (no date)
—Southwest Studies, Scottsdale Community College

Pearl Hart in outlaw garb (left) and in feminine attire for the court —Southwest Studies, Scottsdale Community College

they were brought up for trial. Stashing her tomboy clothes, Hart appeared before the jury in delicate, feminine attire. Playing the consummate coquette and repentant sinner rolled into one, she batted her long lashes and lifted her skirts to reveal her shapely ankles. It worked; the jury found Joe Boot guilty and Pearl Hart innocent!

Outraged, the judge ordered Hart recharged for stealing the stage driver's six-shooter. This time the jury complied and found her guilty. She was sentenced to Yuma Territorial Prison. Boot escaped soon after and was never seen again, but Hart became a celebrity. Journalists came from all over the nation to interview her; easterners were shocked that such a "refined lady" was behind bars. After her release, Hart had a brief show-business career, then returned to Arizona, married a cowboy named Cal Bywater, and settled down to a respectable life near Globe.

In 1909 a new prison opened at Florence, and for a brief time the old prison stood empty. Then, in 1910, a fire burned Yuma's high school, and for the next few years, classes were held in the prison. To this day, the school colors of Yuma High are black and white, and its athletic teams are called the "Criminals." The prison fell into a state of ruin for many years before local citizens began a restoration program. It became a city museum in 1941 and a state park twenty years later.

Arrival of the Railroad

The most dramatic change in the history of Yuma arrived with the railroad in 1877. It was the first time a locomotive rolled into the territory. Naturally the arrival of the iron horse was cause for celebration. Anyone who had crossed the desert on foot, by horse or mule, or in a rocking, jolting stagecoach or wagon could appreciate the wonders of riding in a passenger train.

But Yuma citizens had had to work hard to get their railroad. In May 1877, the Southern Pacific, building east from California, reached the Colorado River and there ran into some Washington-style bureaucratic politicking. Earlier, Maj. Gen. Irwin McDowell, commander of the Military Department of California, had granted permission for construction of a railroad bridge at Yuma. However, Secretary of War J. D. Cameron overruled the department commander, refusing to allow the railroad to cross a federal stream—that is, a navigable river—until some red tape was untangled. In the meantime, permission was granted to build the bridge, but without the railroad tracks.

Chinese workmen spent the hot summer months preparing a grade for the tracks while pile drivers constructed a 667-foot-long bridge across the Colorado. On September 29, 1877, the bridge was completed, except for the rails.

Maj. Tom Dunn, commander of Fort Yuma, had orders not to allow any track laying on the bridge. He put his entire command—consisting of one sergeant and one private—on alert, and posted a sentry at the entrance to the bridge.

At eleven P.M. the guard went off duty, and soon, dark, shadowy figures appeared. With stealth and cunning worthy of an Apache war party, the rail workers began laying track across the bridge. All went well until about 2 A.M., when someone dropped a rail.

Southern Pacific crews completing rail bridge across the Colorado River at Yuma, 1877 —Arizona Historical Society Library

The resounding clatter woke the sleeping soldiers, and the three-man garrison of Fort Yuma sprang into action. Their bayonets fixed, Major Dunn and his men grimly stood their ground; Dunn actually stationed himself on the tracks.

Suddenly, a rumbling came from the darkness. The major found himself face-to-face with the headlights of a locomotive. Concluding that discretion was the better part of valor, the major and his men beat a hasty retreat.

At sunrise the next morning, Engine 31, having successfully traversed the bridge, rolled into Yuma with her whistle screaming. The whole town turned out to witness the historic occasion. The locomotive crept slowly along, blowing off steam, while the gandy dancers laid track ahead of it along Madison Avenue. The Southern Pacific and the federal government each accused the other of high-handedness in the matter. Much chagrined, General McDowell quickly reinforced Fort Yuma with a dozen more soldiers to thwart any further usurping of his military authority.

Engine 31, the first locomotive in Arizona —Arizona State Library

Cesar Chavez

Not long after the coming of the railroad to Yuma in the 1880s, Cesario and Dorotea Chavez migrated to the area from Mexico and homesteaded a small farm. Ownership of the farm passed to Cesario's son Librado, who also operated a small store and served as the elected postmaster. Librado's eldest son, Cesar Estrada Chavez, was born on March 31, 1927. During the Depression, ten-year-old Cesar's happy childhood abruptly came to an end when his father lost their farm and land. To survive, the family turned, like so many other Mexican and Mexican American families, to itinerant crop picking on farms all over the Southwest.

Forever marked by his experiences of migrant life, Chavez went on to win worldwide fame and respect as the founder of the United Farm Workers Union, organized in California in 1962. When he died in 1993, he was still fighting for the rights and quality of life of migrant workers. He had come back to Yuma for a court case brought by a large vegetable-growing company against the Farm Workers. He died in San Luis, Arizona, a small community about twenty miles from Yuma.

I-10
Phoenix—Ehrenberg
148 MILES

To get from Phoenix to Ehrenberg (about sixty-five miles up the Colorado from Yuma), one used to have to travel northwest through Wickenburg, then southwest again through Salome on old highway 60. In 1977, the "Brenda Cutoff" was built along I-10, shaving off many miles and making a straight shot for the California border at Ehrenberg. From the outskirts of Phoenix to the banks of the Colorado at Ehrenburg, there's a lot of wide open space and arid desert to pass through, with range after range of rugged mountains.

The brawny mountain range a few miles south of the freeway is the Sierra Estrella. Between these mountains and the South Mountains farther east, two major rivers come together: the Salt, flowing west out of Phoenix, and the Gila, which comes along from the southeast and skirts Phoenix to the south.

TOLLESON

Tolleson is within the Phoenix city line at exit 133 off I-10. More than fifty descendants of Walter Gist "Daddy Pop" Tolleson, the town's founder, still gather annually in his memory. Daddy Pop owned a general store, the lumber yard, and the post office, and he pretty much ran the town. A strict Baptist, he restricted the sale of liquor in town—there wasn't a saloon there until after his death in 1940.

The tough old man died in his eighties. It's said that he took a swing at somebody with his cane, missed, fell in a hole, and died.

AGUA FRIA RIVER

Near milepost 129, I-10 crosses the Agua Fria River. The name means "Cold Water" in Spanish. Since the river usually runs dry, water is scarce in it, let alone cold water. The headwaters of the Agua Fria are up in the Bradshaw Mountains near Prescott. The river winds its way past Dewey and Black Canyon City on I-17, heading south until it empties into the Gila south of Goodyear.

Billy Moore was the first person in this area to settle on the Agua Fria River. Around 1880 he built a house on the west bank, set up a stage station with corrals and a combined store, saloon, and blacksmith shop, and named the place Cold Water. On the long, hot road from Phoenix, "Uncle" Billy Moore's stage stop was a favorite watering hole. A post office was established at the stage station in 1901 with Moore as postmaster. That lasted until 1905, when the postal inspector discovered Moore was manufacturing his special recipe of home brew on the premises. The post office was relocated.

When the horseless carriage arrived, Moore was too stubborn to give up his team of fine horses. He liked liquor quite a bit and figured that, while an automobile could take him into town, he couldn't trust it to take him home. With horses, Uncle Billy could crawl into the wagon and let his trusty team deposit him at his door. Uncle Billy died at the ripe old age of ninety-two. On the third weekend of October in this area, the Southwest Valley, the citizens hold a parade and rodeo event called Billy Moore Days.

LITCHFIELD PARK AND GOODYEAR

Litchfield Park and Goodyear, both off exit 128 on the western edge of Phoenix, started out as the Agua Fria Ranch. During World War I, the Allies used Egyptian long-staple cotton to manufacture balloon tires—tires with tubes replacing the solid rubber tires of an earlier era. When German blockades cut off cotton supplies, the Allies desperately needed a new source of the fiber. Arizona turned out to have an ideal climate for growing long-staple cotton, and completion of Roosevelt Dam in 1911 ensured a good supply of irrigation water. In 1916 the Goodyear Tire & Rubber Company purchased tracts of land along the normally dry Agua Fria River. Paul W. Litchfield, vice president of the company, gave his name to the site. Today both towns are prosperous retirement communities.

The war created great demand for cotton, not only for tires, but for uniforms, observation balloons, airplane fabric, and a host of other essentials. Cotton produced around Litchfield Park and in other parts of the Salt and Gila River Valleys brought unprecedented prosperity to cotton growers. Laborers, many from the South, poured in to work the fields. By 1916, about 7,000 acres of cotton were in production in the Salt River Valley. By 1918 that number had grown to 69,000 acres; two years later, it was 180,000. Receiving high prices for cotton, farmers put the production of other crops and agricultural products aside. When the war ended, however, and restrictions on Egyptian cotton lifted, prices plummeted from $1.50 per pound of cotton to 28 cents per pound, resulting in the cotton crash of 1920. Farming populations declined by 20 percent during the crash; field workers were particularly devastated.

Today, cotton is still thriving, but it's become the number two crop behind lettuce. Primary markets for Arizona cotton have come to include Taiwan and South Korea.

HASSAYAMPA RIVER

At milepost 105 the interstate crosses the Hassayampa River. Legend has it that a person who drinks from the Hassayampa— known, from then on, as a "Hassayamper"—can never tell the truth again. The river's headwaters in the Bradshaw Mountains south of Prescott were the setting of many a gold strike, and so played a major role in the creation of Arizona Territory in 1863.

A Hassayamper at work (no date)
—Southwest Studies, Scottsdale Community College

BIG HORN, EAGLETAIL, AND
HARQUAHALA RANGES

Between Litchfield Park and US 60, three major ranges of mountains appear to the traveler. The first, coming into view to the north around milepost 88, are the Big Horn Mountains and accompanying wilderness area. The Big Horns take their name from the desert bighorn sheep that live there, a subspecies *(Ovis canadensis nelsoni)* of the cooler-climed Rocky Mountain bighorn sheep. In winter, for moisture, they can survive on the water in vegetation.

Beyond the Big Horns, the Eagletail Mountains rise south of the highway; the Harquahala Mountains appear to the north. Both ranges are in wilderness areas. At the east end of the Eagletails, stately Courthouse Rock protrudes (not to be confused with the famous Oregon Trail landmark). The notorious Clanton family of Tombstone fame supposedly ranched in this area before moving to Cochise County. Harquahala is Mojave for "Water There Is High Up." The Harquahalas have an ecosystem unique among desert mountain ranges.

Through the decades these mountain ranges have offered rich mining—and equally rich folklore. Judging from the legends associated with these mountains, there may be no better place in the world to lose a mine. Stories about the Lost Frenchmen Mine persist to this day. It may be in the Harquahala Mountains . . . or perhaps it was the Eagletails . . . or the Big Horns. Reputable pioneers like King Woolsey and A. H. Peeples both claimed to have encountered the three Frenchmen who worked the mine or to have seen ore samples.

In 1867, three Frenchmen bought supplies at Hooper's store in Yuma and deposited about $8,000 in gold with the storekeeper. They then headed east and camped around Agua Caliente. A small band of Mexican bandits followed them. The next day, aware they were being followed, the Frenchmen led their pursuers on a wild goose chase that ended right back in Agua Caliente for a second night. During the night, the Frenchmen slipped away, separated, and headed in three different directions, successfully eluding further tracking.

In 1889, a Mexican recalled that as a boy he ran away from home and fell in with three Frenchmen. Apparently they let him stay at their camp. Each morning they disappeared into a canyon; each evening they returned carrying cans. Once, the boy sneaked a look into the cans; he saw they were filled with gold nuggets. The next day he followed them and saw where they were hiding the gold. However, the Frenchmen suspected the boy was getting too curious; they beat him, and he ran away.

After this, the Frenchmen vanished and were never seen again. The Mexican believed that Indians must have killed them. He was certain he knew the exact location of the mine, and that he could go straight to it. But he never could find it, and neither could anyone else.

Another famous lost mine in the area is the Belle McKeever. Those who believe in its existence claim it must be the richest gold ledge ever discovered in North America. The mine got its name from the daughter of Abner McKeever. In 1869 the McKeever family had left Texas bound for California on the Gila Trail. Somewhere around today's Gila Bend, Yavapai Indians attacked them. Horrified, young Jim McKeever stood on the other side of the Gila River and watched most of his family die. He also saw his thirteen-year-old sister, Belle, who had escaped on horseback, unwittingly ride back into camp, where warriors captured her and carried her off.

Three soldiers, Pvt. Gene Flanigan, Sgt. Crossthwaite, and Pvt. Joe Wormley, were dispatched from Fort Yuma to pursue the raiders. They weren't prepared for the desert, however, and on the first day, two of their horses died of thirst. Soon after, Wormley became deranged from the heat, but his companions urged him on. The surviving horse led the soldiers to a creek bed. It was dry, but the horse pawed at a spot until it found water. While the men were drinking, they noticed gold nuggets as "big as blackberries" all around them.

Of their location, the soldiers knew only that they were near the Harquahala Mountains. They used drinking cups, knives, and their bare hands to dig up ten pounds of gold. The next day, dysentery set in, but they still managed to gather fifty pounds of gold. Still, they needed to get to help soon. They marked the location, naming it the Belle McKeever after the lost girl, and prepared to head out.

Wormley, still mentally impaired, refused to leave the creek bed; the other two had to force him back into the desert. As the sun beat down, Crossthwaite, too, lost his mind. Finally, they found some shade and stopped, and Flanigan fell asleep. When he awoke, the other two and the horse had vanished. Continuing on, Flanigan came across Crossthwaite's body. A few hours later, rescuers found Flanigan. Wormley was also rescued, but he remembered nothing of the ordeal.

When Flanigan had recuperated, he tried several times to retrace his steps, but he was never able to find the Belle McKeever. According to another version of the story, he was so petrified after his experience in the desert that he went back east and, whatever he was doing, he always had a canteen of water within sight. He died in Philadelphia in 1880. Since then others have tried to locate the Belle McKeever, but without success. It's still out there . . . somewhere.

QUARTZSITE

Quartzsite, off I-10 at its junction with US 95, about twenty miles east of Ehrenberg, was originally known as Tyson's Wells. Charles Tyson found water here in 1856 and built a fort to defend his claim against Mojave Indians. Later, as a stage station, Tyson's Wells offered primitive lodgings on the road between Ehrenberg and Prescott. In *Vanished Arizona,* her account of life on the Arizona frontier in the 1870s, Martha Summerhayes remembers Tyson's Wells—not too favorably. "It reeks of everything unclean, morally and physically."

Tyson's Wells faded for a time but prospered again in the late 1890s, when prospectors began scouring the nearby craggy, cactus-strewn hills for gold. The post office at Tyson's Wells had since closed, and because postal authorities would not allow a branch to reopen with the same name, the new name Quartzite was suggested. Some bureaucrat misspelled the name by adding an "s." Present-day Quartzsite is about nine miles east of the original site of Tyson's Wells.

In the center of Quartzsite stands a monument to one of the most unusual experiments in the history of the westward movement—and a man who was part of it. In 1857 Lt. Ned Beale, a navy officer turned landlubber, charted a proposed railroad route along the thirty-fifth parallel using camels as beasts of burden (see I-40, Lupton–Flagstaff, Part 3).

Since American muleskinners could not speak Arabic and the stubborn camels would not learn English, the government brought in Arabs to handle the camels. The most famous of the Arab drivers, a Syrian named Hadji Ali, soon became known simply as "Hi Jolly."

After the expedition was over, Hi Jolly stayed in Arizona with a few of the camels and used them as pack animals, carrying goods between mining camps and the Colorado River. His business failed, however, and he is said to have released his last camel into the desert around Gila Bend. He married a Tucsonan and had two children. Years later, he moved back to Quartzsite and prospected until his death in 1902. A stone monument marks his grave. In the 1960s Randy Sparks wrote a folk song in his honor, recorded by the New Christy Minstrels.

Today, year-round residents of Quartzsite number around 2,000, but in the winter, thousands of people converge on the town from around the nation and the world—most of them in RVs, which they park in the surrounding desert. With a nod

Tribute to "Hi Jolly" —Courtesy Jeff Kida

toward its mining past, the town has become a center for gem and mineral markets, shows, and amateur collecting.

EHRENBERG

Ehrenberg is seventeen miles west of Quartzsite on merged I-10 and US 95. This Colorado River town owes its success to the capriciousness of the Colorado River: if the river hadn't changed course, leaving another nearby town high and dry, this hot, dusty little town with its meandering main street and its row of adobes facing the river might not exist.

The town that lost out was La Paz, a mining camp established in 1862 when scout Pauline Weaver discovered rich gold placers in the area. Weaver and his friends made their discovery in Arroyo de la Tenaja on January 12, the Feast of Our Lady of Peace, which inspired the name—La Paz means "Peace." Before the rush was over, about $8 million in gold had been gathered in pans, rockers, and sluices.

At one time La Paz boasted 1,500 frontier citizens. It was at its most flourishing in 1863, when Arizona became a territory. That same year, La Paz was named the Yuma County seat. Legislators considered La Paz for the first territorial capital—but it was passed over for Prescott. However, when the gold played out, the town dwindled to 352 residents.

In 1868, the town's fate was sealed when the river changed course, stranding the port of La Paz on dry ground. In 1870 the county seat was moved down the Colorado to Arizona City (Yuma), and Ehrenberg, a town of about 250 south of La Paz, went from a simple ferry landing to the main river port between Parker and Yuma. By 1891 La Paz was a ghost town. The town's meager remains are now on Colorado River Indian Reservation tribal land.

Ehrenberg started out as a ferry landing run by Isaac and William Bradshaw. First known as Bradshaw Ferry Landing, in 1863 the town was renamed Mineral City. In the 1860s Mineral City and Olive City, a mile north, became hotbeds for secessionists and pro-Southern elements. Blacks, Mexicans, Asians, and Indians were barred from owning property. In March 1863 even the mines became segregated when they seceded from the La Paz Mining District and formed the Weave District. Confederate

Ehrenberg, circa 1871 —Arizona Historical Foundation

sympathizers used Olive City as a staging point from which to set out for the east and join the Civil War. Finally a detachment of troops from Fort Mohave set up a camp between La Paz and Olive City to interrupt this flow. Meanwhile, in 1866, the town was renamed for a business partner of Mike and Joe Goldwater, Herman Ehrenberg, who had lived in Mineral City and was ambushed and murdered on his way out of town.

In 1884, prospector Jesus Daniel was appointed postmaster. Daniel was more interested in looking for gold than running the post office. The post office was open for business for a short time on Saturday afternoons, and also on Sunday if Daniel wasn't too hungover. When the government required that he post business hours, Daniel put up the following sign: "This office open when it is open and closed when it is closed."

The government notified Daniel that it was appointing a new postmaster, but Daniel misplaced the registered letter. In 1894 a postal inspector arrived from Denver. He was startled to find sacks of undelivered mail and not a single postage stamp. Daniel explained that he had run out of stamps eight years earlier, but that it had worked fine to simply mark the letters "Collect on the other end."

Goldwater Dynasty

As the main supply point for goods coming up the Colorado for area miners, Ehrenberg was an excellent spot for merchants. It was here that the storied Goldwater dynasty began. Mike and Joe Goldwater were among the first to arrive at the site of the new gold strikes in La Paz. These Polish immigrant brothers had opened a mercantile store in California during the gold rush of 1849. When hard times hit in the early 1860s, the brothers packed up their merchandise and headed for Arizona, settling first in La Paz, then in Ehrenberg.

In time the Goldwaters would establish a chain of stores in Prescott, Parker, Tombstone, Bisbee, Contention, and Phoenix. One of Mike's sons, Morris, became mayor of Prescott (see Prescott, "Prominent Prescottonians") and one of the territory's most

Senator Barry Goldwater at Prescott Frontier Days Parade, 1964
—Sharlot Hall Museum

prominent political figures; he is considered the father of the Democratic Party in Arizona—somewhat ironic in that his nephew was Republican Barry Goldwater. Barry Goldwater, elected to the U.S. Senate in 1952, was a leader in the conservative movement of the early 1960s and the Republican nominee for president in 1964. He died in 1998.

US 60
Phoenix—Wickenburg
55 MILES

WITTMANN

Thirty-five miles northwest of Phoenix, Wittmann was once in the middle of nowhere. In 1920 the railroad attached the name Nada, Spanish for "Nothing," to the station there. Although a few people took up residence, the name Nada, or Nadaburg, stuck for several years, until it was changed to Whittman in 1929. Five years later the spelling was changed.

MORRISTOWN

Morristown, on US 60 just south of its junction with AZ 74, was originally called Vulture Siding. During the prosperous days of the historic Vulture Mine at Wickenburg, about ten miles up the road, wagons took the ore across the desert to the Vulture Siding railroad stop. When George Morris, owner of the Mack Morris Mine, took up residence at Hot Springs Junction, the name changed for the last time, to Morristown.

Around the turn of the twentieth century, the stop was more popularly known as Hot Springs Junction. People traveling to Castle Hot Springs, located in the Hieroglyphic Mountains to the northeast, would get off the train and into a leather-slung stagecoach to cross twenty-one miles of dusty, rock-strewn road. In the early days, before the resort, the springs doubled as bathtub and laundromat for miners. It was said the 160-degree water would, in five minutes, sterilize a pair of long johns a prospector had worn for three months.

WICKENBURG

Before the construction of I-17 in the mid-1960s, a traveler got to Flagstaff from Phoenix via Wickenburg, Prescott, and Ash Fork, then east fifty-two miles to Flagstaff. I-17 eliminated much of this traffic through Wickenburg. I-10 between the California line and Phoenix also removed Wickenburg from the main route between Phoenix and Los Angeles.

Vulture Mine

The story goes that when Henry Wickenburg made his great strike here, he looked up and saw a vulture circling. The experienced prospector found his bonanza after rancher King Woolsey suggested that Wickenburg check out the nearby Harquahala Mountains to the west. It was only a matter of time until Wickenburg's Vulture Mine would turn out to be one of the richest gold strikes in the West, and the richest gold mine in Arizona history.

Henry Wickenburg, born Heinrich Heintzel in Austria in 1820, came to America as a young man to escape political oppression. He changed his name and went to California during the gold rush days. Like many others, he ended up leaving California to work his way back east, landing in Arizona. Wickenburg prospected in central Arizona in 1862, then returned to La Paz, the boomtown on the banks of the Colorado River. Pauline Weaver had struck gold there earlier that year.

In 1863 Pauline Weaver led A. H. Peeples's expedition up the Hassayampa in search of the *madre del oro*—the motherlode. A few miles north of present-day Wickenburg they found gold nuggets strewn across the top of a small mountain, which they dubbed Rich Hill. It is said the gold seekers pocketed $100,000 in nuggets in the first few weeks of the single richest placer strike in Arizona history, on the single richest piece of real estate in Arizona—until the arrival of developers in the twentieth century.

After Weaver's strike, Henry Wickenburg set out on his own, following Woolsey's advice to explore the mountains west of the Hassayampa. He found his glory hole in a mountain twelve miles from the river. He also made the acquaintance of Charles Genung

Henry Wickenburg
(artist unknown)
—Southwest Studies, Scottsdale
Community College

in 1864—another piece of good fortune. Genung knew hard-rock mining, and the Vulture turned out to be a lode mine—that is, the gold was still attached to the ore, as opposed to placer or "free" gold. Wisely, once he had found his ore, Wickenburg decided to sell it for fifteen dollars a ton while it was still in the ground, letting the buyer deal with mining, transporting, and milling it. Those processes took place on the banks of the Hassayampa, where forty *arrastras*—mule-driven ore crushers— operated. Mining equipment for the Vulture arrived at Ehrenberg and was hauled up the Colorado by steamer, then across the desert by wagon to the mine.

Within a year after Wickenburg's discovery, a community named after the discoverer of the Vulture was thriving on the banks of the Hassayampa. Like all boomtowns, the varied assort- ment of citizens included tinhorn gamblers, shady ladies, saloon keepers, dreamers, and schemers. Senator Barry Goldwater told of a time when the mining company failed to pay its bills to his grandfather Mike. The iron-willed Ehrenberg merchant rode over to the Vulture and took over the operation until he had collected enough money to satisfy the debt.

By 1870 the population in Maricopa County's oldest community had grown to nearly 500, not counting the drifters who came with the dust and went with the wind. Wickenburg had grown into the most important city in central Arizona. Wickenburg essentially created Phoenix—at that time a tiny agricultural settlement on the banks of the Salt River—by serving as a market for its livestock and food.

The residents of Wickenburg were so busy trying to strike it rich they didn't have time to build a proper jail, so they used a large old mesquite tree at the corner of Tegner and Center Streets. Incorrigible characters were chained to the jail-tree until they sobered up or served their time in the shade. One regular was George Sayers, a mountain of a man who bellowed like a range bull, even when sober. One time George, also known as the "King of Gunsight" (the town from which he hailed), went on a tear. Finally deputies subdued him and dragged him to the jail-tree. The mesquite was already filled to capacity, however, so they chained George to a huge log. The King of Gunsight spent the night in deep slumber, but when daylight came, he wanted a drink. He shook the mountains with his bellowing, but no one came to his aid. So, shouldering the log—which would have put a pack mule to a supreme test—George walked to the nearest saloon, where he demanded and received a drink, no questions asked.

Another venerable mesquite in the middle of the mining camp served as a hanging tree to thwart high-graders. High-grading—pocketing ore—was always a serious problem at mines. It is estimated that miners stole as much as 40 percent of the rich Vulture's gold—$1 million during its first six years alone. In an answering statistic, over twenty thieves are said to have met their end on the hanging tree.

High-grading was not the only crime associated with mining. About a year after murdering a family at Wittmann in 1886, the Valenzuelas, a Mexican gang active in the area, robbed and murdered three men hauling forty pounds of bullion from the Vulture Mine. A posse trailed the gang to Gila Bend, where they had a shoot-out. One of the murderers, Inocente Valenzuela, was

Vulture Mine buildings today —Author photo

killed, but the other two escaped to Mexico and were never caught. The stolen Vulture Mine gold was found wrapped in a blanket.

The Vulture went on to become the richest gold mine in nineteenth-century Arizona, producing close to $20 million before it closed in 1942. It is said the rock used in the construction of the old buildings would assay out at $20 a ton today. However, Henry Wickenburg did not capitalize on the potential riches. He sold four-fifths of his interest in the mine to Ben Phelps of Philadelphia for $85,000. Furthermore, Wickenburg never received the money owed him, and a string of bad luck plagued the Austrian for the rest of his days. Wickenburg committed suicide in 1905.

Wickenburg Massacre

On November 4, 1871, a stagecoach was attacked in the so-called Wickenburg Massacre. The stage from Wickenburg to Ehrenberg had traveled about nine miles west when assailants unleashed a barrage of gunfire, killing driver "Dutch John" Lentz and five passengers, including a reporter for the *New York Tribune* named Frederick Loring. Two people survived: Mollie Shepherd, a bawdy-house madam carrying $40,000 from the sale of her bordello in Prescott, and army paymaster William Kruger, who was taking a

$100,000 payroll to California. Kruger received a gunshot wound in the shoulder and Shepherd sustained a powder burn on the arm.

The two survivors told conflicting stories of the attack. Kruger claimed he held off nine Apache for several hours with a six-shooter, but examination of the bullet holes in the stagecoach cast doubt on that scenario. In addition, horses, tack, clothing, and ammunition were all left at the scene, and if Indians were responsible, they would have taken these things. The only items missing were the cash and a shovel, leading some to believe the assailants were either Mexican bandits or whites dressed up as Indians.

Nevertheless, Gen. George Crook went to the Date Creek Reservation to investigate whether the Hualapai Indians had robbed the coach. He ended up nearly losing his life. Some renegades attempted to assassinate the general during his parley with the Hualapai chief, but a friendly Hualapai tipped off Crook's soldiers. Meanwhile, observers reported that, as suspects in the Wickenburg incident, the Hualapai seemed to have no more money than usual.

As the Wickenburg case began to unravel, it started to look as though the culprits were Kruger and Shepherd themselves. Prescott locals claimed Kruger was a regular customer at Shepherd's place. A theory developed in which the two murdered the six other people, inflicted superficial wounds on themselves, and buried the loot. But the case against Kruger and Shepherd proved too weak for charges to be pressed, and the pair left for California. There they enjoyed celebrity status, since the massacre had received front-page attention in the papers.

A short time later, in a newspaper interview in California, Kruger said Shepherd died of the wounds she suffered in the massacre. But newsmen could find no record of Shepherd's death. When they sought out Kruger again, they also found that he had vanished from his last address, a hotel.

In December 1872 a man registered in a Phoenix hotel as William Kruger was cut down by a stray bullet fired during a fight between two customers. The victim, the hotel clerk said, had been on his way to the Wickenburg area to do some prospecting. Whether he was the same William Kruger is not known for certain, though he did fit the general description. Who perpetrated the

Wickenburg Massacre remains one of frontier Arizona's many unsolved mysteries.

Walnut Grove Dam Disaster

Up the Hassayampa River from Wickenburg, about twenty miles downstream from Prescott and about eight miles east of Kirkland Junction, Walnut Grove Valley became the site in 1887 of a dam and reservoir. New York miners Wells and DeWitt Bates, owners of the small Marcus gold mine nearby, first conceived of the project to provide water for both mining and agriculture. The dam, built in a narrow gorge, was designed to be 80 feet high, but the water company that ultimately built it in 1887 raised that height to 110 feet.

On February 21, 1890, after a wetter-than-usual winter, the reservoir overfilled and water began cresting the dam. Superintendent Thomas H. Brown could not get the floodgates open, even with dynamite. Unwisely, Brown waited until he had exhausted his options before sending an employee downriver to warn residents the dam might break.

The messenger, Dan Burke—Arizona's ignominious answer to Paul Revere—got as far as Bob Brow's Saloon, also known as Goodwin's Station, where he stopped for a few drinks and a visit to a lady upstairs. Later, Brown dispatched a second messenger, William Akard, but his message also went undelivered: the dam broke during his ride. Akard was never heard from again.

The dam blew around midnight, releasing an epic torrent of water 100 feet tall—including thousands of pounds of rock—roaring down the canyon at over sixty miles an hour. As it rolled along, the flood lost some of its height but little of its force. Two hours later, a forty-foot wall of water swept through Wickenburg and obliterated the little town of Seymour. By the time the water reached the Gila River around Buckeye, witnesses reported it was over two miles wide. Exactly how many people lost their lives was never known.

Brow's Saloon was swept away, including a safe containing $7,000 in gold dust. Somehow the people inside, including Dan Burke, escaped. The next day Burke was arrested, as much for his own protection as on charges of manslaughter. He claimed he had not delivered the message because he got lost. At some point he was released, and he disappeared.

Wickenburg in 1916 (view northeast); the church still stands today. —Desert Caballeros Western Museum

Some Maricopa County residents, Henry Wickenburg among them, sued the Walnut Grove Water Storage Company for damages after the flood. The court dismissed the suit because it wasn't filed in Yavapai County, and for some reason the citizens did not refile.

Saloon owner Bob Brow moved to Prescott and bought the now famous Palace Saloon on Whiskey Row. He is said to have recouped his losses by telling treasure seekers where to find the safe in the sands of the Hassayampa. The details usually took eight shots of whiskey, at 25 cents a shot, to unfold. To this day, people still search for the lost safe on the Hassayampa.

Dude Ranch Capital of the World

During the mid-1920s Wickenburg became known as the "dude ranch capital of the world." About this time the Old West was making the transition from reality into romantic myth. In response to the new nostalgia, men like Jack Burden and Romaine Lowdermilk of Wickenburg established a radical vacation concept—the dude ranch. Much to the surprise of working cattlemen and their hired hands, easterners, it seemed, were ready to pay good money to stay on a ranch, eat the chow, and ride herd on the cows. Burden's Remuda Ranch and Lowdermilk's Kay El Bar Ranch were the first in Wickenburg, and others soon followed.

Around World War II, as many as twelve dude ranches prospered in the area. The cowboys entertained guests around the campfire with their own songs, poems, and stories. Sometimes the exposure brought the cowpunchers to the attention of Hollywood and New York, and they and/or their creations became famous. Gail Gardner, Billy Simon, and Curly Fletcher, among others, had this good fortune. The Kay El Bar, with its picturesque old adobe buildings, is still a working dude ranch.

US 93
Wickenburg—Kingman
130 MILES

BIG SANDY RIVER

Just south of Wikieup, US 93 crossed the Big Sandy River. The Big Sandy originates in the Aquarius Mountains, and at least some of its length is categorized as "wild and scenic." In 2001, a power plant was proposed for a site about two miles east of where US 93 crosses the river, but the permit was denied later that year due to concerns of the Hualapai Nation, environmentalists, and the state.

WIKIEUP

A wickiup is a temporary, dome-shaped brush dwelling built by Apache, Yavapai, and other nomadic or rancheria peoples. Apparently such a dwelling was found at a spring where this small plains community on the Big Sandy River would develop, about thirty miles south of today's I-40. At times the settlement also went by the names Owens and Neal, but neither stuck, so Wikieup was accepted, though misspelled. Nearby Wikieup Canyon is sometimes designated on maps as Wake Up Canyon.

The mountains between Wikieup and the Colorado River are rich in minerals. A number of mines and mining camps, including Planet, McCrackin, American Flag, Signal, and Scatterville, dotted

Apache wickiup —Arizona Historical Society

the area. North of Wikieup, Deluge Wash merges with the Big Sandy. Those familiar with Arizona's desert flash floods know the name Deluge Wash perfectly fits many of the state's desert arroyos.

US 93
Kingman—Hoover Dam
71 MILES

SANTA CLAUS

Santa Claus, about fifteen miles northwest of Kingman on US 93, is perhaps one of the best-known fast-blink communities in America. It never materialized as a metropolis despite the dreams of Nina Talbot. Talbot, a 300-pound Los Angelena who billed herself as the biggest real estate agent in California, planned a

Santa Claus, Arizona
—Southwest Studies, Scottsdale
Community College

subdivision here in the 1930s—a Christmas village in the desert with architecture to match. Nina and her husband Ed took up residence at Santa Claus, where she delighted friends around the country with picturesque Christmas cards from Santa Claus, Arizona. However, the community never took off, and today it is closed.

CHLORIDE

Take the Chloride turnoff east off US 93 to visit this tiny mining town. Named for exposed ore laced with silver chloride—a silver salt used especially in photography—Chloride is the oldest Anglo American mining town in Arizona. It's located in the Cerbat Mountains. *Cerbat,* a Quechan word, refers to bighorn mountain sheep.

Chloride came into existence in 1860, and the town was important enough by 1871 to become the Mohave County seat. Two years later the townspeople moved it a few miles south to Mineral Park, on the Hardyville–Prescott road. Moving whole towns after the ore ran out someplace was not unusual, since building materials were scarce. A rich gold strike in the Cerbats drew many would-be millionaires convinced that Chloride sat right on top of the mother lode and that its streets would be cobbled with gold bricks. By 1900, 2,000 miners lived at Chloride.

The major lode running through the Cerbat Mountains was the Elkhart, a mixture of lead, zinc, and copper, along with some gold and silver. This type of ore made separation complex and difficult. The many mines in the Cerbat Range have included the Golconda, the Payroll, the Golden Gem, the Esmeralda, and the Vanderbilt. Until the 1930s the richest was the Golconda, between Chloride and Kingman, which by that time had produced $6.5 million in ore, mostly zinc. Later the Tennessee, near Chloride, surpassed the Golconda.

The arrival of the Arizona Utah Railroad in 1898 from Kingman to Chloride was cause for celebration. A ballot vote was held to select a woman for the honor of pounding in the silver spike. Each voter had to pay ten cents for a ballot, the proceeds going for a new school. In addition to the silver spike ceremony, the festivities included a drilling contest, always a favorite in a mining camp. Contestants were expected to bore into a granite slab at a rate of "two drinks per minute."

Despite these auspicious beginnings, the Arizona Utah Railroad failed to be profitable and lasted only a few years. Still, Chloride

Loading cattle at Chloride railhead, 1916 —Mohave County Historical Society

could rightly claim to be the first incorporated city in Mohave County, and it continued to thrive until mining declined in the 1940s. Today, Chloride is not a total ghost town; it still has about 200 inhabitants.

WHITE HILLS

Twenty-five miles north of the Chloride turnoff, a back road heads east off of US 93 and ultimately north to Temple Bar. The right fork of this road leads to the ghost town of White Hills, named after the hills themselves. Boom times in the White Hills began in 1892 when an Indian man, Hualapai Jeff, found a sample of rich silver ore and guided Henry Schaeffer, who had been prospecting northeast of the area, to the place where he had found it. Soon Schaeffer and two colleagues had staked claims at the site. The first shipments of ore were said to have averaged 3,000 ounces of silver per ton. Word leaked out and the rush to the White Hills was on.

A Denver syndicate including D. T. Root and David Moffatt investigated the area and bought up the principal claims in late 1892. They installed mining equipment and a mill and by January 1893 there were 600 residents in the camp. By the next year the population had doubled. In 1895 Root and Moffatt sold to an English syndicate for $1.5 million. The English company invested heavily, building a town with electric lights, telephones, running water, and flush toilets. White Hills had become the largest town in Mohave County.

But the ore in the White Hills was spotty, with occasional "teaser" bunches of high-grade ore. At a depth of 650 feet the high-grade ore played out. Shortly after, Moffatt and Root, still owed $26,000 by the English syndicate, sued and got the mine back. As late as the 1970s, attempts were made to turn a profit but there is little production of record. The mine produced somewhere between $2 million and $3 million.

HOOVER DAM

Throughout history, rampaging floods of the Colorado River have periodically devastated the land adjacent to it in what is now Mexico and the United States. In the 1890s, 1916, and 1920, for

Hoover Dam —Southwest Studies, Scottsdale Community College

example, floods rendered the roads in Yuma suitable only for submarines. In 1905 the river hurled its waters into the Imperial Valley and filled the Salton Sea. It took months, and thousands of railroad cars of rock and dirt, to rebuild the river banks and put the river back on course.

To harness the Colorado and to meet Southern California's ravenous appetite for water and electricity, Congress passed the Boulder Canyon Project Act in 1928, authorizing a dam in Black Canyon. The original name was Boulder Dam, but two years after the project began, the Secretary of the Interior ordered the name changed to Hoover in honor of the president. The name was fitting, since the man held more respect as an engineer than as a chief executive. When the Democrats returned to power in 1934, they changed the name back to Boulder. However, President Harry Truman, in a grand gesture of nonpartisan politics, declared the name again and finally to be Hoover Dam.

Chief engineer Frank T. Crowe's mission was to build the largest dam in the world. Early in 1931 Crowe put 3,000 men to work in the 800-foot-deep canyon, where temperatures reached 120 degrees and the rock was hot enough to fry eggs on. Daring workers with jackhammers were suspended on ropes hundreds of feet off the canyon floor, clearing rock before concrete was poured. Then, for the next two years, workers dumped one sixteen-ton bucket of concrete into the forms every sixty seconds. At its peak, the construction project employed 5,000 workers. Ninety-six of them died while working on it. When the job was finished, the dam was taller than a sixty-story skyscraper.

Frank Crowe's time-saving innovations earned him the nickname "Hurry Up" Crowe. One of these was a lighting system that allowed crews to work around the clock. By 1935 construction on the $49-million dam was complete—two years ahead of schedule. The largest dam in the world at that time, Hoover Dam now ranks fifty-second in size worldwide.

Lake Mead
—Southwest
Studies, Scottsdale
Community College

As the lake began to form behind the dam, alarmists falsely predicted the tremendous weight of water would cause serious earthquakes. At first, the 100-mile-long lake was going to be called Lake Powell after John Wesley Powell, the river's first white explorer. However, during the dam's construction, Dr. Ellwood Mead, Commissioner of Reclamation, died. A week later, officials decided to rename the lake in his honor. By volume, Lake Mead is the largest man-made lake in the western hemisphere.

US 60
Wickenburg—Hope
62 MILES

Heading west from Wickenburg, US 60 follows an old well-established wagon road to Ehrenberg. Construction of a railroad in the early 1900s created most of the communities along this route.

HARQUAHALA PEAK
SMITHSONIAN OBSERVATORY

In 1920, the clear skies of Arizona brought Smithsonian scientists to the highest mountain in southwestern Arizona, southwest of Aguila, to build an observatory. Construction required the packing of building materials and other supplies by burro up to Harquahala Peak (5,681 feet), three hours one way. The Harquahala Peak Observatory did not use telescopes. Instead, the scientists who lived and worked there for five years observed solar activity with such devices as theodolites—for measuring angles—and pyrheliometers, which measure heating and cooling. Sent to Washington, the information they collected was compared with data from another observatory and used to forecast weather. The Smithsonian abandoned the observatory in 1925. It is now listed on the National Register of Historic Places. Four-wheel drive is required to reach the observatory, via Eagle Eye Road out of Aguila.

SALOME

Salome is short for the town's full name: "Salome—Where She Danced." In 1904, three men founded the town: Deforest Hall, who changed his name to Dick Wick Hall; Hall's brother Ernest; and Charles Pratt. Dick Wick Hall became the most famous inhabitant, main promoter, and "sage" of Salome, and is responsible for its name. He said the name came about when Charles Pratt's wife Grace Salome attempted to walk across the hot desert sand in bare feet. Soon the temperature was making her "dance" as she attempted to finish her trip unscorched.

Fleeing the cold weather of his Iowa birthplace, Hall came to Wickenburg in 1901 with his brothers to run the local newspaper. He was inspired to change his name to Dick Wickenburg Hall,

In Salome, Arizona
—Courtesy Jeff Kida

later shortening it to Wick. Hall found his Shangri-la in the deserts of western Arizona. In Salome, he opened the Laughing Gas Service Station and Garage, which he ran for two decades. On the walls of the station and along the road for several miles in either direction, humorous signs provoked grins from the bone-weariest traveler and helped make the trip across the searing desert less miserable.

Although Hall's humor touched many travelers on the Los Angeles-to-Phoenix highway, his fame really began to spread when, to pass the time, he began publishing a mimeographed single-sheet newspaper, the *Salome Sun.* He didn't care if people paid for his paper. "I don't need the money," he said, "there's no place here to spend it." At some point someone forwarded a copy of the *Sun* to the *Saturday Evening Post.* The *Post* was the nation's most prestigious and best-paying magazine; every writer dreamed of appearing in it. The *Post* expressed interest in seeing more of Hall's work. He told them he was too busy. They tried again; he ignored them. Finally they asked if he would just send new editions of the *Sun* to them. For the next five years, they printed everything he sent.

Soon most of the civilized world knew of the Salome frog:

> I was Hatched out here by some Mistake—
> Three Hundred Miles from the nearest Lake.
> Salome is a Town of Nineteen Folks
> Who Live on Sunshine, Sand and Jokes.
> And All I can Do is to Think and Sit
> And Wish That I could Get Used to it.
> That's Why I Look so Sad and grim—
> Seven Years Old, and I Can't Swim!

A swimsuit company paid Hall a royalty to let the frog pose in one of their suits. His now expanded reading public also learned of the "Greasewood Golf Lynx," the 247-mile desert golf course, par 16,394, where winter visitors might spend the entire season on just one round of golf and where the clubhouse rented camping equipment, horses, canteens, and maps in addition to golf clubs. He wrote:

> A new record of 46 has been made on the Greasewood Golf Course by J. Bobbinette Jones of Asheville, N.C. This beats the Previous Record of 52 days made by Curley Hanson of Gold Gulch last summer. . . .

Fond readers compared Dick Wick Hall to the great humorists Mark Twain and Will Rogers. Hall was also an entrepreneur who promoted everything from oil wells and gold mines to desert communities, always managing to stay half a step ahead of his creditors. He succeeded in making Salome one of the most famous small towns in the West. Hall died of Bright's disease in 1926 at the age of forty-eight, and is buried in Salome. Each year, the Salome Lions Club remembers him with a community celebration called Dick Wick Days.

HOPE

A community named Johannesberg started out near here, but in 1920, US 60 was built, bypassing the town. So residents relocated to the highway and named their new community Hope, in hopes that they would not have to move again and that their businesses would rebound. In the early 1980s the highway moved again, but this time the people did not give up Hope.

AZ 72
US 60—Parker
49 MILES

BOUSE

Bouse, founded in 1906, was named for George Bouse, a local developer. Until the 1940s, the hamlet basked in obscurity. Then, during World War II, the military decided that the deserts of western Arizona and eastern California were ideal training grounds for the invasion of North Africa. Concerned that "the desert can kill quicker than the enemy," Gen. George Patton established a desert training center near Bouse.

In 1942, thirteen infantry divisions and seven armored divisions moved to Camp Bouse and started training. According to one soldier who trained there, the heat was so intense that "a bottle of beer at 100 degrees Fahrenheit was considered a cool one." The army dismantled Camp Bouse in 1945, but a few foundations and other bits of evidence remain, including tank tracks in the fragile desert.

Three miles north of Bouse, the 59,000-acre Cactus Plain Wilderness Study Area covers the western two-thirds of the Cactus Plain, a sand-dune expanse. Within the area, the color and type of dunes vary. Some are stable; others shift with the wind. The area's uniqueness includes not just the dunes, but also the plants and animals who live there. Death Valley Mormon tea, sand flat milk vetch, and woolly heads are a few of the plants that live there; animals special to the area include the elf owl and several species of lizard.

PARKER

The original town of Parker was four miles downstream of the present city. Established in 1865 at the same time as and as part of the Colorado River Indian Reservation, the town was named for Superintendent of Indian Affairs Gen. Eli Parker. Parker, a Seneca Indian from New York State, was a highly respected officer on Gen. Ulysses S. Grant's staff during the Civil War and was among those present at Lee's surrender at Appomattox.

The town relocated four miles north, still on the reservation, in 1905, when the Arizona & California Railroad built a bridge across the Colorado there. Today, about 3,500 people live in Parker. The town has a casino and a tribal museum and library.

Nellie Bush

One of Parker's most colorful residents was Nellie Bush, the "Queen of the Colorado River." In addition to being the first woman elected to the Arizona Senate (during the 1920s), an airplane pilot, and the only woman licensed to pilot a steamer on the Colorado, Bush was a schoolteacher, school principal, businesswoman, mother, justice of the peace, coroner, and leader in women's club activities. Whatever she accomplished in her life, she did with a can-do attitude. If someone asked her why she was doing it, she said, "Why not?"

Bush was born in 1888 in Missouri. When she was five, her parents moved to Mesa, Arizona. She graduated from Tempe Normal School (Arizona State University) and taught in Mesa and Glendale until she married Joe Bush in 1912. Three years

Nellie Bush
—Southwest Studies,
Scottsdale Community
College

later the couple moved to Parker, where Joe bought the local ferryboat business. With no bridge over the Colorado at the time, automobiles traveling between California and Arizona had to pay $3.50 to cross on the ferry. After that introduction to the Colorado and its rivercraft, Bush obtained her steamboat license and worked as a pilot for seventeen years. She often took her son onboard while she worked. Later she remembered:

> Waves sometimes would be over 8 feet high; often when we were caught on the river in a storm, we'd have to throw overboard some of the ore. Many a time when the sailing was dangerous and I thought about my baby in the pilot house, I've uttered a little prayer, "Now, if you'll just let me get this kid off here alive, I'll never bring him back on board again." But you forgot about that after the danger had passed.

Often enough, Bush had to make the long drive across the dusty desert road to Phoenix. One time her car broke down in the middle of nowhere. She tinkered with the motor for a while and found that the spring in the timer was broken. She removed a spring from her corset, fixed the timer, and went on her way.

In 1920, Bush was elected to the state legislature. She served a total of sixteen years, fourteen as a representative and two as a senator. In 1921 she enrolled in the law school at the University of Arizona. She said, "We lived two blocks from the University campus and two blocks from my son Wesley's school. We would part each morning, my son going one way and I the other. He used to tell people, 'Mother and I are both in the first grade.'"

In law school, the dean forbade Bush and her female classmates to attend class when the subject of rape was being discussed. Approaching the dean, Bush demanded to know if he had heard of a case of rape that didn't involve a woman. "They let us in after that," she said.

In 1931 Bush took up flying when her son, then age sixteen, became interested in airplanes. Both got their flying licenses. They had the only plane in town and built Parker's first airport.

COLORADO RIVER INDIAN RESERVATION

The Indian people who live on the Colorado River Indian Reservation include Mojave, Chemehuevi, Navajo, and Hopi. The Mojave Indians, population 1,100, live along the banks of the Colorado River in western Arizona, California, and Nevada. Their main enterprise today is agriculture. The Mojave were prosperous farmers when the Spanish first encountered them in the sixteenth century, and they had also developed trade routes to the Pacific Ocean. They were once the largest and most warlike of the tribes living along the Colorado. No Spanish missions or settlements were ever located on Mojave lands. War chiefs and shamans were the most influential men within Mojave society. The Mojave allied themselves with the Apache, Yavapai, and Quechan, and their traditional enemies were the Cocopah, Pima, Maricopa, and Tohono O'Odham.

The Chemehuevi Indians are Southern Paiute people, related to the Paiute in southern Nevada. Traditionally, they lived by desert hunting and gathering and by desert farming along the Colorado. They are relative newcomers to Arizona, arriving from the Mojave Desert around 1800. About this time the Mojave succeeded in driving the Maricopa Indians out of the area, which left a vacancy. Since the Chemehuevi got along well with the Mojave, they were allowed to take up residence. Today there are about 530 Chemehuevi on the reservation. Chemehuevi basketry, which uses cottonwood and willow found along the river, is world-famous.

*Mojave runners
(no date)*
—Southwest Studies,
Scottsdale Community
College

US 95 and AZ 95
Yuma—I-40
174 MILES

US 95 heads east out of Yuma, runs parallel to I-8 for ten miles, then turns north. It crosses the Gila River several miles west of Dome. It meets I-10 at Quartzsite, where it turns west and heads into California—but our trip continues north on AZ 95.

YUMA PROVING GROUNDS

The Yuma Proving Grounds form a large U-shaped area around the Kofa National Wildlife Refuge, northeast of Yuma. Public access to the grounds is restricted.

During the spring of 1942, with World War II raging, Gen. George S. Patton established several desert training centers in western Arizona to prepare troops for the rugged North African campaign. Patton, a tough tank commander from the old school, wanted his training grounds to be as rigorous and realistic as possible. The Arizona desert was equal to the task. Several soldiers died in the heat, but in the end the troops went on to prove their mettle against the seasoned veterans of Rommel's Afrika Corps.

At his Yuma Proving Grounds, according to one story, the general, always a stickler for spit, polish, and protocol, came upon a man who was stripped to the waist and working on telephone lines. Patton stopped his jeep and ordered the man to report at once. When the worker strolled up to the general, Patton snapped, "Stand at attention! What is your name and what outfit are you with?" He spiced his interrogation with a few extra, choice expletives. The man waited until Patton was finished, then replied, "My name is John Smith, my outfit is Mountain States Telephone Company, and you can go straight to hell."

KOFA NATIONAL WILDLIFE REFUGE

East of US 95 about thirty miles north of Yuma is the Kofa National Wildlife Refuge. Several back roads off the highway will take you into the refuge. The Kofa refuge takes its name from its primary range of mountains. The range was named for the King of Arizona Mining Company, which used to stamp "K of A" on company property. The active years of gold production at the King of Arizona Mine, in the southwestern part of the mountains, were from 1896 to 1910. In 1897 the company built a five-stamp amalgamation mill at Mohawk, thirty-five miles south of the mine; a year later it also built a cyanide plant to treat tailings. The mine produced $3.5 million in gold before it played out. The old mine itself can be reached via a dirt road off King Road. King Road leaves US 95 at Stone Cabin, a former stage stop.

While most maps refer to these mountains as the Kofas, old-timers around Yuma and La Paz County call them the S. H. (Shithouse) Mountains. This name dates from the 1860s, when soldiers noticed that some of the mountains resembled large houses with smaller buildings in back—and dubbed the mountains accordingly. Later, as more women moved into the area—or whenever a local feared for the delicacy of his listener—the initials served in lieu of the full name. If the listener was curious and inquired further about the meaning of S. H., the local cleared his throat and said it stood for Short Horn. Short Horn even appears on some maps.

The Kofa National Wildlife Refuge covers an area of about 1,000 square miles. A rugged, protected desert environment without paved roads or facilities, its most popular attraction is Palm Canyon. Here, about 100 native California fan palm trees, also known as desert palms, grow in a red-rock ravine. Rare wherever they grow, these are certainly the last wild native California palms in Arizona. Summer temperatures in this area can get up to 120 degrees; rain falls only a few times a year.

LA POSA PLAIN

West of the refuge up to AZ 72, US/AZ 95 passes through the flat desert of the La Posa Plain. Somewhere in the La Posa desert between the La Paz County line and Quartzsite, near milepost 69 on US 95, there's allegedly an outcropping of rich virgin ore known as the Lost Six-Shooter Mine.

In 1884 a man named either Perkins or Jenkins, but P.J. for short, was superintendent of the Planet Mine on the Bill Williams River. After taking some prospective investors to the stage station at Tyson's Wells (Quartzsite), P.J. was caught in a blinding sandstorm on the way home. He dismounted and holed up behind some rocks for protection. When the storm had passed, he looked around and saw what every prospector dreams of: a vein of ore so rich, he could see strings of gold glittering throughout it.

P.J. filled his holster with specimens. Then, leaving his six-shooter and overcoat as markers, he set out across the desert north toward the Bill Williams River. It had been some time since either P.J. or his mare had had water, so he let her loose, figuring she would head for water—and home. He was probably walking behind.

The next day the horse showed up at the Planet Mine, but P.J. was nowhere to be seen. Searchers later found his body half-covered by sand near the old Bouse-to-Parker wagon road. Before dying, he had scribbled this message in a notebook: "Found gold ledge by rocks 15 feet high. Two rocks alike. Knocked off some pieces. Very rich. Dust in air too thick to tell exact location. Think it is above ravine I come up 7 miles."

The ledge was very rich indeed! P.J.'s specimens assayed out at $25,000 in gold per ton. Prospectors searched for the cluster of tall rocks and the seven-mile ravine, but both proved elusive. There have been other gold strikes in the area, but the surroundings never fit P.J.'s description.

POSTON

About twenty-three miles north of Quartzsite, AZ 95 joins up with AZ 72. Twelve miles farther north is Parker; from there, the Mohave Road (Reservation Route 1) heads back out of town to the southwest, parallel to the river, to Poston, on the Colorado River Indian Reservation.

Charles Poston arrived in Arizona in the 1850s. He worked hard to gain territorial status for Arizona, which came in 1863. Arizona's first superintendent for Indian Affairs, he established the Colorado River Indian Reservation in 1865.

The town of Poston gained notoriety much later as the site, from April 1942 to March 1946, of the Colorado River Relocation

Charles D. Poston
—Sharlot Hall Museum

Center, an internment camp on reservation lands for Japanese American families mainly from California.

During this time, with a peak population of 18,000 living behind barbed wire, guarded by the U.S. Army, Poston became Arizona's third-largest city after Phoenix and Tucson. A second Arizona relocation center, Gila River, on leased Pima-Maricopa tribal lands near Phoenix, was home to 13,000 evacuees. Many young male internees went on to join the legendary 442nd Regimental Combat Team. This outfit, made up of Japanese American soldiers, was the most decorated unit in the American army during the war, winning over 3,900 individual decorations.

PARKER DAM AND LAKE HAVASU

Parker Dam, fourteen miles north of the town of Parker on AZ 95, is one of several dams built on the Colorado River since 1909. It was completed in 1938, but not before some interesting encounters took place between hostile factions. Arizona and California have maintained a long-running dispute over the use of Colorado River water. Californians, with greater political clout in Washington, have usually called the plays. This state of affairs infuriated Arizona governor Ben Moeur, a crusty country doctor from Tempe. In 1934, during the building of Parker Dam—designed to deliver some of Arizona's water to the West Coast—Governor Moeur sent the Arizona National Guard to the east bank of the Colorado to intimidate construction workers.

One night a few Guard members went to Parker to ask river pilot Nellie Bush (see Parker) for assistance in an impromptu foray across the river into "enemy" territory. Bush was happy to oblige the Arizona "war effort," placing her two steamers, the *Julie B.* and the *Nellie T.,* at the disposal of the Arizona troops. The mission took place under cover of darkness—which probably explains, in part, why the two craft became entangled in the river's flotsam and jetsam. The red-faced "Arizona Navy" had to be rescued by their California arch-nemeses. Soon afterward, the U.S. Supreme Court forced the Arizona Guard to make a hasty withdrawal.

Parker Dam is the deepest dam in the world—73 percent of it is buried below the original riverbed. Lake Havasu, the reservoir behind the dam, is about forty-five miles long. Along with Hoover and Davis Dams, Parker provides water and power to Los Angeles, San Diego, and communities in the Lower Colorado River Basin.

CENTRAL ARIZONA PROJECT CANAL

The 336-mile Central Arizona Project Canal begins at Lake Havasu and brings water to central and southern Arizona. The 336-mile canal reached Phoenix in 1986 and arrived at its final destination, Tucson, in 1991. Water in the canal flows with the help of gravity whenever possible, but the project also uses fourteen pumping stations to lift the water from 700 feet above sea level at Parker to 1,300 feet at Phoenix and 2,400 feet at Tucson. The water passes through a tunnel in the Buckskin Mountains and an aqueduct for 190 miles to Phoenix, then it has another 143 miles to go to Tucson. During an average year, 1.5 million acre-feet of water travels into central Arizona.

At the beginning of the twentieth century, the seven states in the Colorado River Basin—Arizona, California, Colorado, Nevada, New Mexico, Utah, and Wyoming—divvied up shares of the mighty Colorado's water. In 1922, with the federal government's participation, the seven divided themselves into two groups, upper- and lower-basin members, and 7.5 million acre-feet of water was allotted to each basin. In the lower basin, Arizona, Nevada, and California were to divide that allotment among themselves. However, Arizona disputed its share of the river water, and did not approve a basin-wide agreement until 1944. Currently, Arizona has rights to 2.8 million acre-feet of the water per year; California, 4.4 million acre-feet; and Nevada, 300,000 acre-feet.

In 1946, the idea of bringing Colorado River water to people across Arizona jelled in the Central Arizona Project (CAP). It took years for the idea to gain widespread support, but finally in 1968 President Lyndon Johnson signed the bill that gave the project the go-ahead. Construction began at Lake Havasu in 1973 and was completed around 1992. Since then, the CAP has continued to face challenges. Fewer mines, farmers, and municipalities than expected actually wanted the CAP water. And the quality of the water was different from what customers were used to; it was harder and had more dissolved solids than groundwater. Despite these difficulties, 84,000 customers in Tucson received their first Colorado River water in 1992.

AUBRY LANDING

Just north of Parker Dam is the confluence of the Colorado and Bill Williams Rivers. Though seldom mentioned in history books, this area was the setting for much of Arizona's early history. Juan de Oñate, the great explorer and governor of New Mexico from 1598 to 1609, was one of the first Europeans to come through this area on his way to Yuma Crossing in 1604. During the 1820s such fur trappers as Ewing Young and James O. Pattie plied these streams for beaver. The trapping was excellent, but the Mojave Indians proved too formidable, and after 1830, mountain men generally avoided the area.

Another explorer of renown, François Xavier Aubry, lent his name to an important shipping point at the mouth of the Bill Williams River. Aubry Landing was established in 1864 in honor of the so-called "Skimmer of the Plains." Aubry, a French Canadian, earned that title by riding horseback nonstop from Independence, Missouri, to Santa Fe, a distance of 800 miles, in the amazing time of five days and thirteen hours—all to win a bet.

During his travels in Arizona in the 1850s, Aubry claimed to have encountered a tribe of Indians using rifle balls made of solid gold. He also reported selling a few shirts for $1,500 in gold and swapping a broken-down old mule for one and a half pounds of the yellow metal.

Aubry established a prosperous freighting and livestock business between New Mexico and California. Despite two narrow escapes with Indians in Aubry Valley (near today's Flagstaff), he became convinced that the thirty-fifth parallel was an excellent site for a wagon road and rail line. In those days, recommending one route over another could create enemies when people had vested interests. Aubry's belief in the thirty-fifth parallel led to an altercation in 1854 in a Santa Fe cantina with Richard Weightman, an attorney who preferred the thirty-second parallel for a railroad route. Aubry pulled a revolver, but Weightman was faster and drove a bowie knife into Aubry's belly, killing the great

"Skimmer of the Plains." After Aubry's death, his journals continued to provide future explorers with valuable information on northern Arizona.

The town of Aubry Landing lasted until 1865, when the market for copper dropped. By 1878 all that was left was a post office, hotel, and saloon, all in the same building. William Hardy, the agent for the steamboat company, lived in an old steamboat cabin he had converted into a home. Now all this lies beneath the waters of Lake Havasu.

LAKE HAVASU CITY

Robert P. McCulloch Sr. was a twentieth-century visionary and entrepreneur reminiscent of the enterprising men of the preceding century who made real such dreams as mines, irrigation projects, and towns. McCulloch's founding of Lake Havasu City was one of the last of many bold acts during his productive life. A Stanford engineering graduate and boat racer, McCulloch founded several companies that developed and produced engines and engine components for boats, cars, airplanes, lawnmowers, chainsaws, and other items. He is credited with, among other things, the popularization of the personal-sized chainsaw.

In the late 1950s McCulloch was flying over the Colorado River in western Arizona looking for a test site for his company's outboard motors. At Lake Havasu—created in 1938 by Parker Dam—McCulloch spotted and landed at an old World War II air strip perched on a desert peninsula jutting out into the lake. Later he claimed that, the moment he laid eyes on the place, he envisioned a city there at the foot of the picturesque Mohave Mountains.

In the fall of 1960, McCulloch flew Texan C. V. Wood over the site and said, "Let's build a city." Wood was one of the original creative geniuses behind Disneyland. By 1964, McCulloch had purchased twenty-six acres at the site for about $75 an acre.

McCulloch and Wood turned out to be a perfect match. "Lake Havasu is McCulloch's baby, but Wood is the guy who spanked it and made it breathe," some wag noted at the time. McCulloch's dream was of a planned community centered around recreation, tourism, and retirement. He believed it should be self-supporting, with allotted percentages of different types of businesses.

What really put Lake Havasu City on the map was the acquisition of the 1831 London Bridge in 1968. Legend has it that McCulloch went to France and tried to buy the Eiffel Tower. Predictably, the French told him where to go. So he went to Italy and offered to buy the Leaning Tower of Pisa. He got the same response from the Italians. When he tried England, the British exclaimed, "Have we got a deal for you!" The venerable bridge on the Thames, built in 1831 and bullet-riddled by Luftwaffe gunners in World War II, had begun to sink into the river under the weight of modern-day traffic. The city of London had decided to build a new one.

McCulloch offered $2.46 million and the British took it. The bridge was dismantled and the stones were numbered, hauled by sea to Los Angeles, and trucked to Havasu City. In a ceremony in 1968, London's own lord mayor laid the bridge's cornerstone. Over the next three years, the bridge was reconstructed stone by stone over a mile-long channel cut through the peninsula. The completed bridge was dedicated on October 10, 1971—a date the town commemorates each year with "London Bridge Days." Over the years, the bridge has drawn millions of visitors to the city—some of whom liked the place so much, they bought a home and stayed.

The town was incorporated in 1978, less than a year after its founder's death. In 1980, the *Los Angeles Times* called Lake Havasu City, population 16,000, "the most successful free-standing new town in the United States." Today the population is closer to 45,000. Businesses and schools abound, including a community college.

SELECTED BIBLIOGRAPHY

Acuff, Guy. *Akimult Aw A Tham, the River People: A Short History of the Pima Indians.* Casa Grande, Ariz.: Casa Grande Printing, 1979.

Aguirre, Yjinio. *Echoes of the Conquistadores.* Red Rock, Ariz.: Privately printed, 1983.

Ahnert, Gerald T. *Retracing the Butterfield Overland Trail through Arizona.* Los Angeles: Westernlore Press, 1973.

Altshuler, Constance Wynn. *Chains of Command: Arizona and the Army 1856–1875.* Tucson: Arizona Historical Society, 1981.

Arizona Highways (October 1984).

Arizona Highways (April 1964).

Baeza, Jo (Jeffers). "Tales of the Little Colorado." *Arizona Highways* (September 1965).

Bailey, Lynn R. *Bisbee: Queen of the Copper Camps.* Tucson: Westernlore Press, 1983.

Barnes, Will C. *Apaches and Longhorns.* Los Angeles: Ward Ritchie, 1941.

Bartlett, John R. *Personal Narrative of Exploration and Incidents in Texas, New Mexico, California, Sonora, and Chihuahua, Connected with the United States and Mexican Boundary Commission, during the Years 1850, '51, '52, and '53.* 2 vols. New York: D. Appleton & Co., 1854.

Bourke, John G. *An Apache Campaign in the Sierra Madre.* New York: Scribner's, 1956.

———. *On the Border with Crook.* New York: Scribner's, 1902.

Brandes, Ray. *Frontier Military Posts of Arizona.* Globe, Ariz.: Dale Stuart King Publisher, 1960.

Breakenridge, William. *Helldorado.* Boston: Houghton Mifflin, 1928.

Brooks, Juanita. *Jacob Hamblin, Mormon Apostle to the Indians.* Salt Lake City: Westwater Press, 1980.

———. *John Doyle Lee: Zealot, Pioneer Builder, Scapegoat.* Glendale, Calif.: Arthur H. Clark Co., 1972.

Brophy, Frank C. "The Mystery of San Xavier del Bac." *Arizona Highways* (March 1970).

Browne, J. Ross. *Adventures in Apache Country*. New York: Harper Bros., 1871.

Byrkit, James. *Forging the Copper Collar*. Tucson: University of Arizona Press, 1982.

Carlson, Frances. "James D. Houck, the Sheep King of Cave Creek." *Journal of Arizona History* (Spring 1980).

Chamberlain, Samuel. *My Confession*. New York: Harper and Brothers, 1956.

Chaput, Donald. *Francois X. Aubry: Trader, Trailmaker and Voyageur in the Southwest*. Glendale, Calif.: Arthur H. Clark Co., 1975.

Clarke, Dwight L. *Stephen Watts Kearny, Soldier of the West*. Norman: University of Oklahoma Press, 1961.

Cline, Platt. *Mountain Campus: The Story of Northern Arizona University*. Flagstaff, Ariz.: Northland Press, 1983.

———. *They Came to the Mountain: The Story of Flagstaff's Beginnings*. Flagstaff, Ariz.: Northland Press, 1976.

Connor, Daniel. *Joseph Reddeford Walker and the Arizona Adventure*. Norman: University of Oklahoma Press, 1956.

Cooke, Philip St. George. *The Conquest of New Mexico and California in 1846–1848*. Chicago: Rio Grande Press, 1964.

Corle, Edwin. *The Gila: River of the Southwest*. New York: Rinehart and Co., 1951.

Cremony, John C. *Life among the Apaches*. Glorieta, N.Mex.: Rio Grande Press, 1868.

Crowe, Rosalie, and Sidney Brinckerhoff. *Early Yuma*. Flagstaff, Ariz.: Northland Press, 1976.

Dimock, Brad. *Sunk without a Sound: The Tragic Colorado River Honeymoon of Glen and Bessie Hyde*. Flagstaff, Ariz.: Fretwater Press, 2001.

Dobyns, Henry F., ed. *Journal of Cave Johnson Couts*. Tucson: Arizona Pioneers Historical Society, 1961.

———. *Spanish Colonial Tucson*. Tucson: University of Arizona Press, 1976.

Dunning, Charles H., and Edward Peplow. *Rock to Riches: The Story of American Mining, Past, Present and Future, as Reflected in the Colorful History of Mining in Arizona, the Nation's Greatest Bonanza*. Phoenix: Southwest Publishing Co., 1959.

Eason, Nicholas J. *Fort Verde: An Era of Men and Courage.* Sedona, Ariz.: Tonto Press, 1966.

Egerton, Kearney. *The Fascinating Fourteen: Arizona's Counties.* Phoenix: Branding Iron Press, 1977.

———. *Somewhere Out There . . . Arizona's Lost Mines and Vanished Treasures.* Glendale, Calif.: Prickly Pear Press, 1974.

Faulk, Odie B. *Destiny Road.* New York: Oxford University Press, 1973.

———. *Tombstone: Myth and Reality.* New York: Oxford University Press, 1972.

Favour, Alpheus. *Old Bill Williams.* Norman: University of Oklahoma Press, 1962.

Federal Writers Project. *Arizona.* Joseph Miller, ed. New York: Hastings House, 1956.

Foreman, Grant, ed. *A Pathfinder in the Southwest.* Norman: University of Oklahoma Press, 1968.

Forrest, Earle. *Arizona's Dark and Bloody Ground.* Caldwell, Idaho: Caxton Printers, 1936.

Gilbert, Bill. *Westering Man: The Life of Joseph Walker.* New York: Atheneum, 1983.

Goff, John. *Arizona Biographical Dictionary.* Cave Creek, Ariz.: Black Mountain Press, 1983.

———. "Arizona's National Monuments." *Arizona Highways* (March 1978).

Gordon, Linda. *The Great Arizona Orphan Abduction.* Cambridge: Harvard University Press, 1999.

Granger, Byrd Howell, ed. *Arizona's Names: X Marks the Place.* Tucson: Falconer Publishing Co., 1983.

———. *Will C. Barnes' Arizona Place Names.* Tucson: University of Arizona Press, 1979.

Hall, Sharlot. *First Citizen of Prescott: Pauline Weaver, Trapper and Mountain Man.* Prescott, Ariz.: Sharlot Hall Historical Society, 1977.

Hanchett, Leland L. *Catch the Stage to Phoenix.* Phoenix: Privately printed, 1998.

Harte, John Bret. *Tucson: Portrait of a Desert Pueblo.* Woodland Hills, Calif.: Windsor Publications, 1980.

Heatwole, Thelma. *Arizona off the Beaten Path.* Phoenix: Golden West, 1982.

———. *Ghost Towns and Historical Haunts of Arizona.* Phoenix: Golden West, 1981.

Hinton, Richard. *Handbook to Arizona.* San Francisco: Payot, Upham & Co., 1878; Tucson: Arizona Silhouettes, 1954.

Hobbs, James. *Wild Life in the Far West.* Hartford, Conn.: Wiley, Waterman and Eaton, 1872.

Hopkins, Ernest J., and Alfred Thomas Jr. *The Arizona State University Story.* Phoenix: Southwest Publishing Co., 1960.

Ives, Joseph C. *Report upon the Colorado River of the West, Explored in 1857–1858.* Washington: Government Printing Office, 1861.

Johnson, Wesley. *Phoenix: Valley of the Sun.* Tulsa, Okla.: Continental Heritage Press, 1982.

Kessell, John. *Friars, Soldiers, and Reformers: Hispanic Arizona and the Sonora Mission Frontier, 1767–1856.* Tucson: University of Arizona Press, 1976.

Kollenborn, Tom. *The Apache Trail.* Mesa, Ariz.: World Publishing Corporation, 1998.

Lake, Carolyn, ed. *Under Cover for Wells Fargo: The Unvarnished Recollections of Fred Dodge.* Boston: Houghton Mifflin, 1969.

LeCount, Al, ed. *The History of Tonto.* Punkin Center, Ariz.: Punkin Center Homemakers, 1976.

Levine, Albert J. *From Indian Trails to Jet Trails: Snowflake's Centennial History.* Snowflake, Ariz.: Snowflake Historical Society, 1977.

Lingenfelter, Richard E. *Steamboats on the Colorado.* Tucson: University of Arizona Press, 1978.

Lynch, John, John W. Kennedy, and Robert L. Wooley. *Patton's Desert Training Center.* Fort Meyer, Va.: Council of Abandoned Military Posts, 1982.

Lynch, Richard E. *Winfield Scott: A Biography of Scottsdale's Founder.* Scottsdale, Ariz.: City of Scottsdale, 1978.

Malach, Roman. *Chloride: Mining Gem of the Cerbat Mountains.* Lake Havasu City, Ariz.: Locator Publications, 1978.

Marshall, James. *Santa Fe: The Railroad That Built an Empire.* New York: Random House, 1945.

Martin, Douglas. *Yuma Crossing.* Albuquerque: University of New Mexico Press, 1954.

Maxwell, Margaret. *A Passion for Freedom: The Life of Sharlot Hall.* Tucson: University of Arizona Press, 1982.

McCarty, Kieran. *Desert Documentary* (monograph). Tucson: Arizona Historical Society, 1976.

McElfresh, Patricia Myers. *Scottsdale: Jewel in the Desert.* Woodland Hills, Calif.: Windsor Publications, 1984.

McLaughlin, Herb, and Dorothy McLaughlin. *Phoenix: 1870–1970.* Phoenix: Photographic Associates, 1970.

Merrill, W. Earl. *One Hundred Steps down Mesa's Past.* Mesa, Ariz.: Lofgreen Printing Co., 1970.

Meyers, John M. *Last Chance: Tombstone's Early Years.* New York: E. P. Dutton, 1950.

Miller, Joseph, ed. *Arizona: The Last Frontier.* New York: Hastings House, 1956.

Möllhausen, Baldwin. *Diary of a Journey from the Mississippi to the Coast of the Pacific.* 2 vols. London, 1858.

Mulligan, R. A. "Apache Pass and Old Fort Bowie." *Smoke Signal* (Spring 1965). Tucson Corral of Westerners.

Murphy, Ira. *Brief History of Payson.* Payson, Ariz.: Payson Roundup, 1982.

Myrick, David F. *Railroads of Arizona.* Vols. 1-2. Berkeley, Calif.: Howell-North, 1975, 1980.

———. *Railroads of Arizona.* Vols. 4-5. Wilton, Calif.: Signature Press, 1998, 2001.

Noble, Marguerite. "Payson: One Hundred Years, 1882–1982." *Payson Centennial.* Payson, Ariz.: Rim Country Printery, 1982.

Northern Gila County Historical Society. *Rim Country History.* Payson: Rim Country Printery, 1984.

Ormsby, Waterman L. *The Butterfield Overland Mail.* San Marino, Calif.: Huntington Library, 1955.

Patton, James. *History of Clifton.* Clifton, Ariz.: Greenlee County Chamber of Commerce, 1977.

Plumlee, Tosh. "Arizona's Impossible Railroad." *Arizona Highways* (September 1979).

Poston, Charles. *Building a State in Apache Land.* Tempe, Ariz.: Aztec Press, 1963.

Rolak, Bruno J. "History of Fort Huachuca, 1877–1890." *Smoke Signal* (Spring 1974). Tucson Corral of Westerners.

Ruffner, Lester. *All Hell Needs Is Water.* Tucson: University of Arizona Press, 1972.

———. *Shot in the Ass with Pesos.* Tucson: Tucson Treasure Chest Publications, 1979.

Rusho, W. L., and C. Gregory Crampton. *Desert River Crossing: Historic Lee's Ferry on the Colorado River.* Salt Lake City: Peregrine Smith Inc., 1975.

Russell, Frank. *The Pima Indians.* Tucson: University of Arizona Press, 1975.

Ruxton, George Frederick. *Life in the Far West.* Leroy R. Hafen, ed. Norman: University of Oklahoma, 1951.

Salt River Project. *The Taming of the Salt.* Phoenix, 1979.

Schellie, Don. "Tucson Turns 200." *Arizona Highways* (September 1975).

Schulty, Vernon B. *Southwestern Town: The Story of Willcox, Arizona.* Tucson: University of Arizona Press, 1964.

Sharkey, J. E. "Douglas–Agua Prieta." *Arizona Highways* (September 1975).

Sherman, James, and Barbara Sherman. *Ghost Towns of Arizona.* Norman: University of Oklahoma Press, 1969.

Smith, Dean. *Glendale: Century of Diversity.* Glendale, Ariz.: City of Glendale, 1992.

Sonnichsen, C. L. *Billy King's Tombstone.* Caldwell, Idaho: Caxton Printers, 1942.

———. Tucson: *Life and Times of an American City.* Norman: University of Oklahoma Press, 1982.

Southwest Parks and Monuments Association. *Montezuma Castle.* Globe, Ariz., 1982.

Summerhayes, Martha. *Vanished Arizona.* Philadelphia: Lippincott Co., 1911.

Swanson, James, and Tom Kollenborn. *Superstition Mountain: A Ride through Time.* Phoenix: Arrowhead Press, 1981.

Theobald, John, and Lillian Theobald. *Post Offices and Postmasters.* Phoenix: Arizona Historical Foundation, 1961.

———. *Wells Fargo in Arizona Territory.* Tempe: Arizona Historical Foundation, 1978.

Thrapp, Dan. *Al Sieber: Chief of Scouts.* Norman: University of Oklahoma Press, 1964.

———. *Conquest of Apacheria.* Norman: University of Oklahoma Press, 1967.

Tinker, George. *Northern Arizona and Flagstaff in 1887.* Glendale, Calif.: Arthur H. Clark Co., 1969.

Trafzer, Clifford E. *Yuma: Frontier Crossing of the Far Southwest.* Wichita, Kans.: Western Heritage Books, 1980.

Trimble, Marshall.

———. *Arizona Adventure.* Phoenix: Golden West, 1982.

———. *Arizona: A Panoramic History of a Frontier State.* New York: Doubleday, 1977.

———. *Arizona 2000: A Yearbook for the Millennium.* Flagstaff, Ariz.: Northland Publishing, 1999.

———. *Cavalcade of History.* Tucson: Treasure Chest Publications, 1989.

———. *The CO Bar Ranch.* Flagstaff, Ariz.: Northland Press, 1982.

———. *In Old Arizona.* Phoenix: Golden West, 1985.

Tyler, Daniel. *A Concise History of the Mormon Battalion in the Mexican War.* N.p.: 1881; Glorieta, N.Mex.: Rio Grande Press, 1969.

Udall, Stewart. "In Coronado's Footsteps." *Arizona Highways* (April 1984).

Underhill, Ruth. *The Papago and Pima Indians of Arizona.* Palmer Lake, Colo.: Filter Press, 1979.

Varney, Phil. *Arizona's Best Ghost Towns.* Flagstaff, Ariz.: Northland Press, 1980.

Verde Valley Pioneers Association. *Pioneer Stories of Arizona's Verde Valley.* N.p., 1954.

Wagoner, Jay J. *Early Arizona.* Tucson: University of Arizona Press, 1975.

———. *Arizona Territory: 1863–1912.* Tucson: University of Arizona Press, 1970.

Walker, H. P., and Don Bufkin. *Historical Atlas of Arizona.* Norman: University of Oklahoma Press, 1979.

Weiner, Melissa Ruffner. *Prescott's Yesteryears: Life in Arizona's First Territorial Capitol.* Prescott, Ariz.: Primrose Press, 1978.

———. *Prescott, A Pictorial History.* Virginia Beach, Va.: Donning Co., 1981.

Weir, Bill. *Arizona Handbook.* 7th ed. Emeryville, Calif.: Avalon Travel, 1999.

Whipple, A. W. *The Whipple Report.* Los Angeles: Westernlore Press, 1961.

Williams, Brad, and Choral Pepper. *Lost Legends of the West.* New York: Holt, Rinehart and Winston, 1970.

Wilson, Maggie. "Yoo Hoo, Old Friend: Reflections on a Copper Camp's Past." *Arizona Highways* (September 1983).

Woody, Clara T., and Milton L. Schwartz. *Globe Arizona.* Tucson: Arizona Historical Society, 1977.

Wyllys, Rufus K. *Arizona: History of a Frontier State.* Phoenix: Hobson and Herr, 1950.

Young, Herb. *Ghosts of Cleopatra Hill.* Jerome, Ariz.: Jerome Historical Society, 1964.

———. *They Came to Jerome.* Jerome, Ariz.: Jerome Historical Society, 1972.

WEB SITES

http://www.library.arizona.edu/branches/spc/pams/exotic.html

http://www.outwestnewspaper.com/london.html

http://www.phoenix.about.com

www.desertusa.com

www.geocities.com/rocki47/wittmannsaga.html

www.ghosttowns.com

www.lapahie.com/Henry_Chee_Dodge.cfm

www.library.arizona.edu/images/jpamer/walz.htm

www.library.csi.cuny.edu/westweb/pages/ancient.html

www.nativepubs.com/nativepubs/Apps/bios/0087Wauneka Annie.asp?pic=none

www.smithsonianmag.si.edu/smithsonian/issues97/dec97/bosque.html

www.uspresidency.com/ussenate/ErnestWMcFarland.com/

www.zianet.com/snm/redondo.htm

INDEX

12, 304, 356; Pinal Apache, 165,
356; relationships with other
tribes, 12, 42, 103, 115, 302, 356,
450; at San Carlos Reservation,
19, 64, 356–58; scouts, 75, 102,
381; and the Spanish, 14, 16, 42,
44; White Mountain Apache, 75,
244, 380; whites, conflicts with,
7, 37, 44, 88, 111, 113, 119, 129,
351, 361; wickiups, 437–38.
Mentioned, 4, 104, 107, 121, 364
Apache Junction, 168–69.
Mentioned, 163
Apache Leap, 129
Apache Museum and Cultural
Center, 377
Apache Pass, 64–69, 105; Battle of,
65–69, 75. *Mentioned,* 31, 33
Apache Trail, 234–35. *Mentioned,*
163, 168, 238
Apache Wars (*see also* Apache
Indians; Cochise (chief); Crook,
George; Geronimo (war chief)),
64; end of, 19; and Fort
Huachuca, 100–102; and Fort
Whipple, 258. *Mentioned,* 18, 38,
61
Arab Americans (*see also* camel
drivers, Middle Eastern), 3
Aravaipa Creek, 72, 121
Archaic Culture. *See* Desert Culture
Arcosanti, 200–201
Arizola, 145–47
Arizona (*see also* agriculture;
mining; prehistoric peoples;
Spain/Spanish): geography of, 1–
4, 18; growth of, 4, 7-8, 26-27,
28-29; naming of, 19; native
tribes of, 4, 9, 27 (*see also* Native
Americans; *individual tribes)*;
population of, 3–4, 20, 26, 28;
prehistoric peoples of, 8–12 *(see
also individual groups)*;
statehood, 5, 22–23; state song,
36; state symbols, 5; territorial
capital, 19, 50, 173; tourism in,
26–27
Arizona Canal, 185. *Mentioned,* 175,
187, 189, 236
Arizona Rangers, 54–55, 95, 352, 389

Arizona State University, 171, 173–
75; East, 143
Arizona Strip, 338, 344
Arizona Water Settlements Act, 27,
157
Arizona Women's Hall of Fame, 216
Army Corps of Topographical
Engineers, 18, 37, 108, 139, 224,
271–77, 282, 397–99, 410
Army of the West (*see also* Kearny,
Stephen Watts; Mexican-American
War), 17. *Mentioned,* 136
Ash Fork, 290–93. *Mentioned,* 196,
227, 229, 260, 278
Ashurst, 352–53
Ashurst, Henry Fountain, 352–53
Athabascan language (*see also*
Apache Indians; Navajo Indians),
12, 218, 304, 356, 366
Atlantic & Pacific (Atchison, Topeka
& Santa Fe) Railroad, 22, 213–14,
226, 385. *Mentioned,* 224, 271,
293
Aubry, François Xavier, 457–58.
Mentioned, 296
Aubry Landing, 457–58
Aubry Valley, 296
automobiles, 23–26, 155–56
Aztec Land & Cattle Company, 386–
87. *Mentioned,* 293

Babbitt family, 227–30; Bruce, 230;
C O Bar Ranch, 228–30, 387;
trading company, 228–29, 320
Babocomari Ranch, 104
Baldy, Mount, 282
ball courts, prehistoric, 9, 12, 326
Barcelona, 128
Barnum, Jim, 184–85
Barringer, Daniel, 285
Barth, Solomon, 366–67
Bascom, George, 105
Bascom Affair, 105–6. *Mentioned,*
18, 62, 65
baseball, 27–28, 189, 192
Basha family, 128–29; stores, 128–
29
Beale, Edward "Ned," and Camel
Corps, 3, 224, 275–76, 396, 424.
Mentioned, 297, 298

fight at Stanwix Station, 403;
occupation of Tucson, 48.
Mentioned, 33, 106, 107, 112,
118, 134, 180, 223, 224, 400,
411, 427
Clanton brothers, 93–95, 422
Clark, William Andrews, 263, 264
Clarkdale, 264–65. *Mentioned*, 369
Clifton, 360–63. *Mentioned*, 20, 100,
159, 351
Cluff, Oscar and Alfred, 370
Clum, John, 93, 94, 358
C O Bar Ranch, 228–30. *Mentioned*,
387
Cochise (chief) (*see also* Chiricahua
Apache Indians): 64, 75, 100–
101; and Bascom Affair, 18, 62,
105–6. *Mentioned*, 19, 38, 61, 65,
66, 74, 104
Cochise (town), 62–63
Cochise Culture, 9, 379
Cochise Stronghold, 61–62
Cocopah Indians, 12, 407, 450
code talkers, Navajo, 308–9
Cohonina Culture, 12, 221, 331
Colorado City, 346. *Mentioned*, 411
Colorado Plateau, 2
Colorado River, 395; Central
Arizona Project Canal and, 28,
456–57; in Grand Canyon, 330–
31; Hoover Dam on, 441; and
Lake Powell, 328–29, and Parker
Dam, 451; steamboats on, 395–
99. *Mentioned*, 12, 205, 224, 297,
341, 344, 406, 457, 458
Colorado River Indian Reservation
(*see also* Hopi Indians; Mojave
Indians; Navajo Indians), 450–51.
Mentioned, 426, 448, 454, 455
Colorado River Relocation Center,
454–55
Colossal Cave, 39
Colter, Mary Jane Elizabeth, 253
Comanche Indians, 181, 324, 361
Concho, 380
Congress, 254–55
Cooke, Philip St. George (*see also*
Mormon Battalion), 17, 38, 46
Cooley, Corydon E., 371–72
Coolidge, 136, 137

Coolidge Dam, 356. *Mentioned*, 133,
147, 358
Cooper, Andy. *See* Blevins, Andy
(Cooper)
copper. *See* mines; mining; mining
districts
Copper Queen Hotel, 86
Cordes, 200
Cordes family, 200
Coronado, Francisco Vasquez de,
98–100, 359–60. *Mentioned*, 13,
38, 261, 282, 313, 332, 392–93,
407
Coronado National Monument, 98–
100
Coronado Trail, 359–60
Corral, Tomás, and family, 179
cotton, 23, 26, 420–21; on the Ak-
Chin Reservation, 156; and
Glendale, 190, 192; and the
Pima, 139; and prehistoric
peoples, 40, 180, 220, 283; and
Scottsdale, 176; and World War I,
23, 176, 190, 420–21. *Mentioned*,
33, 148
Courthouse Rock, 422
Courtland, 58–59, 63
Covered Wells, 152
Cowboy Artists of America, 267
cowboys. *See* cattle ranching
Cozzens, Samuel, 225
Crabb, Henry A., 405
Crittenden, George B., 124
Crook, George (*see also* Crook
Military Road): campaign against
Apache, 19, 20, 75–78, 79, 218–
19, 243; and the Wickenburg
Massacre, 434. *Mentioned*, 81,
101, 106, 248, 358, 371
Crook Military Road, 219, 239, 371
Crowe, Frank T., 442–43
Crown King, 196
Cushing, Howard, 135, 165
Cushman, Pauline, 134

dam(s) (*see also* Glen Canyon Dam;
Hoover Dam), 28, 191; Ashurst-
Hayden Diversion, 132–33; on
the Colorado River, 295, 395,
396, 399 (*see also* Hoover Dam);

Fort McDowell, 242–43. *Mentioned,*
169, 180–81, 257, 383
Fort McDowell Indian Reservation
(*see also* Apache Indians; Yavapai
Indians), 242–43. *Mentioned,*
357, 383
Fort Rock, 294
Fort Sumner Reservation. *See*
Bosque Redondo
Fort Thomas, 353–54
Fort Utah, 169
Fort Verde State Historic Park (*see
also* Camp Verde/Fort Verde),
218
Fort Whipple, 258. *Mentioned,* 204
Forty-Mile Desert, 157–58
Fort Yuma, 411. *Mentioned,* 396,
417, 423
Fountain Hills, 240–41
Four Corners (*see also* Navajo
Indian Reservation), 2, 4;
Monument, 321–22; native
inhabitants of, 304, 321.
Mentioned, 320
Franciscans (*see also* Catholic
Church, Garcés, Francisco
Tomás), 14, 15, 314; and Hopi
(Great Pueblo Revolt), 14, 314;
missions, 14–16, 115, 119–20,
408; and Quechans, 15–16, 408.
Mentioned, 43, 136
Fredonia, 342–43
Free, Mickey, 105–6
Fryer, Jere, 134
fur trappers (*see also individual
names),* 16, 17, 259, 280–81,
288, 290, 408, 457. *Mentioned,*
139

Gable, Clark, 294–95, 300
Gadsden, James, 18, 46
Gadsden Hotel, 55–56
Gadsden Purchase, 18, 108, 410
Gálvez Plan, 44–45
Ganado, 307, 310–12
Garcés, Francisco Tomás (*see also*
Franciscans), 15–16, 117, 119–
20; death of (Quechan revolt),
408. *Mentioned,* 43, 136, 154,
297, 326, 332

Gardner, Gail, 208, 437
Genung, Charles, 430–31
Geronimo (town), 354–56
Geronimo (war chief) (*see also*
Chiricahua Apache Indians; San
Carlos Indian Reservation), 20,
73–79, 358; Crook campaign
against, 20, 75–78; Miles
campaign against, 78–79;
surrender of, 20, 53, 68, 78–79.
Mentioned, 24, 61, 102, 218, 351,
354, 381
Geronimo Monument, 73–79
ghost towns: Agua Caliente, 402–3;
Bradshaw City, 196; Bumble Bee,
198–99; Canyon Diablo, 285–86;
Christmas, 124; Congress, 254–
55; Courtland, 58–59; Gleeson,
58; La Paz, 426; McMillenville,
383–84; Mowry, 107; Octave,
255–56; Patagonia, 107; Pearce,
58; Pinal City, 166–67; Stanton,
255–56; Total Wreck, 110;
Weaver, 255–56; White Hills, 441
Gila Bend, 154–56. *Mentioned,* 158,
299, 399
Gila City, 405, 406
Gila River (*see also* Gila Trail), 134,
419; bridge on, 134; cotton-
growing in valley, 148, 420; fur
trapping on, 16, 139; at Gila
Bend, 154; Indians living near
(*see also* Gila River Indian
Reservation), 9, 16, 138, 139,
154, 160, 326; as U.S.-Mexico
boundary, 17, 46, 410.
Mentioned, 17, 18, 32, 72, 123,
148, 157, 273, 353, 399, 401,
403, 406, 419, 423
Gila River Cultural Center, 138
Gila River Indian Reservation (*see
also* Maricopa Indians; Pima
Indians), 137–43
Gila Trail, 193, 399; emigrants on,
117, 144, 401, 410, 411, 423;
attacks on, 401, 411, 423; and
gold rush, 410, 423. *Mentioned,*
157, 271, 277
Glanton, John Joel, 410
Glanton Massacre, 410–11

Gleeson, 58–59. *Mentioned,* 63
Gleeson, John, 58
Glen Canyon Dam, 328–29. *Mentioned,* 2
Glendale, 189–93
Globe, 125–28. *Mentioned,* 20, 87, 165, 195, 384
gold. *See* mines; mining; mining districts
Goldroad, 299. *Mentioned,* 296
gold rush. *See* California
Goldwater: Barry, 28, 135, 211, 429, 431; Mike and Joe, 427, 428–29, 431–32; Morris, 211
Gonzales, Ignacio Elías, 104
Goodfellow, George "Doc," 91–92
Goodwin, John, 280
Goodyear, 419, 420–21
Goodyear Tire & Rubber Company, 420
Goulding, Harry and Mike, 323–24
governors' luncheon, Four Corners, 322
Gowan, Davy, 248–49
Graham, John and Tom (*see also* Pleasant Valley War), 373–76
Graham-Tewksbury feud. *See* Pleasant Valley War
Grand Canyon National Park, 329–38; area of, 329, 336; Bright Angel Trail in, 335; and Colorado Plateau, 2, 282; and Colorado River, 330–31, 395; El Tovar Hotel in, 335–36; explorers in, 100, 325, 329, 332–33, 339, 343, 395; geology of, 330–31; Hyde disappearance in, 337–38; Indians in, 4, 331, 332; Inner Gorge of, 330; Marble Canyon in, 338–39; North Rim of, 343–44; preservation of, 329–30, 336; quotes about, 329–330; South Rim of, 290, 329, 335, 337; tourism in, 27, 333–36; and trains, 290, 335. *Mentioned,* 1, 24, 227, 229, 233, 253, 296, 297, 298, 343, 344, 363
Granite Dells, 207, 258–59
Great Pueblo Revolt, 14, 314
Greenway, John C., 159

Greer, 369
Grey, Zane, 269, 320, 376–77
Griffith, Janice, 251
Grinnell, Henry, 401, 404
Gripe, 352
Grover, Bert, 63
Guadalupe, 148–50
Guadalupe Hidalgo, Treaty of, 17, 46, 146, 409
Guévavi, 113–15. *Mentioned,* 108

Hackberry, 298–99
Hall, Dick Wick, 445–47
Hall, Sharlot, 215–16
Hamblin, Jacob, 326, 342, 363. *Mentioned,* 320, 339, 344
Hance, John, 333–35
Hardyville, 293, 396. *Mentioned,* 205
Harquahala Mountains, 422–23, 430
Harquahala Peak Smithsonian Observatory, 444
Hart, Pearl, 414–16
Harvey, Emerson, 174
Harvey, Fred, 251, 253, 291, 335, 336
Harvey Houses, 251–53, 291
Hashknife Ranch, 386–89
Hassayampa River, 180, 210, 421, 430, 431
Hassayamper, 246, 421
Havasu, Lake, 455–56
Havasupai Indians, 4, 12, 297, 331. *Mentioned,* 332
Hawikuh, 99–100, 332, 359
Hayden, Charles Trumbull, 170–71
Hayes, Ira, 141–43
Heintzelman, Sam, 411
Hell Canyon, 260
highways (*see also* Beeline Highway; roads, historic; Route 66): construction, effects of, 35, 154, 155, 161, 163, 188, 195, 200, 278, 292, 293, 419, 430
Hi Jolly. *See* Ali, Hadji
Hispanics (*see also* Mexico/Mexicans; Spain/Spanish), 3–4, 128, 179, 363, 418, 426. *Mentioned,* 292, 364
Hohokam Indians, 9–10; ball courts, 9, 12, 326, canals, 8, 9–10, 23, 160, 180; Casa Grande and, 136–37;

Montezuma Castle and, 220–21; Montezuma Well and, 221–222; in Oak Creek Canyon, 268; in Petrified Forest, 392; Phoenix and, 180, 181, 184; relationships with other peoples, 10, 138, 221, 379; in the Verde Valley, 217, 221. *Mentioned,* 12, 40, 144, 147

Holbrook, 384–86, 389–91; Blevins shoot-out in, 389–90; Hashknife Ranch in, 386–89. *Mentioned,* 78, 219, 278, 280, 282, 378

Holliday, Doc, 20, 93–5

Homolovi Ruins State Park, 283–84. *Mentioned,* 251

Hon Dah, 370–71

Honeymoon Trail, 326–27

Hooker, Henry Clay, 70–72

Hoover Dam, 441–44. *Mentioned,* 2, 295, 398, 456

Hope, 447

Hopi Indian Reservation (*see also* Hopi Indians), 312–19. *Mentioned,* 2, 8, 303

Hopi Indians (*see also* Hopi Indian Reservation), 312–19; ancient trails, 219, 239; on the Colorado River Indian Reservation, 450; encounter with Coronado, 359; customs and beliefs, 314–16, 331; and the Franciscans, 14, 314; and the Grand Canyon, 331; and the Great Pueblo Revolt, 14, 314; and the Havasupai Indians, 297; and Kin Tiel, 280; kivas, 314, 315; land dispute with Navajo, 310, 316–17; mesas, 313–14, 316; origins, 11, 283, 313, 331; and other religions, 282, 314. *Mentioned,* 2, 4, 100, 284, 342, 366

Houck, 279

Houck, James D., 279

House Rock, 341–42

Howard, Oliver, 19, 61, 64, 357

Hualapai Indian Reservation (*see also* Hualapai Indians), 297–98. *Mentioned,* 278

Hualapai Indians (*see also* Hualapai Indian Reservation; Wickenburg Massacre), 297–98; origins, 12, 331; in Walapai War, 294. *Mentioned,* 282, 437

Hualapai River, 331

Hubbell, John Lorenzo, 310–11

Hubbell Trading Post, 310–12

Humboldt, 202

Humphreys, Mount, 2

Hunter, Sherod, 48, 66, 403

Hyde, Glen and Bessie, 337–38

Indians. *See individual tribe names;* Native Americans; prehistoric peoples

irrigation (*see also* canal(s); dam(s)), 23; ditches, 169, 217, 282; and the Pima, 139; prehistoric, 8, 9–10, 11, 220, 221. *Mentioned,* 33, 156, 171, 175

Isaacson, Jacob, 108

Ives, Joseph, 397, 398–99

"Jackass Mail." *See* San Antonio & San Diego Mail Line

Jackling, D. C., 128

Jacob Lake, 342

jails (*see also* Yuma Territorial Prison): Clifton Cliff, 362–63; "jail tree," 432. *Mentioned,* 59, 134, 262

Japanese, in World War II, 308–9

Japanese Americans: in Glendale, 190–92; and World War II relocation camps, 454–55. *Mentioned,* 3

Jeffords, Thomas Jefferson, 61–62

Jerez, Joe (José), 299

Jerome, 260–64; as boomtown, 20–21. *Mentioned,* 2, 8, 130, 159, 215, 263, 269

Jesuits (*see also* Catholic Church; Kino, Francisco Eusebio), 14, 15, 40–43; missions, 14, 40–43, 113–15, 116, 119. *Mentioned,* 103, 107, 149

Johnson, George, 396–99

Jones, Charles J., 341

Jones, Melvin, 353

Joseph City, 282–83

Augustín de Oiaur, 40, 42, 43;
San Augustín del Tucson; 43; San
Cosme de Tucson, 42; San
Gabriel de Guévavi, 113–16; San
José del Tucson, 42; San Pedro y
San Pablo de Bicuñer, 408; San
Xavier del Bac, 43, 115, 119–20;
Tumacacori, 113–116.
Mentioned, 123
Mitchell, Harry, 173
Mix, Tom, 131–32
Moenave, 326–27
Moenkopi, 282, 318–19
Moeur, Ben, 455
Mofford, Rose Perica, 127
Mogollon Indians, 9, 11, 364, 379.
Mentioned, 12, 221, 392
Mogollon Rim, 2, 244, 369.
Mentioned, 219, 229, 243, 369,
376
Mohave, Lake, 293, 398
Mojave Indians (*see also* Colorado
River Indian Reservation), 450–
51; and Olive Oatman, 299–300,
401; origins, 12; on the San
Carlos Reservation, 358; at
Yuma, 407. *Mentioned,* 140, 173,
273, 296, 298, 422, 424, 457
Möllhausen, Heinrich Baldwin, 271,
397
Molokans, 4, 190–91
Montezuma Castle National
Monument, 219–21. *Mentioned,*
11
Montezuma Well, 221–22
Monument Valley Navajo Tribal
Park, 322–24. *Mentioned,* 2, 27
Moore, Billy, 420
Morenci, 360–63. *Mentioned,* 20,
100, 351
Mormon Battalion, 17, 38, 46, 281;
monument to, 145, 148.
Mentioned, 144, 210, 223
Mormon(s) (*see also* Hamblin,
Jacob; Mormon Battalion;
Mormon War; Young, John W.),
326–27, 344; colonies/
settlements, 169, 282–83, 319,
320, 326, 342–43, 344–45, 347,
363, 364, 366–67, 369, 384, 385;

Indians and, 319, 320, 344, 345,
363; Lehi Pioneers, 169;
Mountain Meadows Massacre,
339–40; Pipe Spring National
Monument/Winsor Castle, 344–
45, 226–27, 319, 385. *Mentioned,*
4, 225, 249, 297
Mormon War, 397
Morristown, 429–30
Mossman, Burt, 352, 388–89
Mountain Meadows Massacre, 339–
40
Mountain View Hotel, 123
movie(s) (*see also* Leo the Lion):
actors from Arizona, 35–36, 127,
131–32, 295, 324, 437; filmed in
Arizona, 104–5, 130, 131, 135,
258–59, 269, 301, 320, 323–24;
portrayals of Arizona in, 33, 72,
90, 130–31, 375; stars visiting
Arizona, 253, 294–95, 300.
Mentioned, 223, 247
Mowry, Sylvester, 107, 118
Murphy, Frank, 196–97, 202
Murphy, Patrick, 98
Murphy, William J., 175, 180, 185,
189. *Mentioned,* 237

Naco, Ariz., 96–98
Naco, Mex., 81, 96–98
National Cowboy Hall of Fame, 72,
213, 389
National Reclamation Act (Newlands
Act), 23, 188, 237
National Trails Highway. *See* Route
66
Na-ti-o-tish, 381–82
Native Americans (*see also*
individual tribe names;
prehistoric peoples), 4, 9, 27.
Navajo Indian Reservation (*see also*
Navajo Indians), 303–10, 316–17.
Mentioned, 320, 322
Navajo Indians (*see also* Colorado
River Indian Reservation), 303–
10; in Canyon de Chelly, 302–3;
code talkers (World War II), 308–
9; land dispute with Hopi, 310,
316–17; legend, Petrified Forest,
391; and the "Long Walk," 303,

Bouse training base during, 447–48; code talkers in, 308–9; Fort Huachuca during, 100, 102; Iwo Jima landing in (Ira Hayes), 142; Japanese detention camps during, 191, 454–55; Papago prisoner-of-war camp during, 177–78; technology and, 26, 28; Yuma Proving Grounds training base during, 451–52. *Mentioned*, 3, 33, 143, 148, 173, 174, 179, 180, 188, 192, 202, 278, 367, 437, 458, 459
Wright, Frank Lloyd, 179–80, 200
Wupatki National Monument, 11–12, 220, 325–26

Yampai, 297
Yampai Indians, 297
Yaqui Indians, 148–50. *Mentioned*, 153
Yavapai Indians (*see also* Camp Verde Indian Reservation; Fort McDowell Indian Reservation), 16, 217–18, 242–43; army

campaigns against, 19, 75, 242–43; miner, 197–98; origins, 12; relationships with other tribes, 19, 140, 217–18, 242–43, 297, 450; and Pauline Weaver, 211; and wickiups, 437. *Mentioned*, 234, 423
Young, 373–76
Young, Ewing, 16, 139, 259, 290, 457
Young, John W., 226–27, 319, 385
Yucca, 295–96
Yuma (*see also* Yuma Territorial Prison), 406–18; missions at, 15, 408. *Mentioned*, 2, 17
Yuma Crossing. *See* Yuma
Yuma Indians. *See* Quechan Indians
Yuma Proving Grounds, 451–52
Yuma Territorial Prison, 414–16. *Mentioned*, 39, 63, 134

Zuni Indians, 368. *Mentioned*, 225, 239, 280, 332, 365
Zuni Reservation, 368
Zuni River, 368

Respected Arizona writer Dean Smith wrote, "Ask the average Arizonan to name an Arizona historian and he's most likely to reply, 'Marshall Trimble.' Then ask him to name an Arizona cowboy, singer, humorist, or storyteller, and he'll still reply, 'Marshall Trimble.'"

Trimble has been the head of the Southwest Studies cultural-historical program at Scottsdale Community College for the past twenty-five years and has taught Arizona and western history for thirty years. As a performer and storyteller, the Ash Fork native specializes in making his beloved state's history and folklore accessible. He has a popular history radio show, *Trimble's Tales,* a regular question-and-answer history column in *True West,* and has appeared on numerous television programs. In addition to *Roadside History of Arizona,* he has written many other books of history and humor (several of them award-winners), among them *Arizona: A Panoramic History of a Frontier State* and *Arizona 2000: A Yearbook for the Millennium.* A folksinger during the 1960s, Trimble continues to entertain with music and stories and has performed with Rex Allen, Waylon Jennings, and the Oak Ridge Boys. In 2000 he represented Arizona in the Library of Congress's Local Legacies program. In 1997 Arizona governor Fife Symington declared him the state's official historian. He continues to travel widely throughout the state, often on the back of a horse. Senator Barry Goldwater wrote, "Arizona's colorful history is alive and well with Marshall Trimble."

We encourage you to patronize your local bookstore. Most stores will order any title they do not stock. You may also order directly from Mountain Press, using the order form provided below or by calling our toll-free, 24-hour number and using your VISA, MasterCard, Discover or American Express.

Some other Roadside History titles of interest:

_____Roadside History of Arizona, Second Edition	paper/$20.00	
_____Roadside History of Arkansas	paper/$18.00	cloth/$30.00
_____Roadside History of California	paper/$20.00	
_____Roadside History of Colorado	paper/$20.00	
_____Roadside History of Idaho	paper/$18.00	
_____Roadside History of Louisiana	paper/$20.00	
_____Roadside History of Montana	paper/$20.00	
_____Roadside History of Nebraska	paper/$18.00	cloth/$30.00
_____Roadside History of Nevada	paper/$20.00	
_____Roadside History of New Mexico	paper/$18.00	
_____Roadside History of Oklahoma	paper/$20.00	
_____Roadside History of Oregon	paper/$18.00	
_____Roadside History of South Dakota	paper/$18.00	
_____Roadside History of Texas	paper/$18.00	
_____Roadside History of Utah	paper/$18.00	
_____Roadside History of Vermont	paper/$15.00	
_____Roadside History of Wyoming	paper/$18.00	cloth/$30.00
_____Roadside History of Yellowstone Park	paper/$10.00	

1-4 books add $4.00, 5 or more books add $6.00 for shipping and handling.

Send the books marked above. I enclose $ _____

Name _____

Address _____

City/State/Zip _____

☐ Payment enclosed (check or money order in U.S. funds)

Bill my: ☐ VISA   ☐ MasterCard ☐ Discover ☐ American Express

Card No._____ Exp. Date:_____

Security code_____ Signature _____

MOUNTAIN PRESS PUBLISHING COMPANY
P.O. Box 2399 • Missoula, MT 59806 • Order Toll-Free 1-800-234-5308
E-mail: info@mtnpress.com • Web: www.mountain-press.com